Canadian Guide to Uniform Legal Citation
7th Edition

7e édition
Manuel canadien de référence juridique

CARSWELL®

∞ The paper used in this publication meets the minimum requirements of American National Standard for Information Sciences—Permanence of Paper for Printed Library Materials, ANSI Z39.48-1984.

ISBN 978-0-7798-2800-5 (bound).—978-0-7798-2799-2 (pbk)

A cataloguing record for this publication is available from Library and Archives Canada.

Printed in Canada by Transcontinental Printing.

Composition: Computer Composition of Canada Inc.

THOMSON REUTERS

CARSWELL, A DIVISION OF THOMSON REUTERS CANADA LIMITED

One Corporate Plaza
2075 Kennedy Road
Toronto, Ontario
M1T 3V4

Customer Relations
Toronto 1-416-609-3800
Elsewhere in Canada/U.S. 1-800-387-5164
Fax 1-416-298-5082
www.carswell.com
E-mail www.carswell.com/email

Officially adopted by:
Officiellement adopté par:

Alberta Law Review
Annals of Air and Space Law
Appeal: Review of Current Law and Law Reform
Canadian Bar Review ~ *Revue du Barreau canadien*
Canadian Journal of Criminology and Criminal Justice
Canadian Journal of Family Law ~ *Revue canadienne de droit familial*
Canadian Journal of Law and Jurisprudence
Canadian Journal of Law and Technology
Constitutional Forum Constitutionnel
Dalhousie Journal of Legal Studies
Dalhousie Law Journal
Health Law Journal
Health Law Review (Alberta)
Indigenous Law Journal
Journal of Law and Equality
Journal of Law and Social Policy
Manitoba Law Journal
McGill International Journal of Sustainable Development Law and Policy ~ *Revue internationale de droit et politique du développement de McGill*
McGill Journal of Law and Health ~ *Revue de droit et santé de McGill*
McGill Law Journal ~ *Revue de droit de McGill*
Osgoode Hall Law Journal
Ottawa Law Review ~ *Revue de droit d'Ottawa*
Queen's Law Journal
Review of Constitutional Studies ~ *Revue d'études constitutionnelles*
Canadian Journal of Law and Society ~ *Revue Canadienne Droit et Société*
Revue de droit de l'Université de Sherbrooke
Revue québécoise de droit international
Saskatchewan Law Review
Singapore Journal of International and Comparative Law
Singapore Journal of Legal Studies
Singapore Law Review
University of British Columbia Law Review
University of New Brunswick Law Journal
University of Ottawa Law and Technology Journal
University of Toronto Faculty of Law Review
University of Toronto Law Journal
Windsor Review of Legal and Social Issues
Windsor Yearbook of Access to Justice

Court of Appeal for New Brunswick ~ *Cour d'appel du Nouveau-Brunswick*
Supreme Court of the Yukon Territory

SUMMARY TABLE OF CONTENTS /
TABLE DES MATIÈRES ABRÉGÉE

English

French

Appendices / *Annexes*

A WORD FROM THE EDITOR

Every four years since 1986, the *McGill Law Journal* has published a new edition of the *Canadian Guide to Uniform Legal Citation*. The *Guide* aims to facilitate efficient legal research by creating a uniform system of rules that will allow authors to accurately communicate their intended message. It is an essential reference tool for all lawyers, judges, law professors, students and publishers. It is essential to have a uniform system of rules in order to perform efficient legal research, as such rules enable the author to accurately communicate his or her intended message to the reader.

Clarity was the key objective in creating the seventh edition of the *Guide*. Regardless of a rule's importance and logic, a rule is only as good as its ability to give clear guidance in practice. Citation rules have thus been articulated in a clear and concise manner in an attempt to allow more flexibility for the *Guide's* users. Punctuation practices have been simplified, a separate chapter on foreign sources has been added, and a number of chapters have been updated. Given the various new electronic legal databases available, we have adapted the citation rules to the current practice, while leaving room for flexibility as future technology and sources develop. We have also extended the applicability of the *Guide* as the rules can now be adjusted for use in a number of languages and jurisdictions.

We would particularly like to thank Me Daniel Boyer (Head Librarian, Nahum Gelber Law Library, McGill University) and Mr. Claudio Antonelli for their support and encouragement in reviewing this *Guide*. We would also like to thank the members of the LexUM team, especially Me Daniel Poulin (Director) and Me Frédéric Pelletier (Legal Counsel), who made valuable contributions to the sections on neutral citations. Last but not least, I would also like to thank the Editor-in-Chief of Volume 55 of the *McGill Law Journal*, Ms. Seo Yun Yang, as well as the entire editorial board, without whom it would have been impossible to complete this work.

We hope you find the new *Guide* helpful and enjoy using it!

Svetlana Samochkine
Cite Guide Editor
McGill Law Journal, Volume 55

If you have any comments or suggestions, please contact us at:

McGill Law Journal
3644 Peel Street
Montreal (Qc), H3A 1W9
Canada

Telephone: (+1) 514.398.7397
Fax: (+1) 514.398.7360
Email: journal.law@mcgill.ca
http://lawjournal.mcgill.ca

TABLE OF CONTENTS

1 GENERAL RULES

➢ The rules in this *Guide* apply to **footnotes**, **in-text citations**, and **bibliographies**.

➢ Use the rules from the English section when writing in English, even if the source being referred to is in another language. Use the French rules only when writing in French.

➢ In citations, omit periods when using an abbreviation or acronym, unless the *Guide* explains otherwise. Follow regular grammatical rules regarding use of periods in all other texts.

➢ The **coloured font** has been used to make some examples in this *Guide* explicit.

➢ If a rule states that parentheses ( ) must be used, do not replace them with brackets [ ] and vice versa.

➢ Underlining may always be used in lieu of italics and vice versa.

1.1 BIBLIOGRAPHIES

LEGISLATION

Anti-terrorism Act, SC 2001, c 41.
Aggregate Resources Act, RSO 1990, c A-8.
National Arts Council Act (Cap 193A, 1992 Rev Ed Sing).
Tobacco Product Control Act, RSC 1985 (4th Supp), c 14.

JURISPRUDENCE

Delgamuukw v British Columbia, [1997] 3 SCR 1010, 153 DLR (4th) 193.
Kendle v Melsom, [1998] HCA 13.
Létourneau c Laflèche Auto Ltée, [1986] RJQ 1956 (Sup Ct).
Nova Scotia (Workers' Compensation Board) v Martin, 2003 SCC 54, [2003] 2 SCR 504.

SECONDARY MATERIAL: MONOGRAPHS

Macklem, Patrick. *Indigenous Difference and the Constitution of Canada* (Toronto: University of Toronto Press, 2001).
Nadeau, Alain-Robert. *Vie privée et droits fondamentaux* (Cowansville, Que: Yvon Blais, 2000).
Smith, Graham JH. *Internet Law and Regulation*, 3d ed (London, UK: Sweet & Maxwell, 2002).
Tan, Cheng Han. *Matrimonial Law in Singapore and Malaysia* (Singapore: Butterworths Asia, 1994).

SECONDARY MATERIAL: ARTICLES

Borrows, John. "With or Without You: First Nations Law (in Canada)" (1996) 41 McGill LJ 629.
————. "Wampum at Niagara: The Royal Proclamation, Canadian Legal History, and Self-Government" in Michael Asch, ed, *Aboriginal and Treaty Rights in Canada: Essays on Law, Equity, and Respect for Difference* (Vancouver: UBC Press, 1997) 155.
Wang Sheng Chang. "Combination of Arbitration with Conciliation and Remittance of Awards – with Special Reference to the Asia-Oceana Region" (2002) 19 J Int Arb 51.
Deleury, E. "Naissance et mort de la personne ou les confrontations de la médecine et du droit" (1976) 17 C de D 265.

➢   Divide bibliographies and tables of authorities of legal texts into the following sections: Legislation, Jurisprudence, and Secondary Materials. If a source does not fit into a defined section, a residual section entitled Other Materials may be used. It may be useful to divide the Secondary Material section into subsections (e.g. Articles, Monographs) and to divide materials into Domestic Sources and Foreign Sources.

➢   Within each section, **list the entries in alphabetical order**. Sort legislation by title, jurisprudence by style of cause and secondary materials by surname of the author.

➢   If a citation directly follows a citation to another work by the same author, replace the author's names with a 3-em dash (see the "Wampum at Niagara" example).

➢   For secondary material included in a bibliography, **the author's surname appears first** to facilitate classification in alphabetical order. Depending on cultural conventions, a surname may appear before, after, or in between given names. If the surname normally appears first (e.g. Wang Sheng Chang), do not place a comma after it. If the given name normally appears first, place a comma after the surname (e.g. Smith, Graham JH). Include any initials present in the author's name as they appear in the publication.

➢   If there is more than one author for a reference, write the given name before the surname for every author except the first one (e.g. Baudouin, Jean-Louis & Pierre-Gabriel Jobin).

➢   If there is a work by a single author and a work by that same author and others (e.g. Baudouin and Baudouin & Jobin), cite the one with a single author first.

➢   Insert a **hanging indent** of ¼ inch or 0.63 cm before each citation. Indent all the lines except the first one.

➢   For secondary materials, follow the rules established in Chapter 6 (except for the order of the names of the author or editor).

1.2   IN-TEXT REFERENCES – MEMORANDUM AND FACTUM

In legal writing, the standard rule is to use footnotes. However, in certain types of documents, citations should be included in the body text.

1.2.1 Memorandum

> In addition to the requirement of an "actionable wrong" independent of the breach sued upon, punitive damages will only be awarded "where the defendant's misconduct is so malicious, oppressive, and high-handed that it offends the court's sense of decency" (*Hill v Church of Scientology of Toronto*, [1995] 2 SCR 1130 at para 196, 186 NR 1, Cory J [*Hill*]). Such behaviour has included defamation (*ibid*), failure to provide medical care (*Robitaille v Vancouver Hockey Club*, [1981] 3 WWR 481, 124 DLR (3d) 228 (BCCA)), and exceptionally abusive behaviour by an insurance company (*Whiten v Pilot Insurance*, 2002 SCC 18, [2002] 1 SCR 595 [*Whiten*]).
>
> Since the primary vehicle of punishment is the criminal law, punitive damages should be scarcely used (*ibid* at para 69). It is also important to underline that there cannot be joint and several responsibility for punitive damages because they arise from the misconduct of the particular defendant against whom they are awarded (*Hill* at para 195).

- ➤ Include the reference immediately after the text, in parentheses.

- ➤ The first time a reference is used, follow the usual rules for footnotes. If a reference is repeated later in the text, include a short form after the first citation (see *Hill*). If a reference is not repeated, do not include a short form (see *Robitaille*).

- ➤ After the first time a reference is used, use only the short form. Include the pinpoint reference (e.g. *Hill* at para 195).

- ➤ Use *ibid* (section 1.4.2) to refer to the immediately preceding reference. Use *supra* (section 1.4.3) when a reference has been mentioned before. Do not use *infra* (section 1.4.4) in a memorandum.

1.2.2 Factum

> 5.   In addition to the requirement of an "actionable wrong" independent of the breach sued upon, punitive damages will only be awarded "where the defendant's misconduct is so malicious, oppressive and high-handed that it offends the court's sense of decency" (*Hill*). Such behaviour has included defamation (*Hill*), failing to provide medical care (*Robitaille*), and exceptionally abusive behaviour by an insurance company (*Whiten*).
>
> > *Hill v Church of Scientology of Toronto*, [1995] 2 SCR 1130 at para 196, 184 NR 1, Cory J [*Hill*].
> >
> > *Robitaille v Vancouver Hockey Club*, [1981] 3 WWR 481, 124 DLR (3d) 228 (BCCA).
> >
> > *Whiten v Pilot Insurance*, 2002 SCC 18, [2002] 1 SCR 595 [*Whiten*].
>
> 6.   Since the primary vehicle of punishment is the criminal law, punitive damages should be scarcely used. It is also important to underline that there cannot be joint and several responsibility for punitive damages because they arise from the misconduct of the particular defendant against whom they are awarded.
>
> > *Whiten, supra* para 5 at para 69.
> >
> > *Hill, supra* para 5 at para 195.

➤ Use the short form in parentheses immediately after the text.

➤ Write the complete reference **at the end of each paragraph**. Indent from both margins and use a smaller font size.

➤ Write the short form, used in the body of the text, in brackets after the first citation.

➤ Organize the references **in the order in which they appear in the text**. Start a new line after each reference. Do not use a semicolon.

➤ Follow the usual rules for *supra* (section 1.4.3). Instead of referring to a footnote number, the number following the *supra* indicates the number of the paragraph in which the source was mentioned for the first time (e.g. *Whiten*, para 5 at para 195). **Do not use *infra*** (section 1.4.4) in a factum.

➤ **Do not use *ibid*** in a factum. At the end of a paragraph, include the pinpoint references that apply to the whole paragraph (e.g. *Whiten v Pilot Insurance*, 2002 SCC 18 at paras 69, 101, 110, [2002] 1 SCR 595).

1.3   FOOTNOTES – RULES

In legal writing, the two most common forms of footnotes are textual footnotes and citation footnotes. **Textual footnotes** contain matters of related interest to the subject but that are sufficiently peripheral that their presence in the body of the paper would detract from the thrust of the argument. **Citation footnotes** are used to indicate sources from which the argument or quotation has been drawn. Both textual and citation information can occur within a single footnote.

1.3.1   When to Footnote

➤ When writing a legal research paper, create footnotes only under the following circumstances: (1) at the first reference to the source; (2) at every subsequent quotation from the source; and (3) at every subsequent reference or allusion to a particular passage in the source. Provide the full citation in the first footnote referring to a source.

1.3.2 How to Indicate a Footnote in the Text

➤ In legal writing, footnotes are indicated by superscripted numbers. Roman numerals and special characters such as *, †, and ‡ are not used.

→ As a general rule, place the footnote number at the end of the sentence after the punctuation.[1]

→ When referring to one word, place the footnote number[2] directly after the word.

→ When quoting from a source, place the footnote number after "the quotation marks"[3] and/or "the punctuation".[4] (This is contrary to the rule applicable in French, where the footnote number precedes the punctuation.)

1.3.3 Where Footnotes Appear

➤ Place footnotes on the same page (if possible) below the text to which they refer. Set them in a **smaller font** with a **horizontal line** separating them from the body of the text.

1.3.4 When to Combine Footnotes

[3] Martin Loughlin, "The Functionalist Style in Public Law" (2005) 55 UTLJ 361; Martin Loughlin, *Public Law and Political Theory* (Oxford: Clarendon Press, 1992).

➤ Never place more than one footnote number at any given point in the text. Instead, combine the citations into one footnote. **Separate different citations in a footnote by a semicolon** and end the entire footnote with a period. If the result is not confusing, citations to multiple sources may generally be combined into one footnote with the footnote number placed at the end of the paragraph. Avoid combining footnotes with several quotations from different sources.

1.3.5 Citation of Non-English Sources

[1] Sylvio Normand, *Introduction au droit des biens* (Montreal: Wilson & Lafleur, 2000) at 40.

[2] *Loi n° 94-653 du 29 juillet 1994*, JO, 30 July 1994, (1994 2ᵉ sem) Gaz Pal Lég 576.

➤ If writing in English, use the English citation rules regardless of the language of the source. Keep the title of the source in the original language and follow that language's rules for capitalization. For all other items in the citation, follow the English rules, particularly the rules on use of punctuation.

1.3.6 Introductory Signals

See *Spar Aerospace Ltd v American Mobile Satellite Corp,* 2002 SCC 78, [2002] 4 SCR 205 [*Spar*]; *Morguard Investments Ltd v De Savoye*, [1990] 3 SCR 1077, 76 DLR (4th) 256. But see *Beals v Saldanha*, 2003 SCC 72, [2003] 3 SCR 416.

➢ Use an introductory signal if it's appropriate to explain the logical relation between the source cited and the proposition stated in the text.

➢ An introductory signal relates to every citation of the same sentence. In the above-mentioned example, the signal see relates to both *Spar* and *Morguard* because they are separated by a semicolon.

➢ Only *c.f.* and *contra* should be italicized because they are non-English words. E.g., however, should be in Roman font because of its common usage in the English language. While not exhaustive, the following list presents some introductory signals:

Spar	There is no introductory signal when the authority cited is being **quoted or explicitly referred to in the text.**
See *Spar*	The authority cited **directly supports** the proposition given in the text.
See especially *Spar*	The authority cited is **the strongest** of several that support the proposition in the text. Use this when listing only the best of many possible sources.
See e.g. *Spar*	*Exempli gratia*, literally "**for example**". The authority cited is one of several that support the proposition given in the text, but the other supporting authorities are not cited.
See generally *Spar*	The authority cited **supports and provides background information** to the proposition in the text.
See also *Spar*	The authority cited provides **added support** for the proposition in the text, but is **not the most authoritative or is not directly on point**.
Accord *Spar*	As with "see also", the authority cited provides **added support** for the proposition in the text. However, in this instance, the authority **directly supports the proposition in the text and is as authoritative as the authority first cited**. "Accord" is also used to indicate that the law of one jurisdiction accords with the law of another.
C.f. *Spar*	*Confer*, literally "compare". The authority cited supports a different proposition, but one that is sufficiently analogous to lend support to the current proposition. **The cited authority lends support to the proposition**.
Compare *Spar*	The authority cited provides a useful contrast to illustrate the proposition being discussed in the text. **The *contrast* lends support rather than the cited authority itself**.
But see *Spar*	The authority cited is in **partial disagreement** with the proposition in the text, but does not directly contradict it.
Contra Spar	The authority cited directly **contradicts** the proposition given in the text.

1.3.7   Parenthetical Information Within Footnotes

> [1] *Roncarelli v Duplessis*, [1959] SCR 121, 16 DLR (2d) 689, Rand J (discretionary decisions must be based on "considerations pertinent to the object of the administration" at 140); *Oakwood Development Ltd v St François Xavier (Municipality)*, [1985] 2 SCR 164, 20 DLR (4th) 641, Wilson J [*Oakwood* cited to SCR] ("[t]he failure of an administrative decision-maker to take into account a highly relevant consideration is just as erroneous as the improper importation of an extraneous consideration" at 174).

> [2] See *Lawson v Wellesley Hospital* (1975), 9 OR (2d) 677, 61 DLR (3d) 445, aff'd [1978] 1 SCR 893, 76 DLR (3d) 688 [*Lawson*] (duty of hospital to protect patient); *Stewart v Extendicare*, [1986] 4 WWR 559, 38 CCLT 67 (Sask QB) [*Stewart*] (duty of nursing home to protect resident).

➢ Following a citation, provide in parentheses a **brief description or quotation of not more than one sentence** if it is helpful to clarify how the cited source supports the in-text proposition. A pinpoint reference must follow the quotation in parentheses (see *Oakwood*).

➢ Begin the parenthetical information with a lower case letter. If the citation begins with a capital letter, change it to lower case in brackets (see *Oakwood*).

➢ Parenthetical information refers to the citation immediately preceding it. Therefore, in the *Lawson* example, the parenthetical information would be placed immediately before aff'd if it is meant to refer only to the court of appeal decision.

1.4   PRIOR AND SUBSEQUENT REFERENCES TO A CITATION

Indicate the full citation only the first time a source appears. Subsequent references refer back to this initial citation.

1.4.1   Establishing a Short Form

1.4.1.1 General Rules

➢ Do not create a short title if there is no further reference to the source in the work.

➢ If the title of a source is short (around three words or less), the full title may be used in all subsequent references (see note 10). If the title of a source is longer, create a short title for subsequent references.

> [1] *Kadlak v Nunavut (Minister of Sustainable Development)*, [2001] Nu J No 1 (Nu Ct J) (QL) [*Kadlak*].
>
> [5] *Kadlak*, *supra* note 1 at para 15.
>
> [7] *R v W (R)*, [1992] 2 SCR 122 at para 1, 74 CCC (3d) 134.
>
> [10] *R v W (R)*, *supra* note 7 at para 3.
>
> [14] James E Ryan, "The Supreme Court and Voluntary Integration" (2007) 121 Harv L Rev 131.
>
> [40] Ryan, *supra* note 14 at 132.

➢ Place the short title in brackets directly after the citation but before any parenthetical information (see *Stewart* in section 1.3.7) and case history (section 3.11). Do not italicize the brackets.

➢ Always italicize the short title for cases or legislation (e.g. *Charter*). Abbreviations of codes such as CCQ are not considered short forms, and thus should not be italicized.

➢ In subsequent footnotes, use the appropriate cross-referencing signals (*supra*, *ibid*) and, where appropriate, the short title to direct the reader back to the footnote containing the full citation (see note 5).

1.4.1.2 Legislation

➢ If a statute has an **official short title**, use only this short title in the initial citation. If the short title is brief, it may also be used in subsequent references (e.g. *Museums Act*).

➢ If a statute has **no official short title**, or if the official short title is too long for subsequent references, create a distinctive short title and indicate it in brackets at the end of the citation.

> [1] *Museums Act*, SC 1990, c 3.
>
> [2] *Nordion and Theratronics Divestiture Authorization Act*, SC 1990, c 4 [*Nordion Act*].
>
> [3] *Canadian Charter of Rights and Freedoms*, Part I of the *Constitution Act, 1982*, being Schedule B to the *Canada Act 1982* (UK), 1982, c 11 [*Charter*].
>
> [4] *Charter of the French language*, RSQ c C-11 [*Bill 101*].

1.4.1.3 Cases

> [1] *R v Van der Peet*, [1996] 2 SCR 507, 137 DLR (4th) 289 [*Van der Peet* cited to SCR].
>
> [7] *Van der Peet*, *supra* note 1 at 510.
>
> [10] *R v Ruzic*, 2001 SCC 24 at para 2, [2001] 1 SCR 687 [*Ruzic*].
>
> [15] *Ruzic*, *supra* note 10 at para 18.

➢ Create a short form by choosing **one of the parties' surnames or a distinctive part of the style of cause**.

➢ If the initial citation includes more than one source, indicate the reporter to which subsequent pinpoint references will be made by including cited to followed by the abbreviation of the reporter.

➢ If there is a pinpoint reference in the initial citation, make all further references to that same source. Do not include cited to in that case (see note 10).

➢ For cases with a neutral citation, do not indicate the reporter to which subsequent references are directed. Paragraph numbers are determined by the court and are uniform for all reporters.

1.4.1.4 Secondary Materials

> ➢ **Use the author's surname** in subsequent references to the source (see notes 2 and 12).

> ➢ If **more than one work by a particular author is cited**, create a short form consisting of the author's name and a shortened form of the title of the work, separated by a comma (see notes 3 and 14). In the short form of the title, maintain the same formatting as the full title—italics for books and quotation marks for articles.

¹ G Blaine Baker, "The Reconstitution of Upper Canadian Legal Thought in the Late-Victorian Empire" (1985) 3 Law & History Rev 219 [Baker, "Reconstitution"].

² John Humphrey, *No Distant Millennium: The International Law of Human Rights* (Paris: UNESCO, 1989).

³ G Blaine Baker, "The Province of Post-Confederation Rights" (1995) 45 UTLJ 77 [Baker, "Post-Confederation Rights"].

¹² Humphrey, *supra* note 2 at 25.

¹³ Rebecca Veinott, "Child Custody and Divorce: A Nova Scotia Study, 1866-1910" in Philip Girard & Jim Phillips, eds, *Essays in the History of Canadian Law*, vol 3 (Toronto: University of Toronto Press, 1990) 273.

¹⁴ Baker, "Post-Confederation Rights", *supra* note 3 at 86.

⁸⁶ Kimberley Smith Maynard, "Divorce in Nova Scotia, 1750-1890" in Girard & Phillips, *supra* note 13, 232 at 239.

> ➢ If there are **two essays from the same book**, refer to the second essay using the original citation of the collection of essays and the name of the editor(s) (see notes 13 and 86).

1.4.2 *Ibid*

¹ See *Canada Labour Relations Board v Halifax Longshoremen's Association, Local 269*, [1983] 1 SCR 245, 144 DLR (3d) 1 [*HLA*].

² *Ibid* at 260. See also *Fraser v Canada (Public Service Staff Relations Board)*, [1985] 2 SCR 455 at 463, 23 DLR (4th) 122 [*Fraser*]; *Heustis v New Brunswick Electric Power Commission*, [1979] 2 SCR 768, 98 DLR (3d) 622 [*Heustis*].

⁵ *Fraser*, *supra* note 2 at 460.

⁶ *Ibid* at 461-62.

⁷ *Ibid*.

⁹⁸ For a more detailed analysis, see *Union des employés de service, Local 298 v Bibeault*, [1988] 2 SCR 1048, 95 NR 161 [*Bibeault* cited to SCR]. The Court cited a "patently unreasonable" standard of review (*ibid* at 1084-85).

⁹⁹ But see *Business Corporations Act*, RSS 1978, c B-10, s 18 [*BCA*].

¹⁰⁰ See *BCA*, *ibid*, s 22.

> ➢ *Ibid* is an abbreviation of the Latin word *ibidem*, meaning "in the same place".

➤ Use *ibid* to direct the reader to the **immediately preceding reference** (not to the whole preceding footnote). Do not provide the number of the footnote in which the preceding reference appears.

➤ *Ibid* may be used **after a full citation** (see note 2), **after a *supra*** (see note 6) or even **after another *ibid*** (see note 7). If there is more than one reference in the previous footnote, use *ibid* only when referring to the very last reference of that footnote.

➤ An *ibid* used without a pinpoint reference refers to the same pinpoint as in the previous footnote (see note 7).

➤ To refer to the previous source within the same footnote, use *ibid* in parentheses (see note 98).

1.4.3 *Supra*

➤ *Supra* is a Latin word meaning "above".

> ¹ *McMillan Bloedel Ltd v British Columbia (AG)* (1996), 22 BCLR (3d) 137, 30 WCB (2d) 446 (CA) [*McMillan*]; *Towne Cinema Theatres Ltd v R*, [1985] 1 SCR 494, 18 DLR (4th) 1 [*Towne Cinema*].
>
> ⁵⁶ *McMillan, supra* note 1 at 147.
>
> ⁵⁷ *Ibid* at 150. See also *Towne Cinema, supra* note 1.
>
> ⁵⁸ *Supra* note 1 at 140.
>
> ⁵⁹ *Ibid*.
>
> ⁶⁰ See also *supra* note 24 and accompanying text.

➤ Use *supra* and the short form to refer a reader to a **previous footnote containing the original full citation**. *Supra* must always refer the reader to the original citation, not to another *supra* or *ibid*.

➤ If the source being referred to is clearly identified in the text (e.g. if the text reads "the court of appeal in *McMillan*⁵⁸"), it is unnecessary to repeat that information in the footnote (see note 58).

➤ To refer to a previous footnote and the text to which the footnote relates, use *supra* note # and accompanying text (see note 60).

➤ To refer only to the text and not to the footnote, use above not *supra* (section 1.4.5).

1.4.4 *Infra*

➤ *Infra* is a Latin word meaning "below".

➤ Use *infra* to refer a reader to a **subsequent footnote**.

➤ The use of *infra* is **strongly discouraged**. Provide the full citation the first time a source is mentioned.

➤ To refer only to the text and not to the footnote, use below instead of *infra* (section 1.4.5).

1.4.5 Above and Below

➤ Use the words above and below to direct the reader to **a portion of the text** and not to the footnotes.

➤ If there are no easily identifiable section or paragraph markers, or if the final pagination of the text is unclear at the time of writing, use the formulation see text accompanying note #.

> [1] See Part III-A, above, for more on this topic.
>
> [2] Further discussion of this case will be found at 164-70, below.
>
> [3] For further analysis of the holding in Oakes, see text accompanying note 41.

1.5   CITING SOURCES THAT QUOTE OR REPRINT THE ORIGINAL SOURCE

It is always preferable to cite directly to an original source. If an original source is quoted in part in another work (the citing source), consult the original work in order to verify the context and accuracy of the reference.

1.5.1 Obscure Original Source

Cited in	*Papers Relating to the Commission appointed to enquire into the state and condition of the Indians of the North-West Coast of British Columbia*, British Columbia Sessional Papers, 1888 at 432-33, cited in Hamar Foster, "Honouring the Queen's Flag: A Legal and Historical Perspective on the Nisga'a Treaty" (1998) 120 BC Studies 11 at 13.

➤ The original source may sometimes be **difficult to find** or may have been **destroyed**. In such exceptional circumstances, it may be necessary to cite to the original source as presented in a citing source. Provide as much information on the original work as possible, followed by cited in and the citation to the citing source.

Reprinted in	George R to Governor Arthur Phillip, Royal Instruction, 25 April 1787 (27 Geo III), reprinted in *Historical Documents of New South Wales*, vol 1, part 2 (Sydney: Government Printer, 1892-1901) 67.

➤ In certain cases, the original version of a document fully reprinted in a collection (e.g. collections reprinting debates, letters, treaties or manuscripts) is **only available in archives**. Provide a complete citation to the original work, followed by reprinted in and the citation to the citing source.

➤ Do not refer to books reprinting excerpts from original sources that are readily available (e.g. textbooks).

✓	*International Covenant on Civil and Political Rights*, (19 December 1966), 999 UNTS 171, 1976 Can TS No 47.
✗	*International Covenant on Civil and Political Rights*, (19 December 1966), 999 UNTS 171, 1976 Can TS No 47, reprinted in Hugh M Kindred et al, eds, *International Law Chiefly as Interpreted and Applied in Canada: Documentary Supplement* (Np: Emond Montgomery, 2000) 87.

1.5.2 Emphasis on the Citing Source

Citing	*Canada (Citizenship and Immigration) v Khosa*, 2009 SCC 12, [2009] 1 SCR 339 at para 38, citing Pierre-André Côté, *Interprétation des lois,* 3d ed (Cowansville, Que: Yvon Blais, 1999) at 91, n 123.

➢ To highlight the fact that a work is referring to the original material (e.g. when the secondary work is more eminent or trustworthy) include the citation to the citing source, followed by citing and by the citation to the original source.

1.6 GENERAL RULES FOR QUOTATIONS

These rules apply to both text and footnotes.

1.6.1 Positioning of Quotations

This principle, which has existed since 1929, is based on a dynamic conception of the constitution "a living tree capable of growth and expansion."[1]

Justice LeBel, writing for the Court, invoked the scenario that Justice Dickson (as he then was) used in *Perka* to explain the concept:

> By way of illustration in *Perka*, Dickson J. evoked the situation of a lost alpinist who, on the point of freezing to death, breaks into a remote mountain cabin. The alpinist confronts a painful dilemma: freeze to death or commit a criminal offence. Yet as Dickson J pointed out at p 249, the alpinist's choice to break the law "is no true choice at all; it is remorselessly compelled by normal human instincts", here of self-preservation.[2]

The *Civil Code of Quebec* begins in a peculiar way, introducing two legal concepts that are meaningless to the common citizen. Article 1 reads as following:

> Every human being possesses juridical personality and has the full enjoyment of civil rights.[3]

➢ Place short quotations of **four lines or fewer** in quotation marks and incorporate them directly into the text.

➢ Indent from both margins and single space quotations of **more than four lines**. Do not use quotation marks. Legislative provisions may be indented even if they are fewer than four lines long.

1.6.2 Format of Quotations

➢ Spelling, capitalization, and internal punctuation in a quotation must be **exactly the same as in the original** source; any changes and additions must be clearly indicated in brackets.

➢ If the sentence becomes grammatically incorrect, make the proper adjustments in brackets (for example, change a lower case letter for an upper case letter).

➢ Use an ellipsis (…) to indicate the omission of a passage from the middle or

In-text
It was clear from this moment that "[t]he centre … of American jurisprudence had changed."[32]
"[A] mixed question of fact and law" must be appealable.[42]

the end of the quoted material. Only use an ellipsis at the beginning of a quotation if the quoted sentence is deliberately left grammatically incomplete.

✓	The petitioner must prove that "[c]onsidering the circumstances, the opposing party will not be able to shift the burden of proof."
✗	The petitioner must prove that "[…] considering the circumstances, the opposing party will not be able to shift the burden of proof."

➢ Where the original source contains an error, **enclose the correction in square brackets**. Do not use [*sic*], which should only be used to draw attention to the original error.

➢ Text may be emphasized by using italics and placing [emphasis added] at the end of the citation. If the text was emphasized in the original copy, place [emphasis in original] at the end of the citation. If there are footnotes in the original text, which are not reproduced in the quote, place [footnotes omitted] at the end of the citation. (The placement of such expressions after the citation in the

Footnotes
[31] *Norris, supra* note 21 [emphasis added].
[32] *Kadlak v Nunavut (Minister of Sustainable Development)*, [2001] Nu J No 1 ¶ 9 (QL) [*Kadlak*] [emphasis in the original].
[77] Lamontagne, *supra* note 65 at 109 [footnotes omitted].

footnote is contrary to the rule applicable in French.) Place these expressions after the establishment of a short form (see note 32).

1.6.3 Quoting a Source in Another Language

➢ If at all possible, use an English version of a source when writing in English and a French

[1] Jacques Ghestin & Gilles Goubeaux, *Traité de droit civil: Introduction générale*, 4th ed (Paris: Librairie générale de droit et de jurisprudence, 1994) at para 669 [translated by author].

version when writing in French. Every Canadian jurisdiction passes statutes in English.

➢ If quoting in another language, a translation may be provided, but is not required. Clearly indicate any translation in the footnote and identify the translator. If the work is translated by a professional, indicate the translator's name (section 6.2.2.5.1). If you, the author, translated the work, include [translated by author].

1.7   WRITING IN A FOREIGN LANGUAGE

The *Guide* is a Canadian work and applies to texts written in the country's two official languages. However, it is possible to adapt these rules to any other language, inspired by the English or the French section. The guidelines are **uniformity** and **facility to retrace a source** for the reader.

➢ **Translate expressions** such as "see", "cited in", "reprinted in", "emphasis added", and "with reference to", but keep the Latin expressions as they are.

➢ Follow the **form** rules, such as the order of elements and the structure of the document.

➢ Follow the **punctuation** rules of the language in which the text is written. If needed, consult a grammar book. Make sure that the form of the punctuation marks remains consistent throughout the text.

➢ For **legislation**, follow the Canadian general form. Use the statute volume and jurisdiction abbreviations as presented in the legislation's official document. Include the court and jurisdiction.

➢ For **jurisprudence**, follow the hierarchy of the sources. Always keep the audience in mind and verify that the readers can have access to the information. Use the abbreviation of the reporter as presented in the source, and always include the court and jurisdiction.

➢ If the abbreviation of the **journal** is not in **Appendix D** of the *Guide*, include the full name of the journal.

Legislation

Legislation

2   LEGISLATION

2.1   STATUTES

2.1.1   General Form

Title,	statute volume	jurisdiction	year,	chapter	(session or supplement),	pinpoint.
Criminal Code,	RS	C	1985,	c C-46		s 745.
Income Tax Act,	RS	C	1985,	c 1	(5th Supp),	s 18(1)(m)(iv)(c).
Charter of human rights and freedoms,	RS	Q		c C-12		s 10.

➤   Do not include a space between the statute volume and the jurisdiction.

➤   For constitutional statutes, see section 2.2.

2.1.2   Sources

➤   Find Canadian legislation in **revised or re-enacted statutes**, **annual volumes**, **loose-leaf consolidations** and **electronic sources**. Use the following table to determine which source to cite for each Canadian jurisdiction.

Legislation

Jurisdiction	Order of the sources to cite from
Canada British-Columbia Saskatchewan Newfoundland and Labrador Northwest Territories Nova Scotia Yukon	Refer to the printed **revised statutes** whenever possible. Refer to the printed **annual volumes** if: → referring to a statute that was enacted since the last revision was published or → referring to a section that has been added or amended since the revision date.
Manitoba	Refer to the **revised statutes** or to the **annual volumes** in the same way as to the former jurisdictions. Optional: refer to the ***Continuing Consolidation of the Statutes of Manitoba*** (CCSM) after the reference to the annual volumes (section 2.1.4).
New Brunswick	*Before 2003:* Refer to the **revised statutes** or to the **annual volumes** in the same way as to the former jurisdictions. -OR- Refer to the **official electronic version** (section 2.1.6). *After 2003:* Use the **official electronic version** (section 2.1.6).
Ontario	Refer to the revised statutes or to the annual volumes in the same way as to the former jurisdictions. -OR- Use the official **electronic version** (e-Laws) (section 2.1.6).
Quebec	Refer to the official loose-leaf consolidation first (section 2.1.4). If necessary, refer to the revised statutes or to the annual volumes in the same way as to the former jurisdictions.

2.1.3   Title

➤ Italicize the title of the statute and place a non-italicized comma after the title.

> *Civil Marriage Act*, SC 2005, c 41.
>
> *Reciprocal Enforcement of Maintenance Orders Act*, SY 1980, c 25, s 5(2).

➤ Provide the **official short title** of the statute. If none is provided, use the title found at the head of the statute. Include The only if it forms part of the title.

> If the title of the statute is provided in the text, do not repeat it in the citation.

> Follow the capitalization of words in the title as set out in the statute. Many English titles of Quebec statutes follow French capitalization rules. Do *not* capitalize letters in these titles to conform to English language capitalization rules.

> Include a year that is part of the title of the statute in italics within the title. Add the year after the jurisdiction even if the year is part of the title.

NB: The statutes of the following jurisdictions are adopted in both English and French: Canada, Manitoba, New Brunswick, Ontario, Quebec, Nunavut, the Northwest Territories, and the Yukon. However, statutes adopted prior to a certain date may exist only in English.

2.1.4 Revised Statutes and Annual Volumes

Revised statutes	*Children's Law Reform Act*, RSO 1990, c C-12.
	An Act respecting immigration to Québec, RSQ c I-0.2, s 3.
Annual volumes	*Agricultural Land Commission Act*, SBC 2002, c 36.

> Both **Revised Statutes** and **Re-enacted Statutes** are abbreviated to RS. For citations to annual volumes, abbreviate **Statutes** to S.

> Use S for Statutes (not O for Ordinances) when referring to any volume, past or present, of Northwest Territories or Yukon legislation.

NB: If a statute cannot be found in the current Revised Statutes, do not assume that it does not exist or that it is no longer relevant. For example, the *Canada Corporations Act* has been replaced by the *Canada Business Corporations Act* for profit-making corporations, but is still in force for non-profit corporations. The *Canada Corporations Act* was not brought forward into the 1985 *Revised Statutes*, but is found in the 1970 revision. The 1970 version as amended is still valid law.

2.1.5 Loose-leafs

Manitoba	*Retirement Plan Beneficiaries Act*, SM 1992, c 31, CCSM c R138, s 14.
Quebec	*Securities Act*, RSQ c V-1.1, s 15.

> Only the provinces of Manitoba, Quebec and Nova Scotia publish an official version of loose-leafs. For Manitoba, always mention the annual volume before the loose-leafs.

> Cite Nova Scotia loose-leafs in the same manner as revised statutes and annual volumes (section 2.1.4).

> Do not place a comma between the name of the volume and the chapter number.

2.1.6   Official electronic version

Ontario	*Law Society Act*, RSO 1990, c L.8, s 26.1(1).
New Brunswick	*Pay Equity Act, 2009*, SNB c P-5.05, s 6(1).

➢ Refer to an official electronic version in the same way as to a printed version (section 2.1.4).

➢ **New Brunswick**: Since 2003, the Queen's Printer for New Brunswick no longer publishes its legislation on paper. It can be found on the government's website (<http://www.gnb.ca/acts>).

➢ **Ontario**: Since November 30, 2008, copies of source laws and consolidated laws accessed from the e-Laws website (<http://www.e-laws.gov.on.ca>) are official copies of the law, unless accompanied by a disclaimer.

2.1.7   Jurisdiction

➢ Place the jurisdiction immediately after the statute volume.

➢ See **Appendix A.1** for the correct abbreviation of legislation.

> *Proceeds of Crime (Money Laundering) and Terrorist Financing Act*, SC 2000, c 17.
>
> *Workers Compensation Act*, SPEI 1994, c 67.

Jurisdiction abbreviations for legislation:

Alberta	A
British Columbia	BC
Canada	C
Lower Canada	LC
Manitoba	M
New Brunswick	NB
Newfoundland (Statutes and Regulations repealed before 6 December 2001 / Gazette published before 21 December 2001)	N
Newfoundland and Labrador (Statutes and Regulations in force on or after 6 December 2001 / Gazette published 21 December 2001 and after)	NL
Northwest Territories	NWT
Nova Scotia	NS
Nunavut (1 April 1999 and after)	Nu
Ontario	O
Prince Edward Island	PEI
Province of Canada	Prov C
Quebec	Q
Saskatchewan	S
Upper Canada	UC
Yukon	Y

2.1.8 Year, Session, and Supplement

Year	*Animal Protection Act*, RSA 2000, c A-41.
Session spanning more than one year	*Government Organization Act, 1983*, SC 1980-81-82-83, c 167.
More than one session in a year	*An Act to amend the Business Licence Act*, SNWT 1985 (3d Sess), c 1.
Supplement	*Customs Act*, RSC 1985, c 1 (2d Supp).
Regnal year	*An Act respecting the Civilization and Enfranchisement of certain Indians*, S Prov C 1859 (22 Vict), c 9.

➢ Place the year after the jurisdiction, followed by a comma. If a session or regnal year follows the year, place the comma after the session or regnal year.

➢ Omit the year when citing the loose-leaf editions of the statutes of Manitoba (CCSM) or Quebec (RSQ), and do not place a comma between the name of the volume and the chapter number (section 2.1.5).

➢ When a **session spans more than one year**, write the full date span of the volume (e.g. 1980-81).

➢ If a **statute volume is divided into several sessions** with independent chapter numbering, place the number of the session (1st, 2d, 3d or 4th) and the abbreviation Sess in parentheses following the year.

➢ Refer to the **supplement** for acts and amendments that were passed during the year in which the *Revised Statutes* were issued, but that were not included in the revision. Place the supplement number and the abbreviation Supp in parentheses after the chapter.

➢ For federal statutes enacted before 1867, and for provincial statutes enacted before the province entered Confederation, give the **regnal year** in parentheses following the calendar year. Otherwise give the calendar year and not the regnal year.

Ann	Ann
Edward	Edw
Elizabeth	Eliz

George	Geo
Victoria	Vict
William	Will

2.1.9 Chapter

➢ Abbreviate chapter to c.

➢ Write the numeric or alphanumeric chapter designation exactly as shown in the statute volume, including dashes and periods.

Holocaust Memorial Day Act, SBC 2000, c 3.
Law Reform Act, SNB 1993, c L-1.2.
Child Welfare Act, 1972, SN 1972, No 37.

NB: Between 1934 and 1975-76, statutes in Newfoundland annual volumes are designated by number. Abbreviate **Number** to No.

2.1.10 Pinpoint

➢ To cite a specific section of a statute, place a comma after the chapter and then indicate the section or sections.

➢ Abbreviate **section** to s and **sections** to ss in the footnotes, but always write the full word in the text. Do not insert at.

➢ Abbreviate further subdivisions of sections (subsections, paragraphs, subparagraphs) to s or ss.

> [1] *Environmental Protection and Enhancement Act*, RSA 2000, c E-12, ss 2, 38-42, 84.
>
> [2] *Legal Profession Act, 1990*, SS 1990, c L-10.1, ss 4(1), 6(2)(b)(i)-(ii), 9.
>
> [3] *Peddlers Act*, RSQ c C-30, s 9, para 2.
>
> [4] *Charter of the French language*, RSQ c C-11, Preamble.
>
> [5] *Access to Information Act*, RSC 1985, c A-1, Schedule II.

➢ Separate **consecutive** sections by a **hyphen** and **non-consecutive** sections by a **comma** (see note 1).

➢ Place each numbered or lettered subsection in parentheses immediately after the section number (see note 2), even when the original version does not include parentheses.

➢ The **provisions of Quebec codes are articles, not sections**. Abbreviate article and articles to art and arts respectively (section 2.3).

➢ Cite an unnumbered or unlettered subdivision like a paragraph, abbreviated as the symbol ¶ or para in the singular and paras in the plural (see note 3). Do not use parentheses.

➢ Do not abbreviate Preamble (see note 4) or Schedule (see note 5).

2.1.11 Amendments, Repeals, and Re-enactments

Presumed to be amended	*Crown Liability and Proceedings Act*, RSC 1985, c C-50.
Indicating amended status	*Emergency Measures Act*, SM 1987, c 11, as amended by SM 1997, c 28. *Municipal Government Act*, RSA 2000, c M-26, s 694(4), as amended by *Municipal Government Amendment Act*, SA 2003, c 43, s 4.
Indicating repealed status	*Family Benefits Act*, RSO 1990, c F.2, as repealed by *Social Assistance Reform Act, 1997*, SO 1997, c 25, s 4(1).
Act amending an earlier act	*An Act to Amend the Labour Standards Act*, SNWT 1999, c 18, amending RSNWT 1988, c L-1.
Act repealing an earlier act	*An Act respecting the James Bay Native Development Corporation*, RSQ 2000, c S-9.1, repealing *An Act to incorporate the James Bay Native Development Corporation*, SQ 1978, c 96.

➤ Citations are presumed to be to the statute **as amended on the date of publication** of the text of the author's text.

➤ Indicate that the statute has been amended only if it is relevant to the point being discussed in the text. When indicating an amendment, cite the original statute first, followed by as amended by and the citation for the amending statute.

➤ When an act has been **repealed**, always indicate the repeal in the citation (as repealed by).

➤ Use amending when referring specifically to a statute that amends an earlier statute, and use repealing when citing a statute that repeals an earlier statute.

➤ Indicate the title of the second statute only if it is different from the title of the first statute, or if it is not included in the title of the first statute cited.

➤ If a statute or part of a statute was repealed and another substituted, cite the original statute first, followed by as re-enacted by and the citation for the new replacement section. Use this term only if the repeal and substitute provision are found in the same section.

Legislation

2.1.12 Appendices

➤ For statutes that appear in an appendix, always provide the official citation first, followed by the citation to the appendix.

Canadian Bill of Rights, SC 1960, c 44, reprinted in RSC 1985, App III.

➤ Introduce the appendix reference with the phrase reprinted in.

➤ Indicate the statute revision or volume to which the appendix is attached (e.g. RSC 1985), followed by a comma and the appendix number.

➤ Abbreviate **Appendix** to App.

➤ Write the appendix number in Roman numerals.

2.1.13 Statutes Within Statutes

➤ Refer first to the title of the statute within the statute. Indicate the relevant part of the containing act and its full citation, introduced by a comma and being.

Enterprise Cape Breton Corporation Act, s 25, being Part II of the *Government Organization Act, Atlantic Canada, 1987*, RSC 1985, c 41 (4th Supp).

➤ Place pinpoint references to section numbers before the citation to the containing act.

2.2   CONSTITUTIONAL STATUTES

Constitution Act, 1867	*Constitution Act, 1867* (UK), 30 & 31 Vict, c 3, reprinted in RSC 1985, App II, No 5.
Canada Act 1982	*Canada Act 1982* (UK), 1982, c 11.
Constitution Act, 1982	*Constitution Act, 1982*, being Schedule B to the *Canada Act 1982* (UK), 1982, c 11.
Charter	*Canadian Charter of Rights and Freedoms*, Part I of the *Constitution Act, 1982*, being Schedule B to the *Canada Act 1982* (UK), 1982, c 11.
Other constitutional statutes	*Saskatchewan Act*, SC 1905, c 42.

➤ Many constitutional statutes were enacted under different names than those used today; use the **new title**. Consult the Schedule to the *Constitution Act, 1982* to determine the new title for the statute. If it is necessary, provide the old title in parentheses at the end of the citation.

➤ Since the *Canada Act 1982* is a British statute, use the rules for the United Kingdom (section 7.1.1).

➢ Since the *Charter* is not an independent enactment, cite it as Part I of the *Constitution Act, 1982*.

➢ If necessary, include a citation to **Appendix II of RSC 1985** after the official citation. Most Canadian constitutional statutes are reprinted in Appendix II.

2.2.1 Pinpoint

Constitution Act, 1867	*Constitution Act, 1867* (UK), 30 & 31 Vict, c 3, s 91, reprinted in RSC 1985, App II, No 5.
Canada Act 1982	*Canada Act 1982* (UK), 1982, c 11, s 1.
Constitution Act, 1982	*Constitution Act, 1982*, s 35, being Schedule B to the *Canada Act 1982* (UK), 1982, c 11.
Charter	*Canadian Charter of Rights and Freedoms*, s 7, Part I of the *Constitution Act, 1982*, being Schedule B to the *Canada Act 1982* (UK), 1982, c 11.
Other constitutional statutes	*Saskatchewan Act*, SC 1905, c 42, s 2.

➢ Place pinpoint references to the *Charter* and the *Constitution Act, 1982* immediately after the title (section 2.1.10).

➢ For any other constitutional statutes, place pinpoint references after the chapter number.

2.3 CODES

Civil Code of Québec	art 1260 CCQ
Civil Code of Québec (1980)	art 435 CCQ (1980)
Civil Code of Lower Canada	art 1131 CCLC
Code of Civil Procedure	art 477 CCP
Code of Penal Procedure	art 104 CPP

➢ **Never use full citations when referring to codes.**

➢ To cite one of the codes illustrated here, use the abbreviated name.

> ➢ To cite another code, write the full title of the code in the first reference, and create a short form if needed (e.g. art 1 *Professional Code* [Prof C]).

> ➢ The provisions of Quebec codes are **articles, not sections**. Abbreviate article to art and articles to arts.

> ➢ Cite an unnumbered or unlettered subdivision like a **paragraph**, abbreviated as the symbol ¶ or para in the singular and paras in the plural (e.g. art 1457, para 2 CCQ).

NB: To cite the **Minister's Comments**, see section 4.2.1.

NB: The **CCQ (1980)** is a series of family law enactments implemented in 1980: *An Act to establish a new Civil Code and to reform family law*, SQ 1980, c 39. Do not confuse this with the *Civil Code of Quebec*, SQ 1991, c 64 (CCQ), which came into force on 1 January 1994, replacing the *Civil Code of Lower Canada* of 1866 (CCLC).

2.4 NUNAVUT

The Territorial Printer of Nunavut does not currently print bound versions of the statutes. Find unofficial Nunavut statutes on the Nunavut Department of Justice website (<http://www.justice.gov.nu.ca>).

2.4.1 Statutes Enacted by Nunavut

> ➢ For statutes enacted by Nunavut after 1 April 1999, provide the standard citation following the general form (section 2.1).

Flag of Nunavut Act, S Nu 1999, c 1.

2.4.2 Statutes Enacted by the Northwest Territories for Nunavut

> ➢ For statutes enacted specifically for Nunavut by the Northwest Territories prior to 1 April 1999 and that do apply only to Nunavut, provide the standard citation followed by: as enacted for Nunavut, pursuant to the *Nunavut Act*, SC 1993, c 28.

Flag of Nunavut Act, S Nu 1999, c 1. *Nunavut Judicial System Implementation Act*, SNWT 1998, c 34, as enacted for Nunavut, pursuant to the *Nunavut Act*, SC 1993, c 28.

2.4.3 Statutes Duplicated for Nunavut

➢   Under section 29 of the federal *Nunavut Act*, SC 1993, c 28, laws from the Northwest Territories were duplicated for Nunavut to take effect on 1 April 1999 (to the extent they would apply in relation to Nunavut).

> *Official Languages Act*, RSNWT 1998, c O-1, as duplicated for Nunavut by s 29 of the *Nunavut Act*, SC 1993, c 28.

➢   Provide the standard citation followed by: as duplicated for Nunavut by s 29 of the *Nunavut Act*, SC 1993, c 28.

2.5   BILLS

	Number,	*title,*	session,	legislature,	jurisdiction,	year,	pinpoint	(additional information) (optional).
Canada	Bill C-26,	*An Act to establish the Canada Border Services Agency,*	1st Sess,	38th Parl,		2005,	cl 5(1)(e)	(as passed by the House of Commons 13 June 2005).
	Bill S-3,	*An Act to amend the Energy Efficiency Act,*	2nd Sess,	40th Parl,		2009,	cl 5	(first reading 29 January 2009).
Provinces and territories	Bill 59,	*An Act to amend the Civil Code as regards marriage,*	1st Sess,	37th Leg,	Quebec,	2004		(assented to 10 November 2004), SQ 2004, c 23.

➢   Add C- before bills originating in the House of Commons and S- before bills originating in the Senate.

➢   **Use the long title of the bill.** Italicize the title and follow the bill's capitalization.

➢   If referring to a provincial bill, include the jurisdiction.

➢   Do not provide the regnal year.

➢   The subdivisions of a bill are **clauses**, abbreviated to cl and cls for plural.

➢   Include additional information as needed (e.g. the date of first reading or the state that the bill has reached at the time of writing). Place the information in parentheses at the end of the citation.

Legislation

➢   If the chapter number of the bill is known, include the future statute citation after the date of assent as an additional information (e.g. (assented to 10 November 2004), SQ 2004, c 23).

2.6   REGULATIONS

Jurisdiction	Unrevised	Revised or re-enacted
Canada	SOR/2000-111, s 4.	CRC, c 1035, s 4.
Alberta	Alta Reg 184/2001, s 2.	—
British Columbia	BC Reg 362/2000, s 4.	—
Manitoba	Man Reg 155/2001, s 3.	Man Reg 368/97R, s 2.
New Brunswick	NB Reg 2000-8, s 11.	—
Newfoundland	Nfld Reg 78/99, s 4.	—
Newfoundland and Labrador	NLR 08/02, s 2.	CNLR 1151/96, s 6.
Northwest Territories	NWT Reg 253-77, s 3.	RRNWT 1990, c E-27, s 16.
Nova Scotia	NS Reg 24/2000, s 8.	—
Nunavut	Nu Reg 045-99, s 2.	—
Ontario	O Reg 426/00, s 2.	RRO 1990, Reg 1015, s 3.
Prince Edward Island	PEI Reg EC1999-598, s 3.	—
Quebec	OC 868-97, 2 July 1997, (1997) GOQ II 3692, s 2.	RRQ 1981, c E-12, r 1, s 4.
Saskatchewan	Sask Reg 67/2001, s 3.	RRS, c C-50-2, Reg 21, OC 359/2000, s 6.
Yukon	YOIC 2000/130, s 9.	—

2.6.1   Federal Regulations

2.6.1.1   Revised Regulations

➢   Abbreviate **Consolidated Regulations of Canada** to CRC.

➢   Indicate the year of revision of the revised regulations (optional). Citations are assumed to be to the latest revision.

Title,	CRC,	chapter,	pinpoint	(year) (optional).
Migratory Birds Regula-tions,	CRC,	c 1035,	s 4	(1978).

2.6.1.2 *Unrevised Regulations*

Title (optional),	SOR/	year-regulation number,	pinpoint.
Offset of Taxes by a Refund or a Rebate (GST/HST) Regulations,	SOR/	91-49,	s 4.
Canadian Aviation Security Regulations,	SOR/	2000-111,	s 4.

> ➤ Find federal regulations promulgated after the Consolidation **in Part II of the** ***Canada Gazette***. Do not include a direct citation to the *Gazette*.

> ➤ Indicate the title (optional).

> ➤ Abbreviate **Statutory Orders and Regulations** to SOR.

> ➤ For regulations starting with the year 2000, include the four digits of the year. For years up until 1999, use only the last two digits (e.g. write 98 and not 1998).

2.6.2 Provincial and Territorial Regulations

> ➤ Include the title of the regulations (optional) in italics at the beginning of the citation, followed by a comma.

> ➤ Some jurisdictions use all four digits to indicate the year starting with the year 2000.

NB: Alberta, British Columbia, New Brunswick, Nova Scotia, Nunavut, Prince Edward Island, and the Yukon do not publish revised versions of their regulations.

2.6.2.1 *Alberta, British Columbia*

> ➤ Cite the Alberta and British Columbia loose-leaf consolidation in the same manner as unrevised regulations (section 2.6).

Jurisdiction	Reg	number/ year,	pinpoint.
Alta	Reg	184/2001,	s 2.
BC	Reg	184/2001,	s 6.

2.6.2.2 Manitoba

	Jurisdiction	Reg	number/year,	pinpoint.
Not re-enacted	Man	Reg	155/2001,	s 3.
Re-enacted	Man	Reg	468/88R.	s 2.

➢ Most of Manitoba's regulations were re-enacted in English and in French in **1987** and **1988**. There has been no revision since.

➢ To indicate a re-enacted regulation, insert R immediately following the year.

2.6.2.3 New Brunswick

Jurisdiction	Reg	year-number,	pinpoint.
NB	Reg	2000-8,	s 11.

➢ The New Brunswick regulations were last revised in **1963**.

2.6.2.4 Newfoundland and Labrador

➢ All references to Newfoundland were retroactively amended to Newfoundland and Labrador. Indicate Newfoundland only for regulations repealed before 6 December 2001.

2.6.2.4.1 Unrevised

➢ Write Nfld Reg to indicate regulations repealed before 6 December 2001. Use NL for other regulations.

Jurisdiction	R	number/last two digits of year,	pinpoint.
NL	R	8/02,	s 2.

2.6.2.4.2 Revised

➢ Newfoundland and Labrador regulations were revised and consolidated in 1996. Use CNLR to indicate a **Consolidated Newfoundland and Labrador Regulation**.

CNLR	number/year of consolidation,	pinpoint.
CNLR	1151/96,	s 6.

➢ Use CNR for **Consolidated Newfoundland Regulation** to indicate regulations repealed before 6 December 2001.

2.6.2.5 Northwest Territories

2.6.2.5.1 Unrevised

Jurisdiction	Reg	number-last two digits of year,	pinpoint.
NWT	Reg	253-77,	s 3.

2.6.2.5.2 Revised

RRNWT	year of revision,	chapter,	pinpoint.
RRNWT	1990,	c E-27,	s 16.

2.6.2.6 Nova Scotia

Jurisdiction	Reg	number/year,	pinpoint.
NS	Reg	24/2000,	s 8.

2.6.2.7 Nunavut

➢ Consult the *Nunavut Gazette* for all regulations since 1 April 1999.

Jurisdiction	Reg	number-last two digits of year,	pinpoint.
Nu	Reg	045-99,	s 2.

➢ Consult the *Revised Regulations of the Northwest Territories* (1990) and *The Northwest Territories Gazette*, Part II, for all regulations made prior to 1 April 1999.

➢ No official revised version of the Nunavut Regulations has been issued.

2.6.2.8 Ontario

2.6.2.8.1 Unrevised

Jurisdiction	Reg	number/last two digits of year,	pinpoint.
O	Reg	426/00,	s 2.

2.6.2.8.2 Revised

RRO	year of revision,	Reg	number,	pinpoint.
RRO	1990,	Reg	1015,	s 3.

Legislation

2.6.2.9   Prince Edward Island

➢ EC is the abbreviation for **Executive Council**. There is no space between EC and year-number.

Jurisdiction	Reg	ECyear-number	pinpoint.
PEI	Reg	EC1999-598,	s 3.

2.6.2.10 Quebec

2.6.2.10.1 Unrevised

OC	number-year,	date,	*Gazette* citation,	pinpoint.
OC	1240-2000,	25 October 2000,	(2000) GOQ II, 6817,	s 2.

➢ To cite the *Gazette officielle du Québec*, see section 2.7.1.

2.6.2.10.2 Revised

RRQ 1981,	number,	rule number,	pinpoint.
RRQ 1981,	c C-11,	r 9,	s 10.

2.6.2.11 Saskatchewan

2.6.2.11.1 Unrevised

Jurisdiction	Reg	number/year	pinpoint.
Sask	Reg	67/2001,	s 3.

2.6.2.11.1 Revised

RRS	chapter,	number,	OC number/year (if available),	pinpoint.
RRS,	c C-502,	Reg 21,	OC 359/2000,	s 6.

2.6.2.12 Yukon

Jurisdiction	O/C	year/number,	pinpoint.
Y	O/C	2000/130,	s 9.

➢ Abbreviate **Order in Council** to OIC.

2.7   OTHER INFORMATION PUBLISHED IN *GAZETTES*

2.7.1   General Form

Title (additional information),	(year)	*Gazette* abbreviation	part of *Gazette,*	page,	additional information) (optional).
Ministerial Order 36/91,	(1991)	A Gaz	I,	1609,	s 6.
Notice (City of Abbotsford),	(2004)	C Gaz	I,	2520.	
OC 309/2001,	(2001)	A Gaz	I,	1752	(*Provincial Parks Act*).

➤ Include a space between the *Gazette* abbreviation and the year (e.g. C Gaz 1995).

➤ Indicate the title of the item if appropriate. If the item is numbered in some way, include the number with the title, as it appears in the *Gazette*. Include the statutory instrument number (SI) if there is one. Include the name of the person or body concerned by a notice in parentheses after the title (optional).

➤ Indicate the part of the *Gazette* following the abbreviation. If the *Gazette* is **not published in parts**, add a comma after the abbreviation and cite the page number (e.g. GOQ, 74).

➤ Include additional information, such as the name of the statute under which an order in council is made (see *Provincial Parks Act*).

Legislation

Abbreviations of *Gazettes*:

The Alberta Gazette	A Gaz
The British Columbia Gazette	BC Gaz
Canada Gazette	C Gaz
Gazette officielle du Québec	GOQ
The Manitoba Gazette	M Gaz
New Brunswick: The Royal Gazette	NB Gaz
Northwest Territories Gazette	NWT Gaz
The Newfoundland Gazette (before 21 December 2001)	N Gaz
The Newfoundland and Labrador Gazette (21 December 2001 and after)	NL Gaz
Nova Scotia: Royal Gazette	NS Gaz
Nunavut Gazette	Nu Gaz
The Ontario Gazette	O Gaz
Prince Edward Island: Royal Gazette	PEI Gaz
The Saskatchewan Gazette	S Gaz
The Yukon Gazette	Y Gaz

NB: The PDF of the *Canada Gazette* has been official since 1 April 2003 at <http://canadagazette.gc.ca>.

2.7.2 Orders in Council

An Order in Council is an instrument issued by the executive, which implements a government decision (such as the creation of a regulation).

2.7.2.1 Federal

Title (if available),	PC year-number or SI/year-number,	*Gazette* citation	(additional information) (optional).
	PC 1997-627,	(1997) C Gaz II, 1381.	
Withdrawal from Disposal Order (North Slave Region NWT),	SI/97-42,	(1997) C Gaz II, 1338.	

➢   Include the title in italics, if applicable.

➢   Abbreviate **Privy Council** to PC.

➢   Include the statutory instrument (SI) number, if there is one.

> Provide additional information (e.g. the title of the act under which the order in council is made) if necessary.

2.7.2.2 *Provincial and Territorial*

Title (if available),	Order in Council number,	*Gazette* citation	(additional information) (optional).
	OIC 1989/19,	(1989) Y Gaz II, 57.	
Town of Paradise Order,	OC 99-529,	(1999) N Gaz II, 451	(*Municipalities Act*).
Regulation respecting the lifting of the suspension and the application of section 41.1 of the Act respecting labour standards for certain employees,	OIC 570-93,	(1993) GOQ II, 2607.	

> Include the title of the instrument if available.

> Use the abbreviation for **Order in Council** as it appears in the relevant *Gazette*.

> Use the Order in Council number as it appears in the *Gazette*. This may include the year or the last two digits of the year.

> Provide additional information, such as the title of the act under which the order in council is made.

Legislation

2.7.3 Proclamations and Royal Instructions

Citation of law that entered into force or issuer of proclamation or instruction,	type of document,	date,	SI/year- number,	*Gazette* or other citation.
Sex Offender Information Registration Act, SC 2004, c 10,		proclaimed in force 15 December 2004,	SI/2004- 157,	(2004) C Gaz II, 2021.
	Proclamation,	1 April 1991,		(1991) S Gaz I, 1174.
George R,	Proclamation,	7 October 1763 (3 Geo III),		reprinted in RSC 1985, App II, No 1.
George R to Governor Arthur Phillip,	Royal Instruction,	25 April 1787 (27 Geo III),		reprinted in *Historical Documents of New South Wales*, vol 1, part 2 (Sydney: Government Printer, 1892-1901) 67.

➢ Use the words Proclamation or Royal Instruction if it is appropriate in the context.

➢ Include the date, followed by the *Gazette* or any other citation.

➢ To cite the federal proclamations dating from 1972, include the statutory instrument (SI) number.

2.8 MUNICIPAL BY-LAWS

	Municipality,	by-law or revised by-law	number,	*title*	(date),	pinpoint.
Unrevised	City of Whitehorse,	by-law	No 97-42,	*Zoning By-law*	(11 May 1998),	s 1.
Revised	City of Montreal,	revised by-law	C S-0.1.1,	*By-law Concerning Collection Services,*		s 5.

> ➢ Include the by-law number. Provide the full title if no short title is available.

2.9 RULES OF PRACTICE

Jurisdiction (if applicable),	issuing body (if applicable),	*title*,	pinpoint.
		Federal Court Immigration Rules,	r 18.
Manitoba,		*Court of Queen's Bench Rules,*	r 275.2.
	Commission québécoise des libérations conditionnelles, IC 570-93,	*Règles de pratique,*	r 10(4).

> ➢ Rules of practice (or rules of court) are procedural regulations governing judiciary and administrative bodies.

> ➢ Include the jurisdiction and issuing body unless it is part of the title of the rules.

> ➢ Do not indicate Canada for the rules of the Supreme Court of Canada or the Federal Court.

> ➢ Abbreviate **rule** as r.

> ➢ To cite to the Quebec *Code of Civil Procedure* or *Code of Penal Procedure*, see section 2.3.

Legislation

2.10 SECURITIES COMMISSIONS RULES

Title,	commission	document,	bulletin (if applicable)	(date),	pinpoint.
Mutual Reliance Review System for Exemptive Relief Applications,	OSC	NP 12-201		(26 August 2005),	s 6.
Proposed Amendments to Multilateral Instrument 52-109 Certification of Disclosure in Issuers' Annual and Interim Filings and Companion Policy 52-109CP,	MSC	Notice 2005-19		(1 April 2005).	
CSA Notice — Amendments to NI 31-101 National Registration System and NP 31-201 National Registration System,	OSC	CSA Notice,	29 OSCB 3955	(2006),	at 3956.

> Cite securities national instruments, national policies and other documents to **provincial securities commissions**.

> Abbreviate **National Policy** as NP and **National Instrument** as NI.

> For amendments, proposed rules, staff notices, requests for comments, and other commission documents, cite to the **securities commission bulletin** or similar publication, if available.

Jurisprudence

3   JURISPRUDENCE

3.1   SOURCES

Hierarchy of sources:

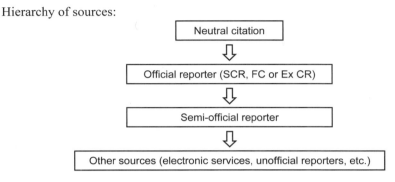

> ➤ Whenever possible, provide the reader with **at least two sources** to make sure the information is appropriately **identified** and **accessible**. Include as many sources as might be useful.

> ➤ **Before citing less authoritative sources, make sure that more authoritative sources are not available** (e.g. do not cite an electronic service before citing an official reporter).

> → Always provide the neutral citation if it is available.

> → After the neutral citation, provide the official reporters (SCR, FC or Ex CR).

> → If the neutral citation and/or official reporters are not available, provide the semi-official reporters.

> → Lastly, provide other sources (electronic services, unofficial reporters, etc.).

> ➤ Choose the **other sources** carefully and keep in mind their accessibility to readers.

> → For printed reporters, prefer **general reporters** that **cover a large geographic area** and that are **more readily available** (section 3.7.2).

> → For electronic services, prefer research databases that are **widely accessible** (section 3.8).

> ➤ Consult the following table to determine which sources to cite depending on what is available.

Jurisprudence

Sources available	Rule	Example
Neutral citation only	Cite to neutral citation and electronic source if available	*Adoption – 091*, 2009 QCCQ 628 (available on QL).
Neutral citation and printed reporter(s)	Include neutral citation and then cite to the most authoritative printed reporter available	*R v Latimer*, 2001 SCC 1, [2001] 1 SCR 3.
Official reporter and other reporter(s)	Cite to official reporter, including the most authoritative reporter as a parallel citation	*Baker v Canada (Minister of Citizenship and Immigration)*, [1999] 2 SCR 817, 174 DLR (4th) 193.
Unofficial reporter(s) and/or electronic service(s)	Cite to the two most accessible sources. Cite a paper reporter before an electronic reporter	*Coldmatic Refrigeration of Canada Ltd v Leveltek Processing LLC* (2005), 70 OR (3d) 758 (available on CanLII) (Ont CA).
No source available	Follow rules for unreported decisions in section 3.12	*Commission des droits de la personne du Québec c Brasserie O'Keefe* (13 September 1990), Montreal 500-05-005826-873 (Qc Sup Ct).

3.2   GENERAL FORM

3.2.1   Neutral Citation Available

Style of cause,	neutral citation	pinpoint,	other source,	judge (if applicable)	[short title].
Fisher v Fisher,	2008 ONCA 11	at paras 52-59,	88 OR (3d) 241,	Lang JA	[*Fisher*].
Stewart v Berezan,	2007 BCCA 150	at paras 11, 15,	64 BCLR (4th) 152,	Donald J	[*Stewart*].

3.2.2   Neutral Citation Not Available

Style of cause	(year of the decision) (if necessary),	reporter	pinpoint,	other source,	(jurisdiction) (if necessary)	judge (if applicable)	[short title].
Gordon v Goertz,		[1996] 2 SCR 27	at para 13,	134 DLR (4th) 321,		McLachlin J	[*Gordon*].
R v Dimic	(1998),	54 CRR (2d) 290		(available on CanLII),	(Ont CA)		[*Dimic*].

3.3   STYLE OF CAUSE

> The style of cause is a shorter version of the title, referring to a decision informally.

> **When the style of cause is provided by the reporter, keep it as is**. If the decision does not indicate the style of cause, follow the rules of sections 3.3.1 to 3.3.18.

> If the style of cause is indicated in the text, do not repeat it in the footnote.

> Italicize both the names of the parties and the *v* or *c* that separates their names.

> The use of the *v* and *c* in the style of cause indicates the language of the decision. If the decision of the tribunal is in English, use *v*. If the decision of the tribunal is in French, use *c*. If the decision is bilingual, use *v* if you are writing in English.

Decision in English	*Pacific Developments Ltd v Calgary (City of)*
Decision in French	*Traverse Trois-Pistoles Escoumins Ltée c Quebec (Commission des Transports)*
Bilingual decision	*Committee for the Equal Treatment of Asbestos Minority Shareholders v Ontario (Securities Commission)*

3.3.1 Names of Parties

✓	*Toneguzzo-Norvell v Savein Best v Best*
✗	*Jessica Teresa Toneguzzo-Norvell v Nelson Savein T Best v M Best*

> Use **surnames**; omit given names or first initials.

> Where more than one person is on either side of the action, use only the first person's name.

> Omit expressions such as et al that indicate multiple parties.

> Capitalize the first letter of a party name and the first letter of all words, other than prepositions, conjunctions, and words in procedural phrases (e.g. *in re*; *ex rel*).

> Translate into English descriptions such as city but do not translate words forming part of the name of a party, such as University, and abbreviations such as Ltd or LLP.

> Do not include The, Le, La, L', or Les as the first word of a party name, even if it is part of a company name. Include these words if they are part of the name of an object proceeded against *in rem* (such as aircraft or ships, e.g. *The Mihalis Angelos*).

3.3.2 Person Represented by Guardian or Tutor

Williams (Guardian ad litem of) v Canadian National Railway
Dobson (Litigation guardian of) v Dobson

3.3.3 Names of Companies and Partnerships

➤ Always include Ltd, ltée, Limited, srl, or LLP. Do not translate these identifying words or abbreviations.

➤ If it is clear from the name that a party is a company, do not include Inc or Co. However, if it is not clear from the name that the party is a company, or if these identifying words or abbreviations do not come at the end of the name of the company (e.g. Union Oil Co of Canada), include the appropriate identifying words. Include these words if they form an integral part of the name of the company. In such cases, Corporation is abbreviated to Corp.

✓	*Sloan v Union Oil Co of Canada Ltd*
	Metson v RW de Wolfe Ltd
	Prowse Chowne LLP v Northey
	National Party of Canada v Canadian Broadcasting Corp
	Wickberg v Shatsky & Shatsky
✗	*Sloan v Union Oil*
	Metson v de Wolfe

➤ Include given names and initials that form part of a company or firm name. Also include the names of all partners in a partnership.

➤ When a company has a bilingual name, use the name of the company in the language of the decision. If the decision is bilingual, use the name of the company in the language in which you are writing.

3.3.4 Countries, Federal Units, Provinces, and Municipalities

Country	✓	*United States v Burns*
	✗	*The United States of America v Burns*
Province, State		*Mercier v Alberta (AG)*
Municipality		*Bay Colony Ltd v Wasaga Beach (Town of)*
		Markle v Toronto (City of)
		Toronto Dominion Bank v Alfred (Township of)

➤ Use the **common name of a country**, not its formal name or abbreviation.

➤ Omit Province of, State of, People of, or any other similar identifiers.

➤ Include identifiers such as City of, County of, District of, or Township of in parentheses.

3.3.5 Wills and Estates

Name of estate	Kipling v Kohinsky Estate
Name of estate if no plaintiff or defendant is included in the style of cause	Re Eurig Estate

> ➢ Do not use the names of executors.

> ➢ The term Re should precede the name of the estate.

3.3.6 Bankruptcies and Receiverships

Chablis Textiles (Trustee of) v London Life Insurance *Confederation Trust Co (Liquidator of) v Donovan*

> ➢ Use the name of the bankruptcy or company in receivership followed by Trustee of, Receiver of, or Liquidator of in parentheses.

3.3.7 Statute Titles

Jurisdiction is obvious from the name of the statute	Re Canadian Labour Code
Jurisdiction cannot be discerned from the name of the statute	Reference Re Fisheries Act (Canada)

3.3.8 The Crown—Criminal Cases

> ➢ Use R to refer to the Crown in criminal cases. It should also replace expressions such as The Queen, Regina, The Crown, or The Queen in Right of.

R v Blondin

3.3.9 The Crown—Civil Cases

Attorney General (AG)		Schreiber v Canada (AG)
Minister of National Revenue (MNR)		Buckman v MNR
Other government bodies		Susan Shoe Industries Ltd v Ontario (Employment Standards Officer)
Do not repeat the name of the jurisdiction	✓	Laurentian Bank of Canada v Canada (Human Rights Commission)
	✗	Laurentian Bank of Canada v Canada (Canadian Human Rights Commission)
Do not include the name of an individual representing a government body	✓	Canada (Combines Investigation Branch, Director of Investigation and Research) v Southam
	✗	Lawson AW Hunter (Director of Investigation and Research of the Combines Investigation Branch) v Southam

➤ In civil cases, **use the name of the jurisdiction** to signify the Crown in right of Canada or a province.

➤ Place the name of the government body (such as an agency, commission, or department) in parentheses after the name of the jurisdiction.

➤ Abbreviate the **Minister of National Revenue** to MNR, the **Deputy Minister of National Revenue** to Deputy MNR, and **Attorney General** to AG.

➤ To cite a federal or provincial **administrative tribunal**, see section 3.13.

➤ Do not include the name of an individual representing a government body.

3.3.10 Crown Corporations

Westaim Corp v Royal Canadian Mint

➤ Do not include the name of the jurisdiction before the name of the Crown corporation.

3.3.11 Municipal Boards and Bodies

Johnson v Sarnia (City of) Commissioners of Police

3.3.12 School Boards

✓	*Prince Albert Rural School Division No 56 v Teachers of Saskatchewan*
✗	*Board of Education of Prince Albert Rural School Division No 56 v Teachers of Saskatchewan*

➤ Omit such terms as Board of Education, Board of Trustees, or Governors of. Include only the name of the institution.

3.3.13 Unions

✓	*Canadian Autoworkers Union, Local 576 v Bradco Construction*
✗	*CAU, Local 576 v Bradco Construction*

➤ Do not abbreviate union names, as such abbreviations vary widely.

3.3.14 Social Welfare Agencies

Doe v Metropolitan Toronto Child and Family Services
EP v Winnipeg (Director of Child and Family Services)

➢ Include the name of the community where the aid agency is based unless it forms part of the name of the agency.

3.3.15 Parties' Names that are Undisclosed

➢ If the names of the parties are not disclosed in the case, use initials where available, or the title and numerical description provided by the reporter.

Droit de la famille - 1544
M v H

3.3.16 If The Case Is Known Under Two Names—The *Sub Nom* Rule

Reference Re Resolution to Amend the Constitution, [1981] 1 SCR 753, (*sub nom Reference Re Amendment of the Constitution of Canada (Nos 1, 2 and 3)*) 125 DLR (3d) 1.

➢ Use the style of cause **provided in the first reporter of the reference**.

➢ If **another source cited refers to the parties by different names**, enclose this style of cause in parentheses introduced by the phrase *sub nom*. Place the parentheses immediately before the citation for the reporter using those names.

➢ *Sub nom* is the abbreviated version of *sub nomine*, which is Latin for "under the name of".

3.3.17 One Party Acting for Someone Else—The *Ex Rel* Rule

➢ Where a third party enters the suit to act on behalf of one of the parties, note this by using the phrase *ex rel*.

Ryel v Quebec (AG) ex rel Société immobilière du Québec

➢ *Ex rel* is the abbreviated version of *ex relatione*, which is Latin for "upon relation or information".

3.3.18 Procedural Phrases and Constitutional References

Constitutional	*Reference Re Firearms Act*
Other	*Re Gray* *Ex parte James:* *Re Condon*

➢ Use *Reference Re* for constitutional cases only; in all other cases, use *Re* alone before the subject.

> ➤ Shorten *In re*, *In the matter of*, and *Dans l'affaire de* to *Re*.

> ➤ Write *Ex parte* in full. The expression indicates that the named party is the one that has brought the action.

3.4   YEAR OF DECISION

When a decision has a neutral citation, do not write the year in parentheses after the style of cause. **Apply the following rules if there is no neutral citation**:

Year of reporter is not indicated	Provide the year of decision in parentheses	*R v Borden* (1993), 24 CR (4th) 184 (NSCA).
Year of reporter and year of decision different	Provide both years	*Joyal c Hôpital du Christ-Roi* (1996), [1997] RJQ 38 (CA).
Year of reporter and year of decision are the same	Provide the year of the reporter	*Cadbury Schweppes v FBI Foods Ltd*, [1999] 1 SCR 142. ✗ *Cadbury Schweppes v FBI Foods Ltd* (1999), [1999] 1 SCR 142.

> ➤ Provide the year of the decision in parentheses after the style of cause and followed by a comma.

> ➤ **Use parentheses** for the **year of the decision**. Follow the parentheses by a comma.

> ➤ **Use brackets** for the **year of the reporter**. Precede the brackets by a comma.

3.5   NEUTRAL CITATION

The number of the neutral citation emanates from the court — **never create a neutral citation** when an official one is unavailable. Each Canadian court and a growing number of administrative tribunals have adopted the neutral citation. The date of implementation for each entity is available at **Appendix B-2**.

The neutral citation can be used to identify a particular case independently from the electronic database or reporter in which it is published. Nevertheless, a neutral citation should always be followed by a citation to another reporter, since it does not tell the reader where to find the case.

For more information on neutral citation, see the document of the Canadian Citation Committee, *The Preparation Citation and Distribution of Canadian Decisions* at <http://lexum.org/ccc-ccr/preparation/en/>.

Style of cause,	neutral citation,			traditional citation,	optional elements.	
	year	tribunal identifier	decision number		paragraph number	note.
R v Law,	2002	SCC	10,	[2002] 1 SCR 227.		
R v Senko,	2004	ABQB	60,	352 AR 235	at para 12.	
Ordre des arpenteurs-géomètres du Québec c Tremblay,	2001	QCTP	24,			n 14.
Effigi Inc v Canada (AG),	2004	FC	1000		¶ 34-35, 40.	

> The neutral citation is assigned by the court and cannot be changed.

> The jurisdiction and level of court are usually apparent in a neutral citation. It is not necessary to include other abbreviations of jurisdictions and courts.

> If the reader might not recognize the jurisdiction of the tribunal identifier, include the country's neutral three letter **ISO-3166-1 alpha-3** reference code before the neutral citation (e.g. *R v Law*, CAN 2002 SCC 10). The code is GBR for the United Kingdom, FRA for France, AUS for Australia, NZL for New Zealand, SGP for Singapore and ZAF for South Africa.

> Some databases provide citations that resemble neutral citations but that should be treated as case identifiers provided by the service only (e.g. Quicklaw).

Jurisprudence

3.5.1 Year

The core of the citation begins with the year in which the decision was rendered by the court. If the date of the decision is fixed later, the year in the citation may refer to the year the case is entered into the court register.

3.5.2 Tribunal Identifier

The tribunal identifier is assigned by the court and can be up to eight characters in length. It is composed of three elements. With the exception of the Northwest Territories, the identifier begins with a prefix of **two characters**.

Alberta	AB
British Columbia	BC
Manitoba	MB
New Brunswick	NB
Newfoundland and Labrador	NL (NF – before 2002)
Northwest Territories	NWT
Nova Scotia	NS
Nunavut	NU
Ontario	ON
Prince Edward Island	PE
Quebec	QC
Saskatchewan	SK
Yukon	YK

➤   The usual acronym of the tribunal or court follows this prefix. Omit the reintroduction of any letters representing the jurisdiction (e.g. the "Tribunal des professions du Québec" is QCTP and not QCTPQ).

3.5.3 Decision Number

➤   The sequence number is assigned by the court. This number comes back to "1" on 1 January of every year.

3.6   PINPOINT

3.6.1   General Form

➤ Place the pinpoint reference **after the neutral citation**. If there is no neutral citation, place it after the first page of the reporter.

➤ Always refer to **paragraphs** if there is a neutral citation. If there is no neutral citation,

> *R v Proulx*, 2000 SCC 5 at para 27, [2000] 1 SCR 61.
>
> *Bousquet v Barmish Inc* (1991), 37 CPR (3d) 516 at 527 (FCTD).
>
> *Schofield v Smith* (2003), 119 NBR (2d) 130 at 135ff.
>
> *Vriend v Alberta (AG)*, [1998] 1 SCR 493 at 532-34, 156 DLR (4th) 385.
>
> *R c Kouri*, [2004] RJQ 2061 at 2368, 2370 (CA).

refer to a page number or a paragraph and indicate the cited reporter (section 3.6.2). Begin a page or paragraph pinpoint with at or ¶. Do not place a comma before at and do not use p to indicate the page number. Cite paragraphs by using para, paras, or ¶.

➤ To indicate a **general area** rather than a specific set of pages or paragraphs, place ff (the abbreviation of "and following") immediately after the number (see *Schofield*). It is preferable, however, to cite a specific set of pages or paragraphs.

➤ Separate **consecutive page or paragraph numbers** by a hyphen, retaining at least the two last digits (e.g. 32-35, not 32-5).

➤ Separate **non-sequential page or paragraph numbers** by a comma (e.g. 160, 172).

3.6.2   Cited Reporter

> *R v Gimson*, [1991] 3 SCR 692, 62 OAC 282 [*Gimson* cited to SCR].
>
> *Delgamuukw v British Columbia*, 79 DLR (4th) 185, [1991] 3 WWR 97 (BCSC) [*Delgamuukw* cited to DLR].
>
> *Université du Québec à Trois-Rivières v Larocque*, [1993] 1 SCR 471 at 473, 101 DLR (4th) 494 [*Larocque*].
>
> *R v Sharpe*, 2007 BCCA 191, 219 CCC (3d) 187 [*Sharpe*].

➤ The page and paragraph numbering often differ from one reporter to the other. The reader must know to which reporter the pinpoint references cite.

➤ Cite the pinpoint reference to the **most official reporter, mentioned first**. For every subsequent pinpoint, cite to the same reporter.

➤ After the short title, add cited to, followed by the abbreviation of the reporter (see *Delgamuukw*).

➢ Do not specify the source of the pinpoint in the subsequent references if there is a pinpoint reference the first time a case is mentioned (see *Laroque*). It is implied that the subsequent references will follow the same model and cite to the same reporter.

➢ Do not specify the source of the pinpoint when there is a neutral citation with numbered paragraphs (see *Sharpe*). In this case, the paragraph numbers are set by the court and not by the individual publishers.

3.7   PRINTED REPORTER

3.7.1   Year of Reporter

Reporter organized by year	one volume published per year	*Hébert c Giguère*, [2003] RJQ 89.
	several volumes published per year	*Reference re Secession of Quebec*, [1998] 2 SCR 217.
Reporter published in volumes numbered in series		*R v Innocente*, 2003 NSCA 50, 214 NSR (2d) 295.

➢ Reporters are published either in volumes organized by year of publication (e.g. SCR, RJQ) or in volumes numbered in series (e.g. DLR, CCC).

→ If the reporter volumes are numbered by **year of publication**, enclose the year in brackets.

→ Some reporters organized by year of publication publish **several volumes per year** (e.g. SCR). Indicate the year in brackets followed by the volume number.

→ If the reporter volumes are numbered in **series**, no year is needed to identify the reporter volume.

➢ Note that **some reporters have changed their mode of organization**.

→ The **Supreme Court Reports** were organized by volume from 1877-1923 (e.g. 27 SCR). Then, from 1923-1974, they were organized by year (e.g. [1950] SCR). Since 1975, they have been organized by year with several volumes per year (e.g. [1982] 2 SCR).

→ Prior to 1974, the **Ontario Reports** were organized by year of publication (e.g. [1973] OR). Since 1974, they have been published in a numbered series (e.g. 20 OR).

3.7.2 Reporter

> Bakken v Harris (2005), 261 Sask R 46 (QB).

> ➤ Abbreviate the name of the reporter according to the list in **Appendix C**.

3.7.2.1 Official Reporters

➤ Official reporters are published by the Queen's Printer.

➤ Whenever there is a discrepancy between two versions of the same case, the version in the official reporter takes precedence.

List of official reporters:

Canada Supreme Court Reports (1970-present) Canada Law Reports: Supreme Court of Canada (1923-1969) Canada Supreme Court Reports (1876-1922)	SCR
Federal Court Reports (1971-present)	FCR
Exchequer Court of Canada Reports (1923-1970) Exchequer Court of Canada Reports (1875-1922)	Ex CR

3.7.2.2 Semi-Official Reporters

➤ Semi-official reporters are published under the auspices of a provincial or territorial bar association.

List of the semi-official reporters (as of 2009):

Alberta	Alberta Reports (1976-present) NB: Alberta Law Reports (5th) (Alta LR (5th)) is unofficial.	AR
British Columbia	No published semi-official reporter.	--
Manitoba	No published semi-official reporter.	--
New Brunswick	New Brunswick Reports (2d) (1969-present)	NBR (2d)
Newfoundland and Labrador & Prince Edward Island	Newfoundland & Prince Edward Island Reports (1971-present)	Nfld & PEIR
Nova Scotia	Nova Scotia Reports (2d) (1969-present)	NSR (2d)
Nunavut	No published semi-official reporter.	--
Ontario	Ontario Reports (3d) (1991-present)	OR (3d)
Quebec	Recueils de jurisprudence du Québec (1986-present)	RJQ
Saskatchewan	No published semi-official reporter.	--
Northwest Territories	No published semi-official reporter.	--
Yukon	No published semi-official reporter.	--

Jurisprudence

For a complete listing of semi-official reporters including those published prior to 2009, see **Appendix C-2**.

3.7.2.3 Unofficial Reporters

➤ To choose the appropriate reporter, follow these general guidelines:

→ **General reporters** (e.g. Western Weekly Reports) are preferred to specific reporters (e.g. Canadian Criminal Cases).

→ Reporters covering a **large geographic area** (e.g. Dominion Law Reports) are preferred to reporters covering a smaller geographic area (e.g. Saskatchewan Reports).

→ Reporters that are **most readily available** (e.g. Dominion Law Reports) are preferred to more obscure reporters.

➤ See **Appendix C-3** for a list of unofficial reporters.

3.7.3 Series

Series number	*Rohani v Rohani* (2004), 34 BCLR (4th) 62 (CA).
	✗ *Rohani v Rohani* (2004), 34 BCLR (4ᵗʰ) 62 (CA).
New series	*Citizen's Mining Council of Newfoundland and Labrador Inc v Canada (Minister of the Environment)* (1999), 29 CELR (NS) 117 (FCTD).

➤ If the reporter has been published in more than one series, indicate the series in parentheses, between the reporter abbreviation and the first page of the judgment.

➤ Abbreviate **New Series** or *Nouvelle série* to NS.

➤ Do not put the series number in superscript (e.g. (4th) and not (4ᵗʰ)).

3.7.4 First Page

Reference re Secession of Quebec, [1998] 2 SCR 217.

➤ Indicate the number of the first page of the decision after the reporter.

3.8   ELECTRONIC SERVICES

➤ Before citing to an electronic service, make sure it is the most appropriate source (section 3.1).

➤ Do not cite to an electronic service to which the majority of readers will not have access. For example, avoid Azimut if writing for an audience outside of Quebec.

➤ Include the paragraph number for the pinpoint reference. **Do not cite the page numbers** reproduced in the electronic source, as these are specific to the service used and can vary in different forms (e.g. txt, html).

➤ Abbreviations for electronic services can be found in **Appendix E**.

3.8.1   Published Judgments and Judgments with a Neutral Citation

Reference to a printed reporter or neutral citation	(available on	name of the electronic service).
Desputeaux c Éditions Chouette (1987) Inc, [2001] RJQ 945	(available on	Azimut).
R v Wilkening, 2009 ABCA 9	(available on	WL Can).

➤ When a judgment **has been published in a printed reporter and/or has a neutral citation**, write the neutral citation or the printed reporter, then write in parentheses available on, followed by the name of the electronic service.

3.8.2   Unpublished Judgments With No Neutral Citation

3.8.2.1 CanLII

Style of cause,	identifier given by service	pinpoint	(jurisdiction and/or court) (if applicable).
Kellogg v Black Ridge Gold Ltd,	1993 CanLII 2848	at para 15	(NWT SC).

➤ The Canadian Legal Information Institute (CanLII) is freely accessible on <http://www.canlii.org>.

3.8.2.2 Quicklaw

Style of cause,	identifier given by service	(Quicklaw)	pinpoint	(jurisdiction and/or court) (if applicable).
Fuentes v Canada (Minister of Citizenship and Immigration),	[1995] FCJ no 206	(QL)	at para 10	(TD).

> ➢ Find the Quicklaw identifier below the style of cause. Do not confuse it with printed reporters (e.g. AJ for Alberta Judgments, BCJ for British Columbia Judgments, OJ for Ontario Judgments).

> ➢ Make sure that the judgment was not published elsewhere in the database. QuickCITE lists all the sources for any particular judgment.

3.8.2.3 Westlaw Canada

Style of cause,	identifier given by service	(WL Can)	pinpoint	(jurisdiction and/or court) (if applicable).
Underwood v Underwood,	1995 CarswellOnt 88	(WL Can)		(Ont Gen Div).

> ➢ In June 2009, the database Westlaw*e*Carswell changed its name to Westlaw Canada.

> ➢ If the only identifier is the one provided by Westlaw Canada, the judgment is otherwise unreported.

3.8.2.4 Azimut

Style of cause	(year),	identifier given by service	(Azimut)	pinpoint	(jurisdiction and/or court) (if applicable).
Desputeaux c Éditions Chouette	(2001),	AZ-50085400	(Azimut)	at para 19	(QC CA).

> ➢ Azimut is a service created by the Société québécoise d'information juridique (SOQUIJ). If the prospective readers are not from Quebec, do not cite Azimut.

3.8.2.5 Lexis

Style of cause,	identifier given by service	pinpoint	(jurisdiction and/or court) (if applicable).
Davies v MNR,	1997 Can Tax Ct LEXIS 5874	at 5.	

> ➢ If the only identifier is the one provided by Lexis, the judgment is otherwise unreported.

3.8.2.6 *Westlaw*

Style of cause,	identifier given by service	pinpoint	(jurisdiction and/or court) (if applicable).
Fincher v Baker,	1997 WL 675447	at 2	(Ala Civ App).

> ➢ If the only identifier is the one provided by Westlaw, the judgment is otherwise unreported.

3.8.2.7 *BAILII*

Style of cause,	identifier given by service	(BAILII)	pinpoint	(jurisdiction and/or court) (if applicable).
London Borough of Harrow v Johnstone,	[1997] UKHL 9	(BAILII)	at para 6.	

> ➢ Do not confuse BAILII's identifier with a neutral citation. Add (BAILII) after the identifier to avoid confusion.

3.8.2.8 *Lawnet*

Style of cause,	(year),	database identifier given by service	(Lawnet)	pinpoint	(jurisdiction and/or court).
Beryl Claire Clarke and Others c Silkair (Singapore) Pte Ltd,	(2001),	Suit Nos 1746, 1748-1752 of 1999	(Lawnet)	at para 10	(Sing HC).

3.8.2.9 *Other Services*

> ➢ Refer to electronic services that have comprehensive indexes, search tools, and professional editors.

3.8.2.9.1   Service with Its Own Identifier

Style of cause,	(year) (if applicable),	database identifier given by service	(electronic service) (if applicable)	pinpoint	(jurisdiction and/or court).
Abitibi-Consolidated Inc v Doughan,		EYB 2008-139174	(REJB)	at para 23	(Qc Sup Ct).

> ➢ Add the year and the name of the electronic service only if the information is not already included in the database identifier.

➢ If the abbreviation of the electronic service is not included in **Appendix E** of the *Guide*, use the most commonly used name. For example, write REJB and not Répertoire électronique de jurisprudence du Barreau.

3.8.2.9.2   Service with No Identifier

Style of cause,	(year)	pinpoint	(jurisdiction and/or court)	(available on	name of the electronic service).
R v Woollin,	(1998)	at para 23	(HL)	(available on	Justis).

3.9   JURISDICTION AND COURT

Taylor v Law Society of Prince Edward Island (1992), 97 DLR (4th) 427 (PEISC (AD)).

Ballard v Ballard (2001), 201 Nfld & PEIR 352 (Nfld SC (TD)).

O'Brien v Centre de location Simplex ltée (1993), 132 NBR (2d) 179 (CA).

Boisjoli c Goebel, [1982] CS 1 (Qc).

Dobson (Litigation Guardian of) v Dobson, [1999] 2 SCR 753.

➢ The jurisdiction and court should be indicated if:

→ there is **no neutral citation** (which indicates both jurisdiction and court level); **and**

→ this information **is not evident from the title of the reporter** (see O'Brien).

➢ Indicate the jurisdiction and court in parentheses, following every source.

➢ If the court is bilingual, use English abbreviations. If the court renders judgments only in French, use the French abbreviations.

➢ There is no space in an abbreviation consisting solely of upper case letters. Leave a space when an abbreviation consists of both upper case letters and lower case letters (e.g. BCCA; Ont Div Ct; NS Co Ct; Alta QB).

➢ Use the abbreviations for the jurisdictions found in **Appendix A-1** and the court abbreviations in **Appendix B**.

3.10 JUDGE

> If relevant, a reference to the name of the judge may be included. Add dissenting if it's a dissenting opinion.

R v Sharpe, 2001 SCC 2, [2001] 1 SCR 45 at para 24, McLachlin CJC.

Gosselin c Québec (PG), [1999] RJQ 1033 (CA), Robert JA, dissenting.

> Do not insert a comma between the name of the judge and the office.

Office abbreviations:

CJC	Chief Justice of Canada
CJA	Chief Justice of Appeal
CJ	Chief Justice, Chief Judge
JA	Justice of Appeal, Judge of Appeals Court
JJA	Justices of Appeal, Judges of Appeals Court
J	Justice, Judge
JJ	Justices, Judges
LJ	Lord Justice
LJJ	Lord Justices
Mag	Magistrate

3.11 CASE HISTORY

3.11.1 Prior History

Affirming	*Law v Canada (Minister of Employment and Immigration)*, [1999] 1 SCR 497, aff'g (1996), 135 DLR (4th) 293 (FCA).
Reversing	*Wilson & Lafleur ltée c Société québécoise d'information juridique*, [2000] RJQ 1086 (CA), rev'g [1998] RJQ 2489 (Sup Ct).

> Cite the prior history of the case as the last element of the citation if it is relevant to the argument.

> Separate different decisions with a comma.

> Abbreviate affirming to aff'g. Abbreviate reversing to rev'g.

> Both aff'g and rev'g refer to the first citation.

> If the decision is affirming or reversing the prior decision on grounds other than those being discussed, use aff'g on other grounds or rev'g on other grounds.

3.11.2 Subsequent History

Affirming	*R v Paice*, [2004] 5 WWR 621 (CA), aff'd 2005 SCC 22, [2005] 1 SCR 339.
Reversing	*Ontario English Catholic Teachers' Association v Ontario (AG)* (1998), 162 DLR (4th) 257 (Ont Gen Div), rev'd (1999), 172 DLR (4th) 193 (Ont CA), rev'd 2001 SCC 15, [2001] 1 SCR 470.

> ➢ Cite the subsequent case history if it was appealed to other courts.

> ➢ Place the subsequent case history as the last element of the citation.

> ➢ Separate different decisions with a comma.

> ➢ Abbreviate **affirmed** to aff'd and **reversed** to rev'd.

> ➢ If the decision was affirmed or reversed on grounds other than those being discussed, use aff'd on other grounds or rev'd on other grounds.

> ➢ Both aff'd and rev'd refer back to the first citation. In *Ontario English Catholic Teachers' Association*, the use of rev'd preceding the Supreme Court citation indicates that the Supreme Court agreed that the judgment of the Ontario Court of Justice, General Division, should have been reversed; it did not reverse the decision of the Ontario Court of Appeal.

3.11.3 Prior and Subsequent History

Affirming	*Ardoch Algonquin First Nation v Ontario* (1997), 148 DLR (4th) 126 (Ont CA), rev'g [1997] 1 CNLR 66 (Ont Gen Div), aff'd 2000 SCC 37, [2000] 1 SCR 950.
Reversing	*Canada v Canderel Ltd*, [1995] 2 FC 232 (CA), rev'g [1994] 1 CTC 2336 (TCC), rev'd [1998] 1 SCR 147.

> ➢ Apply the rules for prior and subsequent history listed above.

> ➢ All affirming and reversing decisions refer back to the first citation.

>> → In *Ardoch*, the Ontario Court of Appeal reversed a decision by the lower court, and the reversal was later affirmed by the Supreme Court of Canada.

>> → In *Canderel Ltd*, the Federal Court of Appeal reversed the decision of the Tax Court of Canada, but was itself reversed by the Supreme Court of Canada (i.e. the Supreme Court of Canada upheld the Tax Court's decision).

> ➢ Place prior history before subsequent history.

3.11.4 Leave to Appeal

	Citation of the decision for which leave to appeal is requested,	court,	citation of the decision as to the appeal.
Requested	*White Resource Management Ltd v Durish* (1992), 131 AR 273 (CA),	leave to appeal to SCC requested.	
Granted	*Westec Aerospace v Raytheon Aircraft* (1999), 173 DLR (4th) 498 (BCCA),	leave to appeal to SCC granted,	[2000] 1 SCR xxii.
Refused	*Procter & Gamble Pharmaceuticals Canada Inc v Canada (Minister of Health)*, 2004 FCA 393,	leave to appeal to SCC refused,	30714 (April 21, 2005).
As of Right	*Whiten v Pilot Insurance* (1996), 132 DLR (4th) 568 (Ont Gen Div),	appeal as of right to the CA.	

➢ The list of the decisions on leave to appeal to the **Supreme Court of Canada** can be found at the beginning of the SCR. The decisions are available on CanLII for cases after 2005.

➢ Decisions on leave to appeal to **court of appeal** are sometimes available in printed reporters and electronic services.

➢ Include the citation of the decision for which leave to appeal is requested.

➢ Indicate the court to which the appeal is requested. If available, indicate whether leave was granted or refused and include the citation for that decision.

➢ If a printed reporter is unavailable or the motion is not yet published, provide the **docket number** followed by the date in parentheses.

3.12 UNREPORTED JUDGMENTS WITHOUT A NEUTRAL CITATION

Style of cause	(date),	judicial district	docket number	JE number (Quebec only) (if available)	(jurisdiction and court).
R v Crête	(18 April 1991),	Ottawa	97/03674		(Ont Prov Ct).
Lalancette c Gagnon	(18 April 1995),	Montreal	500-02-019902-944,	JE 95-1255	(CQ).

➢ Indicate the style of cause, the full date of the decision in parentheses followed by a comma, the judicial district, and the docket number. Place the jurisdiction and court in parentheses at the end of the citation.

➢ **For Quebec cases**, include the ***Jurisprudence Express*** (JE) number (if available) preceded by a comma after the docket number.

3.13 ADMINISTRATIVE BODIES AND TRIBUNALS

3.13.1 Decisions in Printed Reporters

Adversarial	*Clarke Institute of Psychiatry v Ontario Nurses' Assn (Adusei Grievance)* (2001), 95 LAC (4th) 154 (OLRB).
Non-adversarial	*Re Writers' Union of Canada Certification Application (Certification)* (1998), 84 CPR (3d) 329 (Canadian Artists and Professional Relations Tribunal).

➢ Indicate the style of cause, whether it is adversarial or non-adversarial. Where there is no style of cause, use the decision number instead.

➢ Include the abbreviation as provided by the administrative body or tribunal in parentheses at the end of the citation if it is not evident from the title of the cited reporter (if an abbreviation cannot be found, use the full name).

➢ Abbreviate provinces and territories to the shortest provincial abbreviations (the Ontario Securities Commission is abbreviated OSC, and the Newfoundland and Labrador Human Rights Commission is abbreviated NLHRC). Note that abbreviations of a printed reporter (e.g. OSC Bull) may be different from the abbreviation of the agency (e.g. OSC).

3.13.2 Online Decisions

Style of cause	(date),	decision number (if applicable),	online:	administrative body or tribunal	<address>.
Acuity Funds Ltd et al	(13 March 2009),		online:	OSC	<http://www.osc.gov.on.ca>.
13th Street – a new specialty channel	(14 December 2000),	2000-449,	online:	CRTC	<http://www.crtc.gc.ca>.
The Commissioner of Competition v Elkhorn Ranch & Resort Ltd	(23 November 2009),	CT-2009-018,	online:	Competition Tribunal	<http://www.ct-tc.gc.ca>.

➢ Enclose the date of the decision in parentheses after the style of cause. Place a comma after the date.

➢ If applicable, include the decision number followed by online: and the abbreviation used by the administrative body or tribunal. These abbreviations usually do not contain periods. Note that most abbreviations consist of single letters for each important word in the name. Abbreviate provinces and territories to the shortest provincial abbreviations (e.g. the Ontario Securities Commission is abbreviated OSC and the Newfoundland and Labrador Human Rights Commission is abbreviated NLHRC).

➢ Write the address of the **home page** of the website. Do not specify the precise link of the decision.

3.14   Arguments and Documents at a Hearing

Factum	Reference re Secession of Quebec, [1998] 2 SCR 217 (Factum of the Appellant at para 16).
Oral pleading	Vriend v Alberta, [1998] 1 SCR 493 (Oral argument, Appellant).
Public Settlement Agreement	Mulroney v Canada (AG) [Settlement Agreement], [1997] QJ No 45 (Qc Sup Ct) (QL).
Evidence	R v Swain, [1991] 1 SCR 933 (Evidence, Dr Fleming's recommendation that the appellant be released in the community).

➢ When referring to a **factum**, provide the full citation of the case. Then, indicate in parentheses Factum of, the party (Appellant or Respondent), and the page number or paragraph number. A short form can be established following the first reference to the document (e.g. Factum of the Appellant at para 16 [FOA]).

➢ When referring to an **oral argument**, provide the full citation of the case, then place Oral argument and the party in parentheses.

➢ When referring to a **public settlement agreement**, provide the style of cause, followed by Settlement Agreement in brackets before the other elements of the citation. If the agreement was announced through a news release, see section 6.16.

➢ When referring to **evidence**, provide the full citation of the case, followed by Evidence in parentheses with a brief statement identifying the item.

➢ When referring to a **trial transcript**, use the rules for citing unreported judgments (section 3.12).

4 Government Documents E-69

4   GOVERNMENT DOCUMENTS

4.1   PARLIAMENTARY PAPERS

This section applies to documents directly published by a parliamentary body. For every federal government document, indicate the jurisdiction (Canada) only when other citations to international materials may confuse the reader.

4.1.1 Debates

Jurisdiction,	legislature,	*title,*	legislative session,	volume and/or number	(date)	pinpoint	(speaker) *(if any).*
		House of Commons Debates,	37th Parl, 1st Sess,	No 64	(17 May 2001)	at 4175	(Hon Elinor Caplan).
		Debates of the Senate,	39th Parl, 2nd Sess,	No 44	(1 April 2008)	at 1017	(Noël A Kinsella).
Ontario,	Legislative Assembly,	*Official Report of Debates (Hansard),*	37th Parl, 2nd Sess,	No 53	(18 October 2001)	at 2819	(Julia Munro).
Yukon,	Legislative Assembly,	*Hansard*	30th Leg, 2nd Sess,	No 18	(22 November 2000)	at 552	(Peter Jenkins).

➢ Indicate the jurisdiction (if a province) and the legislature, unless this information is mentioned in the title of the debates. Do not superscript st, nd and th.

➢ Write the title, in italics, as it appears on the title page of the document.

➢ Place the volume and/or document number, if any, after the title, preceded by a non-italicized comma.

➢ Include the full date in parentheses followed by the pinpoint.

➢ Include the name of the speaker in parentheses at the end of the citation (if any).

4.1.2 Journals

Jurisdiction,	legislature,	*title*,	legislative session,	volume and/or number	(date)	pinpoint	(speaker) (if applicable).
	Senate,	*Journals of the Senate,*	39th Parl, 1st Sess,	No 108	(14 June 2007).		.
	House of Commons,	*Journals,*	40th Leg, 2nd Sess,	No 36	(30 March 2009)	at 588.	
Saskatchewan,	Legislative Assembly,	*Journals of the Legislative Assembly,*	23rd Leg, 3rd Sess,	vol 105	(9 March 1998)	at 7.	
		Journals of the House of Assembly of Lower-Canada,	8th Parl, 2nd Sess,	vol 25	(26 January 1816)	at 15	(Thomas Douglass).

> ➢ Indicate the jurisdiction (if a province) and the legislature, unless this information is mentioned in the title of the journals.

> ➢ Cite the title, in italics, as it appears on the title page.

> ➢ Place the volume and/or document number after the title, preceded by a non-italicized comma.

> ➢ Include the full date in parentheses followed by the pinpoint.

> ➢ Include the name of the speaker in parentheses at the end of the citation.

4.1.3 Order Papers

Jurisdiction,	legislature,	*title*,	legislative session,	number	(date)	pinpoint.
	House of Commons,	*Order Paper,*	39th Leg, 1st Sess,	No 175	(20 June 2007).	
Québec,	National Assembly,	*Feuilleton et préavis,*	38th Leg, 1st Sess,	No 79	(6 May 2008).	

> ➢ Indicate the jurisdiction if a province.

> ➢ At the federal level, the *Order Paper* and the *Notice Paper* are two parts of a single publication. Only cite the specific part in the title.

4.1.4 Sessional Papers

Jurisdiction,	legislature,	"title of report"	by	author	in	*title,*	number	(year)	pinpoint
	Parliament,	"Report of the Chief Inspector of Dominion Lands Agencies"	by	HG Cuttle	in	*Sessional Papers,*	No 25	(1920)	at 3.
Ontario,	Legislative Assembly,	"Report on Workmen's Compensation for Injuries"	by	James Mavor	in	*Sessional Papers,*	No 40	(1900)	at 6-7.

➢ Indicate the jurisdiction (if a province) and the legislature, unless this information is mentioned in the title of the report.

➢ Indicate the title of the report in quotation marks after the legislature.

➢ If an author is given, place by and the name after the title of report.

➢ If the sessional paper is numbered, cite the number after the title, preceded by a comma.

➢ Indicate the year and not the full date in parentheses.

4.1.5 Votes and Proceedings

Jurisdiction,	legislature,	*title,*	legislative session,	volume and/ or document number	(date)	pinpoint.
Quebec,	National Assembly,	*Votes and Proceedings,*	39th Leg, 1st Sess,	No 175	(18 June 2009).	
Ontario,	Legislative Assembly,	*Votes and Proceedings,*	38th Leg, 2nd Sess,	No 79	(14 December 2005).	

➢ Indicate the jurisdiction (if a province) and the legislature, unless this information is mentioned in the title.

➢ Cite the title, in italics, as it appears on the title page of the document.

➢ Indicate the number of the legislative session.

➢ Place the volume and/or document number, if any, after the number of the legislature, preceded by a comma.

4.1.6 Reports Published in Debates

Jurisdiction,	legislature,	issuing body,	"title of report"	in	*title*,	number	(date)	pinpoint.
Ontario,	Legislative Assembly,	Standing Committee on regulations and private bills,	"Election of Chair"	in	*Official Report of Debates (Hansard)*,	No T-6	(26 September 2001)	at 41.

➢ Indicate the jurisdiction if a province.

➢ For debates, follow the rules from section 4.1.1. After the name of the legislature, add the name of issuing body and the title of the report. Place the title of the report in quotation marks.

➢ Place the number of the paper, if any, after the title, preceded by a comma.

4.1.7 Reports Published Separately

Jurisdiction,	legislature,	issuing body,	*title*	(date)	pinpoint	(Chair) (if applicable).
	House of Commons,	Standing Committee on Agriculture and Agri-Food,	*Labelling of Genetically Modified Food and its Impact on Farmers: Report of the Standing Committee on Agriculture and Agri-Food*	(June 2002)		(Chair: Charles Hubbard).

➢ Indicate the jurisdiction if a province.

➢ After the name of the legislature, add the name of issuing body, followed by the title of the report in italics.

➢ Provide the complete date as provided by the report in parentheses.

➢ If the Chair is indicated on the cover page, add the information in parentheses.

➢ This section applies to reports directly published by a parliamentary body. If the report is published by any other body, see section 4.2 on non-parliamentary reports.

4.2 NON-PARLIAMENTARY PAPERS

This section applies to documents published under a separate cover that do not emanate directly from a legislative body.

4.2.1 General Form

Jurisdiction,	issuing body,	*title*,	volume (if applicable)	(publication information)	pinpoint	(additional information) (optional).
Canada,	Royal Commission on Electoral Reform and Party Financing,	*Reforming Electoral Democracy,*	vol 4	(Ottawa: Communication Group, 1991)	at 99	(Chair: Pierre Lortie).
		Report of the Parliamentary Ad Hoc Committee on AIDS,		(Ottawa: Ad Hoc Committee on AIDS, 1990)	at 5.	
Quebec,	Ministère de la justice,	*Commentaires du ministre de la justice,*	vol 1	(Quebec: Publications du Québec, 1993)	at 705.	

➤ Include the jurisdiction unless it is mentioned in another element of the citation.

➤ Write the issuing body unless it is mentioned in the title of the report.

➤ If there is an indication of the nature of the publication on the title page, include it in parentheses immediately after the title. For example: "Statistics Canada, *Market Research Handbook* (Socio-economic guide), (Ottawa: Small Business and Special Surveys Division, 2001) at 167".

➤ If there is a volume, cite it after the title, preceded by a comma.

➤ Provide publication information according to the rules of sections 6.2.5-6.2.9.

➤ The name of the Commissioner or Chair may be included in parentheses at the end of the citation.

4.2.2   Interpretation Bulletins

Department,	Interpretation Bulletin	IT-number,	"title"	(date)	pinpoint.
Canada Revenue Agency,	Interpretation Bulletin	IT-459,	"Income Tax Act Adventure or Concern in the Nature of Trade"	(8 September 1980).	
Canada Revenue Agency,	Interpretation Bulletin	IT-525R,	"Performing Artists"	(17 August 1995).	
Canada Revenue Agency,	Interpretation Bulletin	IT-244R3,	"Gifts by Individuals of Life Insurance Policies as Charitable Donations"	(6 September 1991)	at para. 4.

➢ **ITs** are income tax interpretation bulletins published by the Canada Revenue Agency.

➢ If the bulletin has been revised insert R after the IT number. The number of revisions is indicated by the number following the R (par ex. R3).

➢ When interpretation bulletins are divided into paragraphs, pinpoint to a paragraph.

4.2.3 Reports of Inquiries and Commissions

4.2.3.1 Reports Published in a Single Volume

Jurisdiction,	issuing body,	title	(publication information)	pinpoint.
	Commission of Inquiry into the Sponsorship Program and Advertising Activities,	Who is Responsible? Fact Finding Report	(Ottawa: Public Works and Government Services Canada, 2005)	at 33.

➢ Do not indicate the name of the commission if it is already mentioned in the title of the report.

4.2.3.2 Reports Published in Multiple Volumes

4.2.3.2.1   Volumes with a Single Title

Jurisdiction,	issuing body,	title,	volume	(publication information)	(President) (if applicable)	pinpoint.
		Commission of Inquiry on the Blood System in Canada: Final Report,	vol 1	(Ottawa: Public Works and Government Services Canada, 1997)		at 100.

➢ To cite a report published in multiple volumes with a single title, include the volume number after the title. To distinguish the volumes, indicate vol or any other appellation used in the report (such as book).

➤ Do not repeat the volume number in subsequent references unless there is a citation to a different volume anywhere else in the citing document (e.g. *Blood System Report*, vol 2, *supra* note 5 at 64).

4.2.3.2.2   Volumes with Different Titles

Citation for volume 1	;	citation for volume 2
Report of the Royal Commission on Aboriginal Peoples: Looking Forward, Looking Back, vol 1 (Ottawa: Supply and Services Canada, 1996)	;	*Report of the Royal Commission on Aboriginal Peoples: Restructuring the Relationship*, vol 2 (Ottawa: Supply and Services Canada, 1996) at 14.

➤ To cite a report published in multiple volumes with different titles, include a full citation for each volume separated by a semicolon. Treat the title of the volume as a subtitle of the entire work.

➤ Subsequent references must include the volume number following the short title (e.g. *Aboriginal Peoples Report*, vol 2, supra note 4 at 32).

4.2.3 Annual Reports and Release Bulletins

Issuing body,	*title,*	volume, number and/ or **chapter** (if any)	(publication information)	pin-point.
Statistics Canada,	*The Daily,*		(Ottawa: StatCan, 31 July 2009)	at 5.
Health Canada,	*Health Policy Research Bulletin,*	No 13	(Ottawa: Health Canada, 2007)	at 3.
Atomic Energy of Canada Limited,	*Annual Report,*		(Mississagua (Ont): AECL, 2006)	at 11.
Communications Canada,	*Telecommunications in Canada: An Overview of the Carriage Industry,*		(Ottawa: Communications Canada, 1992)	at 21.
Office of the Auditor General of Canada,	*Report of the Auditor General of Canada to the House of Commons,*	ch 8	(Ottawa: OAG, 2008).	

➤ Include the volume, number or chapter as indicated in the edition.

➤ Include the full date as provided.

➤ If the issuing body and the editors are the same entity, use the official abbreviation in the publication information (see the Statistics Canada and Office of the Auditor General of Canada examples).

4.2.5   Individual Authors or Editors

Issuing body,	title	by	author or editor	(publication information).
Agriculture and Agri-Food Canada,	The Health of Our Water: Toward Sustainable Agriculture in Canada	by	DR Coote & LJ Gregorich, eds	(Ottawa: Minister of Public Works and Government Services Canada, 2000).

➢ If there are individual authors or editors, include by after the title, followed by their names.

4.3   PUBLIC PAPERS OF INTERGOVERNMENTAL CONFERENCES

Name of conference or committee,	title,	document number	(location of conference:	date of conference).
Meeting of the Continuing Committee of Ministers on the Constitution,	The Canadian Charter of Rights and Freedoms—Discussion Draft, July 4, 1980,	Doc 830-81/027	(Ottawa:	8-12 September 1980).
Federal-Provincial-Territorial Meeting of Ministers Responsible for Justice,	Dealing with Impaired Driving in Prince Edward Island: A Summary 1986-1997,	Doc 830-600/021	(Montreal:	4-5 December 1997).

➢ Indicate the name of the conference or committee in full, followed by the title of the paper and the document number.

➢ Provide the location and full date of the conference in parentheses.

5   INTERNATIONAL MATERIALS

5.1   INTERNATIONAL DOCUMENTS

5.1.1   Treaties and Other International Agreements

Title,	parties (if applicable),	date of signature,	treaty series reference,	other source	(other information) (optional).
Treaty Relating to Boundary Waters and Questions Arising with Canada,	United States and United Kingdom,	11 January 1909,	36 US Stat 2448,	UKTS 1910 No 23.	
Convention for the Protection of Human Rights and Fundamental Freedoms,		4 November 1950,	213 UNTS 221 at 223,	Eur TS 5	[*ECHR*].
International Covenant on Civil and Political Rights,		19 December 1966,	999 UNTS 171, arts 9-14,	Can TS 1976 No 47, 6 ILM 368	(entered into force 23 March 1976, accession by Canada 19 May 1976) [*ICCPR*].
North American Free Trade Agreement Between the Government of Canada, the Government of Mexico and the Government of the United States,		17 December 1992,	Can TS 1994 No 2,	32 ILM 289	(entered into force 1 January 1994) [*NAFTA*].
General Agreement on Tariffs and Trade,		30 October 1947,	58 UNTS 187,	Can TS 1947 No 27	(entered into force 1 January 1948) [*GATT 1947*].

➢ Write the complete title of the treaty. When the names of the signatories appear in the title of a treaty, shorten them to reflect common usage (e.g. United Kingdom, not United Kingdom of Great Britain and Northern Ireland) but do not abbreviate them (e.g. UK).

➢ If the names of the parties to a bilateral treaty are not mentioned in the title, include the shortened (but not abbreviated) names of the parties after the title, between commas. The names of the parties to a multilateral treaty may be included in parentheses at the end of the citation.

➢ Provide the date when the treaty was first signed or opened for signature.

➢ Provide the treaty series citation after the date. It is preferable to provide a parallel citation for treaties, referring to treaty series in the following order of preference: (1) *United Nations Treaty Series* [UNTS] or *League of Nations Treaty Series* [LNTS]; (2) official treaty series of a state involved (e.g. *Canada Treaty Series* [Can TS], *United Kingdom Treaty Series* [UKTS]); (3) other sources of international treaties (e.g. *International Legal Materials* [ILM]).

➢ Provided additional information at the end of the citation (e.g. the names of the parties to a multilateral treaty, the date of entry into force, the number of ratifications, and the status of particular countries).

Treaty series and their abbreviations:

Air and Aviation Treaties of the World	AATW
Australian Treaty Series	ATS
British and Foreign State Papers	UKFS
Canada Treaty Series	Can TS
Consolidated Treaty Series	Cons TS
Documents juridiques internationaux	DJI
European Treaty Series	Eur TS
International Legal Materials	ILM
Journal officiel	JO
League of Nations Treaty Series	LNTS
Organization of American States Treaty Series	OASTS
Recueil des traités d'alliance, de paix, de trêve, de neutralité, de commerce, de limites, d'échange, et plusieurs autres actes à la connaissance des relations étrangères des puissances et États de l'Europe	Rec TA
Recueil des traités de la Société des Nations	RTSN
Recueil des traités des Nations Unies	RTNU
Recueil des traités du Canada	RT Can
Recueil des traités et accords de la France	RTAF
Recueil général des traités de la France	Rec GTF
Série des traités et conventions européennes	STE
Treaties and other International Agreements of the United States of America 1776-1949	TI Agree *(formerly USBS)*
United Kingdom Treaty Series	UKTS
United Nations Treaty Series	UNTS
United States Statutes at Large	US Stat
United States Treaties and Other International Acts Series	TIAS
United States Treaties and Other International Agreements	UST

5.1.1.1 Australian Treaty Neutral Citation

The Australian Commonwealth government has adopted a method of neutral citation for treaties that should precede citation to a printed source. The form consists of the publication year in brackets, the identifier, and the document number. This citation should follow the treaty name and the year of signing.

Identifiers for neutral citation:

Australian Treaty Series	ATS	*Agreement on the Conservation of Albatrosses and Petrels*, 19 June 2001, [2004] ATS 5.
Australian Treaty National Interest Analysis	ATNIA	
Australian Treaty not yet in force	ATNIF	

5.1.2 United Nations Documents

Every UN document does not always contain all the elements found in the examples below. Adapt the citation and provide the information necessary to identify the document clearly.

Abbreviations of commonly used words and phrases:

Decision	Dec	Plenary	Plen
Document	Doc	Recommendation	Rec
Emergency	Emer	Regulation	Reg
Meeting	Mtg	Resolution	Res
Mimeograph(ed)	Mimeo	Session	Sess
Number	No	Special	Spec
Official Records	OR	Supplement	Supp

5.1.2.1 Charter of the United Nations

The *Charter of the United Nations* does not require a full citation. Cite it as: *Charter of the United Nations*, 26 June 1945, Can TS 1945 No 7.

5.1.2.2 Official Records

Official records published by UN organizations contain three parts: **Meetings**, **Supplements**, and **Annexes**. The official records are identified by the particular body's acronym followed by OR. Provide the full names of UN bodies that have no official acronym.

Official acronyms of the principal United Nations bodies:

Economic and Social Council	ESC
First Committee, Second Committee, etc.	C1, C2, etc.
General Assembly	GA
Security Council	SC
Trade and Development Board	TDB
Trusteeship Council	TC
United Nations Conference on Trade and Development	UNCTAD

5.1.2.2.1   Meetings

UN body's acronym and OR,	session number or number of years since the body's inception,	meeting,	UN doc number (and sales number if applicable)	(year of document) (if applicable)	pin-point	[provisional].
UNCTAD TDBOR,	23d Sess,	565th Mtg,	UN Doc TD/B/ SR.565	(1981).		
UNSCOR,	53d Year,	3849th Mtg,	UN Doc S/ PV.3849	(1998)		[provisional].
UNESCOR,	1984,	23d Plen Mtg,	UN Doc E/1984/ SR.23.			

➤ Indicate UN (unless UN is part of the body's acronym) followed by the **UN body's acronym** and OR (**Official Records**). Do not add a space between UN and the acronym.

➤ Provide the **session number** after the name of the body. If the session number is not available, give the year of the body since its inception. If neither the session number nor the year of the body are available, provide the calendar year.

➤ Provide the **meeting number** after the sessional information.

➤ Provide the **UN document number** after the meeting number. If a document has more than one document number, indicate all the numbers, separated by a hyphen. Give the **sales document number** after the document number in parentheses (e.g. Sales No #) (if applicable).

➤ Provide the **calendar year** in parentheses after the UN document number, unless it has been indicated previously.

➤ Indicate **provisional documents** by placing [provisional] at the end of the citation.

5.1.2.2.2   Supplements

UN resolutions, decisions, and reports appear as supplements to documents published in the Official Records.

	Author (if applicable),	Title,	UN body Res or Dec number,	UN body's acronym and OR,	Session number or calendar year,	Supp No,	UN Doc number,	(calendar year)	1st page and pinpoint.
Resolution		Universal Declaration of Human Rights,	GA Res 217(III),	UNGAOR,	3d Sess,	Supp No 13,	UN Doc A/810,	(1948)	71.
Decision		Protection of the heritage of indigenous people,	ESC Dec 1998/ 277,	UNESCOR,	1998,	Supp No 1,	UN Doc E/1998 /98,		113 at 115.
Reports	Commission on Crime Prevention and Criminal Justice,	Report on the Ninth Session,		UNESCOR,	2000,	Supp No 10,	UN Doc E/2000 /30.		
		Report of the UN Commissioner for Refugees,		UNGAOR,	15th Sess,	Supp No 11,	UN Doc A/4378/ Rev.1,	(1960).	

➢ Provide the title in italics. Write the author of reports if not mentioned in the title.

➢ For decisions and resolutions, provide the **decision or resolution number** after the title.

➢ Indicate UN (unless UN is part of the body's acronym) followed by the **UN body's acronym** and OR (**Official Records**). Do not add a space between UN and the acronym. For resolutions and decisions, provide this information after the resolution or decision number. For reports, provide this information immediately after the report's title.

➢ Provide the **session number** after the UN body's official records acronym. If the session number is not available, give the **year of the body since its inception**. If neither the session number nor the year of the body is available, provide the **calendar year**.

➢ Provide the **supplement number** and the UN document number after the sessional information.

➢ Provide the **calendar year** in parentheses after the UN document number, unless it has been indicated previously.

➢ Conclude the citation with the first page number and pinpoint. Add a comma when there is no information provided between the UN document and the first page.

5.1.2.2.3   Annexes

Title,	UN body's acronym and OR,	session number or number of years since the body's inception,	Annex, agenda item no,	UN Doc number	(year) (if applicable)	1st page (if applicable) and pinpoint.
Protectionism and structural adjustment,	UNCTAD TDBOR,	32d Sess,	Annex, Agenda Item 6,	UN Doc TD/B/1081	(1986)	at 23.
USSR: Draft Resolution,	UNESCOR,	3d year, 7th Sess,	Annex, Agenda Item 7,	UN Doc E/884/Rev.1	(1948)	at para 3.

➢ Provide the title of the document in italics.

➢ Provide the UN body's acronym and OR (**Official Records**) after the title. Do not add a space between UN and the acronym.

➢ Provide the **session number** after the UN body's acronym. If the session number is not available, give the **year of the body since its inception**. If neither the session number nor the year of the body is available, provide the **calendar year**.

➢ Indicate Annex and the agenda item number, followed by the UN document number.

➢ Provide the calendar year in parentheses after the UN document number, unless it has been indicated previously.

➢ Conclude the citation with the first page number if the document is part of a bound collection of documents. Add a comma when there is no information provided between the UN document and the first page.

5.1.2.3 Mimeographs

➢ A mimeograph is an official document of the UN. Refer to it only when the document has not been reproduced in the Official Reports. Mimeographs are available at <http://documents.un.org>.

UNSC, Disarmament Commission, *Questions About Arms Manufacturing in Eastern Iraq*, UN Doc S/CN.10/L.666 (July 1993) [mimeo restricted].

➢ Follow the rules for supplements, at section 5.1.2.2.2. Indicate mimeo and place it in brackets at the end of the citation. If applicable, include provisional, limited, or restricted in the same brackets.

5.1.2.4 Periodicals

➢ When referring to periodical articles published by the UN, follow the rules for citing articles (section 6.1). If it is unclear from the title of the periodical that the UN is the publisher, include UN and the particular body responsible for the publication in parentheses at the end of the citation.

> CP Romulo, "External Debt in Central America" (1987) CEPAL Review No 32 (UN, Economic Commission for Latin America and the Caribbean).

5.1.2.5 Yearbooks

➢ Cite UN yearbooks using the same rules as for collections of essays, at section 6.3. Give the UN document number of the article cited and of the yearbook, if available.

> "Report of the Commission to the General Assembly on the work of its thirty-ninth Session" (UN Doc A/42/10) in *Yearbook of the International Law Commission 1987*, vol 2, part 2 (New York: UN, 1989) at 50 (UNDOC.A/CN 4/SER.A/1987/Add. 1).

5.1.2.6 Sales Publications

> UN, *Recommendations on the Transport of Dangerous Goods*, 9th ed (New York: UN, 1995) at 18.

➢ Cite sales publications using the rules for books, at section 6.2.

5.1.3 European Union Documents

European Union regulations, directives, decisions, debates, and other documents are published in the ***Official Journal of the European Union*** (OJ). The OJ is published every working day in every official language. It consists of two related series (**the L series for legislation** and **the C series for information and notices**) and a supplement (**the S series for public tenders** which is available only in electronic format as of 1 July 1998). The title replaced the *Official Journal of the European Communities* as of 1 February 2003.

5.1.3.1 *Regulations, Directives, and Decisions*

Legislation from the European Communities includes instruments referred to as regulations, directives, and decisions. They are published in the legislation (**L**) series of the *Official Journal of the European Union.*

	EC,	*title,*	[year of journal]	OJ,	series and issue number /1st page	pin-point.
Regulations	EC,	*Commission Regulation (EC) 218/2005 of 10 February 2005 opening and providing for the administration of an autonomous tariff quota for garlic from 1 January 2005,*	[2005]	OJ,	L 39/5	at 6.
Directives	EC,	*Commission Directive 2004/29/EC of 4 March 2004 on determining the characteristics and minimum conditions for inspecting vine varieties,*	[2004]	OJ,	L 71/22.	
Decisions	EC,	*Commission Decision 98/85/EC of 16 January 1998 concerning certain protective measures with regard to live birds coming from, or originating in Hong Kong and China,*	[1998]	OJ,	L 15/45	at 46.

➢ Write EC for **European Community** and provide the full title of the instrument in italics.

➢ The **instrument number** is included in the title. The number in **directives and decisions** consists of the year and a sequential number (e.g. 98/85 or 2004/29). Note that only the last two digits of the year are used until 1998. Beginning with 1999, all four digits are used.

➢ To cite **regulations**, write the sequential number first, followed by the last two digits of the year until 1998 and the full year starting in 1999 (e.g. 2514/98).

➢ Indicate the **OJ series**, then the issue number and the first page of the instrument, separated by a slash (e.g. L 15/45). Cite EC legislation to the **L** series of the *Official Journal of the European Union.*

5.1.3.2 *Debates of the European Parliament*

EC,	*date of sitting or title,*	[year]	OJ	Annex issue number/first page	pinpoint.
EC,	*Sitting of Wednesday, 5 May 1999,*	[1999]	OJ	Annex 4-539/144	at 152.

➢ The debates of the European Parliament can be found in the Annex to the *Official Journal of the European Union* (OJ).

➢ Write EC and provide the title of the document or the date of the sitting.

➢ Provide the year the sitting was reported in brackets, followed by OJ, then Annex and the **issue number**. A slash (/) separates the issue number from the first page (e.g. 4-539/144).

5.1.3.3 *Other Documents*

Information and notices	EC, *Explanatory note concerning Annex III of the EU-Mexico Agreement (Decision 2/2000 of the EU-Mexico Joint Council)*, [2004] OJ C 40/2.
General publications	EC, Commission, *Report from the Commission to the Council and the European Parliament* (Luxembourg: EC, 1995).
Periodicals	EC, *External Trade: Monthly Statistics* (1994) No 1 at 16.

➢ Write EC as the author of all EC documents. If available, provide a more precise authoring body.

➢ Cite the *Official Journal of the European Union: Information and Notices* (**C series**) in the same manner as other sections of the official journal.

➢ For **general publications**, see Chapter 6 of this *Guide*.

➢ For **periodicals**, italicize the title of the periodical and indicate the issue number after the year.

5.1.4 Council of Europe Documents

Documents from the Council of Europe can be found in the following official publications.

Official publication	Abbreviation
Documents: Working Papers	Documents
Information Bulletin on Legal Affairs	Inf Bull
Official Report of Debates	Debates
Orders of the Day and Minutes of Proceedings	Orders
Texts Adopted by the Assembly	Texts Adopted

	Council of Europe,	body,	sessional information,	*title* (if applicable),	official publication	(year)	pin-point.
Debates	Council of Europe,	PA,	2001 Ordinary Sess (First Part),		Debates, vol 1	(2001)	at 67.
Texts Adopted	Council of Europe,	CA,	21st Sess, Part 3,		Texts Adopted, Rec 585	(1970)	at 1.
Orders and minutes	Council of Europe,	CA, Part 2,	21st Sess,		Orders, 10th Sitting	(1969)	at 20.
Working Papers	Council of Europe,	PA,	2000 Ordinary Sess (Third Part),	*Situation of lesbians and gays in Council of Europe member states,*	Documents, vol 5, Doc 8755	(2000)	at 1.
Series	Council of Europe,	Committee of Ministers,		*Recommendation R(82)1,*	(1980) 12 Inf Bull 58.		

➢ Write Council of Europe, followed by the particular body responsible for the instrument. Abbreviate **Parliamentary Assembly** to PA, and **Consultative Assembly** to CA.

➢ Provide the sessional information followed by the title of the document, if applicable.

➢ Indicate the official publication in abbreviated form.

➢ Indicate the year of publication in parentheses after the official publication.

➢ To cite periodicals (Inf Bull), see section 6.1.

5.1.5 Organization of American States Documents

OAS,	issuing body,	session number (if applicable),	*title,*	OAS document number	(year)	pin-point.
OAS,	General Assembly,	2d Sess,	*Draft Standards Regarding the Formulation of Reservations to Multilateral Treaties,*	OR OEA/Ser.P/AG/ Doc.202	(1972).	
OAS,	Inter-American Commission on Human Rights,		*Draft of the Inter-American Declaration on the Rights of Indigenous Peoples,*	OR OEA/Ser.L/V/ II.90/Doc.14, rev 1	(1995)	at 1.

➢ **OAS documents do not have an author**. Include the particular issuing body, if one exists, unless it is clear from the title of the report.

➢ Where applicable, put the session or meeting number after the name of the issuing body.

➢ Use the official title of the document.

➢ Place OR before the OAS document number. The document number begins with the letters OEA (Organización de los Estados Americanos) and not OAS.

➢ Conclude the citation with the year of the document in parentheses.

5.1.6 World Trade Organization (WTO) and the General Agreement on Tariffs and Trade (GATT) Documents

	GATT or WTO,	title,	Decision, Recommendation, or Document number,	session number,	BISD	online information.
Decisions and recommen- dations		*Accession of Guatemala,*	GATT CP Decision L/6824,	47th Sess,	38th Supp BISD (1991) 16.	
		Freedom of Contract in Transport Insurance,	GATT CP Recommendation of 27 May 1959,	15th Sess,	8th Supp BISD (1960) 26.	
Reports	GATT,	*Report of the Panel adopted by the Committee on Anti-Dumping Practices on 30 October 1995,*	GATT Doc ADP/137,		42d Supp. BISD (1995) 17.	
	WTO,	*Report of the Working Party on the Accession of Bulgaria,*	WTO Doc WT/ ACC/BGR/5 (1996),			online: WTO <http://docsonline.wto.org>.
Meetings	WTO, General Council,	*Minutes of Meeting* (held on 22 November 2000),	WTO Doc WT/ GC/M/60,			online: WTO <http://docsonline.wto.org>.

➢ **Decisions and recommendations do not have an author**. GATT and WTO are the authors of all reports. Include the particular issuing body, if one exists, unless it is clear from the title of the report.

➢ Give the decision, recommendation, or document number. If none, give the full date of the decision or recommendation. Abbreviate **Contracting Parties** to CP, **Decision** to Dec and **Recommendation** to Rec.

➢ Where possible, cite GATT documents to the *Basic Instruments and Selected Documents* (BISD), followed by the year in parentheses and the first page of the document.

➢ If a report is printed independently with no document number, use the rules for books, at section 6.2 (e.g. GATT, *The International Markets for Meat: 1990/91* (Geneva: GATT, 1991)).

5.1.7 Organisation for Economic Co-operation and Development (OECD) Documents

	OECD, authoring body (if applicable),	*title,*	series title,	working paper number or other publication information,	Doc No	(publication information or year).
Series	OECD, Development Assistance Committee,	*Japan (No 34),*	Development Cooperation Review Series,			(Paris: OECD, 1999).
Working Papers	OECD, Economics Department,	*Encouraging Environmentally Sustainable Growth in Australia,*		Working Paper No 309,	Doc No ECO/WKP (2001) 35	(2001).
Periodical	OECD,	*OECD Economic Surveys: China,*		Economic Surveys, vol 2005, No 13,		(2005).

➢ Indicate OECD and the authoring body, followed by the title in italics.

➢ If the document is a work in a series, provide the series title.

➢ If the document is a working paper, provide the working paper number, if applicable, and the OECD document number. Note that the document number begins with OCDE, in French or English.

➢ Include other information such as the volume number for a periodical or series.

➢ Provide the publication information in parentheses at the end of the citation. For periodicals, provide the month of publication, if applicable.

5.2   CASES

See Appendix A-5 for a list of abbreviations of international organizations and their reporters.

5.2.1 Permanent Court of International Justice (1922-1946)

To cite acts and rules of the PCIJ, write the title, volume number, and name of publication, followed by the first page or document number (e.g. *Revised Rules of the Court* (1926), PCIJ 33 (Ser D) No 1).

5.2.1.1 Judgments, Orders, and Advisory Opinions

	Style of cause (names of parties)	(year),	type of decision,	reporter	case No	pinpoint.
Judgments	Panevezys-Saldutiskis Railway Case (Estonia v Lithuania)	(1939),		PCIJ (Ser A/B)	No 76	at 16.
Orders	Panevezys-Saldutiskis Railway Case (Estonia v Lithuania)		Order of 30 June 1938,	PCIJ (Ser A/B)	No 75	at 8.
Advisory Opinions	Case of the Customs Régime Between Germany and Austria	(1931),	Advisory Opinion,	PCIJ (Ser A/B)	No 41	at 3.

➢ Indicate the style of cause and, for judgments and orders, the names of the parties involved.

➢ For judgments and advisory opinions, provide the year of the decision in parentheses after the style of cause.

➢ Specify if the document is an order or an advisory opinion. If referring to an order, provide the full date. In such a case, no year is required after the style of cause.

➢ Provide the PCIJ series followed by the case number. **Judgments of the PCIJ** are published in *Series A: Collection of Judgments* (PCIJ (Ser A)) and in *Series A/B: Judgments, Orders and Advisory Opinions* (PCIJ (Ser A/B)). **Orders** and **advisory opinions** are published in *Series B: Collection of Advisory Opinions* (PCIJ (Ser B)) and in *Series A/B: Judgments, Orders and Advisory Opinions* (PCIJ (Ser A/B)).

5.2.1.2 Pleadings, Oral Arguments, and Documents

Style of cause (names of parties),	"title of document"	(date),	reporter	case No,	first page	pinpoint.
Lighthouses Case Between France and Greece (France v Greece),	"Oral argument of Professor Basdevant"	(5 February 1934),	PCIJ (Series C)	No 74,	222	at 227.
Pajzs, Csáky, Esterházy Case (Hungary v Yugoslavia),	"Application Instituting Proceedings"	(1 December 1935),	PCIJ (Series C)	No 79,	10	at 12.

➢ Indicate the style of cause and, in parentheses, the names of the parties involved.

➢ Provide the official title of the document, followed by the full date in parentheses.

➢ Indicate the PCIJ Series and the case number. Pleadings, oral arguments, and other documents from **before 1931** are published in *Series C: Acts and Documents Relating to Judgments and Advisory Opinions Given by the Court* (PCIJ (Series C)), and **from 1931 on** in *Series C: Pleadings, Oral Statements and Documents* (PCIJ (Series C)). **Basic Documents**, **Annual Reports** and **Indices** are published in series D through series F.

➤ Place a comma between the case number and the first page of the document. Include a pinpoint, if necessary.

5.2.2 International Court of Justice (1946-present)

To cite acts and rules of the ICJ, write the title, volume number, and name of publication, followed by the first page or document number (e.g. *Travel and Subsistence Regulations of the International Court of Justice*, [1947] ICJ Acts & Doc 94).

5.2.2.1 Judgments, Orders, and Advisory Opinions

Refer to the ICJ website <http://www.icj-cij.org> (section 5.3) for ICJ judgments, opinions, or orders not yet printed.

	Style of cause (names of parties),	type of decision,	[year of reporter]	reporter	first page	pinpoint.
Judgments	*Case concerning East Timor (Portugal v Australia),*		[1995]	ICJ Rep	90	at 103.
Orders	*Fisheries Jurisdiction Case (Spain v Canada),*	Order of 8 May 1996,	[1996]	ICJ Rep	58.	
Advisory Opinions	*Legality of the Threat or Use of Nuclear Weapons Case,*	Advisory Opinion,	[1996]	ICJ Rep	226	at 230.

➤ Begin with the style of cause and the names of the parties involved. Although the ICJ Reports sometimes separates the parties' names with a slash (*El Salvador/ Honduras*), always separate them with a *v* (*Portugal v Australia*). Names of the parties are not provided for advisory opinions.

➤ Specify if the document is an order or an advisory opinion. If referring to an order, provide the full date.

➤ Provide the year of the reporter in brackets, followed by the reporter and the first page. Judgments, orders, and advisory opinions of the ICJ are published in the court's official reporter: ***Reports of Judgments, Advisory Opinions and Orders*** (ICJ Rep).

5.2.2.2 Pleadings, Oral Arguments, and Documents

Style of cause (names of parties),	"title of document"	(date),	[year of reporter]	reporter (vol)	first page	pin-point.
Case concerning Right of Passage over Indian Territory (Portugal v India),	"Oral argument of Shri MC Setalvad"	(23 September 1957),	[1960]	ICJ Pleadings (vol 4)	14	at 23.
Fisheries Jurisdiction Case (Spain v Canada),	"Application Instituting Proceedings Submitted by Spain"	(28 March 1995),		ICJ Pleadings	3.	

➢ Indicate the style of cause and, in parentheses, the names of the parties.

➢ After the style of cause, provide the title of the document as indicated in the reporter, followed by the date in parentheses.

➢ Indicate the reporter and the first page of the document. The ICJ publishes pleadings and other documents in *Pleadings, Oral Arguments and Documents* (**ICJ Pleadings**). If there is a volume number, cite it in Arabic numerals (e.g. 1, 2, 3) before the number of the first page.

➢ After 1981, ICJ Pleadings do not indicate the date of publication of the reporter. Pleadings are available on the ICJ website: <http://.icj-cij.org>.

5.2.3 Court of Justice of the European Communities and European Court of First Instance

	Style of cause,	case number,	[year of reporter]	reporter	first page	pinpoint,	other source.
ECJ	Commission v Luxembourg,	C-26/99,	[1999]	ECR	I-8987	at I-8995.	
CFI	Kesko v Commission,	T-22/97,	[1999]	ECR	II-3775	at II-3822.	

➢ Write the style of cause. Abbreviate the names of institutions (e.g. Council rather than Council of the European Communities).

➢ Write the case number. C- indicates a decision of the Court of Justice of the European Communities, also known as the **European Court of Justice** (ECJ). T- indicates a decision of the **European Court of First Instance** (CFI).

➢ Cite the reporter and indicate the first page of the case. Decisions of the ECJ and the CFI are published in the Courts' official reporter *Reports of Cases before the Court of Justice and the Court of First Instance*. Cite it as the **European Court Reports** (ECR).

➢ Precede page numbers by I for **ECJ decisions** and by II for **CFI decisions**.

➢ Use the *Common Market Law Reports* (CMLR) or the *Common Market Reporter* (CMR) as other sources.

5.2.4   European Court of Human Rights and European Commission of Human Rights

5.2.4.1 Before 1999

Style of cause	(year of judgment),	volume number	reporter	first page,	other source.
Kurt v Turkey	(1998),	74	ECHR (Ser A)	1152,	27 EHRR 373.
Spencer v United Kingdom	(1998),	92A	Eur Comm'n HR DR	56,	41 YB Eur Conv HR 72.

➤   Indicate the style of cause followed by the year of the decision in parentheses.

➤   Provide the volume number of the official reporter before the name of the reporter, followed by the name of the reporter and the first page of the judgment. Cite the official reporters of the Court and Commission: *European Court of Human Rights, Series A: Judgments and Decisions* (ECHR (Ser A)); *Collection of Decisions of the European Commission of Human Rights* (Eur Comm'n HR CD (1960-1974)); *Decisions and Reports of the European Commission of Human Rights* (Eur Comm'n HR DR (1975-1999)).

➤   Use the *Yearbook of the European Convention on Human Rights* (YB Eur Conv HR) or the *European Human Rights Reports* (EHRR) as other sources.

5.2.4.2 1999 and Later

Protocol No 11 to the Convention for the Protection of Human Rights and Fundamental Freedoms came into force on 1 November 1998 and replaced the old court and commission with a new full-time court.

Style of cause,	application No,	[year]	vol number	reporter	first page,	other source.
Allard v Sweden,	No 35179/97,	[2003]	VII	ECHR	207,	39 EHRR 321.
Cyprus v Turkey,	No 25781/94,	[2001]	IV	ECHR	1,	35 EHRR 731.

➤   Add [GC] at the end of the style of cause before the comma if the judgment was given by the Grand Chamber of the Court.

➤   Other information may also be added in parentheses after the style of cause, before the comma: (dec) for a **decision on admissibility**, (preliminary objections) for a judgment concerning only **preliminary objections**, (just satisfaction) for a judgment concerning only **just satisfaction**, (revision) for a judgment concerning **revision**, (interpretation) for a judgment concerning **interpretation**, (striking out) for a judgment **striking the case out**, or (friendly settlement) for a judgment concerning a **friendly settlement**.

➤   If there is more than one application number, include only the first number.

> For unreported decisions, give the application number followed by the date the judgment was rendered (e.g. *Roche v United Kingdom*, No 32555/96 (19 October 2005)).

5.2.5 Inter-American Court of Human Rights

5.2.5.1 *Judgments, Orders, and Advisory Opinions*

	Style of cause (name of state concerned)	(year of judgment),	type of decision and number,	reporter	case or report No,	pinpoint,	other source.
Judgments	*Neira Alegria Case (Peru)*	(1996),		Inter-Am Ct HR (Ser C)	No 29,	at para 55,	*Annual Report of the Inter-American Court of Human Rights: 1996*, OEA/ Ser.L/V/III.19/doc.4 (1997) 179.
Advisory Opinions	*Reports of the Inter-American Commission on Human Rights (Art 51 of the American Convention on Human Rights) (Chile)*	(1997),	Advisory Opinion OC-15/97,	Inter-Am Ct HR (Ser A)	No 15,	at para 53,	*Annual Report of the Inter-American Commission on Human Rights: 1997*, OEA/Ser.L/V/ III.39/doc.5 (1998) 307.

> Indicate the style of cause. If the case involves an individual state, include the name of that state in parentheses.

> Provide the date of the decision in parentheses.

> Specify if the document is an **advisory opinion** and provide the advisory opinion number.

> Provide the reporter and case number. The Inter-American Court of Human Rights publishes **judgments** in *Inter-American Court of Human Rights, Series C: Decisions and Judgments* (Inter-Am Ct HR (Ser C)) and **advisory opinions** in *Inter-American Court of Human Rights, Series A: Judgments and Opinions* (Inter-Am Ct HR (Ser A)).

> Use the **annual report of the court,** the *International Legal Materials* (ILM) or use the *Inter-American Yearbook on Human Rights* as other sources.

5.2.5.2 Pleadings, Oral Arguments, and Documents

Style of cause (name of the state concerned),	type of decision and number,	"title of document"	(date of document),	reporter and (series)	first page	pin-point.
Proposed Amendments to the Naturalization Provisions of the Constitution of Costa Rica,	Advisory Opinion OC-4/84,	"Verbatim Record of Public Hearing"	(7 September 1983),	Inter-Am Ct HR (Ser B)	23.	

➢ Indicate the style of cause. If the name of the state concerned is not already included in the style of cause, write the name in parentheses.

➢ Specify if it is an **advisory opinion** and give the advisory opinion number.

➢ Include the title of the document in quotation marks, followed by the full date in parentheses.

➢ Provide the reporter and first page. The Inter-American Court of Human Rights published pleadings, oral arguments, and other documents in *Inter-American Court of Human Rights, Series B: Pleadings, Oral Arguments and Documents* (Inter-Am Ct HR (Ser B)).

5.2.6   Inter-American Commission on Human Rights

Style of cause	(year of judgment),	Inter-Am Comm HR,	case or report No,	pinpoint,	annual report,	document number.
Sánchez v Mexico	(1992),	Inter-Am Comm HR,	No 27/92,		Annual Report of the Inter-American Commission on Human Rights: 1992-93,	OEA/Ser.L/V/II.83/ doc.14 104.

➢ Indicate the style of cause followed by the year of decision in parentheses.

➢ Indicate Inter-Am Comm HR followed by the case or report number.

➢ Decisions of the Inter-American Commission on Human Rights are published in the commission's annual reports. Cite the commission's annual report and the document number. The document number starts with the letters OEA (Organización de les Estados Americanos) and not OAS, no matter the language of the document.

5.2.7   International Criminal Tribunals

This section provides guidelines for citing documents created by:

→   the International Criminal Court;

→   the International Criminal Tribunal for the former Yugoslavia;

→   the International Criminal Tribunal for Rwanda;

→   the Special Court for Sierra Leone; and

→   the Special Panels for Serious Crimes (East Timor).

Style of cause,	case number,	title of document (version)	(date of document)	pinpoint	(tribunal),	source.
Prosecutor v Zdravko Mucic (Celebici Camp Case),	IT- 96-21-*Abis,*	Judgment on Sentence Appeal	(8 April 2003)	at para 8	(International Criminal Tribunal for the former Yugoslavia, Appeals Chamber),	(WL).
Prosecutor v Théoneste Bagosora,	ICTR-98-41-I,	Minutes of Proceedings	(2 April 2002)		(International Criminal Tribunal for Rwanda, Trial Chamber),	online: ICTR <http://www.ictr.org>.
Deputy General Prosecutor for Serious Crimes v Sito Barros,	01/2004,	Final Judgment	(12 May 2005)	at para 12	(Special Panels for Serious Crimes (East Timor)),	online: Judicial System Monitoring Program <http://www.jsmp. minihub.org>.

➢   Include the **given name** of the accused where available in the style of cause.

➢   If there are **multiple accused** in the style of cause, use only the name of the first accused in the style of cause.

➢   Include **informal designation** in parentheses, after the title, if necessary (e.g. *Celebici Camp Case*).

➢   The title reflects the nature of the document, which can vary considerably. Indicate whether the document cited is the **public version** (designated Public or Public redacted) or the **confidential version** to which public access is limited.

➢   For websites, see section 5.3. The official Internet sites of the adjudicative bodies report only a limited portion of available documents. Some commercial electronic services provide wider coverage.

➢   If the name of the website is the same as that of the tribunal, use only the initials when identifying the website (e.g. ICTR).

5.2.8   General Agreement on Tariffs and Trade (GATT) 1947 Panel Reports

Style of cause (complainant)	(year of decision),	GATT Doc number,	BISD volume and (year)	first page and pinpoint,	other source.
Republic of Korea—Restrictions on Imports of Beef (Complaint by New Zealand)	(1989),	GATT Doc L/6505,	36th Supp BISD (1990)	234.	
United States—Countervailing Duties on Fresh, Chilled and Frozen Pork from Canada (Complaint by Canada)	(1991),	GATT Doc DS7/R,	38th Supp BISD (1990-91)	30.	

> Indicate the style of cause followed by the name of the complainant(s) in parentheses.

> Provide the year of the decision in parentheses followed by a comma and the GATT document number.

> Cite the GATT's **BISD (*Basic Instruments and Selected Documents*)** by providing the supplement number, followed by BISD, the year in parentheses, and the initial page of the document.

> Include pinpoint references to paragraphs immediately after the document reference.

> For Internet citations, see section 5.3.

5.2.9   World Trade Organization (WTO) Panel and Appellate Body Reports

	Style of cause (complainant)	(year of decision),	WTO Doc number	pinpoint	(type of report),	other source.
Panel Report	*United States—Sections 301-310 of The Trade Act of 1974 (Complaint by the European Communities)*	(1999),	WTO Doc WT/DS152/R	at para 3.1	(Panel Report),	online: WTO <http://docsonline.wto.org>.
Appellate Body Report	*India—Patent Protection for Pharmaceutical and Agricultural Chemical Products (Complaint by the United States)*	(1997),	WTO Doc WT/DS50/AB/R		(Appellate Body Report),	online: WTO <http://docsonline.wto.org>.

> Provide the style of cause, followed by the names of the complainants. If the **complaints are treated as one** in the report, provide the names of all complainants after the style of cause. If there are **many complainants** and each complaint is treated separately, provide only the name of the complainant to which the report

is destined. If there are more than three complainants, provide the name of one complainant followed by et al.

➢ Provide the year of the decision in parentheses, followed by the WTO document number. A report can have more than one document number (e.g. WT/DS 8, 10, 11/AB/R). In the document number, WT/DS indicates **World Trade Dispute Settlement**, AB indicates an **Appellate Body**, and R indicates **report**. If the case involves more than one complainant, different reports may be addressed to particular complainants. In such cases, the last element of the document number will indicate the name of the particular complainant to which the report is destined (e.g. WT/DS27/R/USA).

➢ Following the WTO document number, specify in parentheses whether it is a Panel Report or an Appellate Body Report.

➢ For Internet citations, see section 5.3.

5.2.10 Canada-United States Free Trade Agreement Panels

	Style of cause	(year of decision),	file number,	reporter	(type of panel),	other source.
Published	Re Red Raspberries from Canada	(1990),	USA-89-1904-01,	3 TCT 8175	(Ch 19 Panel),	online: NAFTA Secretariat <http://www.nafta-sec-alena.org>.
Unpublished	Re Fresh, Chilled or Frozen Pork from Canada	(1991),	ECC-91-1904-01USA,		ECC,	online: NAFTA Secretariat <http://www.nafta-sec-alena.org>.

➢ After the style of cause, provide the date of the decision in parentheses, followed by the file number. Indicate a reporter reference, if the panel is published.

➢ Abbreviate the various panels as follows: Ch 18 Panel (**Canada-United States Trade Commission Panel under Chapter 18**), Ch 19 Panel (**Canada-United States Binational Panel under Chapter 19**), and ECC (**Extraordinary Challenge Committee**).

➢ For Internet citations, see section 5.3.

5.2.11 North American Free Trade Agreement (NAFTA) Binational Panels

	Style of cause (names of parties)	(year of decision),	file number	(type of panel),	other source.
Review of US Agency Final Determination	Re Certain Softwood Lumber from Canada (United States v Canada)	(2005),	ECC-2004-1904-01USA	(ECC),	online: NAFTA Secretariat <http://www.nafta-sec-alena.org>.
Review of Mexican Agency Final Determination	Re Polystyrene and Impact Crystal from the United States of America (United States v Mexico)	(1995),	MEX-94-1904-03	(Ch 19 Panel),	online: NAFTA Secretariat <http://www.nafta-sec-alena.org>.
Review of Canadian Measures	Re Tariffs Applied by Canada to Certain US-Origin Agricultural Products (United States v Canada)	(1996),	CDA-95-2008-01	(Ch 20 Panel),	online: NAFTA Secretariat <http://www.nafta-sec-alena.org>.

➤ Indicate the style of cause, followed by the names of the parties involved in parentheses.

➤ Provide the year of the decision in parentheses. Include the file number and refer to a reporter if possible.

➤ Provide information of the chapter under which the complaint was brought. Abbreviate **Chapter 19 Binational Panel** to Ch 19 Panel, **Chapter 20: Arbitral Panel** to Ch 20 Panel, and **Chapter 19 Extraordinary Challenge Committee** to ECC.

➤ For Internet citations, see section 5.3.

5.2.12 International Arbitration Cases

	Style of cause or Case No	(year of decision),	reporter and pinpoint	(framework),	(names of arbitrators) (optional).
Names of parties available	Southern Pacific Properties v Egypt	(1992),	32 ILM 933 at 1008	(International Centre for Settlement of Investment Disputes),	(Arbitrators: Dr Eduardo Jiménez de Aréchaga, Mohamed Amin El Mahdi, Robert F Pietrowski Jr).
Names of parties not revealed	Case No 6248	(1990),	19 YB Comm Arb 124 at 129	(International Chamber of Commerce).	

➤ Indicate the style of cause including the parties' names, if available. If parties are reported anonymously, indicate the case number.

➤ Indicate the year of the decision in parentheses, followed by the citation to a reporter.

➤ Specify which organization is responsible for providing the arbitration framework or mechanism, in parentheses at the end of the citation.

> Provide names of arbitrators in parentheses at the end of the citation (optional).

5.2.13 World Intellectual Property Organization (WIPO) Arbitration Cases

5.2.13.1 Uniform Domain Name Dispute Resolution Policy (UDRP)

Style of cause,	case number	<domain name>	(WIPO Arbitration and Mediation Center (UDRP)).
CareerBuilder, LLC v Names for sale,	D2005-0186	<careersbuilder.com>	(WIPO Arbitration and Mediation Center (UDRP)).

> After the style of cause, include the case number and the domain name that is the subject of the arbitration.

5.2.14 International Law Cases Decided Before National Courts

Style of cause,	domestic reporter,	International Reporter	(country and court).
Re Noble and Wolf,	[1949] 4 DLR 375,	[1948] Ann Dig ILC 302	(Can, Ont CA).
Lindon v Commonwealth of Australia (No 2),	(1996), 136 ALR 251,	118 ILR 338	(Austl, HC).
Institute of Chartered Accountants in England and Wales v Commissioners of Customs and Excise,	[1999] 2 All ER 449,	[1999] 2 CMLR 1333	(UK, HL).

> Cite a national reporter if a national court decides an international case. Provide a second citation to an internationally available reporter, e.g. the *Annual Digest and Reports of Public International Law Cases* (Ann Dig ILC), the *International Law Reports* (ILR), the *Common Market Law Reports* (CMLR), or the *Common Market Reporter* (CMR). After 1950, the Ann Dig ILC became the ILR.

> Indicate the country and the jurisdiction where the case was held, and specify the court that made the decision.

5.3   WEBSITES

Traditional citation,	online:	name of website	<URL>.
US, Commission on Security and Cooperation in Europe, *Presidential Elections and Independence Referendums in the Baltic States, the Soviet Union and Successor States* (Washington, DC: The Commission, 1992) at 53,	online:	Commission on Security and Cooperation in Europe	<http://www.csce.gov>.
Convention on the Rights of the Child, 20 November 1989, 1577 UNTS 3,	online:	United Nations Treaty Collection	<http://untreaty.un.org>.

➢   Provide the full traditional citation, followed by a comma. Add online: and the name of the website, followed by the URL.

➢   Cite the URL of the **home page of the website**.

➢   Many online articles expire after a short period of time. Cite to online sources only if the source provides an archive of material for a reasonable period of time, preferably several years.

➢   Include a paragraph number as a pinpoint reference, if available. If the page numbering of a printed source is reproduced in the electronic source, reference may be made to those page numbers.

6   Secondary Sources and Other Materials E-105

6   SECONDARY SOURCES AND OTHER MATERIALS

6.1   PERIODICALS

6.1.1   General Form

Author,	"title of article"	(year)	volume	abbreviation of journal	page	pinpoint	(electronic service) (if applicable).
John Borrows,	"Creating an Indigenous Legal Community"	(2005)	50	McGill LJ	153	at 155	(QL).

6.1.2   Author

6.1.2.1   Single Author

➢   Indicate the author's name **as it is presented on the title page of the article**. Include all names and initials used, but do not add a space between two

> Lynn A Iding, "In a Poor State: The Long Road to Human Rights Protection on the Basis of Social Condition" (2003) 41 Alta LR 513.
>
> HW Arthurs, "The Political Economy of Canadian Legal Education" (1998) 25 JL & Soc'y 14.

initials. Do not substitute names when initials are used, and do not substitute initials when names are used.

➢   Include titles such as The Honourable, Madam Justice, Rabbi, Professor, or Lord if they appear on the title page. Do not include authors' degrees or other credentials.

6.1.2.2   Joint Authors

> David Weissbrodt & Muria Kruger, "Norms on the Responsibilities of Transnational Corporations and Other Business Enterprises with Regard to Human Rights" (2003) 97 AJIL 901.
>
> Rafael La Porta et al, "Law and Finance" (1998) 106 Journal of Political Economy 1113 at 1152.

➢   Include up to three authors.

→   If there are two authors, separate the authors' names with an ampersand (&).

→   If there are three authors, separate the first two authors with a coma and place an ampersand (&) before the last one.

→   If there are more than three authors, include only the first author's name and et al.

> For collaborations other than full joint authorship, follow the usage on the title page.

6.1.3   Title of Article

> Place the title of the article **in quotation marks**.

> Do not put a comma after the title.

> Separate a title from a subtitle with a colon. Do not use an em-dash (—) or an en-dash (–).

Suzanne A Kim, "'Yellow' Skin, 'White' Masks: Asian American 'Impersonations' of Whiteness and the Feminist Critique of Liberal Equality" (2001) 8 Asian LJ 89.

Darcy L MacPherson, "Extending Corporate Criminal Liability?: Some Thoughts on Bill C-45" (2005) 30 Man LJ 253.

> Capitalize the title according to the conventions of the language of the title.

> Follow the punctuation rules of the language of the title. Always use double quotation marks (e.g. "Title") around the title if you are writing in English.

> For further rules on language and punctuation of titles, see section 6.2.3.

6.1.4   Year of Publication

| Journal organized by volume | David M. Brown, "Freedom From or Freedom For?: Religion As a Case Study in Defining the Content of Charter Rights" (2000) 33 UBC L Rev 551. |
| Journal organized by year | Frédéric Pollaud-Dulian, "À propos de la sécurité juridique" [2001] RTD civ 487. |

> If a journal is **organized by volume number,** indicate the year of publication **in parentheses**.

> A journal is **not organized by volume number, but rather by year**, provide the year **in brackets**.

6.1.5   Volume, Issue and Series

Author, "title of article" (year of publication)	volume	:	issue	title of journal	series (if applicable)	first page of article.
David Lametti, "Publish and Profit?: Justifying the Ownership of Copyright in the Academic Setting" (2001)	26	:	2	Queen's LJ		497.
Peter Hanford, "Edward John Eyre and the Conflict of Laws" (2008)	32	:	3	Melbourne UL Rev		822.
RRA Walker, "The English Property Legislation of 1922-6" (1928)	10	:	1	J Comp Legis & Int'l L	(3d)	1.

➤ Place the volume number after the year of publication, followed by a colon and the issue number. **Always indicate the issue number** if there is more than one issue, whether or not the issues of a volume are consecutively paginated.

➤ Indicate the **series number** (if applicable) in parentheses after the title of the journal.

6.1.6 Title of Journal

> Janet Conway, "Civil Resistance and the 'Diversity of Tactics' in the Anti-Globalization Movement: Problems of Violence, Silence, and Solidarity in Activist Politics" (2003) 41 Osgoode Hall LJ 505.
>
> Meaghan Sunderland, "Criminal Law Reform in the People's Republic of China: Any Hope for Those Facing the Death Penalty?" (2002) 8 Appeal 18.

➤ Abbreviate the title of the periodical according to the list of abbreviations in **Appendix D**. Also consult **Bieber's Dictionary of Legal Abbreviations**. If the abbreviation is not found, write the complete title of the journal.

➤ Do not italicize the title or the abbreviation.

6.1.6.1 France

Author,	"title of article"	publication information.
Fabrice Leduc,	"La détermination du prix, une exigence exceptionnelle ?"	(1992) JCP I 3631.

➤ See sections 6.1.2 and 6.1.3 to cite the author and title of articles published in French general reporters. See the list of reporters in **Appendix C-3**.

➤ Cite the reporter as set out in section 3.7.

Reporter abbreviations:

Actualité juridique de droit administratif	AJDA
Bulletin des arrêts de la Cour de cassation, chambre civile	Bull civ
Gazette du Palais	Gaz Pal
Recueil Dalloz and Recueil Dalloz et Sirey (1945-present)	D
Recueil des décisions du Conseil d'État or Recueil Lebon	Rec
Semaine juridique (1937-present)	JCP

6.1.7 First Page of Article

➤ Indicate the first page of the article after the title of the journal. Do not include "at".

> Joseph Eliot Magnet, "National Minorities and the Multinational State" (2001) 26 Queen's LJ 397.

6.1.7.1 *Article Published in Parts*

Publication in two separate volumes	RA Macdonald, "Enforcing Rights in Corporeal Moveables: Revendication and Its Surrogates" (1986) 31 McGill LJ 573 & (1986) 32 McGill LJ 1.
Publication in two separate parts of the same volume	Edward W Keyserlingk, "The Unborn Child's Right to Prenatal Care" (1982) 3 Health L Can 10 & 31.

➤ If parts of the article are published in **different volumes**, provide the author and the title as usual. Include both full citations, separated by an ampersand (&).

➤ If the article is published in parts of **one volume**, include both first page numbers, separated by an ampersand (&).

6.1.8 Pinpoint

Bradley J Freedman & Robert JC Deane, "Trade-marks and the Internet: A Canadian Perspective" (2001) 34 UBC L Rev 345 at 399.
SM Waddams, *The Law of Contracts*, 5th ed (Toronto: Canada Law Book, 2005) at para 292.
Louise Arbour & Fannie Lafontaine, "Beyond Self-Congratulation: The Charter at 25 in an International Perspective" (2007) 47 Osgoode Hall LJ 239 at 259, n 63.

➤ Place the pinpoint reference after the publication information.

➤ Prefer paragraph pinpoints to page pinpoints. Begin a page or paragraph pinpoint with at or ¶. Cite paragraphs by using para, paras, or ¶. Do not include p to indicate the page number.

➤ Separate **consecutive** page or paragraph references by a hyphen. For multiple-digit numbers, retain at least the last two digits at all times (e.g. 159-60 or 32-35, but not 32-5).

➤ Separate **non-consecutive** page numbers or paragraphs by a comma (e.g. at 35, 38).

➤ To indicate a **general section** of the text without referring to specific pages or paragraphs, use ff following the page or paragraph number(s). It is preferable, however, to cite a specific set of pages or paragraphs.

➤ To pinpoint to a specific footnote, abbreviate **footnote** to n (e.g. at 99, n 140) and **footnotes** to nn (e.g. at 142, nn 73-75). If page numbers are not available because the article is online, simply cite to the footnote number (e.g. at n 140).

➤ Use the same number format as the text (e.g. 5-6; v-vi).

6.2   BOOKS

6.2.1   General Form

Author,	*title,*	edition	other elements	(place of publication:	publisher,	year of publication)	pin-point	(electronic service) (if applicable).
Philip Girard,	*Bora Laskin: Bringing Law to Life*			(Toronto:	University of Toronto Press for the Osgoode Society for Canadian Legal History,	2005)	at 20.	
Margaret Somerville,	*Death Talk: The Case against Euthanasia and Physician-Assisted Suicide*			(Montreal:	McGill-Queen's University Press,	2001)	at 78.	
Martha Derthick,	*Up in Smoke: From Legislation to Litigation in Tobacco Politics,*	2d ed		(Washing-ton, DC:	CQ Press,	2005).		

> Provide any other element in the "other elements" section between the edition and the place of publication. Their order of presentation is the following: **name of editor or compiler** (section 6.2.2.3), **name of translator** (section 6.2.2.5), **total number of volumes or number of cited volume** (section 6.2.4), **volume title, series title and volume number within series, loose-leaf** (section 6.2.6).

6.2.2   Author

6.2.2.1   Single Author

> Indicate the author's name **as it is presented on the title page of the book**. Include all names and initials used, but note that there is no space between two initials. Do not substitute names when initials are used, and do not substitute initials when names are used.

Ellen Anderson, *Judging Bertha Wilson*: Law as Large as Life (Toronto: University of Toronto Press for the Osgoode Society for Canadian Legal History, 2001).

Rt Hon Lord Denning, *What Next in the Law* (London, UK: Butterworths, 1982).

H Patrick Glenn, *Legal Traditions of the World* (Oxford: Oxford University Press, 2000).

David Fraser, *Cricket and the Law: the Man in White is Always Right* (London, UK: Routledge, 2005).

➤ Include **titles** such as The Honourable, Madam Justice, Rabbi, Professor, or Lord if they appear on the title page. Do not include authors' degrees or other credentials.

6.2.2.2 Joint Authors

> [1] Monique Mattei Ferraro & Eoghan Casey, *Investigating Child Exploitation and Pornography: The Internet, the Law and Forensic Science* (Boston: Elsevier/Academic Press, 2005).
>
> [9] Joel Bakan et al, *Canadian Constitutional Law*, 3d ed (Toronto: Emond Montgomery, 2003).
>
> [10] Pierre-Gabriel Jobin with the collaboration of Nathalie Vézina, *Baudouin et Jobin : Les obligations*, 6th ed (Cowansville, Que: Yvon Blais, 2005).

➤ Include **up to three authors**, separating the first two authors' names with a comma, and the last two with an ampersand (&).

➤ If there are **more than three authors**, include only the first author's name and et al.

➤ For **collaborations** other than full joint authorship, follow the usage on the title page of the book (see note 10).

6.2.2.3 Editor of a Collection

➤ Indicate the name of the editor before the title of the collection.

➤ List **up to three editors**; if there are more than three indicate the first followed by et al.

> David Dyzenhaus & Mayo Moran, eds, *Calling Power to Account: Law, Reparations and the Chinese Canadian Head Tax Case* (Toronto: University of Toronto Press, 2005).

➤ Abbreviate **editor** to ed and **editors** to eds, preceded and followed by a comma.

➤ To cite an **essay in particular**, and not the collection in general, include the name of the author and the title of the essay before the name of the editor (section 6.3).

6.2.2.4 Editor or Reviser of the Text of Another

6.2.2.4.1   Author's Name is Part of the Title

Editor	ed,	title,	edition	(publication information).
HG Beale,	ed,	*Chitty on Contracts,*	29th ed	(London, UK: Sweet & Maxwell, 2004).

➤ If the author's name is part of the title, treat the editor as the author, followed by ed.

6.2.2.4.2   Author's Name is Not Part of the Title

Author,	title,	edition	by	editor	(publication information).
SA De Smith,	*Judicial Review of Administrative Action,*	5th ed	by	Lord Woolf & Jeffrey Jowell	(London, UK: Sweet & Maxwell, 1995).

➢ If the author's name is not part of the title, indicate the editor after the edition.

➢ Precede the name(s) of editor(s) name with ed by. If there is a numbered edition, mention it (e.g. 5th ed by).

➢ Provide the names of both the author(s) and the editor(s) as they appear in the publication.

6.2.2.5 *Translator*

➢ Translate languages likely to be unfamiliar to readers. The original language of a quotation may be provided in the footnote.

6.2.2.5.1   Published Translation

Author,	title,	translated by	name of translator	(publication information)	[modified by author] (if applicable).
Averroës,	*The Book of the Decisive Treatise Determining the Connection Between the Law and Wisdom,*	translated by	Charles E Butterworth	(Provo, Utah: Brigham Young University Press, 2001).	

➢ For published translations, include the translator's name, preceded by translated by, before the publication information.

➢ If it is necessary to modify the translation, indicate this with [modified by author] after the publication information, but before the final period.

➢ If providing both the editor or reviser's information (section 6.2.2.4) and the translator's information (section 6.2.2.5), always provide the editor's information first.

6.2.2.5.2   Providing a Translation

Author,	title,	(publication information)	pinpoint	[translated by author].
María José Falcón y Tella,	*La desobediencia civil,*	(Madrid: Marcial Pons, 2000)	at 28	[translated by author].

➢ When writing and providing a translation for ease of understanding, cite to the work and insert [translated by author] **in the footnote** (and not after the translated text, as required in the French rule). The expression refers to you, the author, and not to the author of the work being cited.

6.2.3 Title

> [1] Petri Mäntysaari, *Comparative Corporate Governance: Shareholders as a Rule-maker* (New York: Springer, 2005).
>
> [2] Janet Dine, Companies, *International Trade and Human Rights* (New York: Cambridge University Press, 2005).
>
> [3] WR Cornish & G de M Clark, *Law and Society in England, 1750-1950* (London, UK: Sweet & Maxwell, 1989).
>
> [4] Cesare Beccaria, *Dei delliti e delle pene* [On Crimes and Punishment], 5th Ed (London, UK: Transaction Publishers, 2009).
>
> [5] Waldo Ansaldi, ed, *Democracy in Latin America: A Boat Adrift* (in Spanish) (Buenos Aires: Fondo de Cultura Económica, 2007).

> ➤ Indicate the title in full, in italics. Use the spelling and punctuation of the published title, with the following exceptions:
>
>   → precede subtitles by a colon (notes 1 and 5); and
>
>   → place a comma before dates included at the end of the title (note 3).
>
> ➤ Capitalize the title according to the conventions of the language of the title.
>
> ➤ If the title of a work is in a language other than English, French, or a language that will be familiar to readers, use **either** of the following rules:
>
>   → Provide the title in the original language, followed by a translation of the title into English (note 4). Place the translation in non-italic font, in brackets with no punctuation between the original title and translation. Transliterate titles in languages that are not written in Latin characters, such as Chinese and Hebrew (e.g. Menachem Elon, *Ha-Mishpat Ha-Ivri* [Jewish Law]).
>
>   → Provide a translation of the title in English in italics, followed by the name of the original language of the text in parentheses (note 5). Do not include any punctuation between the translation of the title and the parentheses.

6.2.3.1 Published Proceedings of Conferences or Symposia

> ➤ Treat information about the conference or symposium as part of the title. Place this information in italics after a comma.

> Paul Brand, Kevin Costello & WN Osborough, eds, *Adventures of the Law: Proceedings of the Sixteenth British Legal History Conference, Dublin, 2003* (Dublin: Four Courts Press in association with the Irish Legal History Society, 2005).

6.2.4   Volume Number

6.2.4.1 Books in English

6.2.4.1.1   Volumes Published Under Separate Titles

➢ Place the volume before the publication information.

> David Gillies, Telecommunications Law, vol 1 (London, UK: Butterworths, 2003).

➢ Provide the volume number in Arabic numerals (e.g. 1, 2, 3), even if the book itself uses Roman numerals.

➢ Insert a comma between the title and the volume number.

6.2.4.1.2   Volumes Published Under a Single Title

➢ If the volumes are subdivisions of a single title, insert the volume after the publication information.

> Karl Marx, Capital: A Critical Analysis of Capitalist Production, ed by Friedrich Engels, translated by Samuel Moore & Edward B Aveling (London, UK: Swan Sonnenschein, 1908) vol 1 at 15.

➢ Do not put a comma between the publication information and the volume.

➢ Provide the volume number in Arabic numerals (e.g. 1, 2, 3) even if the book itself uses Roman numerals.

6.2.4.2 Books in French

Author,	title,	tome and/or volume,	edition	editor (if applicable)	(publication information).
Jean Carbonnier,	Droit civil : les obligations,	t 4,	22d ed		(Paris: Presses Universitaires de France, 2000).
Henri Mazeaud et al,	Leçons de droit civil,	t 3, vol 1,	7th ed	by Yves Picod	(Paris: Montchrestien, 1999).

➢ French legal writing may be divided into **tomes** (t), with each tome further subdivided into **volumes** (v).

➢ Use only Arabic numerals (e.g. 1, 2, 3) for tome and volume numbers.

➢ Tome and volume information appears after the title.

6.2.5 Edition

➤ If the work has appeared in several editions, place the number of the edition (e.g. 8th ed) after the title. Do not superscript the st, d or th following the number.

➤ Abbreviate **edition** to ed.

> Richard Clayton & Hugh Tomlinson, eds, *Civil Actions Against the Police*, 3d ed (London, UK: Sweet & Maxwell, 2004).
>
> Carlos L Israels & Egon Guttman, *Modern Securities Transfer*, revised ed (Boston: Warren, Gorham & Lamont, 1971).

➤ If the work has been revised but no edition number is given, insert revised ed after the title.

6.2.6 Books in Loose-leaf Form

Author,	title,	loose-leaf (consulted on	date of consultation),	(publication information),	pinpoint.
Georges Audet et al,	*Le congédiement en droit québécois en matière de contrat individuel de travail*,	loose-leaf (consulted on	18 April 2009),	(Cowansville, Que: Yvon Blais, 1991),	ch 5 at 71.
Madeleine Lemieux,	*Tribunaux administratifs du Québec : Règles et législation annotées*,	loose-leaf (consulted on	28 August 2009),	(Cowansville, Que: Yvon Blais, 2002),	ch R9 at 85.
Robert W Hillman,	*Hillman on Lawyer Mobility: The Law and Ethics of Partner Withdrawals and the Law Firm Breakups*,	loose-leaf (consulted on	4 October 2009),	2d ed (Austin: Wolters Kluwer, 1998),	ch 2 at 85.

➤ This section applies to **books that are continually updated**. For legislation in loose-leaf format, see section 2.1.5.

➤ After the title, write loose-leaf and put consulted on in parentheses, followed by the date of consultation.

➤ Use the publication date that appears on the copyright page, even if it differs from a date that appears elsewhere in the loose-leaf manual. Use the chapter and the page number to pinpoint if available.

6.2.7 Place of Publication

➤ Indicate the place of publication as it appears on the title page or on the verso of the title page. Use an **English form** of a name if it exists (e.g. Munich and not München; Prague and not Praha).

> Bruce MacDougall, *Queer Judgments: Homosexuality, Expression, and the Courts in Canada* (Toronto: University of Toronto Press, 2000).
>
> Lee Edwards, ed, *Bringing Justice to the People: the Story of the Freedom-Based Public Interest Law Movement* (Washington, DC: Heritage Books, 2004).

> If **more than one place of publication** is listed, include the first place only.

> If **no place of publication** is listed, write np.

> If additional information is required to identify the place of publication (e.g. the province, state, or country) include that information, in abbreviated form, after the place of publication. If a location could be confused with another, provide additional information (e.g. London, Ont and London, UK).

> See the commonly used Canadian province abbreviations of **Appendix A-1** and the American state abbreviations of **Appendix A-2**.

6.2.8 Publisher

✓	Martha M Ertman & Joan C Williams, *Rethinking Commodification: Cases and Readings in Law and Culture* (New York: New York University Press, 2005).
	Ellen Anderson, *Judging Bertha Wilson: Law as Large as Life* (Toronto: University of Toronto Press for The Osgoode Society for Canadian Legal History, 2001).
✓	Gaëlle Breton-LeGoff, *L'influence des organisations non gouvernementales (ONG) sur la négociation de quelques instruments internationaux* (Cowansville, Que: Yvon Blais, 2001).
✗	Gaëlle Breton-LeGoff, *L'influence des organisations non gouvernementales (ONG) sur la négociation de quelques instruments internationaux* (Cowansville, Que: Les Éditions Yvon Blais inc, 2001).

> Write the publisher's name **as it appears on the title page**.

> Do not abbreviate the publisher's name (e.g. University Press and not UP).

> Omit the definite article (the) even if it is the first word of the name.

> Omit terms that identify corporate status (e.g. Ltd, Inc).

> Omit the words "Publishing" or "Publishers" and "éditions" unless it is part of an indivisible whole (e.g. Éditions de l'Homme; Verlag).

> Write Press in English and Presses in French if included as the publisher's name on the title page.

> For references to **copublishers**, provide the places of publication first, followed by the names of the publishers and the year. Separate the places of publication from the names of the publishers by a semicolon. See the example below.

(First place of publication,	second place of publication;	first publisher,	second publisher,	year).
(Latzville, BC,	Montreal;	Oolichan Books,	Institute for Research on Public Policy,	1992).

> If a publisher is **working for an organization** write for immediately before the organization's name (e.g. Janet E Gans Epner for The Commission on Women in the Profession).

> If **no publisher** is listed, write no publisher.

6.2.9   Year of Publication

> Indicate the year of the **current edition**, not of the first edition. Generally, use the most recent copyright date, unless a year of publication is given explicitly.

> Michael Hames-García, *Fugitive Thought: Prison Movements, Race and the Meaning of Justice* (Minneapolis: University of Minnesota Press, 2004).

> Do not cite the year of printing.

> If **no year is listed**, write [nd].

6.2.10 Pinpoint

> Place the pinpoint after the publication information.

> **Prefer paragraph pinpoints** to page pinpoints. Begin a page or paragraph pinpoint with at para, at paras, or ¶. Do not include p to indicate the page number.

> Separate **consecutive** page or paragraph references by a hyphen, and retain at least the last two digits at all times (e.g. 159-60 or 32-35, but not 32-5).

> Ronald Joseph Delisle & Don Stuart, eds, *Evidence: Principles and Problems*, 6th ed (Toronto: Carswell, 2001) ch 4 at 450ff.

> Kent Roach, *Constitutional Remedies in Canada* (Aurora, Ont: Canada Law Book, 1994) ¶ 12.30.

> Donald Bloxham, *Genocide on Trial: War Crimes Trials and the Formation of Holocaust History and Memory* (Oxford: Oxford University Press, 2001) at 43, n 139.

> Beth Harris, *Defending the Right to a Home: The Power of Anti-Poverty Lawyers* (Aldershot: Ashgate, 2004) at 45.

> **Non-consecutive** page numbers are separated by a comma (e.g. 35, 38).

> To indicate a **general section** of the text use ff following the page or paragraph number(s). It is preferable, however, to cite a specific set of pages or paragraphs.

> Abbreviate **chapter** and **chapters** to ch. The rule is different for legislation (section 2.1.9).

> To pinpoint to a specific footnote, abbreviate **footnote** to n (e.g. at 43, n 139) and **footnotes** to nn (e.g. at 43, nn 139-41). If page numbers are not available, refer to the footnote number (e.g. at n 140).

> Write numbers (page, paragraph, or other) as they appear in the text (e.g. 5-6; v-vi).

6.3   COLLECTIONS OF ESSAYS

Author of essay,	"title of essay"	in	editor (if applicable),	ed,	title of book	(publication information)	first page of essay	pin- point.
Gabriel J Chin,	"Race, the War on Drugs and Collateral Consequences of Criminal Conviction"	in	Christopher Mele & Teresa A Miller,	eds,	*Civil Penalties, Social Consequences*	(New York: Routledge, 2005)	43	at 45.
Adelle Blackett,	"Promoting Domestic Workers' Human Dignity through Specific Regulation"	in	Antoinette Fauve-Chamoux,	ed,	*Domestic Service and the Formation of European Identity: Understanding the Globalization of Domestic Work, 16th-21st Centuries*	(Bern: Peter Lang SA, Éditions scientifiques européennes, 2005)	211	at 215.
Guénaël Mettraux,	"Preface"	in	Suénaël Mettraux,	ed,	*Perspectives on the Nuremberg Trial*	(New York: Oxford University Press, 2008)	xi.	

➢ Place the name of the author and the title of the essay before the collection.

➢ Introduce the collection with in.

➢ Follow the name(s) of the editor(s) of the collection by ed or eds, placed between commas. Some collections have no named editor. Do not provide any editor in such cases.

➢ Provide the title of the collection in italics, followed by the publication information.

➢ Indicate the first page of the essay and any applicable pinpoint references after the publication information.

➢ If referring to the **foreword, preface, introduction, or conclusion** of a book, indicate it as if it were an entry in a collection of essays. Use Foreword, Preface, etc. or the title of that section in lieu of the title of the essay (see the Guénaël Mettraux example).

6.4   DICTIONARIES

6.4.1   General Dictionaries

Title,	edition,	sub verbo	"keyword".
The Oxford English Dictionary,	2d ed,	sub verbo	"law".
Black's Law Dictionary,	7th ed,	sub verbo	"promissory estoppel".

> ➢ Provide the title of the dictionary in italics.

> ➢ Indicate the edition or year.

> ➢ *Sub verbo* is Latin for "under the word".

6.4.2   Specialized Dictionaries

Editor or author,	ed (if applicable),	title,	edition (if applicable)	(publication information)	sub verbo	"keyword".
F Allard et al,	eds,	Private Law Dictionary of Obligations and Bilingual Lexicons,		(Cowansville, Que: Yvon Blais, 2003)	sub verbo	"code".
Hubert Reid,		Dictionnaire de droit québécois et canadien,		(Montreal: Wilson & Lafleur, 1994)	sub verbo	"hypothèque".

> ➢ Cite the specialized dictionary as if it were a book. See section 6.2.

> ➢ *Sub verbo* is Latin for "under the word".

6.5   ENCYCLOPEDIC DIGESTS

6.5.1   Canadian Encyclopedic Digest

> ➢ The CED is published in loose-leaf format and provides a broad narrative of the law. Each volume is organized by subject matter (e.g. criminal law, family law).

CED	(series	edition),	volume,	title	section.
CED	(Ont	4th),	vol 1,	title 2	at § 10.

> ➢ Write CED, not the name of the encyclopedic digest in full.

> ➢ Indicate the series: **Ontario CED** (Ont) or **Western CED** (West).

6.5.2 Common Law

> *Halsbury's Laws of England*, vol 34, 4th ed (London, UK: Butterworths, 1980) at 60, para 71.
>
> *American Jurisprudence*, vol 17A, 2d ed (Rochester, NY: Lawyer's Cooperative, 1991) "Contracts", § 97.

➤ Follow the rules for books in section 6.2, but **do not include the author's name**.

➤ Where available, **use the paragraph or section numbers** instead of page numbers. Use § for American digests.

➤ If the section in question has a title, include it in quotation marks, after the publication information (see *American Jurisprudence*).

6.5.3 France

6.5.3.1 General Form

Title of collection,	edition (if applicable),	subject heading	by	author of the section of the encyclopædia,	pinpoint.
Juris-classeur civil,		art 3, fasc N	by	Phillipe Malaurie,	No 38.
Encyclopédie juridique Dalloz : Répertoire de droit civil,	2d ed,	"Publicité foncière"	by	Marc Donnier,	No 528.

➤ Whenever possible, refer to the *Juris-classeur civil*.

➤ Provide the full title of the collection in italics.

➤ If **more than one edition** of the encyclopædia has been published, include the number of the edition.

➤ Do not introduce the pinpoint with "at".

➤ Establish a short form (section 1.4.1) by using the abbreviated title of the encyclopædia.

Abbreviations of the principal encyclopædias:

Encyclopédie juridique Dalloz : Répertoire de droit administratif	*Rép admin*
Encyclopédie juridique Dalloz : Répertoire de droit civil	*Rép civ*
Encyclopédie juridique Dalloz : Répertoire de droit commercial	*Rép com*
Juris-classeur administratif	*J-cl admin*
Juris-classeur civil	*J-cl civ*
Juris-classeur civil annexe	*J-cl civ annexe*
Juris-classeur commercial	*J-cl com*
Juris-classeur commercial: Banque et crédit	*J-cl com BC*
Juris-classeur répertoire notarial	*J-cl rép not*
Juris-classeur responsabilité civile	*J-cl resp civ*

6.5.3.2 Subject Headings

Organized alphabetically	*Encyclopédie juridique Dalloz : Répertoire de droit civil*, "Parenté-alliance" by Janine Revel.
	Juris-classeur civil annexes, "Associations", fasc 1-A, by Robert Brichet.
Organized by articles of a code	*Juris-classeur civil*, art 3, fasc 4 by Yves Luchaire.
	Juris-classeur civil, art. 1354 to 1356, fasc 20 by Daniel Veaux.
Organized by volume	*Juris-classeur commercial : Concurrence consommation*, vol 1, fasc 360 by Véronique Sélinsky.

➢ **Organized alphabetically**: Include the keyword indicating the section in quotation marks. If there is a fascicle number corresponding to the section, insert fasc followed by the number.

➢ **Organized by articles of a code**: Provide the article number under which the section is classified. Use the same form as is used in the collection. If applicable, indicate fasc followed by the number.

➢ **Organized by volume**: Provide the number of the volume in which the section is found. If applicable, indicate fasc followed by the number.

➢ Regardless of the system of classification of the subject headings, indicate the number of the fascicle after the volume number, separated by a comma.

➢ Do not cite the date of the revision of the fascicle.

6.6   CODES OF PROFESSIONAL CONDUCT

Issuing body,	title of the code,	publication information,	pinpoint.
The Canadian Bar Association,	CBA Code of Professional Conduct,	Ottawa: CBA, 2006,	ch III, commentary 1.
The Law Society of Manitoba,	Code of Professional Coduct,	Winnipeg: Law Society of Manitoba, 2007,	ch 6.1(1)(f).

➢ If the issuing body and the editor is the same entity, use the official abbreviation in the publication information (e.g. CBA for The Canadian Bar Association).

➢ Some codes of professional conduct are enacted by legislation. Cite them like regular laws (section 2.1) (e.g. *Professional Code*, RSQ c C-26).

6.7   ARBITRATION CASES

➢ For **international arbitration** cases, see section 5.2.12. For **WIPO** cases, see section 5.2.13.

6.7.1   Published Arbitration Cases

Style of cause or case number	(year of decision),	reporter	pinpoint	(names of arbitrators) (optional).
California State University v State Employers Trade Council – United	(2009),	126 Lab Arb (BNA) 613		(Arbitrator: Bonnie G Bogue).

➢ Indicate the style of cause or the case number, followed by the year of the decision in parentheses.

➢ If the case is published in a printed reporter, cite the arbitration reporter in the same manner as jurisprudence reporter (section 3.7).

➢ Add the **name of the arbitrator** in parentheses (optional).

6.7.2   Unpublished Arbitration Cases

Style of cause or case number	(year of decision),	identifier given by service	(service) (if applicable)	pin-point	(names of arbitrators) (optional).
Winona School District ISD 861 Winona v Winona Education Association	(2006),	2006 WL 3876585	(WL Can)		(Arbitrator: Daniel J Jacobowski).

➢ Indicate the style of cause or the case number, followed by the year of the decision in parentheses.

➢ If the case is published on an electronic service, write the identifier given by the service. Add the abbreviation of the service in parentheses if it's not already included in the identifier.

➢ Add the **name of the arbitrator** in parentheses (optional).

6.8   BOOK REVIEWS

Author of book review,	"title of book review", (if applicable)	Book Review of	*title of book being reviewed*	by	author or editor of book reviewed,	citation information.
Heather Jensen,		Book Review of	*Girl Trouble: Female Delinquency in English Canada*	by	Joan Sangster,	(2004) 67 Sask L Rev 658.
Christopher Heer, Michael Hong & Jason J Kee,		Book Review of	*Intellectual Property Disputes: Resolution and Remedies*	by	Ronald E Dimock, ed,	(2004) 62 UT Fac L Rev 93.
Larry Lee,	"Reading the Seattle Manifesto: In Search of a Theory",	Book Review of	*Whose Trade Organization? Corporate Globalization and the Erosion of Democracy: An Assessment of the World Trade Organization*	by	Lori Wallach & Michelle Sforza,	(2003) 79 NYUL Rev 2305.

➢ If the review has a title, include it after the author of the review, followed by a comma.

➢ Insert Book Review of before the title of the book reviewed. Change the expression to Book Note of if that terminology is used in the publication.

➢ After the title of the book being reviewed, indicate the name of the author of the book introduced with by.

→ If the title of the review includes **both the title of the book reviewed and its author**, do not repeat this information. Instead, just write Book Review, leaving out "of".

→ If the title of the review includes *either* the author or the title, but not both, then all the information should be indicated after Book Review of, even if some of it will be repeated.

➢ If the book being reviewed has an editor instead of an author, write ed after the name of the editor of the book reviewed and a comma (e.g. Ronald E Dimock, ed).

6.9   CASE COMMENTS AND COMMENTS ON LEGISLATION

	Author,	"title" (if applicable),	type of comment	on	style of cause or title of law or bill (if applicable),	(citation).
Case Comment	Jessie L Givener,	*"Lavoie v Canada*: Reconciling Equality Rights and Citizenship-based Law",	Case Comment			(2003-2004) 35 Ottawa L Rev 277.
Legislative Comment	John Boston,	*"The Prison Litigation Reform Act*: The New Face of Court Stripping",	Legislative Comment	on	Pub L No 104-134, 110 Stat 1321-66 (1996),	(2001) 67 Brook L Rev 429.

> ➢ Indicate the title of the comment (if available) in quotation marks.

> ➢ For **case comments**, indicate Case Comment. Also include the style of cause preceded by on, unless it is in the title.

> ➢ For **legislative comments**, indicate Legislative Comment. Also include the title of the law or bill preceded by on, unless it is in the title.

6.9.1   France

6.9.1.1 Annotation

Author,	Annotation of	court,	date of decision,	(year of publication)	reporter	section	first page.
Christophe Caron,	Annotation of	Cass com,	28 avril 2004,	(2004)	JCP	II	2045.

> ➢ Add a space between each item of information (e.g. (2004) JCP II 2045).

> ➢ Introduce the case citation with Annotation of.

> ➢ See section 7.3.2 for the rules on citing French jurisprudence.

6.9.1.2 Comments Published in General Reporters

Author,	"title"	(year of publication)	reporter	section	first page	pinpoint.
Dominique Karsenty,	"La réparation des détentions"	(2003)	JCP	I	225	at 227.
Florence Bussy,	"Nul ne peut être juge et partie"	(2004)	D	Chron	1745	at 1750.

> ➢ Add a space between each item of information (e.g. (2004) D Chron 1745 at 1750).

> ➤ After the title, indicate the reporter information according to the rules at section 7.3.2.

6.10 COMMENTS, REMARKS, AND NOTES

Author (if applicable),	"title" (if applicable),	type of document,	(citation).
Thomas M Franck,	"Criminals, Combatants, or What – An Examination of the Role of Law in Responding to the Threat of Terrorism",	Editorial Comment,	(2004) 98 AJIL 686.
Eric J Feigin,	"Architecture of Consent: Internet Protocols and Their Legal Implications",	Note,	(2004) 56 Stan L Rev 901.

> ➤ Include the type of document (Note, Comments or Remarks) before the citation information. Do not enclose it in quotation marks. If the document has a title, place the title in quotation marks.

6.11 HISTORICAL LEGAL MATERIALS

6.11.1 Roman Law

Collection	Abbreviation	Example
Laws of the Twelve Tables	XII Tab	XII Tab 8.2
Institutes of Gaius	G	G 3.220
Code of Theodosius	Cod Th	Cod Th 8.14.1
Institutes of Justinian	Inst	Inst 4.4 pr (translated by Birks & McLeod)
Digest of Justinian	Dig	Dig 47.10.1 (Ulpian)
Codex of Justinian	Cod	Cod 6.42.16
Novels	Nov	Nov 22.3

> ➤ Refer to the **traditional divisions of the work** (generally book, title, section), not to the page number of the particular edition or translation. There are no spaces between the numbers of the different divisions.

> ➤ The abbreviation pr means "*principium*" or "beginning" and refers to the unnumbered material before the first section of a title. It is preceded by a space.

> ➤ For **Justinian's *Digest***, indicate the author of the passage in question parenthetically after the citation.

➤ Indicate the particular edition or translation used in parentheses at the end of the citation (e.g. (translated by Birks & McLeod)).

6.11.2 Canon Law

Collection	Abbreviation	Example
Decretum of Gratian	Decr (optional)	Part 1: D 50 c 11 Part 2: C 30 q 4 c 5 Part 2, De poenitentia: De poen D 1 c 75 Part 3: De cons D 1 c 5
Decretals of Gregory IX (*Liber extra*)	X	X 5.38.12
Decretals of Boniface VIII (*Liber sextus*)	VI	VI 5.2.16
Constitutions of Clement V (*Clementinae*)	Clem	Clem 3.7.2
Extravagants of John XXII (*Extravagantes Johannis XXII*)	Extrav Jo XII	Extrav Jo XII 14.2
Common Extravagants (*Extravagantes communes*)	Extrav Com	Extrav Com 3.2.9
Codex Iuris Canonici (1917)	1917 Code	1917 Code c 88, § 2
Codex Iuris Canonici (1983)	1983 Code	1983 Code c 221, § 1

➤ Refer to the traditional divisions of the work, not the page number of the particular edition or translation.

➤ Use Arabic numerals (e.g. 1, 2, 3) to indicate the divisions, regardless of the usage of the edition or translation.

➤ Indicate the particular edition or translation used in parentheses at the end of the citation.

6.11.3 Talmudic Law

➤ Indicate Babylonian or Jerusalem Talmud.

➤ Italicize the tractate.

Talmud,	tractate,	pinpoint.
Babylonian Talmud,	*Bava Metzia*,	11b.
Jerusalem Talmud,	*Sanhedrin*,	Mish 1 Hal 5.

➤ When using the Babylonian Talmud, refer to the **traditional pagination** (Vilna edition) and not to the page number given by the publisher or translator. It is always assumed that the cited text is the Vilna edition. When using a different edition (e.g. Warsaw), indicate the edition in parentheses following the pinpoint.

➢ Use Arabic numerals (e.g. 1, 2, 3) to indicate the leaf number and a or b to indicate the page.

➢ When referring to a **particular edition or translation**, indicate the publication information in parentheses following the pinpoint (sections 6.2.2.5.1 and 6.2.5).

➢ When providing a translation, insert [translated by author] after the initial citation and pinpoint (section 6.2.2.5.2).

➢ Pinpoint the **Jerusalem Talmud** to the Mishna (Mish) and the Halacha (Hal) and not to the page, as there are various editions with different pagination. Pinpoint to a page if the full publication information in parentheses can be provided, as set out in sections 6.2.6 to 6.2.8.

6.12 UNPUBLISHED MANUSCRIPTS

6.12.1 General Form

Author,	*title*	(date of creation)	[unpublished,	archived at	location].
Irwin Cotler,	*Canadian Charter of Rights and Freedoms*	(1998)	[unpublished,	archived at	McGill University Faculty of Law Library].

➢ Include the title according to the genre. If it is an article, place the title in quotation marks. If it is a book, place the title in italics.

➢ Include the date of creation in parentheses after the title.

➢ Indicate that the manuscript is unpublished by enclosing unpublished, archived at and the location of the manuscript in brackets.

6.12.2 Forthcoming Manuscripts

Author,	title,	publication information	[forthcoming in	projected date of publication].
Joshua AT Fairfield,	"Anti-social contracts: The Contractual Governance of Virtual Worlds,"	53 McGill LJ	[forthcoming in	2008].
Alain Supiot,	*Le Nouvel âge du droit social*	Seuil	[forthcoming in	October 2009].

➢ Indicate the title according to the type of manuscript. If the manuscript is an article, place the title in quotation marks. If the manuscript is a book, place the title in italics.

➢ Include the publication information according to the classification of the document, but do not indicate the year of publication.

➢ Indicate that the manuscript has not yet been published by enclosing forthcoming in and with the projected date of publication in brackets, if available.

6.12.3 Theses and Dissertations

Author,	*title*	(degree,	institution,	year)	[unpublished].
Julie Desrosiers,	*L'isolement, le retrait et l'arrêt d'agir dans les centres de réadaptation pour jeunes*	(DCL Thesis,	McGill University Institute of Comparative Law,	2005)	[unpublished].
C Morneau,	*L'éthique dans les entreprises multinationales : Une étude développementale des codes d'éthique*	(M Sc mémoire,	HEC Montreal,	2006)	[unpublished].

➢ After the author's name and the title of the thesis or dissertation, indicate the degree for which it was written, the institution, and the year in parentheses. If the degree or institution is unknown, include the **field of study** (e.g. law, political science, economics).

➢ At the end of the citation include [unpublished].

➢ If the thesis has been published, cite the published source. Follow the corresponding rules of the *Guide* for that publication.

➢ Cite theses issued by microform services (e.g. University Microfilms International) in the same manner as published books, with the service in lieu of publisher.

6.13 ADDRESSES AND PAPERS DELIVERED AT CONFERENCES

Speaker,	"title" (if available) or Address	(lecture series, paper, or other information	delivered at the	conference or venue,	date),	publication information or [unpublished].
Chris Tollefson,	"The Implications of *Okanagan Indian Band* for Public Interest Litigants: A Strategic Discussion Paper"	(Paper	delivered at the	AGM of the Court Challenges Program of Canada, Winnipeg,	19 November 2005),	[unpublished].
John Borrows,	"Creating an Indigenous Legal Community"	(John C Tait Memorial Lecture in Law and Public Policy,	delivered at the	Faculty of Law, McGill University,	14 October 2004),	(2005) 50 McGill LJ 153.

➢ If the address has a title, provide the title. If it has **no title**, indicate Address.

➢ Include the lecture series in which the address was delivered, if available.

➢ Indicate the **location** or institution where the address was delivered or the paper presented.

➢ Provide the publication information, preceded by a comma, if the address has been published.

➢ If the address is **unpublished**, insert [unpublished] at the end of the citation. Indicate, if available, where a transcript of the unpublished address is available (section 6.12.1).

➢ If the address is **published as a collection**, cite it in the same manner as a collection of essays (section 6.3).

6.14 COURSE MATERIALS

Professor,	*title*,	type of document (if applicable),	(faculty,	date or year)	pinpoint.
Lara Khoury & Geneviève Saumier,	*Coursepack: Extra-contractual Obligations/ Torts,*		(Faculty of Law, McGill University,	2003)	at 20.
Jean-Sébastien Brière,	*Droit des brevets,*	Coursepack,	(Faculté de droit, Université de Sherbrooke,	Fall 2008)	at 331.

➢ Write the type of document if it's not already included in the title:

→ **Coursepacks** are booklets of material put together by professors for a particular class. Although it is always preferable to cite to the original material, if the citation or pinpoint is unavailable, one may cite to the coursepack.

→ **Lecture notes** are notes written by the professor for use in a particular class.

6.15 MAGAZINES

Author (if available),	"title of article",	*title of magazine*	volume number: issue number.	(date)	first page of article,	pin-point,	electronic source (if applicable).
	"Mugabe's self-defeated foes",	*The Economist*	377:8453	(19 November 2005)	66.		
Luiza Ch Savage,	"Judges Are Like Umpires",	*Maclean's*		(26 September 2005)	36,		online: Macleans.ca <http://www.macleans.ca>.
Benjamin Phelan,	"Buried Truths",	*Harper's Magazine*	309:1855	(December 2004)	70.		

> Include the name of the author of the article, if available, followed by the title of the article in quotation marks.

> Provide the name of the magazine in italics. Enclose any other optional identifying information, such as the place of publication, in brackets and italics immediately following the name of the magazine.

> Include the **volume number** and **issue number**, separated by a colon. Add no spaces between the numbers and the colon.

> Insert the **full date** in parentheses. If the date is a timespan rather than a precise date, indicate the **first day of coverage** (e.g. 22 November not 22-28 November).

6.16 NEWSPAPERS, NEWSWIRES, AND OTHER NEWS SOURCES

Author,	"title of article",	*newspaper*	(date)	page	electronic source (if applicable).
Naomi Wolf,	"Take the shame out of rape",	*The Guardian*	(25 November 2005)		online: Guardian Unlimited <http://www.guardian.co.uk>.
	"Ottawa eyes six candidates in search of new Supreme Court judge",	*Canadian Press*	(17 October 2005)		(QL).
	"Ruling on baby with three mothers",	*BBC News*	(10 November 2005)		online: BBC News <http://news.bbc.co.uk>.
Bill Curry,	"PM, premiers work out deal on aboriginal health care",	*The Globe and Mail*	(26 November 2005)	A4.	
Karen Montheith,	"CIPO contemplating changes – Extensions of time in examinations",		(30 September 2009)		online: Canadian Trademark Blog <http://www.trademarkblog.ca>.

➢ Provide the name of the author, if available, followed by the title of the article in quotation marks.

➢ Provide the name of the newspaper, newswire, or other source in italics.

➢ If geographic information is required to identify the source, indicate it within brackets in the title (e.g. *Business Times [of Singapore]* or *The [Montreal] Gazette*).

Newspapers:

➢ If geographic information is required to identify a newspaper, indicate the city within brackets in the title.

➢ If pages are numbered by section, provide the section's identifier (e.g. A4).

➢ If the article is contained on a single page, do not repeat that page for a pinpoint.

Newswires:

➢ A newswire is a service transmitting the latest news via satellite and various electronic media.

➢ Replace the newspaper name in italics with the newswire name in italics.

➢ For further information on citing to electronic sources, see section 6.21.

6.16.1 Editorials and Letters to the Editor

Author (if applicable),	"title of the editorial" (if applicable),	style of document,	*newspaper*	(date)	page,	electronic source (if applicable).
	"Accountability Begins at Home",	Editorial,	*The New York Times*	(21 November 2005)		online: The New York Times <http://www.nytimes.com>.
Harold von Cramon,		Letter to the Editor,	*The [Montreal] Gazette*	(26 September 2005)	A26.	
Ken Lum,		Letter to the Editor,	*The Vancouver Sun*	(6 December 2004)	A10.	

➢ Indicate Letter to the Editor after the author of a letter to the editor.

➢ Indicate Editorial after the title of an editorial.

➢ Italicize the name of the newspaper, magazine, or other source. Enclose any other optional identifying information, such as the place of publication, in brackets and italics (e.g. *Business Times [of Singapore]* or *The [Montreal] Gazette*).

6.17 NEWS RELEASES

Issuing body,	type of document,	document number,	"title" (optional)	(date)	electronic source (if applicable).
Indian and Northern Affairs,	News Release,	2-02688,	"Inuit Firms Secure Three Contaminated Sites Contracts"	(6 July 2005).	
Canadian Council for Refugees,	Media Release,		"CCR decries security policy's impact on refugees"	(28 April 2004)	online: CCR <http://www.ccrweb.ca>.
United Nations,	Press Release,	SG/SM/12548-OBV/820-WOM/1764,	"Secretary-General, Marking International Day of Rural Women, Calls for Scaling Up Investments in Resources, Infrastructure, Services to Improve Rural Women's Lives"	(15 October 2009)	online: UN Meetings Coverage & Press Releases <http://www.un.org/en/unpress>.

➤ Indicate the type of document as it appears at the top of the page (e.g. News Release).

➤ If the document is **numbered**, provide the number immediately after the type of document.

➤ Include the **date** at the end of the citation, before the electronic source.

6.18 LETTERS, MEMORANDA, AND INTERVIEWS

Letter or Interview	persons involved	(date)	further information.
Letter from	Sir Robert Wilmot to Lord George Sackville	(16 November 1753)	in James Walton, ed, "*The King's Business": Letters on the Administration of Ireland 1740-1761, from the Papers of Sir Robert Wilmot* (New York: AMS Press, 1996).
Interview of	Edward Beauvais by Douglas Sanderson	(29 May 1948)	on *This Week*, CBC Radio, Toronto, CBC Radio Archives.
	PE Moore, Acting Superintendent of Medical Services, Indian Affairs Branch, to EL Fairclough, Minister of Citizenship	[nd]	Hull, Indian and Northern Affairs Canada (6-24-3, vol 2).

➤ Include the parties' names, followed by the date the letter was written. If there is **no date available**, place [nd].

➤ Indicate an **interview** or **memorandum** by writing Interview of or Memorandum from and the parties' names at the beginning of the citation.

> ➤ If the position of a person involved is not obvious or is not mentioned in the text, include as much detail on the position as necessary, preceded by a comma (e.g. PE Moore, Acting Superintendent of Medical Services, Indian Affairs Branch).

> ➤ If the author is not the interviewer, include the name of the interviewer. If the author (you) is the interviewer, it is not necessary to do so.

> ➤ If the letter, memorandum, or interview is published, appears online, or is held in an archive, include the appropriate citation for such sources.

6.19 ARCHIVAL MATERIALS

Title of document and (other information),	location of archive,	name of archive	(classification number)
Daniel Tracey v Jean Baptiste Bourtron dit Larochelle (23 December 1830),	Montreal,	Archives Nationales du Québec	(files of the Court of Quarter Sessions).
Chief Andrew Paull to TA Crerar (22 June 1944),	Ottawa,	National Archives of Canada	(RG 10, vol 6826, file 496-3-2, pt 1).

> ➤ If a document is located in an archive, provide as much information on the document as possible using the traditional citation rules, followed by the archival information.

6.20 INTELLECTUAL PROPERTY

6.20.1 Patents

"Title of Invention,"	country	Patent No,	PCT patent No	(filing date),	pinpoint.
"Violin Shoulder Cradle,"	Can	Patent No 2414383,	PCT Patent No PCT/US2001/021243	(29 June 2001),	clm 10.
"Parallel network processor array,"	US	Patent No 6854117,		(31 October 2000),	fig 9.

> ➤ Indicate the **title of the invention** in quotation marks.

> ➤ Indicate the abbreviation of the **country where the patent was granted** and the **patent number**.

> ➤ If a patent was granted through the **Patent Cooperation Treaty** (PCT), use the same form for citation (PCT Patent No).

> ➤ Indicate the **filing date**.

> If necessary, include both the country and the PCT patent numbers, separated by a comma.

> Pinpoint to the abstract (abstract), a claim number (clm) or a figure (fig).

> For **patent applications**, write application filed on before the **filing date** (e.g. application filed on 30 August 2008).

6.20.2 Trade-marks

"Trade-mark",	registrant,	country	registration number	(registration date)	status.
"Kellog's Cinnamon Mini Buns à la Cannelle",	Kellog Company,	Can	No TMA424258	(4 March 1994)	expunged.
"Lego",	Lego Juris A/S,	USA	78882203	(3 June 2008)	live.

> Indicate the **trade-mark** in quotation marks.

> Indicate the abbreviation of the **country where the trade-mark was registered**.

> Write the **registration number**. The format of the number varies for every jurisdiction.

> Indicate the registration date in parentheses.

> Write the **status** of the trade-mark in the register. Write dead or live for United States trade-marks, and registered or expunged for Canada.

6.20.3 Copyright

"Title of the protected work"	(type of work)	owner of the copyright,	country	registration number	(registration date).	status.
"Twilight"	(music)	Mary Chapin Carpentier,	USA	Pau002997899	(20 December 2005).	
"Agrippa : Le livre noir"	(literary)	Éditions Michel Quintin,	Can	1056747	(11 March 2003)	registered.

> Indicate the **title of the protected work** in quotation marks.

> In Canada, the type of work includes original literary, artistic, dramatic and musical works, performer's performances, sound recordings and communication signals, as well as mechanical contrivance.

> Indicate the **owner of the copyright** and the **abbreviation of the country** where the copyright was issued.

➢ Write the **registration number**. The format of the number varies for each jurisdiction.

➢ Indicate the **registration date** in parentheses.

➢ Indicate the status (registered or expunged) of the copyright in the register.

6.21 ELECTRONIC SOURCES

6.21.1 Electronic Services

Traditional citation	(electronic service and database).
Kristin Savell, "Human Rights in the Age of Technology: Can Law Reign in the Medical Juggernaut?" (2001) 23 Sydney L Rev 423	(Lexis).
Alan D Gold, *Expert Evidence in Criminal Law: The Scientific Approach* (Toronto: Irwin Law, 2003)	(QL).

➢ Provide the full citation, followed by the electronic service in parentheses.

➢ If a publisher is not listed, or if the text is not published anywhere other than in the electronic service, cite the online service as the publisher (e.g. (Kingston, Ont: QL, 2001)).

➢ Do not cite to an electronic service that the majority of readers will not be able to access. For example, do not cite to Lawnet (Singapore) when writing for a Canadian audience.

➢ For a list of electronic services and their abbreviations, see **Appendix E**.

6.21.2 Online Journals (eJournals)

Traditional citation,	online:	(year)	volume: issue (if applicable)	journal	article number	pinpoint	<URL>.
Grant Yang, "Stop the Abuse of Gmail!",	online:	(2005)		Duke L & Tech Rev	14	at para 5	<http://www. law. duke.edu/ journals/dltr/>.
Kahikino Noa Dettweiler, "Racial Classification or Cultural Identification?: The Gathering Rights Jurisprudence of Two Twentieth Century Hawaiian Supreme Court Justices",	online:	(2005)	6:1	Asian Pac L & Pol'y J	5		<http://www. hawaii.edu/aplpj>.

> Some journals are published exclusively online with their own system of citation.

> Cite the journal according to this internal system. Include the URL of the home page of the journal at the end of the citation.

6.21.3 Websites

Traditional citation,	online:	name of website	<URL>.
Henry Samuel, "March for girl set alight after marriage refusal" *The Daily Telegraph* (28 November 2005),	online:	The Telegraph Group	<http://www.telegraph.co.uk>.
Theodore de Bruyn, *A Plan of Action for Canada to reduce HIV/AIDS-related stigma and discrimination,*	online:	Canadian HIV/AIDS Legal Network	<http://www.aidslaw.ca>.
EPA Science and Technology, *Tiny new technology to clean up big pollution problems,*	online:	US Environmental Protection Agency	<http://www.epa.gov>.
"Defamation in the Internet Age" (1 June 2008) (podcast),	online:	Osler	<http://www.osler.com>.

> Provide the full traditional citation, followed by a comma. Add online: and the name of the website, followed by the URL.

> Write the full URL of the **home page** of the website. If the specific page is not likely to move or would be too hard to find from the home page, write the URL of the page (e.g. a PDF file).

> Some websites may not include the names of authors or formal titles for written work. In these cases, exercise your best judgment and include basic, critical information in place of the traditional citation (see EPA example).

> Many online articles expire after a short period of time. Cite to online sources only if the source provides an archive of material for a reasonable period of time, preferably several years.

> Cite **podcasts** like any other internet site and add (podcast) after the traditional citation (see Osler example). If provided, write the name of the speaker instead of the author.

> Include a paragraph number as a pinpoint reference, if available. If the page numbering of a printed source is reproduced in the electronic source, reference may be made to those page numbers.

6.21.4 Other Digital Media

Traditional citation,	type of digital media:	*title of the media if different*	(publication information).
Peter W Hogg & Mary Ellen Turpel, "Implementing Aboriginal Self-Government: Constitutional and Jurisdictional Issues",	CD-ROM:	*For Seven Generations: An Information Legacy of the Royal Commission on Aboriginal Peoples*	(Ottawa: Libraxus, 1997).
The Paper Chase, 1973,	DVD:		(Beverly Hills, Cal: 20th Century Fox Home Entertainment, 2003).

➢ Provide the traditional citation for the document being cited, followed by a comma.

➢ Indicate the type of digital media (e.g. CD-ROM, DVD, BluRay, MiniDisc) after the comma. If the title of the media is different from the title in the traditional citation, add a colon.

➢ Indicate the title of the disc in italics, followed by a comma and the update, if applicable.

➢ In parentheses, provide the publication information for the digital medium. Include the place of publication, the publisher, and the year of publication.

Foreign Sources

Foreign Sources

Foreign Sources

7   FOREIGN SOURCES

To cite a source from a country that is not listed in this chapter, use the Canadian rules of the previous chapters as a guideline.

7.1   UNITED KINGDOM

For general rules, see *Oxford Standard for Citation of Legal Authorities*.

For jurisprudence, see Donald Raistrick, *Index to Legal Citations and Abbreviations*, 2d ed (London, UK: Bowker-Saur, 1993).

7.1.1   Legislation

7.1.1.1   *Statutes*

➢   Include (UK) after the title of the statute to indicate its origin.

➢   Before 1963: When the title includes a year, place a comma

Before 1963	*Statute of Westminster*, 1931 (UK), 22 & 23 Geo V, c 4, s 2.
1 January 1963 and after	*Terrorism Act 2000* (UK), c 11, s 129.

before the year. Cite the regnal year in Arabic numerals (e.g. 1, 2, 3) and the number following the abbreviation for the monarch in Roman numerals (Geo V).

➢   1 January 1963 and after: When the title includes a year, do not place a comma before the year. When the title does not include a year, indicate the calendar year after (UK), proceeded by a comma.

7.1.1.1.1   Northern Ireland

7.1.1.1.1.1   Legislation Passed by the United Kingdom

Before 1963	*Public Health (Ireland) Act, 1878* (UK), 41 & 42 Vict, c 52.
1 January 1963 and after	*Northern Ireland Act 1998* (UK), 1998, c 47, s 5.

➢   Cite legislation applying to Northern Ireland passed by the United Kingdom in the same manner as United Kingdom legislation.

7.1.1.1.1.2   Legislation Passed by Northern Ireland

1921-1972	*Criminal Law Amendment (Northern Ireland)* Act, RSNI 1923, c 8.
	National Insurance Act, NI Pub Gen Acts 1946, c 23, s 7.
1999-present	*Family Law Act (Northern Ireland)* 2001, (NI), 2001, c 12.

➢ Abbreviate Northern Ireland Public General Acts to NI Pub Gen Acts.

➢ Abbreviate Statutes Revised, Northern Ireland to RSNI.

➢ The United Kingdom passed legislation for Northern Ireland from 1972-1999. On 19 November 1998, the Northern Irealnd Assembly was created and empowered to pass legislation as of 2 December 1999. For legislation passed by the Assembly after 1999, include (NI) after the title of the statute to indicate its origin. Note that after 2 December 1999, the United Kingdom can still pass legislation affecting Northern Ireland.

NB: The Northern Ireland Assembly and the Executive have been suspended as of 14 October 2002. Responsibility and control of Northern Ireland Departments have been assumed by the *Secretary of State for Northern Ireland* and the *Northern Ireland Office*.

7.1.1.1.2   Scotland

Before 1998	*Contract (Scotland) Act 1997* (UK), 1997, c 34.
	Scotland Act 1998 (UK), 1998, c 46, s 4.
1998-present	*Standards in Scotland's Schools etc. Act*, ASP 2000, c 6, s 2.

➢ Cite legislation from before 1998 in the same manner as United Kingdom legislation.

➢ Note that Acts passed by the United Kingdom still apply to Scotland if the legislation pertains to a reserved or non-devolved matter.

➢ From 19 November 1998, abbreviate Acts of Scottish Parliament to ASP.

7.1.1.1.3   Wales

Government of Wales Act 1998 (UK), 1998, c 38, s 3.

➢ The United Kingdom passes legislation pertaining to Wales. Cite this legislation in the same manner as United Kingdom legislation.

7.1.1.2 Bills

7.1.1.2.1   United Kingdom

Bill number,	title,	session,	year,	pinpoint	(additional information) (optional).
Bill 45,	*London Olympics Bill*,	2005-2006 sess,	2005,		(1st reading 14 July 2005).
Bill 40,	*Harbours Bill [HL]*,	2005-2006 sess,	2005,	s 2.	

➤ For bills that originate in the House of Lords, indicate [HL] (not italicized) in the title.

7.1.1.2.2   Northern Ireland

Number,	title,	session,	year,	pinpoint	(additional information) (optional).
NIA Bill 15/00,	A Bill to amend the Game Preservation (Northern Ireland) Act 1928,	2001-2002 sess,	2001,	s 2	(Committee Stage Extension 29 October 2001).
NIA Bill 17/07,	Child Maintenance Bill,	2007-2008 sess,	2008,	s 12.	

7.1.1.2.3   Scotland

Number,	title,	session,	year,	pinpoint	(additional information) (optional).
SP Bill 42,	Human Tissue (Scotland) Bill,	sess 2,	2005,	s 6	(1st reading 3 June 2005).
SP Bill 17,	Climate Change (Scotland) Bill,	sess 3,	2008,	s 3(2)(b)	(State 1 debate 6-7 May 2009).

7.1.1.3 Regulations

7.1.1.3.1   United Kingdom

	Title (optional),	SR & O or SI	year/number.
Before 1948	Public Health (Prevention of Tuberculosis) Regulations 1925,	SR & O	1927/757.
1948 and after	The Welfare Food (Amendment) Regulations 2005,	SI	2005/688.

➤ Including the title of the regulation is optional.

➤ For regulations before 1948, abbreviate **Statutory Rules & Orders** to SR & O. For regulations after 1948, abbreviate **Statutory Instruments** to SI.

7.1.1.3.2   Northern Ireland Regulations and Orders

Title (optional),	SR & O or SI	year/number	(NI number).
The Proceeds of Crime (Northern Ireland) Order 1996,	SI	1996/1299	(NI 9).
The Tax Credits 2001 (Miscellaneous Amendments No. 8) (Northern Ireland) Regulations,	SI	2001/3086.	
Cheese Regulations (NI) 1970,	SR & O	1970/14.	
Dangerous Substances in Harbour Areas Regulations (Northern Ireland) 1991,	SR	1991/509.	

➤ Including the title of the regulation is optional.

➤ A regulation or order passed by the UK is contained in the *Statutory Instruments* (SI).

➤ A regulation passed by the Northern Ireland Assembly is called a *Statutory Rule* (SR).

➤ Northern Ireland regulations are also included in *Statutory Regulations and Orders* (abbreviated SR & O) beginning in 1922.

➤ If there is a **Northern Ireland Order number**, include it after the year/number to indicate that the order was passed by the Northern Ireland Assembly.

7.1.1.3.3   Scotland

Cite Scottish regulations in the same manner as United Kingdom regulations (section 7.1.1.3.1).

7.1.1.3.3.1   Regulations Passed by the United Kingdom

Title (optional),	SR & O or SI	year/number.
Employment Tribunals (Constitution and Rules of Procedure) (Scotland) Regulations 2001,	SI	2001/1170.
Local Government Pension Scheme Amendment (Scotland) Regulations 2009,	SI	2009/93.

7.1.1.3.3.2   Regulations Passed by the Scottish Parliament

Title (optional),	Scot SI	year/number.
National Health Service (General Ophthalmic Services) (Scotland) Amendment Regulations 2001,	Scot SI	2001/62.
Plastic Materials and Articles in Contact with Food (Scotland) Regulations 2009,	Scot SI	2009/30.

➤ Abbreviate *Scottish Statutory Instruments* to Scot SI.

7.1.1.3.4   Wales

Title (optional),	SR & O or SI	year/number	(W number).
Children's Homes Amendment (Wales) Regulations 2001,	SI	2001/140	(W 6).

➤ After the year/number, include the Welsh regulation number to indicate that the regulation was passed by the National Assembly for Wales.

7.1.2 Jurisprudence

7.1.2.1 General Form

Style of cause	(year of decision),	neutral citation	[year of reporter]	vol	repor-ter	page	court.
R v Woollin	(1998),		[1999]		AC	82	HL (Eng).
Campbell v MGN Ltd,		[2004] UKHL 22,	[2004]	2	AC	457.	

➢   Cite the **Law Reports** (section 7.1.2.5.1) in preference to the **Weekly Law Reports** (WLR) or the **All England Law Reports** (All ER).

➢   See **Appendix B** for a list of courts and their abbreviations, and **Appendix C-3** for a list of United Kingdom reporters and their abbreviations.

7.1.2.2 Neutral Citation

➢   Many courts in the United Kingdom have officially adopted a system of neutral citation. The form is the same as that of Canadian neutral citation (section 3.5), with the exception that the year is placed in brackets.

7.1.2.3 Appeal Courts

> ¹ *Campbell v MGN Limited*, [2004] UKHL 22.
>
> ² *Copping v Surrey County Council*, [2005] EWCA Civ 1604 ¶ 15.

House of Lords	[year] UKHL number
Privy Council	[year] UKPC number
England and Wales Court of Appeal (Civil Division)	[year] EWCA Civ number
England and Wales Court of Appeal (Criminal Division)	[year] EWCA Crim number

➢   The neutral citations for the Appeal Courts and the Administrative Court of the High Court became official on 11 January 2001.

➢   Place the year of the decision in brackets followed by the court identifier and the case number.

7.1.2.4 High Court

[Year]	court	number	(division)	pinpoint.
[2005]	EWHC	1974	(Admlty)	¶ 10.
[2005]	EWHC	2995	(Comm).	

➢   Neutral citations to the High Court were **officially adopted on 14 January 2002**.

➢   For cases heard in the High Court, the division of the Court is placed in parentheses *after* the case number.

➢   NB: Cases heard by the Administrative Court in 2001 should follow the form year EWHC Admin number, similar to the Court of Appeal (section 7.1.2.3).

➤ Pinpoint to paragraphs and use ¶ or at para.

High Court Divisions and Abbreviations:

Chancery Division	Ch
Patents Court	Pat
Queen's Bench Division	QB
Administrative Court	Admin

Commercial Court	Comm
Admiralty Court	Admlty
Technology & Construction Court	TCC
Family Division	Fam

7.1.2.5 *Reporter*

7.1.2.5.1   Law Reports

➤ *Law Reports* are divided into series. Do not refer to the *Law Reports*, but rather to the series.

➤ Since there is no separate reporter for the Court of Appeal, include CA (the abbreviation of Court of Appeal) at the end of each citation to a case heard in that court.

Law Reports and abbreviations:

Appeal Cases (House of Lords and Judicial Committee of the Privy Council)	AC
Chancery (Chancery Division and appeals therefrom in the Court of Appeal)	Ch
Common Pleas	CP
Family (1972 - present)	Fam
Industrial Courts Reports (1972-1974) and Industrial Cases Reports (1975 - present)	ICR
Probate (1891-1971) (Family Division, Probate, Divorce, and Admiralty Division, appeals therefrom, and Ecclesiastical Courts)	P
Queen's (King's) Bench (Queen's (King's) Bench Division and appeals therefrom in the Court of Appeal)	QB (KB)
Law Reports Restrictive Practices (1957-1972) (National Industrial Relations Court and Restrictive Practices Court, appeals therefrom, and decisions of the High Court relevant to industrial relations)	LR RP

7.1.2.5.1.1   From 1875-1890

Akerblom v Price, Potter, Walker & Co (1881), 7 QBD 129 (CA) [*Akerblom*].

➤ Include D for Division after the reporter to distinguish the 1875-1890 series of reporters from the later series with the same name.

7.1.2.5.1.2   From 1865-1875

> Rylands v Fletcher (1868), LR 3 HL 330.

➢ Include LR for Law Reports before the volume number to distinguish the 1865-1875 series of reporters from the later series with the same name.

7.1.2.5.1.3   From 1537-1865

➢ Cite to the nominate reporter whenever possible and always provide a parallel citation to **English Reports** (ER) where available.

> Lord Byron v Johnston (1816), 2 Mer 28, 35 ER 851 (Ch).

➢ The *English Reports* and *All England Reports Reprints* are reprints.

7.1.2.6 *Yearbooks*

Style of cause	(year),	yearbook	term	regnal year	monarch,	plea number,	folio number.
Waldon v Marshall	(1370),	YB	Mich	43	Edw III,	pl 38,	fol 33.

➢ Abbreviate Michaelmas to Mich, Hilary to Hil, Easter to Pach, and Trinity to Trin.

➢ Indicate the regnal year in Arabic numerals (e.g. 1, 2, 3).

➢ Cite the monarch using Roman numerals.

➢ Abbreviate plea to pl.

➢ Abbreviate folio to fol.

7.1.2.7 Reprints

➤ When citing to a reprint, provide as much information about the original yearbook entry as possible. Cite to the location where the reprint is found.

Yearbook citation	reprinted in	citation.
Beauver v Abbot of St Albans (1312), YB Mich 6 Edw II,	reprinted in	(1921) 38 Selden Soc 32.

7.1.2.8 Scotland, Ireland and Northern Ireland

Scotland	*M'Courtney v HM Advocate*, [1977] JC 68 (HCJ Scot).
Ireland	*Johnson v Egan*, [1894] 2 IR 480 (QBD).
Northern Ireland	*R v Crooks*, [1999] NI 226 (CA).

➤ Where the jurisdiction is not obvious from the title of the reporter, and there is no neutral citation, abbreviate Scotland to Scot, Ireland to Ir, and Northern Ireland to NI Enclose the abbreviation in parentheses at the end of the citation.

➤ As each volume is divided according to the court reported and each section is paginated separately, include the name of the court.

➤ See **Appendix B** for court abbreviations and **Appendix C** for reporter abbreviations.

7.1.2.9 Neutral Citation

➤ The rules for neutral citation are the same for Scotland, Ireland, and Northern Ireland. The rules are similar to those of Canadian neutral citation with the exception that the year is placed in square brackets. See sections 3.7.2 and 3.10.2.1.

7.1.2.9.1 Scotland

➤ As the neutral citation does not indicate the jurisdiction, add Scot for Scotland in parentheses at the end of the entire citation (following all parallel citations).

Smith v Brown, [2005] HCJT 2 (Scot).

Kinross v Dunsmuir, [2005] HCJAC 3 ¶ 12 (Scot).

McBride v MacDuff, [2005] CSOH 4 (Scot).

High Court of Justiciary	[year] HCJT number
Court of Criminal Appeal	[year] HCJAC number
Court of Session, Outer House	[year] CSOH number
Court of Session, Inner House	[year] CSIH number

7.1.2.9.2 Ireland

High Court	[year] IEHC number
Supreme Court	[year] IESC number
Court of Criminal Appeal	[year] IECCA number

Finnigan v O'Dair, [2006] IEHC 4.

Mackey v Mackey, [2005] IESC 2 ¶4.

7.1.2.9.3 Northern Ireland

McDonnell v Henry, [2005] NICA 17.

Barkley v Whiteside, [2004] NIQB 12 ¶ 12.

High Court:

Queen's Bench Division	[year] NIQB number
Family Division	[year] NIFam number
Chancery Division	[year] NICh number

7.1.2.10 *Judge*

Lord Justice	LJ
Lord Justices	LJJ
Master of the Rolls	MR
Lord Chancellor	LC
Vice Chancellor	VC
Baron	B
Chief Baron	CB

7.1.3 Government Documents

Indicate UK at the beginning of the citation.

7.1.3.1 Debates

7.1.3.1.1   **Before 1803**

UK,	house,	*Parliamentary History of England,*	volume,	column	(date)	(speaker) (optional).
UK,	HC,	*Parliamentary History of England,*	vol 17,	col 1357	(27 May 1774).	
UK,	HL,	*Parliamentary History of England,*	vol 2,	col 791	(24 May 1641).	

➢   For debates prior to 1803, cite to the ***Parliamentary History of England***.

➢   Abbreviate **House of Commons** to HC and **House of Lords** to HL.

➢   Indicate the speaker (if provided) in parentheses at the end of the citation.

7.1.3.1.2   **1803 and After**

UK,	house,	*title,*	series or session (if applicable),	volume,	column	pinpoint	(date)	(speaker) (optional).
UK,	HL,	*Parliamentary Debates,*	5th ser,	vol 442,	col 6		(3 May 1983)	(Baroness Masham of Ilton).
UK,	SP,	*Official Report,*	sess 1 (2000),	vol 7, No 6,	col 634		(22 June 2000)	(Peter Peacock).
UK,	NIA,	*Official Report,*				at 500	(24 October 2000).	
UK,	NAW,	*Official Record,*				at 27	(19 July 2001).	

➢   Indicate the speaker (if provided) in parentheses at the end of the citation.

➢   After UK, indicate the house.

Houses' abbreviations:

House of Commons	HC
House of Lords	HL
National Assembly for Wales	NAW
Northern Ireland Assembly	NIA
Scottish Parliament	SP

7.1.3.2 Journals

UK,	*journal,*	volume	(date)	pinpoint.
UK,	*Journal of the House of Commons,*	vol 234	(9 December 1977)	at 95.
UK,	*Journal of the House of Lords,*	vol 22	(10 January 1995)	at 89.

➤ Do not repeat the house, since it is already included in the title of the journal.

7.1.3.3 Parliamentary Papers

UK,	house,	"title",	sessional or command paper number	in *Sessional Papers,*	vol	(year)	first page	pinpoint	(president) (if any).
UK,	HC,	"Report of the Committee on the Law Relating to Rights of Light",	Cmnd 473	in *Sessional Papers,*	vol 17	(1957-58)	955		(President: CE Harman).
UK,	HC,	"Monopolies and Mergers Commission Report on the Supply in the U.K. of the Services of Administering Performing Rights and Film Synchronisation Rights",	Cm 3147	in *Sessional Papers*		(1995-96)	1.		

➤ Indicate the title as it appears on the title page of the report.

➤ Place the sessional number or command paper number after the title of the paper.

➤ Cite to the **House of Commons' bound *Sessional Papers*** unless the paper only appears in the House of Lords' *Sessional Papers*.

➤ Place the volume number, if specified, after *Sessional Papers*, preceded by a comma.

➤ Include the name of the president (if provided) in parentheses at the end of the citation.

➤ **The proper abbreviation of Command is essential for identifying the document.** It is indicated on the title page of each *Command Paper*:

1833-1869	1st series (1-4222)	c
1870-1899	2d series (1-9550)	C
1900-1918	3d series (1-9239)	Cd
1919-1956	4th series (1-9889)	Cmd
1957-1986	5th series (1-9927)	Cmnd
1986-present	6th series (1-)	Cm

➤ Indicate the first page of the paper after the date.

➤ Pinpoint to the internal pagination of the paper.

7.1.3.4 Non-parliamentary Papers

UK,	issuing body,	*title*	(nature of paper) (if applicable)	authors (if applicable)	(publication information).
UK,	Royal Commission on Criminal Procedure,	*Police Interrogation: The Psychological Approach*			(London: Her Majesty's Stationery Office, 1980).
UK,	Royal Commission on the Press,	*Studies on the Press*	(Working Paper No 3)	by Oliver Boyd-Barrett, Dr Colin Seymour-Ure & Professor Jeremy Turnstall	(London: Her Majesty's Stationery Office, 1978).
UK,	Law Commission,	*The Illegality of Defence in Tort*	(Consultation Paper No 160)		(London: Her Majesty's Stationery Office, 2001).
UK,		*Report of the Committee on Homosexual Offences and Prostitution*			(London: Her Majesty's Stationery Office, 1957).

➢   Cite non-parliamentary papers in the same manner as Canadian non-parliamentary papers, according to the rules at section 4.2.

➢   Do not write the issuing body if it is already in the title (see the *Report of the Committee on Homosexual Offences and Prostitution* example).

7.2   UNITED STATES

See the latest edition of *The Bluebook: A Uniform System of Citation*.

7.2.1   Legislation

7.2.1.1 Federal and State Constitutions

US Const art III, § 2, cl 3.

US Const amend XIV, § 1.

NM Const art IV, § 7.

➢   Abbreviate article to art, section to §, and sections to §§.

➢   A paragraph within a section is labeled a clause, and is abbreviated to cl or cls in the plural.

➢   Abbreviate amendment to amend.

➢   Abbreviate preamble to pmbl.

➢   Indicate article and amendment numbers in capital Roman numerals. Indicate section and clause numbers in Arabic numerals (e.g. 1, 2, 3).

➢   See **Appendix A-2** for a list of state abbreviations.

7.2.1.2 Federal and State Statutes

Order of preference of sources:

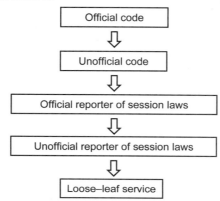

7.2.1.2.1   Codes

➤ A code in the United States is a consolidation and codification by subject matter of the general and permanent federal or state laws.

➤ An official code is a code of the laws of the United States organized under 50 subject titles, prepared under the supervision of an appropriate government authority (e.g. federal Department of Justice).

➤ The official federal code is the *United States Code* (USC).

➤ To determine whether a state code is official or unofficial consult the *Bluebook*.

➤ An unofficial code is a code of the laws of the United States prepared by a private publisher. Unofficial federal codes include:

→ the *United States Code Service* (USCS) and

→ the *United States Code Annotated* (USCA).

	Title (exceptionally),	division of code (if applicable)	abbreviated code name	title number (if applicable)	section	(publisher (if applicable)	supplement (if applicable)	year).
Official codes	*Americans with Disabilities Act,*	42	USC		§ 12101			(1990).
			Minn Stat		§ 169.94			(2004).
			IRC		§ 61			(2000).
Unofficial codes		8	USCA		§ 1182	(West		1997).
			Pa Stat Ann	tit 63	§ 425.3	(West	Supp	1986).
			Wis Stat Ann		§ 939.645	(West	Supp	1992).

➢ Once a statute has been codified, its original title is not usually cited. **Include the title only for a special reason** (e.g. because it is commonly known by that name). Italicize the title.

➢ If the code is **divided** into separate numbered titles, chapters, or volumes, include the number of that division. When citing federal codes, indicate the division before the code abbreviation.

➢ Do not italicize the abbreviated name of the code. For citations to the Internal Revenue Code, it is possible to replace 26 USC with IRC.

➢ When citing to an unofficial code, include the name of the publisher before the year, or before Supp where applicable.

➢ When citing a supplement found in a pocket insert, place Supp before the year.

➢ Include the year of publication of the code in parentheses at the end of the citation. When citing a **bound volume**, provide the year that appears on the spine of the volume. When citing a **supplement**, provide the year that appears on the title page of the supplement.

7.2.1.2.2   Session Laws

Session laws are the statutes passed by a session of Congress, bound and indexed chronologically. Session laws track the historical development of a law.

Title or date of enactment,	public law number or chapter number,	section (optional),	session laws reporter	first page of act	pinpoint to reporter	(year) (if not in title)	(codification information) (optional).
The Indian Child Welfare Act of 1978,	Pub L No 95-608,		92 Stat	3069			(codified as amended at 25 USC § 1901-1963 (1988)).
Antiterrorism and Effective Death Penalty Act of 1996,	Pub L No 104-132,	§ 327,	110 Stat	1214	at 1257	(1997).	
Act of 25 April 1978,	c 515,	§ 3,	1978 Ala Acts	569	at 570.		

➢ Provide the name of the statute in italics. If it has no name, identify it by the date of its enactment in roman type, not italics (Act of 25 April 1978). If no date of enactment is available, identify it by the date on which the act came into effect (Act effective [date]).

➢ Provide the public law number, introduced by the abbreviation Pub L No, or the chapter number of the statute, introduced by c. The number before the hyphen in the public law number is the session. The number following the hyphen is the identifier.

> To cite a **particular section**, indicate the section number directly after the public law number or the chapter number. Include a pinpoint to the reporter.

> For federal statutes, the **official reporter** is the *Statutes at Large*, abbreviated to Stat. The abbreviation of the reporter is preceded by the volume number, followed by the first page of the act. To determine whether a reporter of state session laws is official or unofficial, consult the *Bluebook*.

> Indicate a **pinpoint** following the citation to the first page of the act. Include a pinpoint to the particular section after the public law number or the chapter number.

> Indicate the year the **statute was enacted** in parentheses at the end of the citation, unless the year is part of the name of the statute. The year in the title might not coincide with the year in which the statute was published, in which case you must provide both. See the *Antiterrorism and Effective Death Penalty Act of 1996* example.

> **Codification information** for the law should be provided if it is available. If a single statute is divided and codified under many subject-headings of the code, indicate this with parenthetical information at the end of the citation ((codified as amended in scattered sections of 26 USC)).

7.2.1.2.3   Unofficial Reporters of Session Laws

Title,	public law number,	[volume]	unofficial reporter	pinpoint,	session law citation.
Veteran's Benefits Improvements Act of 1996,	Pub L No 104-275,	[1996]	USCCAN	3762,	110 Stat 3322.

> The most important unofficial reporter of session laws is the *United States Code Congressional and Administrative News*, abbreviated to USCCAN.

> When citing to the USCCAN, indicate the volume and page number of the *Statutes at Large* (Stat) in which the law will subsequently appear.

7.2.1.3 *Uniform Codes, Uniform Acts, and Restatements*

> **Uniform Codes** and **Uniform Acts** are proposed legislation, published by the National Conference of Commissioners of Uniform State Laws, to be adopted in all state legislatures, districts, and protectorates. **Restatements** are reports of the state of US common

Title	section	(year of adoption).
UCC	§ 2-012	(1995).
Uniform Partnership Act	§ 23	(1969).
Restatements of Security	§ 51	(1941).
Restatement (Second) of the Law of Property	§ 15	(1977).

law on given topics and interpretation of statutes, published by the American Law Institute.

➢ Italicize the title, unless it is a code.

➢ Do not place a comma after the title of a code or a restatement.

➢ When more than one restatement has been produced, indicate the number in parentheses.

➢ At the end of the citation, in parentheses, indicate the year of adoption, promulgation, or latest amendment, which often appears on the title page.

7.2.1.4 Bills and Resolutions

7.2.1.4.1   Federal Bills

US,	Bill	house	number,	*title*,	Congress number,	year,	pinpoint	(status, if enacted).
US,	Bill	HR	1,	*No Child Left Behind Act of 2001,*	107th Cong,	2001,		(enacted).
US,	Bill	S	7,	*Prescription Drug Benefit and Cost Containment Act of 2003,*	108th Cong,	2003,	s 107.	

➢ Abbreviate House of Representatives as HR and Senate as S.

7.2.1.4.2   Federal Resolutions

US,	type of resolution	number,	*title*,	Congress number,	year	(status, if enacted).
US,	HR Con Res	6,	*Expressing the Sense of the Congress Regarding the Need to Pass Legislation to Increase Penalties on Perpetrators of Hate Crimes,*	107th Cong,	2001.	
US,	HR Res	387,	*Providing for consideration of the bill (HR 3283) to enhance resources to enforce United States trade rights,*	109th Cong,	2005	(enacted).

Abbreviations of the type of resolution:

House Concurrent Resolutions	HR Con Res
House Resolutions	HR Res
House Joint Resolutions	HRJ Res
Senate Concurrent Resolutions	S Con Res
Senate Resolutions	S Res
Senate Joint Resolutions	SJ Res

7.2.1.4.3 State Bills and Resolutions

US,	type of bill or resolution	number,	*title,*	year or legislature number,	number or designation of legislative session,	state,	year,	pinpoint	(status, if enacted).
US,	AB	31,	*An Act to Add Section 51885 to the Education Code, Relating to Educational Technology,*	1997-98,	Reg Sess,	Cal,	1996,	s 1.	
US,	SR	10,	*Calling for the Establishment of a Delaware State Police Community Relations Task Force,*	141st Gen Assem,	Reg Sess,	Del,	2001,		(enacted).

➤ In addition to Regular Sessions, state legislatures may hold **First**, **Second**, and **Third Extraordinary Sessions**. Abbreviate these as 1st Extra Sess, 2d Extra Sess, and 3d Extra Sess, respectively. **Special Sessions** may be abbreviated Spec Sess.

➤ Abbreviate the state according to the list in **Appendix A-2**.

7.2.1.5 Regulations

7.2.1.5.1 The Code of Federal Regulations

The *Code of Federal Regulations* is the codification of the regulations of the United States, organized under the same 50 subject titles as the United States Code.

Title (exceptionally),	volume	reporter	section	(year).
EPA Effluent Limitations Guidelines,	40	CFR	§ 405.53	(1980).
	47	CFR	§ 73.609	(1994).

➤ Indicate the title of the rule or regulation when it is commonly known under that name.

➤ When possible, cite federal rules and regulations to the *Code of Federal Regulations.*

➤ The *Code of Federal Regulations* (CFR) is the official compilation of the federal government.

NB: For a list of official state administrative compilations, consult the *Bluebook.*

7.2.1.5.2   Administrative Registers

Administrative registers report, among other things, administrative regulations enacted by government authorities.

Title (if applicable),	volume	Fed Reg	page	(year)	(codification information	pinpoint).
	44	Fed Reg	12437221	(1979)	(to be codified at 29 CFR	§ 552).
Outer Continental Sheld Air Regulation Consistency Update for California,	70	Fed Reg	19472	(2009)	(to be codified at 40 CFR	§ 55).

> ➤ When rules and regulations have not been codified, cite them to an administrative register.

> ➤ For federal rules and regulations, cite the *Federal Register* (Fed Reg).

> ➤ Include the number of the volume, the abbreviation of the register, the page number, and the year.

> ➤ When possible, at the end of the citation indicate where the rule or regulation will appear in the official compilation.

NB: To identify state administrative registers, and for more information on citing American legislation, consult the *Bluebook*.

7.2.2 Jurisprudence

7.2.2.1 General Form

Style of cause,	vol	reporter	(series)	page	pinpoint	(jurisdiction and/or court	year of decision)	(other information) (if applicable).
Texas Beef Group v Winfrey,	11	F Supp	(2d)	858		(ND Tex	1998).	
Dell Computer Corp,	121	FTC		616	at 619		(1996).	
Distribution Center of Columbus,	83	Lab Arb Rep (BNA)		163			(1984)	(Seidman, Arb).

> ➤ Administrative adjudications and arbitrations are cited in the same manner as other cases.

> ➤ For arbitrations, place the name of the arbitrator followed by a comma and Arb in parentheses at the end of the citation.

7.2.2.2 *Style of Cause*

➤ Indicate the style of cause according to the rules in section 3.3.

➤ For a state or country, use the common name, not the full formal name or abbreviation.

✓	California v United States Larez v Los Angeles (City of)
✗	State of California v United States of America Larez v LA

➤ If the case involves a city whose name could be mistaken for a state, enclose the relevant identifying information in parentheses: New York (City of) or Washington (DC).

7.2.2.3 *Neutral Citation*

There is currently **no one uniform standard for neutral citation** in the United States, although some jurisdictions have adopted such citations. Use the *Bluebook* for details.

7.2.2.4 *Reporter and Series*

➤ After the style of cause, provide the volume number, the reporter abbreviation, the series number, and the first page of the case. There is always a space between the reporter abbreviation and the series number.

> *Murray v Earle*, 405 F (3d) 278 (5th Cir 2005).
>
> *Scott v Sanford*, 60 US (19 How) 393 (1857).

➤ *US Reports* **prior to 1875** are also numbered consecutively for each editor. Place this number and the editor's name in parentheses after US.

Abbreviations of editors:

Wallace	Wall
Black	Black
Howard	How
Peters	Pet
Wheaton	Wheat
Cranch	Cranch
Dallas	Dall

Foreign Sources

Abbreviations of principal reporters:

Atlantic Reporter	A
California Reporter	Cal
Federal Reporter	F
Federal Supplement	F Supp
Lawyers' Edition	L Ed 2d
New York Supplement	NYS
North Eastern Reporter	NE
North Western Reporter	NW
Pacific Reporter	P
South Eastern Reporter	SE
South Western Reporter	SW
Southern Reporter	So
Supreme Court Reporter	S Ct
United States Reports	US
United States Law Week	USLW

➢ For the United States Supreme Court, cite reporters in the following order of preference: **US → S Ct → L Ed 2d → USLW**.

➢ For federal courts, cite to F or F Supp.

➢ For state courts, cite to a regional reporter in preference to a state reporter.

➢ See **Appendix C** for a list of common reporters and their abbreviations.

7.2.2.5 Pinpoint

United States v McVeigh, 153 F3d 1166 at 1170 (10th Cir 1998). *McVeigh, supra* note 1 at 1173.

➢ Place at before a pinpoint reference.

7.2.2.6 Court

7.2.2.6.1   Federal Courts

United States Supreme Court	*Bush v Gore*, 531 US 98 (2000).
	Boy Scouts of America v Dale, 68 USLW 4625 (US 28 June 2000).
Courts of Appeal	*United States v Kaczynski*, 154 F 3d 930 (9th Cir 1998).
District Courts	*A&M Records v Napster*, 114 F Supp 2d 896 (ND Cal 2000).

➢ The **United States Supreme Court** does not require an abbreviation unless the citation is to the *United States Law Week* (USLW). When citing to the USLW, place US and the full date in parentheses at the end of the citation.

➢ For Courts of Appeal cite the numbered circuit.

➢ Abbreviate the **District of Columbia Circuit Court** to DC Cir and the **Federal Circuit Court** to Fed Cir.

➢ For district courts provide the abbreviated name of the district.

7.2.2.6.2   State Courts

➢ Provide the court and the jurisdiction in parentheses, using the abbreviations from **Appendices A-2 and B**.

➢ Omit the jurisdiction if it is obvious from the name of the reporter.

➢ Omit the court if it is the highest court in its jurisdiction.

> *Peevyhouse v Garland Coal & Mining*, 382 P 2d 109 (Okla Sup Ct 1963).
>
> *Truman v Thomas*, 165 Cal Rptr 308 (1980).
>
> *Hinterlong v Baldwin*, 308 Ill App 3d 441 (App Ct 1999).

7.2.2.7 Year of Decision

➢ Place the year of decision in parentheses at the end of the citation. If there is also a court abbreviation, combine the two within the same parentheses ((App Ct 1999)).

7.2.3   Government Documents

Indicate US at the beginning of the citation.

7.2.3.1 Debates

US,	*Cong Rec*,	edition,	volume,	part,	pinpoint	(date)	(speaker) (optional).
US,	*Cong Rec*,		vol 125,	15,	at 18691	(1979).	
US,	*Cong Rec*,	daily ed,	vol 143,	69,	at H3176	(22 May 1977)	(Rep Portman).

➢ Cite congressional debates after 1873 to the ***Congressional Record*** (Cong Rec).

➢ For information on how to cite earlier congressional debates, consult the *Bluebook*.

➢ Use the **daily edition** only if the debate is not yet in the bound edition.

7.2.3.2 Committee Hearings

7.2.3.2.1   Federal

US,	*title,*	Congress number	(publication information)	pinpoint	(speaker) (optional).
US,	*Federal Property Campaign Fundraising Reform Act of 2000: Hearing on HR 4845 Before the House Committee of the Judiciary,*	106th Cong	(2000)	at 2-3.	
US,	*Assisted Suicide: Legal, Medical, Ethical and Social Issues: Hearing Before the Subcommittee on Health and Environment of the House Committee on Commerce,*	105th Cong	(Washington, DC: United States Government Printing Office, 1997)	at 2	(Dr C Everett Koop).

➢ Always cite the year of publication, and provide further publication information if available.

7.2.3.2.2   State

US,	*title,*	number of the legislative body or, if not numbered, the year,	legislature number or designation,	state	(publication information)	pin-point	(speaker) (optional).
US,	*Rico Litigation: Hearing on S 1197 Before the Senate Comm. On Commerce and Econ Dev,*	41st Legis,	1st Reg Sess 5,	Ariz	(1993)		(Barry Wong, policy analyst).

➢ Abbreviate the state according to the list in **Appendix A-2**.

➢ Always cite the year of publication, and provide further publication information if available.

7.2.3.3 Reports and Documents

7.2.3.3.1   Federal

7.2.3.3.1.1   Numbered Documents and Reports

US,	issuing body,	title	(number)	(publication information)	pinpoint.
US,		*Secrecy: Report of the Commission on Protecting and Reducing Government Secrecy: Pursuant to Public Law 236, 103rd Congress*	(S Doc No 105-2)	(Washington, DC: US Government Printing Office, 1997)	at 3.
US,	Senate Committee on the Budget, 111th Cong,	*Concurrent Resolution on the Budget FY 2010*		(Washington, DC: US Government Printing Office, 2009)	at 213.

> Indicate the issuing body unless it is named in the title of the report.

> Always cite the year of publication, and provide further publication information if available.

Abbreviations of numbers:

Documents	Reports
HR Doc No	HR Rep No
HR Misc Doc No	HR Conf Rep No
S Doc No	S Rep No
S Exec Doc No	

7.2.3.3.1.2   Unnumbered Documents and Committee Prints

US,	issuing body,	title,	Committee Print (if relevant)	(publication information)	pinpoint.
US,	Staff of House Committee on Veterans' Affairs, 105th Cong,	*Persian Gulf Illnesses: An Overview,*	Committee Print	(1998)	at 15.
US,	National Commission on Children,	*Beyond Rhetoric: A New American Agenda for Children and Families,*		(Washington, DC: The Commission, 1991)	at 41.

➢ Include the Congress number with the issuing body, if relevant.

➢ Always cite the year of publication, and provide further publication information if available.

7.2.3.3.2   State

	US,	issuing body,	*title*	(number) (if applicable)	(publication information)	pinpoint.
Numbered Documents and Reports	US,	California Energy Commission,	Existing Renewable Resources Account, vol 1	(500-01-014V1)	(2001).	
Unnumbered Documents	US,	Washington State Transport Commission,	*Washington's Transportation Plan 2003-2022*		(Washington State Department of Transportation, 2002).	

➢ Provide the document number, if available.

➢ Always cite the year of publication, and provide further publication information if available.

7.3   FRANCE

7.3.1   Legislation

7.3.1.1   Statutes and Other Legislative Instruments

Title,	JO,	publication date	(NC) (if applicable),	page	other source.
Loi n° 99-493 du 15 juin 1999,	JO,	16 June 1999,		8759,	(1999) D Lég 3.7.
Ordonnance n° 2001-766 du 29 août 2001,	JO,	31 August 2001		13946,	(2001) D Lég 2564.
Décret du 5 décembre 1978 portant classement d'un site pittoresque,	JO,	6 December 1978	(NC),	9250.	

➢ Cite the title of the statute in French, but provide the date of publication and all related information in English.

➢ If the legislation has a number, then the descriptive title is optional. If the legislation does not have a number, include its descriptive title in full.

➢ Always cite first to the *Journal officiel de la République française*, abbreviated to JO, followed by the publication date and the page number. For JO supplements, place (NC) for *numéro complémentaire* after the publication date. For a list of earlier versions of the *Journal officiel*, see section 4.4.2.

➢ When possible, provide a citation to a French reporter, according to the rules at section 7.3.2.10.

7.3.1.2 Codes

Code civil des Français (1804-1807)	art 85 CcF
Code Napoléon (1807-1814)	art 85 CN
Code civil (1815-)	art 1536 C civ
Code pénal	art 113-10 C pén
Nouveau Code de procédure civile	art 1439 NC proc civ
Code de propriété intellectuelle	art 123(8) CPI
Code de procédure pénale	art 144(2) C proc pén

➢ Never use full citations when referring to codes.

➢ To cite to one of the codes illustrated here, use the abbreviated name.

➢ To cite to another code, write the full title of the code at the first reference, and create a short form if needed (e.g. art 1 *Code de la consommation* [C cons]).

7.3.2 Jurisprudence

➢ Always use the **page numbers at the top** of the pages of *La semaine juridique* and not the numbers at the bottom.

7.3.2.1 General Form

Court (if applic-able)	city (if applic-able),	date,	style of cause (if applic-able),	(year of publica-tion)	reporter	section (if applic-able),	page and/or decision number	(Annota-tion) (if applicable).
Cour de Cassation	Cass civ 2ᵉ		14 June 2001,	(2001)	D	Jur,	3075	(Annotation Didier Cholet).
Court of Appeal	CA	Paris,	12 January 2000,	(2000)	JCP	II,	10433	(Annotation Philippe Pierre).
Court of First Instance	Trib gr inst	Mans,	7 September 1999,	(2000)	JCP	II,	10258	(Annotation Colette Saujot).

7.3.2.2 Court

7.3.2.2.1   Courts of First Instance

Court	city,	date,	style of cause (if applicable),	(year of public-ation	session) (if applicable)	reporter	section (if applicable)	page	(Annota-tion) (if applicable).
Trib admin	Nantes,	27 November 1981,	Mme Robin,	(1981)		Rec		544.	
Trib gr inst	Paris,	10 September 1998,		(1999	1re sem)	Gaz Pal	Jur	37.	

> Indicate the city where the court sits after the name of the court.

Abbreviations of the names of the courts:

Tribunal administratif	Trib admin
Tribunal civil or Tribunal de première instance (Civil court of original general jurisdiction, prior to 1958)	Trib civ
Tribunal commercial	Trib com
Tribunal correctionnel	Trib corr
Tribunal de grande instance (Civil court of original general jurisdiction, after 1958)	Trib gr inst
Tribunal d'instance (Small claims court, after 1958)	Trib inst

For a more complete list, see **Appendix B**.

7.3.2.2.2   Court of Appeal

CA	city,	date,	style of cause (if applic-able)	(year of publica-tion	session) (if applic-able)	reporter	section	page,	decision number	(Annotation).
CA	Orléans,	23 October 1997,		(1999	1re sem)	Gaz Pal	Jur	217,		(Annotation Benoît de Roquefeuil).
CA	Paris,	21 mai 2008,	K c E et Sté nationale de télévision France 2	(2008)		JCP	Jur	390,	No 06/07678.	

7.3.2.2.3   Cour de cassation

Chamber,	date,	(year of publication)	reporter	section	page,	decision number (if applicable).
Cass civ 1re,	30 March 1999,	(1999)	Bull civ	I	77,	No 118.
Cass crim,	24 February 2009,	(2009)	D Jur		951,	No 08-87.409.

Abbreviations of chambers:

Chambre civile	Cass civ 1re
	Cass civ 2^e
	Cass civ 3^e
Chambre commerciale	Cass com
Chambre sociale	Cass soc
Chambre criminelle	Cass crim
Chambre des requêtes	Cass req
Chambres réunies (before 1967)	Cass Ch réun
Assemblée plénière (after 1967)	Cass Ass plén
Chambre mixte	Cass mixte

7.3.2.2.4   Conseil d'État

Court,	date,	style of cause,	(year of publication)	reporter	page.
CE,	27 January 1984,	*Ordre des avocats de la Polynésie française*,	(1984)	Rec	20.

➤ Abbreviate *Conseil d'État* to CE.

7.3.2.2.5   Conseil constitutionnel

Court,	date,	style of cause,	(year of publication)	reporter	page,	decision number.
Cons const,	25 June 1986,	*Privatisations*,	(1986)	Rec	61,	86-207 DC.

➤ Abbreviate **Conseil constitutionnel** to Cons const.

➤ Indicate the decision number at the end of the citation.

7.3.2.3 Style of Cause

Cass civ 1re, 5 February 1968, *Ligny-Luxembourg*, (1968 1re sem) Gaz Pal Jur 264.

➤ **Omit the style of cause except in the following circumstances:**

→ when citing a decision from an administrative tribunal or the Conseil d'État (but not in every case);

→ when citing an unpublished decision or one that is summarized in the *Sommaire* section of a reporter;

→ to avoid confusion (e.g. where two decisions were rendered on the same day by the same court);

→   when the case is better known by the names of the parties than by the usual information.

➢   When the style of cause is included, italicize it and place it after the date, set off by commas.

7.3.2.4 Year

Paris, 5 February 1999, (1999 2ᵉ sem) Gaz Pal Jur 452.

➢   Include the year of publication in parentheses, before the abbreviation of the reporter.

7.3.2.5 Session

➢   When citing the *Gazette du Palais* (Gaz Pal), indicate the session number in the parentheses, after the year of publication.

7.3.2.6 Reporter

Court,	date,	year of publication of reporter	session number) (if applicable)	reporter	section	page and/ or decision number.
Cass civ 3ᵉ,	23 June 1999,	(2000)		JCP	II	10333.
Cass soc,	3 February 1998,	(1998	1ʳᵉ sem)	Gaz Pal	Jur	176.

➢   Add a space between every information ((2000 1ʳᵉ sem) Gaz Pal Jur 176).

Common French reporters:

Actualité juridique de droit administratif	AJDA
Bulletin de la Cour de cassation, section civile	Bull civ
Gazette du Palais	Gaz Pal
Recueil Dalloz and Recueil Dalloz et Sirey (1945-present)	D
Recueil des décisions du Conseil d'État or Recueil Lebon	RCE or Rec
Semaine Juridique (1937-present)	JCP

See **Appendix C** for more French reporter abbreviations.

7.3.2.7 Section

➢   When the sections in the volume are numbered, indicate the section number in Roman numerals after the year of publication.

Foreign Sources

➤ When the sections are not numbered, provide the abbreviation of the section title.

➤ Do not include the section when citing the **Recueil Lebon** (Rec) or the **Actualité juridique de droit administratif** (AJDA).

Abbreviation of section titles:

Assemblée plénière	Ass plén
Chambre mixte	Ch Mixte
Chambres des requêtes	Req
Chambres réunies	Ch réun
Chroniques	Chron
Doctrine	Doctr
Informations rapides	Inf
Jurisprudence	Jur
Législation, Lois et décrets, Textes de lois, etc.	Lég
Panorama de jurisprudence	Pan
Sommaire	Somm

7.3.2.8 Page and Decision Number

Semaine juridique	Ass plén, 6 November 1998, (1999) JCP II 10000 bis.
Bulletin de la Cour de cassation	Cass civ 2ᵉ, 7 June 2001, (2001) Bull civ II 75, No 110.

➤ Indicate the page number after the section or the year of publication.

➤ For the **Semaine Juridique**, provide the decision number (e.g. 10000 bis).

➤ For the **Bulletin de la Cour de cassation** cite both the page and decision number separated by a comma and a space.

7.3.2.9 Pinpoint

Trib gr inst Narbonne, 12 March 1999, (1999 1ʳᵉ sem) Gaz Pal Jur 405 at 406.

➤ Pinpoint citations are rarely used given the brevity of most decisions. If required, it is always placed after the page number and introduced by at.

7.3.2.10 Other Sources

First citation,	other source.
Cass civ 1ʳᵉ, 26 May 1999, (1999) Bull civ I 115, No 175,	(1999) JCP II 10112.
Cass crim, 21 janvier 2009, (2009) Bull crim 74, n° 08-83.492,	(2009) D Jur 374.

7.3.2.11 *Annotations, Reports, and Conclusions*

Cass civ 1ʳᵉ, 6 juillet 1999, (1999) JCP II 10217 (Annotataion Thierry Garé).

> ➤ Any annotation or other writing appended to or included with a case must be indicated at the end of the citation, in parentheses.

> ➤ Write Annotation, Report, or Conclusion followed by the author's name.

7.3.3 Government Documents

Indicate France at the beginning of the citation of every government document.

7.3.3.1 *Debates*

7.3.3.1.1 From 1787 to 1860

France,	*Archives parlementaires,*	series,	tome,	date,	pinpoint	(speaker) (optional).
France,	*Archives parlementaires,*	1st series,	t 83,	5 January 1794,	s 3.	

> ➤ Cite to *Archives parlementaires : Recueil complet des débats législatifs et politiques des chambres françaises*, using the short title *Archives parlementaires*.

> ➤ Indicate the series after the title. The first series covers 1787-1799, the second 1800-1860.

> ➤ Pinpoint to sections, not to articles.

> ➤ Add the name of the speaker (if provided) in parentheses at the end of the citation.

7.3.3.1.2   1871 to the Present

France,	*journal,*	house,	Débats parlementaires,	division,	number and date,	pin-point,	(speaker) (optional).
France,	JO,	Assemblée nationale,	Débats parlementaires,	Compte rendu intégral,	2nd session of 10 February 2004,	at 1570,	(Pascal Clément).
France,	JO,	Sénat,	Débats parlementaires,	Compte rendu intégral,	Session of 20 November 2003.		

> ➤ From 1871 to the present, parliamentary debates are published in the ***Journal officiel de la République française***, abbreviated *JO*.

> → Indicate the house, followed by Débats parlementaires.
> → 1871-1880: omit both the house and Débats parlementaires.

→ 1943-1945; 1945-1946; 1947-1958: indicate only Débats de [name of house].

Names of houses according to the period:

1881-1940	Chambre des députés	1880-1940	Sénat
1943-1945	Assemblée consultative provisoire		
1945-1946	Assemblée constituante		
1947-1958	Assemblée de l'Union française	1946-1958	Conseil de la République
1958-	Assemblée nationale	1958-	Sénat

➢ Indicate the division only from 1980 to the present for the Assemblée nationale, and from 1983 to the present for the Sénat. The divisions are Compte rendu intégral and Questions écrites remises à la Présidence de l'Assemblée nationale et réponses des ministres for the Assemblée nationale, and Compte rendu intégral and Questions remises à la Présidence du Sénat et réponses des ministres aux questions écrites for the Sénat.

➢ Indicate the number (if provided) and the date of the session followed by the pinpoint.

➢ The name of the speaker may be added in parentheses at the end of the citation.

7.3.3.2 Earlier Versions of the Journal officiel

France,	title,	year or date of publication,	tome or volume	pinpoint.
France,	Journal officiel de l'Empire français,	1868,	t 1	at 14.
France,	Gazette nationale, ou le Moniteur universel,	1 July 1791,	t 9	at 3.

➢ **Before 1871**, parliamentary debates, parliamentary documents, and non-parliamentary documents were generally published in the various precursors to the *Journal officiel de la République française*:

1789-1810	Gazette nationale, ou le Moniteur universel
1811-1848	Moniteur universel
1848-1852	Moniteur universel, Journal officiel de la République
1852-1870	Journal officiel de l'Empire français

➢ The citation form varies according to the organization of the journal. In general, the citation should include at least the title, the year in question or the date of publication, the tome or volume (if any), and the pinpoint.

7.3.3.3 *Parliamentary Documents*

7.3.3.3.1   Travaux et réunions parlementaires

France,	house,	issuing body,	"title",	Compte rendu or *Bulletin*	(date)	(President) (optional).
France,	Assemblée nationale,	Délégation aux droits des femmes,	"Auditions sur le suivi de l'application des lois relatives à l'IVG et à la contraception",	Compte rendu No 4	(6 November 2001)	(President: Martine Lignières-Cassou).
France,	Sénat,	Commission des affaires étrangères,	"Auditions de M. Dominique de Villepin, Ministre des affaires étrangères",	*Bulletin* de la semaine du 27 janvier 2003	(28 January 2003)	(President: André Dulait).

> ➢ Indicate the title of the *travaux*, then the number of the corresponding *Compte rendu* (for *travaux* of the Assemblée nationale) or the date of the *Bulletin* (for *travaux* of the Sénat). Unlike Compte rendu, *Bulletin* should be in italics.

> ➢ Add the name of the president (if provided) in parentheses at the end of the citation.

7.3.3.3.2   Rapports d'information (Reports)

France,	house,	issuing body (if applicable),	title,	by author(s),	report number	(date)	pinpoint.
France,	Sénat,	Délégation pour l'Union européenne,	*Le projet de traité établissant une Constitution pour l'Europe,*	by Hubert Haenel,	Report No 3	(1 October 2003)	at 4.
France,	Assemblée nationale,		*Rapport d'information déposé en application de l'article 145 du Règlement par la mission d'information commune sur le prix des carburants dans les départements d'outre-mer,*	by Jacques Le Guen & Jérôme Cahuzac,	Report No 1885	(23 July 2009)	at p 63.

7.3.3.4 *Non-parliamentary Documents*

France,	issuing body,	title,	report number or volume,	publication information	pinpoint	(additional information) (optional).
France,		*Commission d'enquête sur la sécurité du transport maritime des produits dangereux ou polluants,*	Report No 2535, vol 1,			(5 July 2000 President: Daniel Paul).
France,	Conseil économique et social,	*La conjoncture économique et sociale en 2005,*		Avis et rapports du Conseil économique et social, *JO*, No 2005-09	at I-8	(1 June 2005 report by Luc Guyau).
France,	Ministère de la justice,	*Bulletin officiel,*	No 82		at 3	(1 April-30 June 2001).

➤ Follow the rules for Canadian non-parliamentary documents in section 4.2.

7.4   AUSTRALIA

7.4.1   Legislation

7.4.1.1 *Statutes*

Title	(jurisdiction),	pinpoint.
Corporations Act 2001	(Cth).	
Electricity Reform Act 2001	(NT).	
Marine Pollution Act 1987	(NSW),	s 53(1)(d).

➤ Cite the act's official short title in italics. Include the year of act as part of the title.

➤ Place the abbreviation of the jurisdiction after the title.

Abbreviations of jurisdictions:

Commonwealth	Cth
Australian Capital Territory	ACT
New South Wales	NSW
Northern Territory	NT
Queensland	Qld
South Australia	SA
Tasmania	Tas
Victoria	Vic
Western Australia	WA

Statutory compilations:

Acts of Parliament of the Commonwealth of Australia	*Queensland Statutes*
Laws of the Australian Capital Territory, Acts	*South Australia Statutes*
Statutes of New South Wales	*Tasmanian Statutes*
Northern Territory of Australia Laws	*Acts of the Victorian Parliament*
Laws of the Northern Territory of Australia	*Victorian Statutes*
Queensland Acts	*Statutes of Western Australia*

7.4.1.2 Delegated Legislation (Regulations)

Title	(regulatory compilations or session laws),	pinpoint.
Admiralty Rules 2002	(Cth),	r 5(b).
Income Tax Regulations (Amendment) 1996	(Cth).	
Education Regulation 2005	(ACT),	s 5.

➢ Regulations and Rules generally follow the same style as statutes (section 7.4.1.1).

Compilations of regulations:

Commonwealth Statutory Rules
Laws of the Australian Capital Territory, Subordinate Legislation
New South Wales Rules, Regulations, and By-Laws
Queensland Subordinate Legislation
Tasmanian Statutory Rules
Victorian Statutory Rules, Regulations, and By-Laws
Western Australia Subsidiary Legislation

7.4.2   Jurisprudence

7.4.2.1 General Form

Style of cause,	*(year),*	neutral citation,	[year of reporter]	vol	reporter	page	(court) (if required).
Neilson v Overseas Projects Corporation of Victoria Ltd,		[2005] HCA 54.					
Macleod v Australian Securities and Investment Commission,		[2002] HCA 37,		211	CLR	287.	
Standard Portland Cement Company Pty Ltd v Good,	(1983),			57	ALJR	151	(PC).
Thwaites v Ryan,	(1983),		[1984]		VR	65	(SC).

7.4.2.2 Neutral Citation

Many Australian courts have adopted the neutral citation. Neutral citation in Australia follows the same format as Canadian neutral

[year]	court	number	pinpoint.
[2005]	HCA	54	¶ 15.

citation (section 3.5) except that the year is placed in square brackets.

7.4.2.3 Reporter

7.4.2.3.1   Law Reports

Abbreviations of the series for the *Law Reports*:

Commonwealth Law Reports (1903-present)—Official	CLR
Australian Law Reports (1973-present)	ALR
Federal Court Reports (1984-present)—Official	FCR
Federal Law Reports (1956-present)	FLR
Australian Law Journal Reports (1958-present)	ALJR
New South Wales Law Reports (1971-present)—Official	NSWLR
Queensland State Reports (1902-1957)—Official	Qd SR
Queensland Reports (1958-present)—Official	Qd R
South Australia State Reports (1922-present)—Official	SASR
Tasmanian Law Reports (1896-1940)—Official	Tas LR
Tasmanian State Reports (1941-1978)	Tas R
Tasmanian Reports (1979-present)—Official	Tas R
Victorian Law Reports (1875-1956)	VLR
Victorian Reports (1957-present)—Official	VR
Western Australia Law Reports (1899-1959)	WALR
Western Australia Law Reports (1960-present)—Official	WAR
Australian Capital Territory Reports (1973-present)	ACTR
Northern Territory Reports (1978-present)	NTR
Northern Territory Law Reports (1992-present)	NTLR

➢ For **Privy Council** (PC) and **High Court of Australia** (HCA) decisions, cite to (in order of preference): CLR, ALR.

➢ For other federal court decisions, cite to the official FCR before FLR.

➢ For Australian States and Territories, cite to the official state or territorial court reporter when possible.

Foreign Sources

7.4.2.4 *Jurisdiction and Court*

Abbreviations of the courts:

Court	Abbreviation and identifiers
Privy Council (Australia)	PC
High Court of Australia	HCA
Federal Court of Australia	FCA
Supreme Court of Queensland—Court of Appeal	QCA
Supreme Court of Queensland	QSC
Supreme Court of the Australian Capital Territory	ACTSC
Supreme Court of New South Wales	NSWSC
Supreme Court of New South Wales—Court of Appeal	NSWCA
Supreme Court of Tasmania	TASSC
Supreme Court of Victoria—Court of Appeal	VSCA
Supreme Court of Victoria	VSC
Supreme Court of Southern Australia	SASC
District Court of Southern Australia	SADC
Supreme Court of Western Australia	WASC
Supreme Court of Western Australia—Court of Appeal	WASCA
Supreme Court of the Northern Territory	NTSC

➢ For state and territorial courts, if the jurisdiction is evident from the reporter cited, only indicate the level of court.

7.4.3 Government Documents

Place **Austl** at the beginning of the citation.

7.4.3.1 *Debates*

Austl,	jurisdiction,	house,	*Parliamentary Debates*	(date)	pinpoint	(speaker) (optional).
Austl,	Commonwealth,	House of Representatives,	*Parliamentary Debates*	(17 September 2001)	at 30739	(Mr Howard, Prime Minister).
Austl,	Victoria,	Legislative Assembly,	*Parliamentary Debates*	(23 October 1968)	at 1197.	

➢ After **Austl**, indicate the jurisdiction. See **Appendix A-3** for Australian abbreviations.

➢ Always indicate the reporter as Parliamentary Debates.

7.4.3.2 Parliamentary Papers

Austl,	jurisdiction,	title,	number	(year)	pinpoint.
Austl,	Commonwealth,	Department of Foreign Affairs Annual Report 1975,	Parl Paper No 142	(1976)	at 5.
Austl,	Commonwealth,	Community Affairs Legislation Committee – Senate Standing – Compliance Audits on Medicare Benefits,	Parl Paper No 118.		

> ➢ The number is preceded by **Parl Paper No.**

7.4.3.3 Non-Parliamentary Papers

Austl,	jurisdiction,	issuing body,	title	(nature of paper)	by author(s) (if applicable)	(publication information)	pinpoint.
Austl,	Common-wealth,	Royal Commission into Aboriginal Deaths in Custody,	Report of the Inquiry into the Death of Stanley John Gollan		by Commissioner Elliott Johnston	(Canberra: Australian Government Publishing Service, 1990)	at 31.
Austl,	Common-wealth,	Law Reform Commission,	Annual Report 1998	(Report No 49)		(Canberra: Australian Government Publishing Service, 1988).	

7.4.3.4 Ministerial Documents

Author,	jurisdiction,	title,	document service,	number	(date)	pinpoint.
Paul Keating,	Commonwealth (Austl),	Opening of the Global Cultural Diversity Conference,	Ministerial Document Service,	No 172/94-95	(27 April 1995)	at 5977.

> ➢ If additional information is required to identify the jurisdiction as within Australia, include **Austl** in parentheses following the jurisdiction named and before the comma preceding the title.

7.5   NEW ZEALAND

7.5.1   Legislation

7.5.1.1 *Statutes*

Title	(NZ),	year/number,	volume RS	first page.
Abolition of the Death Penalty Act 1989	(NZ),	1989/119,	41 RS	1.
Kiwifruit Industry Restructuring Act 1999	(NZ),	1999/95.		

> ➤ Provide the volume number followed by RS (for Reprint Series).

7.5.1.2 *Delegated Legislation (Regulations)*

Title	(NZ),	year/number or Gazette year,	*Gazette* page	vol RS	page.
Kiwifruit Export Regulations 1999	(NZ),	1999/310.			
Ticketing of Meat Notice 1979	(NZ),	Gazette 1979,	2030.		
High Court Amendment Rules (No 2) 1987	(NZ),	1987/169,		40 RS	904.

> ➤ Provide the volume number followed by RS (for Reprint Series).

7.5.2   Jurisprudence

7.5.2.1 *General Form*

Style of cause,	(year of decision),	neutral citation	[year of reporter]	volume	reporter	page	(jurisdiction and/or court) (if applicable).
R v Clarke,		[2005] NZSC 60.					
Pfizer v Commissioner of Patents,			[2005]	1	NZLR	362	(HC).

7.5.2.2 *Neutral Citation*

> ➤ The Supreme Court of New Zealand officially adopted the use of neutral citation for judgments rendered

[Year]	court	number of decision	pinpoint.
[2005]	NZSC	46	¶ 4.

during and after 2005. Neutral citation in New Zealand follows the same format as Canadian neutral citation (section 3.5) except that the year is placed in square brackets.

Foreign Sources

7.5.2.3 Reporter

7.5.2.3.1   Law Reports

➤ *Law Reports* are divided into series. **Reference is not made to the *Law Reports* but rather to the series**.

➤ There is no separate reporter for the **Judicial Committee of the Privy Council** (post-1932), the **Court of Appeal**, or the **High Court**. Include abbreviations PC, CA, or HC at the end of each citation to a case heard in that court.

Abbreviations of the series for the *Law Reports*:

New Zealand Law Reports (1883-present) (Privy Council, Supreme Court of New Zealand, Court of Appeal, High Court)	NZLR
New Zealand Privy Council Cases (1840-1932)	NZPCC
Gazette Law Reports (1898-1953) (Court of Appeal, Supreme Court (High Court), Court of Arbitration)	GLR
District Court Reports (1980-present)	NZDCR
Magistrates' Court Decisions (1939-1979)	MCD
Magistrates' Court Reports (1906-1953)	MCR
Book of Awards (1894-1991) (Arbitration Court, Court of Appeal)	BA
Employment Reports of New Zealand (1991-present) (Court of Appeal, Labour Court, Aircrew Industrial Tribunal)	ERNZ
New Zealand Industrial Law Reports (1987-1990) (Labour Court, Court of Appeal, Aircrew Industrial Tribunal)	NZILR
Judgments of the Arbitration Court of New Zealand (1979-1986) (Arbitration Court, Court of Appeal)	NZAC
New Zealand Family Law Reports (1981-present) (Privy Council, Court of Appeal, High Court, Family Court, Youth Court, District Court)	NZFLR
Criminal Reports of New Zealand (1993-present) (Court of Appeal, High Court)	CRNZ

7.5.2.4 Court

Privy Council (New Zealand)	PC
New Zealand Supreme Court – established in 2004	NZSC
New Zealand Court of Appeal	NZCA
New Zealand High Court	NZHC
District Court of New Zealand	DCNZ
Magistrates' Court of New Zealand	Mag Ct NZ
Coroners Court	Cor Ct
New Zealand Employment Court	NZ Empl Ct
Environment Court	Env Ct
Family Court of New Zealand	Fam Ct NZ
Maori Land Court / *Te Kooti Whenua Maori*	Maori Land Ct
Maori Appellate Court	Maori AC
New Zealand Youth Court	NZYC
Waitangi Tribunal / *Te Rōpū Whakamana i te Tiriti o Waitangi*	Waitangi Trib

NB: The ***Supreme Court Act 2003*** established the Supreme Court of New Zealand and abolished appeals from New Zealand to the Privy Council.

7.5.3   Government Documents

Indicate NZ at the beginning of the citation.

7.5.3.1 Debates

NZ,	*Hansard,*	stage: subject	(question number)	date	(speaker) (optional).
NZ,	*Hansard,*	Questions To Ministers: Biosecurity Risk-Motor Vehicle and Equipment Imports	(No 3)	1 March 2000	(Ian Ewen-Street).

➢   *Hansard* provides the type of stage: Questions to Ministers, Debate-General, Report of [a named] Committee or Miscellaneous.

➢   Indicate the title of the debate as the subject (e.g. Labour, Associate Minister-Accountability). If the stage and the subject are the same, do not repeat the information.

7.5.3.2 Parliamentary Papers

NZ,	"title",	date,	session	(chair) (optional)	shoulder number.
NZ,	"Report of the Government Administration Committee, Inquiry into New Zealand's Adoption Laws",	August 2001,	46th Parliament	(Dianne Yates, Chair).	
NZ,	"Report of the Game Bird Habitat Trust Board for the year ended 31 August 1999",	February 2000,			C.22.

➤ Do not add a space between the prefix of the shoulder and the actual number. The prefix of the shoulder number indicates the subject group, as follows:

Subject groups
A. Political and Foreign Affairs
B. Finance and Revenue
C. Environment and Primary Production
D. Energy and Works
E. Welfare and Justice
F. Communications
G. General
H. Commissions, Royal Commissions

7.6   SINGAPORE

7.6.1   Legislation

NB: If there is no other indication that the legislative document is from Singapore, write Rev Ed Sing instead of Rev Ed.

7.6.1.1 Constitutional Documents

➤ Cite constitutional amendments in the same manner as ordinary legislation.

➤ Revised Edition is abbreviated to Rev Ed.

> *Constitution of the Republic of Singapore* (1999 Rev Ed), art 12(1).
>
> *Independence of Singapore Agreement 1965* (1985 Rev Ed).
>
> *Republic of Singapore Independence Act* (1985 Rev Ed), No 9 of 1965, s 2.

7.6.1.2 *Statutes*

Statutes from the Revised Edition	*Penal Code* (Cap 224, 1985 Rev Ed Sing), s 34.
Statutes not yet assigned a *Revised Edition* chapter number	*United Nations Act 2001* (No 44 of 2001, Sing), s 2.

➢   ***Revised Edition of the Statutes of the Republic of Singapore*** is abbreviated to Rev Ed Sing.

➢   Cap refers to Chapter. For recent acts that have not yet been assigned a chapter number in a revised edition, use the act number as in the example above. The act number is not to be confused with the Acts Supplement number, which is a number given to each supplement of the Government *Gazette* publishing subsequent amendments to the act.

➢   For legislation **prior to 15 August 1945**, the following abbreviations should be inserted after the title of the statute:

→   For legislation enacted during the **Straits Settlements period** (1 April 1867 to 15 February 1942) use (SS).

→   For legislation enacted by the **Japanese Military Administration** during the occupation of Singapore (15 February 1942 to 15 August 1945) use (JMA).

➢   For legislation enacted **after 15 August 1945**, write (Sing) to cite legislation passed during the following periods:

→   British Military Administration;

→   Colony of Singapore;

→   State of Singapore, both before and during federation with Malaysia; and

→   Republic of Singapore.

7.6.1.3 *Amendments and Repeals*

Penal Code (Cap 224, 1985 Rev Ed Sing), s 73, as amended by *Penal Code (Amendment) Act*, No 18 of 1998, s 2.

Control of Imports and Exports Act (cap 56, 1985 Ref Ed Sing), as amended by *Regulation of Imports and Exports Act 1995* (No 24 of 1995).

➢   For further information, see section 2.1.1.8.

7.6.1.4 English Statutes Applicable in Singapore

> English statutes now applicable in Singapore under the *Application of English Law Act* (Cap 7A,

Misrepresentation Act (Cap 390, 1994 Rev Ed Sing), s 2.
Hire-Purchase Act (Cap 125, 1999 Rev Ed), s 5.

1994 Rev Ed Sing) may be cited to their Singapore revised edition in the same manner as Singapore statutes.

7.6.1.5 Subsidiary Legislation (Rules, Regulations, Notifications, Orders)

7.6.1.5.1   Revised

Title	(Chapter number, legislation type and number, year Rev Ed Sing),	pinpoint.
Housing and Development Conveyancing Fees Rules	(Cap 129, R 2, 1999 Rev Ed Sing),	r 2.
Telecommunications (Class Licenses) Regulations	(Cap 323, Reg 3, 2000 Rev Ed Sing),	reg 10.

> When citing to revised subsidiary legislation, the chapter (Cap) refers to the chapter number of the parent legislation.

> For legislation type, use Reg for **regulation**, R for **rule**, N for **notification** or O for **order**, followed by the number.

> The year indicated should refer to the Revised Edition where the subsidiary legislation is found.

> **Revised Edition** is abbreviated to Rev Ed.

> Pinpoint using reg for **regulation**, r for **rule**, o for **order** or n for **notification**. Note that the type of pinpoint may differ from the type of instrument (e.g. a rule may contain orders).

7.6.1.5.2   Unrevised

Title	(S number/year Sing),	pinpoint.
United Nations (Anti-Terrorism Measures) Regulations 2001	(S 561/2001 Sing),	reg 3.
Monetary Authority of Singapore (Merchant Banks – Annual Fees) Notification 2005	(S 405/2005 Sing),	n 2(2).
Payment and Settlement Systems (finality and Netting) (Designated System) Order 2002	(S 620/2002 Sing),	o 3(a).

7.6.2 Jurisprudence

7.6.2.1 General Form

Style of cause,	(year of decision),	neutral citation,	[year of reporter]	volume	reporter	page	(court) (if applicable).
Er Joo Nguang v Public Prosecutor,			[2000]	2	SLR	645	(HC).
Firstlink Energy Pte. Ltd v Creanovate Pte Ltd,		[2006] SGHC 19.					
Re Ong Yew Teck,	(1960),			26	MLJ	67	(Sing HC).

➢ In Singapore, unlike Canada, because of the plurality of cultural practices governing names, always provide the full name of individuals.

➢ Include the abbreviation Sing in parentheses at the end of the citation unless the citation is from the *Singapore Law Reports* or its reissue.

7.6.2.2 Neutral Citation

➢ Singapore courts have officially adopted a neutral citation. The form is the same as that of Canadian neutral citation, with the exception that the year is placed in brackets (section 3.5).

[year]	court	decision number	pinpoint.
[2005]	SGCA	55	[11].

➢ Provide the paragraph number in brackets (e.g. [11]).

➢ The Supreme Court established that citation to the Singapore Law Reports prevail over the neutral citation.

7.6.2.3 Reporters

Abbreviations of the principal reporters:

Singapore Law Reports	SLR
Singapore Law Reports (Reissue) (1965-2002)	SLR (R)
Malayan Law Journal	MLJ
Criminal Law Aid Scheme News	CLASN
Straits Settlements Law Reports	SSLR

➢ *Singapore Law Reports (Reissue)* for the years 1965-2002 changed in the headnotes and numbered the paragraphs. The reissued volumes are as authoritative as the original *Singapore Law Reports*.

Foreign Sources

7.6.2.4 Court

Court abbreviations:

Court	abbrev	identifier
Court of Appeal	CA	SGCA
High Court	HC	SGHC
District Court	Dist Ct	SGDC
Magistrates' Court	Mag Ct	SGMC

➢   District Courts have no subdivisions.

7.6.2.5 Unreported Decisions without Neutral Citation

Style of cause	(date),	case number	(jurisdiction and/or court) (if applicable).
Public Prosecutor v Loh Chai Huat	(31 May 2001),	DAC No 36923 of 2000	(Sing Dist Ct).

7.6.3   Government Documents

7.6.3.1 Parliamentary Debates

Parliamentary Debates Singapore: Official Report,	volume	column	(date)	(speaker) (optional).
Parliamentary Debates Singapore: Official Report,	vol 73	at col 2436	(15 October 2001)	(Professor S Jayakumar).
Parliamentary Debates Singapore: Official Report,	vol 80	at col 2293	(13 February 2006)	(Professor Ivan Png Paak Liang).

7.6.3.2 Supreme Court Practice Directions

Practice directions are issued by the courts to regulate litigation. Until 1994, they were issued as discrete documents. Since then, they have been consolidated into a publication known as the *Supreme Court Practice Directions*.

7.6.3.2.1 Consolidated Practice Directions

Sing,	The Supreme Court Practice Directions	(year)	part	section.
Sing,	The Supreme Court Practice Directions	(2007)	part XV	s 123(1).

7.6.3.2.2 Amendments to Practice Directions

Sing,	Supreme Court PD	number	of year,	section.
Sing,	Supreme Court PD	No 1	of 2008,	s 7.

➢   Abbreviate **Practice Directions** to PD.

7.7   SOUTH AFRICA

7.7.1 Legislation

7.7.1.1 *Statutes*

Title,	(S Afr),	number	of year,	pinpoint.
Constitution of the Republic of South Africa, 1996,		No 108	of 1996.	
Consumer Protection Act,	(S Afr),	No 68	of 2008,	s 33.

7.7.1.2 *Amendments and Repeals*

Constitution of the Republic of South Africa, nº 108 of 1996 as amended by *Constitution of the Republic of South Africa Amendment Act,* nº 3 of 1999.

➤   For further information, see section 2.1.11.

7.7.1.2 *Bills*

Number,	title,	(S Afr),	session,	parliament,	year,	pinpoint.
B30-2005,	*Precious Metals Bill,*	(S Afr),	3d sess,	3d Parl,	2005.	
B26-2005,	*Nursing Bill,*	(S Afr),	3d sess,	3d Parl,	2005,	s 17.

7.7.2 Jurisprudence

7.7.2.1 *General Form*

Style of cause	(year of decision),	[year of reporter]	volume	reporter	page,	pin-point	(jurisdiction and/or court) (if applicable).
Oosthuizen v Stanley		[1938]		AD	322,		(S Afr SC).
Messina Associated Carriers v Kleinhaus		[2001]	3	S Afr LR	868,		(SCA).

➤   Cite to the **South African Law Reports** or to the **Butterworths Constitutional Law Reports** if possible.

7.7.2.2 Neutral citation

➢ Some South African courts have officially adopted a neutral citation. The form is the same as that of Canadian neutral citation (section 3.5), with the exception that the year is placed in brackets.

[year]	court	number	paragraph.
[2006]	ZACC	25	at para 1.

7.7.2.3 Reporters

Abbreviations of the principal reporters:

All South African Law Reports	All SA
Butterworths Constitutional Law Reports	B Const LR
South African Law Reports, Appellate Division (1910-1946)	S Afr LR, AD
South African Law Reports (1947-present)	S Afr LR

For a complete listing of all reporters, see **Appendix C**.

7.7.2.4 Court

Abbreviations of the courts:

Bophuthatswana High Court	Boph HC
Cape Provincial Division	Cape Prov Div
Ciskei High Court	Ciskei HC
Constitutional Court of South Africa	S Afr Const Ct
Durban and Coast Local Division	D&C Local Div
Eastern Cape Division	E Cape Div
Labour Court of South Africa	S Afr Labour Ct
Labour Court of Appeal of South Africa	S Afr Labour CA
Land Claims Court of South Africa	S Afr Land Claims Ct
Natal Provincial Division	Natal Prov Div
Northern Cape Division	N Cape Div
Orange Free State Provincial Division	OFS Prov Div
South-Eastern Cape Division	SE Cape Div
Supreme Court of Appeal of South Africa	S Afr SC
Transkei High Court	Transkei HC
Transvaal Provincial Division	Transv Prov Div
Venda High Court	Venda HC
Witwatersrand Local Division	Wit Local Div

7.7.3 Government Documents

7.7.3.1 Debates

S Afr,	Hansard,	House,	date	pinpoint	(speaker) (optional).
S Afr,	Hansard,	National Assembly,	9 February 2009	at 1	(MJ Ellis).

7.7.3.2 Reports, Discussion Papers and Issue Papers

Title,	Commission (if applicable),	Project number (if applicable)	(date)	pinpoint.
Truth and Reconciliation Commission of South Africa Report,			(29 October 1998)	at ch 1, para 91.
Report on Trafficking in Persons,	South African Law Reform Commission,	Project No 131	(August 2008)	at 23.
Domestic Violence,	South African Law Reform Commission,	Project No 100	(30 May 1997)	at 14.

➢   Write the name of the commission if it is not included in the title of the report.

INDEX

MOT DE LA RÉDACTRICE

À tous les quatre ans depuis 1986, la *Revue de droit de McGill* publie une nouvelle édition du *Manuel canadien de référence juridique*. Il s'agit d'un outil de référence précieux dans le milieu juridique, tant pour les avocats et les juges que pour les professeurs, les étudiants et les membres des revues de droit provenant tant du Canada que d'ailleurs. Un système de règles uniformes est crucial pour permettre la recherche efficace de jurisprudence, de législation et de tout autre document juridique. Sans ces règles, il régnerait une discordance entre le message communiqué par un auteur et la compréhension de son lecteur.

Le mot d'ordre lors de l'élaboration de la septième édition du *Manuel* était la clarté. En effet, peu importe sa pertinence et sa logique, une règle maladroitement communiquée n'a que peu d'utilité pratique. Les idées ont donc été exprimées de manière concise et directe, accordant plus de flexibilité à l'utilisateur. De plus, la ponctuation a été simplifiée, un chapitre séparé a été créé pour les sources étrangères et de nombreux documents ont été mis à jour. Compte tenu de l'essor croissant de la recherche juridique électronique, nous avons mieux adapté nos règles aux besoins actuels des utilisateurs, tout en laissant la porte ouverte aux technologies à venir. Nous avons aussi étendu la portée du *Manuel* : les règles peuvent désormais être ajustées à un grand nombre de langues et de juridictions.

Nous tenons particulièrement à remercier Me Daniel Boyer (directeur, Bibliothèque de droit Nahum Gelber, Université McGill) et Claudio Antonelli pour avoir révisé la totalité du *Manuel* et pour leur soutien et leurs encouragements. Merci également aux membres de l'équipe de LexUM, notamment à Me Daniel Poulin (directeur) et à Me Frédéric Pelletier (conseiller juridique), qui ont contribué aux sections sur références neutres. Je tiens également à remercier la rédactrice en chef du volume 55 de la *Revue*, Mlle Seo Yun Yang, ainsi que tous les rédacteurs, sans qui il m'aurait été impossible de terminer le travail.

Nous espérons que vous trouviez le nouveau *Manuel* utile et que vous parcourriez ses pages avec plaisir !

Svetlana Samochkine
Rédactrice du Manuel de référence
Revue de droit de McGill, volume 55

Pour tout commentaire ou toute suggestion, n'hésitez pas à nous contacter:

Revue de droit de McGill
3644, rue Peel
Montréal (Qc) H3A 1W9
Canada

Téléphone : (+1) (514) 398-7397
Télécopieur : (+1) (514) 398-7360
Courriel : journal.law@mcgill.ca
http://lawjournal.mcgill.ca

TABLE DES MATIÉRES

6   Doctrine et autres documents F-107

1   RÈGLES FONDAMENTALES

➢ Les règles établies dans ce *Manuel* s'appliquent aux **notes de bas de page**, aux **références dans le texte** et aux **bibliographies**.

➢ Utiliser les règles de la partie française pour écrire en français, et ce, même lorsque la source originale est dans une autre langue. N'utiliser les règles de la partie anglaise que pour écrire en anglais.

➢ Lorsqu'un acronyme ou une abréviation est employé dans une phrase complète, suivre les règles grammaticales usuelles dans l'usage des **points**. Omettre ces points dans les notes de bas de page et les références dans le texte de type « mécanique ».

➢ Les **caractères en couleur** de ce *Manuel* mettent les exemples en évidence.

➢ Si la règle impose des parenthèses ( ), ne pas les remplacer par des crochets [ ] et vice-versa.

➢ Le soulignement peut toujours remplacer l'italique et vice-versa.

1.1   BIBLIOGRAPHIES

LÉGISLATION

Barristers and Solicitors Act, RSBC 1979, c 26.
Loi antiterroriste, LC 2001, c 41.
Loi de 1991 sur les sages-femmes, LO 1991, c 31.
Loi sur les sociétés et fiducies du Québec, LRQ c S-29.0.

JURISPRUDENCE

Delgamuukw c Colombie-Britannique, [1997] 3 RCS 1010, 153 DLR (4e) 193.
Kendle v Melsom, [1998] HCA 13.
Cass civ 1re, 26 juin 2001, (2001) D Jur 2593 (note V Avena-Robardet).
Létourneau c Laflèche Auto Ltée, [1986] RJQ 1956 (CS).
Nouvelle-Écosse (Workers' Compensation Board) c Martin, 2003 CSC 54, [2003] 2 RCS 504.

DOCTRINE : MONOGRAPHIES

Lafond, Pierre-Claude. *Précis de droit des biens*, Montréal, Thémis, 1999.
Médina, Annie. *Abus de biens sociaux : Prévention, détection, poursuite*, Paris, Dalloz, 2001.
Nadeau, Alain-Robert. *Vie privée et droits fondamentaux*, Cowansville (Qc), Yvon Blais, 2000.
Tan, Cheng Han. *Matrimonial Law in Singapore and Malaysia*, Singapore, Butterworths Asia, 1994.

DOCTRINE : ARTICLES

Lamontagne, Denys-Claude. « L'imbrication du possessoire et du pétitoire », (1995) 55 R du B 661.
Lamontagne, Denys-Claude. « L'influence du droit public sur le droit immobilier », [1986] RDI 401.
Turp, Daniel. « Le droit au Québec à l'autodétermination et à l'indépendance : la loi sur la *clarté* du Canada et la loi sur les *droits fondamentaux* du Québec en collision » dans Marie-Françoise Labouz, dir, *Intégrations et identités nord-américaines : Vues de Montréal*, Bruxelles, Bruylant, 2001, 137.
Wang Sheng Chang. « Combination of Arbitration with Conciliation and Remittance of Awards – with Special Reference to the Asia-Oceana Region » (2002) 19 J Int Arb 51.

➢ Diviser les bibliographies et les listes d'autorités de textes juridiques en sections (par ex. législation, jurisprudence et doctrine). Si certaines sources ne correspondent pas à l'une de ces catégories, ajouter une section résiduelle (autres sources). Il peut être utile de diviser la section contenant la doctrine en sous-sections (par ex. monographies, périodiques et ouvrages collectifs). Il est également possible de diviser les sources entre sources internes et sources étrangères.

➢ Dans chaque section, classer les sources par **ordre alphabétique**. Classer la législation selon le titre de la loi, la jurisprudence selon l'intitulé et la doctrine selon le nom de famille de l'auteur.

➢ Pour la doctrine contenue dans une bibliographie, présenter le **nom de famille de l'auteur en premier** pour faciliter le classement par ordre alphabétique. Attention : l'ordre du prénom et du nom de famille change selon les traditions culturelles (avant, après ou entre les prénoms). Si le nom de famille apparaît en premier sur l'édition, omettre la virgule après ce nom (par ex. Wang Sheng Chang). Si le prénom apparaît en premier, mettre une virgule après le nom (par ex. Smith, Graham JH). Laisser toutes les initiales telles quelles.

➢ S'il y a une référence avec plus d'un auteur, écrire le prénom avant le nom de famille pour tous les auteurs excepté le premier (par ex. Baudouin, Jean-Louis et Pierre-Gabriel Jobin).

➢ S'il y a une référence à une œuvre par un seul auteur, ainsi qu' à une œuvre par cet auteur et d'autres auteurs (par ex. Baudouin et Baudouin et Jobin), écrire celle avec un seul auteur d'abord.

➢ Ajouter un **retrait** de ¼ de pouce ou 0.63 cm avant chaque reference (mettre en retrait toutes les lignes sauf la première).

➢ Suivre les règles du chapitre 6 pour toute information d'une référence à la doctrine (excepté pour l'ordre des noms de l'auteur ou du directeur d'un ouvrage collectif).

1.2   RÉFÉRENCES DANS LE TEXTE : NOTE DE SERVICE ET FACTUM

La règle habituelle exige l'utilisation de notes en bas de page pour la rédaction de textes juridiques. Toutefois, dans certains types de documents, les références doivent être incluses **dans le corps même du texte**.

1.2.1 Note de service

En plus des conditions pour « méfait donnant ouverture à un droit d'action » indépendamment de la violation pour laquelle on poursuit, les dommages-intérêts punitifs seront accordés lorsque la conduite du défendeur est si « malveillante, opprimante et abusive qu'elle choque le sens de dignité de la cour » (*Hill c Église de scientologie de Toronto*, [1995] 2 RCS 1130 au para 196, 186 NR 1, juge Cory [*Hill*]). Une telle conduite comprend la diffamation (*ibid*), l'omission de fournir des soins médicaux (*Robitaille v Vancouver Hockey Club*, [1981] 3 WWR 481, 124 DLR (3ᵉ) 228 (BCCA)), et exceptionnellement les comportements abusifs des compagnies d'assurance (*Whiten c Pilot Insurance*, 2002 CSC 18, [2002] 1 SCR 595 [*Whiten*]).

Puisque le premier mécanisme punitif est le droit criminel, la modération doit primer dans les recours aux dommages punitifs (*ibid* au para 69). Il faut aussi noter qu'il ne peut y avoir responsabilité solidaire à l'égard de dommages-intérêts punitifs, car seul le responsable de la mauvaise conduite doit être condamné à les verser (*Hill* au para 195).

> ➤ Inclure la référence immédiatement après le texte, entre parenthèses.

> ➤ La première fois qu'une référence apparaît, suivre les règles habituelles pour les notes de bas de page. Si la référence sera répétée par la suite, créer un titre abrégé après la première référence (voir *Hill*). Si la référence n'est pas répétée, ne pas créer de titre abrégé (voir *Robitaille*).

> ➤ À partir de la deuxième apparition d'une référence, utiliser uniquement le titre abrégé. Ajouter la référence précise (par ex. *Hill* au para 195).

> ➤ Utiliser *ibid* (section 1.4.2) pour indiquer la référence précédente immédiatement. Utiliser *supra* (section 1.4.3) pour indiquer que la référence a déjà été mentionnée plus tôt. **Ne pas utiliser *infra*** (section 1.4.4) dans une note de service.

1.2.2 Factum

> 5.   En plus des conditions pour « méfait donnant ouverture à un droit d'action » indépendamment de la violation pour laquelle on poursuit, les dommages-intérêts punitifs seront accordés lorsque la conduite du défendeur est si « malveillante, opprimante et abusive qu'elle choque le sens de dignité de la cour » (*Hill*). Une telle conduite comprend la diffamation (*Hill*), l'omission de fournir des soins médicaux (*Robitaille*), et exceptionnellement les comportements abusifs des compagnies d'assurance (*Whiten*).
>
>> *Hill c Église de scientologie de Toronto* [1995] 2 RCS 1130 au para 196, 186 NR 1, juge Cory [*Hill*].
>>
>> *Robitaille v Vancouver Hockey Club*, [1981] 3 WWR 481, 124 DLR (3ᵉ) 228 (BCCA) [*Robitaille*].
>>
>> *Whiten c Pilot Insurance*, 2002 CSC 18, [2002] 1 RCS 595 [*Whiten*].
>
> 6.   Puisque le premier mécanisme punitif est le droit criminel, la modération doit primer dans les recours aux dommages punitifs (*Whiten*). Il faut aussi noter qu'il ne peut y avoir responsabilité solidaire à l'égard de dommages-intérêts punitifs, car seul le responsable de la mauvaise conduite doit être condamné à les verser (*Hill*).
>
>> *Whiten*, *supra* para 5 au para 69.
>>
>> *Hill*, *supra* para 5 au para 195.

➢ Écrire le titre abrégé entre parenthèses immédiatement après le texte.

➢ Indiquer la référence complète **à la fin du paragraphe**. Mettre en retrait les marges de gauche et de droite et utiliser une plus petite police de caractères.

➢ Écrire le titre abrégé, utilisé dans le corps du texte, en italiques et entre crochets, après la première référence complète.

➢ Mettre les références **dans l'ordre de leur apparition dans le texte**. Changer de ligne après chaque référence (ne pas mettre de point-virgule).

➢ Suivre les règles habituelles pour l'utilisation du *supra* (section 1.4.3). Toutefois, au lieu de se référer au numéro d'une note de bas de page, l'indicatif suivant le *supra* se réfère au numéro du paragraphe dans lequel est apparue la source pour la première fois (par ex. *Whiten, supra* para 5 au para 69). **Ne pas utiliser *infra*** (section 1.4.4) dans un factum.

➢ **Ne pas utiliser *ibid*** (section 1.4.2) dans un factum. À la fin du paragraphe, inclure les références précises s'appliquant à tout le paragraphe (par ex. *Whiten c Pilot Insurance*, 2002 CSC 18, [2002] 1 RCS 595 aux paras 69, 101, 110).

1.3   RÈGLES CONCERNANT LES NOTES DE BAS DE PAGE

Les notes de bas de page des textes juridiques sont habituellement des notes discursives ou des notes de référence. Les **notes discursives** regroupent les commentaires pertinents, mais assez périphériques risquant ainsi de dévier le lecteur du sujet principal. Les **notes de référence** indiquent les sources desquelles proviennent les arguments ou les citations. L'information discursive et de référence peut être combinée dans une même note.

1.3.1 La création des notes de bas de page

➢ Créer des notes de bas de page dans les cas suivants : (1) à la première référence à la source en question ; (2) à chaque référence ou allusion à un passage particulier de la source ; et (3) à chaque citation ultérieure tirée de la source. Fournir la référence complète dans la première référence à la source uniquement.

1.3.2 L'indication des notes de bas de page dans le texte

➢ Indiquer les notes de bas de page par des numéros en chiffres arabes (par ex. 1, 2, 3) en exposant. Ne pas utiliser de chiffres romains ou de caractères tels que *, † et ‡.

→ De préférence, mettre le numéro de la note de bas de page à la fin d'une phrase, mais avant la ponctuation[1].

→ Pour faire référence à un seul mot, placer le numéro de la note[2] immédiatement après le mot en question.

→ Si le mot est suivi d'un signe de ponctuation[3], le numéro précède la ponctuation.

→ S'il s'agit d'une citation placée « entre guillemets »[4], le numéro suit les guillemets et précède la ponctuation. (Cet ordre diffère de celui exigé pour les textes anglais, dans lesquels le numéro suit la ponctuation.)

1.3.3 L'emplacement des notes de bas de page

➢ Les notes de bas de page figurent au bas de la page, sous le texte, et se trouvent autant que possible sur la même page que le texte auquel elles correspondent. Distinguer les notes de bas de page du texte par une **plus petite police de caractères** et par une séparation du texte à l'aide d'une **ligne horizontale**.

1.3.4 La combinaison des notes de bas de page

➢ Ne jamais mettre plus d'un numéro de note à un même endroit dans le texte. Combiner plutôt les références en une seule note de bas de page. Lorsque plusieurs références figurent dans une même note, elles sont séparées par un point-virgule et la note se termine par un point.

> [7] *Godbout c Longueuil (Ville de)*, [1997] 3 RCS 844 ; *Aubry c Vice-Versa*, [1998] 1 RCS 591.

➤ Si cela n'entraîne aucune confusion, il est possible de combiner les références à plusieurs documents en une note dont le numéro est placé à la fin du paragraphe. Éviter la combinaison s'il s'agit de citations provenant de sources différentes.

1.3.5   Les références aux sources non françaises

➤ L'écriture en français exige le respect des règles de référence françaises, quelle que soit la langue dans laquelle la source est rédigée.

> [1] David Kairys, dir, *The Politics of Law: A Progressive Critique*, 3e éd, New York, Basic Books, 1998 à la p 76.
>
> [2] *Credit Union Act*, SNS 1994, c 4.

➤ Conserver le titre (incluant l'usage des majuscules et de la ponctuation) dans la langue d'origine. Pour tout autre élément de la référence, respecter les règles françaises, particulièrement en ce qui a trait à l'usage de la ponctuation.

1.3.6   Formules introductives

> Voir *Spar Aerospace ltée c American Mobile Satellite Corp*, 2002 CSC 78, [2002] 4 RCS 205 [*Spar*] ; *Morguard Investments Ltd c De Savoye*, [1990] 3 RCS 1077, 76 DLR (4e) 256. Voir toutefois *Beals c Saldanha*, 2003 CSC 72, [2003] 3 RCS 416.

➤ Les formules introductives permettent d'expliquer le lien logique entre la source à laquelle se réfère la note et l'idée énoncée dans le texte.

➤ Chaque formule introductive se rapporte à **toutes les références de la même phrase**. Dans l'exemple ci-dessus, la formule voir introduit à la fois *Spar* et *Morguard*, car ces références sont séparées par un point-virgule.

➤ Mettre toutes les formules dans une police romaine, excepté *contra*, qui est en italique. Sans être exhaustive, la liste suivante présente quelques formules :

Spar	Il n'y a pas de formule introductive lorsque l'autorité en question est citée dans le texte ou est explicitement mentionnée dans le texte.
Voir *Spar*	L'autorité en question **appuie l'idée** exprimée dans le texte.
Voir notamment *Spar*	L'autorité en question est **la plus concluante parmi plusieurs références** qui soutiennent l'idée exprimée dans le texte. Utiliser cette formule lorsque seules les meilleures sources sont présentées.
Voir par ex *Spar*	L'autorité en question en est **une parmi plusieurs appuyant l'idée** exprimée dans le texte.
Voir généralement *Spar*	L'autorité en question fournit des **renseignements généraux** sur le sujet.
Voir aussi *Spar*	L'autorité en question **s'ajoute à d'autres** qui appuient l'idée exprimée dans le texte, mais elle **n'est pas la plus concluante et n'est pas entièrement à propos**.
En accord avec *Spar*	Comme avec la formule « voir aussi », l'autorité en question s'ajoute à d'autres qui appuient l'idée exprimée dans le texte. Toutefois, dans ce cas-ci, **l'autorité appuie directement l'idée exprimée dans le texte et a autant de poids que la première autorité**. Le terme « accord » est également utilisé pour indiquer que la loi d'une indication géographique correspond avec la loi d'une autre indication géographique.
Comparer *Spar*	L'autorité en question offre une **comparaison intéressante** servant à illustrer l'idée exprimée dans le texte.
Voir toutefois *Spar*	L'autorité en question est en **désaccord partiel** avec l'idée exprimée dans le texte, mais elle ne la contredit pas directement.
Contra *Spar*	L'autorité en question **contredit directement** l'idée exprimée dans le texte.

1.3.7   Information entre parenthèses dans les notes de bas de page

[1] *Roncarelli c Duplessis*, [1959] RSC 121, 16 DLR (2ᵉ) 689, juge Rand (une décision discrétionnaire « *[must] be based on considerations pertinent to the object of the administration* » à la p 140) ; *Oakwood Development Ltd c St. François Xavier (Municipalité)*, [1985] 2 RCS 164, 20 DLR (4ᵉ) 641, juge Wilson [*Oakwood* avec renvois aux RCS] (« [l]'omission d'un organe de décision administrative de tenir compte d'un élément très important constitue une erreur au même titre que la prise en considération inappropriée d'un facteur étranger à l'affaire » à la p 174).

[2] Voir *Protection de la jeunesse – 631*, [1993] RDF 535 (le parent a obtenu l'accès au journal intime de son adolescent) ; *Droit de la famille – 2206*, [1995] RJQ 1419 (CS) [*DDF 2206*] (le parent a enregistré la conversation téléphonique entre l'enfant et son père).

[3] *R c Robillard* (2000), [2001] RJQ 1, 151 CCC (3ᵉ) 296 (CA) (le juge de la Cour supérieure a erré en déclarant que la réception en preuve des communications non confidentielles était susceptible de déconsidérer l'administration de la justice), infirmant [1999] JQ n° 5583 (CS).

➢ Lorsque l'idée affirmée ou infirmée par une cause manque de clarté, il peut être utile de fournir **entre parenthèses** une **brève description d'une phrase ou moins**.

Une citation courte de la cause peut également être incluse entre parenthèses, suivie de la référence précise (voir *Oakwood*).

➢ L'information entre parenthèses poursuit l'idée de la phrase précédente et débute par une minuscule. S'il s'agit d'une citation qui débute par une majuscule, changer la première lettre par une minuscule entre crochets (voir *Oakwood*).

➢ L'information entre parenthèses concerne la référence précédente. Ainsi, l'information entre parenthèses doit être placée après la décision à laquelle l'information se réfère (voir *Robillard*).

1.4 RÉFÉRENCES ULTÉRIEURES ET ANTÉRIEURES

Lorsqu'une source apparaît plus d'une fois, **ne mentionner la référence complète que la première fois**. Les références ultérieures renvoient à cette première référence.

1.4.1 Titre abrégé

1.4.1.1 Modèle de base

➢ Ne pas créer de titre abrégé si la référence n'est mentionnée qu'une fois dans le texte.

➢ Si le titre d'une source est court (environ trois mots ou moins), le titre complet peut être utilisé dans toutes les références ultérieures (voir note 10). Si le titre d'une source est plus long, créer un titre abrégé et l'utiliser dans toutes les références ultérieures.

➢ Mettre le titre abrégé entre crochets à la fin de la référence, avant l'information entre parenthèses (voir *DDF 2206* à la section 1.3.7) et les étapes successives de la cause (section 3.11). Ne pas mettre les crochets en italique.

> [4] *Lamborghini (Canada) inc c Automobili Lamborghini SPA* (1996), [1997] RJQ 58 (CA) [*Lamborghini*].
>
> [21] *Lamborghini*, *supra* note 4 à la p 66.
>
> [7] *R c W (R)*, [1992] 2 SCR 122 au para 1, 74 CCC (3e) 134.
>
> [10] (*R c W (R)*, *supra* note 7 au para 3).
>
> [41] Christine Gagnon, « Les effets de la publication de la déclaration de copropriété » dans *La copropriété divise*, 2e éd, Cowansville (Qc), Yvon Blais, 2007 [Gagnon].
>
> [80] Gagnon *supra* note 41 à la p 1.

➢ Placer les titres abrégés de législation et de jurisprudence en italique (par ex. *Charte*). Toutefois, les abréviations comme CcQ ne sont pas considérées comme des titres abrégés et ne doivent pas être placées en italique. Il est tout de même possible d'utiliser *Code* en tant que titre abrégé. Si un seul code est mentionné dans le texte, il n'est pas nécessaire d'inclure cette forme abrégée entre crochets après la première référence.

➢ Toutes les références ultérieures (*supra, ibid*) doivent être précédées du titre abrégé de la source pour guider le lecteur à la note de la référence complète (voir note 80).

1.4.1.2 Législation

> [1] *Code criminel*, LRC 1985, c C-46.
>
> [2] *Charte des droits et libertés de la personne*, LRQ c C-12 [*Charte québécoise*].
>
> [3] *Loi sur la Gendarmerie royale du Canada*, LRC 1985 (2ᵉ supp), c 8 [*Loi sur la GRC*].
>
> [4] *Charte canadienne des droits et libertés*, partie I de la *Loi constitutionnelle de 1982*, constituant l'annexe B de la *Loi de 1982 sur le Canada* (R-U), 1982, c 11 [*Charte canadienne*].

➢ Si une loi a un **titre abrégé officiel**, lui seul devrait être fourni dans la première référence. Si ce titre abrégé officiel est suffisamment court, il peut être utilisé pour les références ultérieures (par ex. *Code criminel*).

➢ Si une loi n'a **pas de titre abrégé officiel ou que celui-ci est trop long** pour les références ultérieures, il peut être abrégé par un titre distinctif indiqué entre crochets à la fin de la référence.

1.4.1.3 Jurisprudence

➢ Choisir une partie distincte de l'intitulé ou le nom de l'une des parties pour créer un titre abrégé.

➢ Si la référence originale se réfère à plus d'une source, indiquer le recueil utilisé pour les références précises subséquentes à l'aide de la mention avec renvois aux, suivie de l'abréviation du recueil.

> [1] *R c Van der Peet*, [1996] 2 RCS 507, 137 DLR (4ᵉ) 289 [*Van der Peet* avec renvois aux RCS].
>
> [7] *Van der Peet*, *supra* note 1 à la p 512.
>
> [10] *R c Ruzic*, 2001 CSC 24 au para 2, [2001] 1 RCS 687 [*Ruzic*].
>
> [15] *Ruzic*, *supra* note 10 au para 18.

➢ Si une référence précise est indiquée dans la référence originale, cela sous-entend que toutes les références subséquentes seront effectuées à la même source. Ne pas inclure avec renvois aux dans ce cas (voir note 10).

➢ Pour les causes ayant une référence neutre, il n'est pas nécessaire d'indiquer à quel recueil appartiennent les références ultérieures. La numérotation des paragraphes est uniforme pour tous les recueils.

1.4.1.4 Doctrine

[1] Aline Grenon, « La protection du consommateur et les sûretés mobilières au Québec et en Ontario : Solutions distinctes ? » (2001) R du B can 917 [Grenon, « Protection »].

[2] Marie-Thérèse Chicha, *L'équité salariale : Mise en œuvre et enjeux*, 2e éd, Cowansville (Qc), Yvon Blais, 2000.

[3] Aline Grenon, « Le crédit-bail et la vente à tempérament dans le *Code civil du Québec* » (1994) 25 RGD 217 [Grenon, « Crédit-bail »].

[12] Chicha, *supra* note 2 à la p 183.

[13] Louise Rolland, « La simulation dans le droit civil des obligations : Le mensonge révélateur » dans Nicholas Kasirer, *Le faux en droit privé*, Montréal, Thémis, 2000 à la p 93.

[14] Grenon, « Protection », *supra* note 1 à la p 923.

[86] Philippe Jestaz, « Faux et détournement d'institution en droit français de la famille » dans Kasirer, *supra* note 13 à la p 13.

➤ Pour faire référence à de la doctrine dans une référence ultérieure, indiquer le **nom de famille de l'auteur** (voir notes 2 et 12).

➤ Si **plusieurs ouvrages d'un même auteur** sont mentionnés, utiliser le nom de famille de l'auteur et un titre abrégé (voir notes 3 et 14). Respecter la forme typographique du titre du document dans le titre abrégé, soit l'utilisation d'italique pour les livres ou l'utilisation des guillemets pour les articles.

➤ Pour faire référence à **un autre article d'un même ouvrage collectif**, écrire au long le nom de l'auteur et de l'article. Écrire ensuite la référence du premier article en mentionnant le nom du directeur de l'ouvrage collectif (voir note 86).

1.4.2 Ibid

[1] Voir *Lapointe c Hôpital Le Gardeur*, [1992] 1 SCR 382, 90 DLR (4e) 27 [*Lapointe*].

[2] *Ibid* à la p 2629. Voir aussi *Laferrière c Lawson*, [1991] 1 RCS 541 à la p 592, 78 DLR (4e) 609 [*Laferrière*] ; *Wilson c Rowswell*, [1970] RCS 865, 1 DLR (3e) 737 [*Wilson*].

[5] *Laferrière*, *supra* note 2 à la p 595.

[6] *Ibid*.

[7] *Ibid* à la p 262.

[98] Voir aussi *Pelletier c Roberge*, [1991] RRA 726, 41 QAC 161 [*Pelletier*]. *Pelletier* emploie la théorie de la perte de chance en droit québécois (voir *ibid* à la p 737).

[99] Voir toutefois la *Loi sur les compagnies*, LRQ c C-38, art 77 [*LSC*].

[100] Voir la *LSC*, *ibid*, art 79.

➤ *Ibid* est l'abréviation du latin *ibidem* qui signifie « au même endroit ».

➤ Utiliser *ibid* pour indiquer la **référence immédiatement précédente** (et non la note de bas de page au complet). Ne pas indiquer le numéro de la note référée.

Règles fondamentales

➤ Utiliser *ibid* **après une référence complète** (voir note 2), **après un *supra*** (voir note 6) ou même **après un autre *ibid*** (voir note 7). S'il y a plus d'une référence dans la note de bas de page précédente, utiliser *ibid* uniquement pour indiquer la toute dernière référence de cette note.

➤ Quand *ibid* est utilisé sans référence précise, *ibid* indique la même référence précise que la note précédente (voir note 6).

➤ Pour faire référence à la source précédente dans une même note, utiliser *ibid* entre parenthèses (voir note 98).

1.4.3 *Supra*

➤ *Supra* est le mot latin pour « ci-dessus ».

➤ Utiliser *supra* et le titre abrégé pour indiquer la référence précédente contenant la référence complète. *Supra* indique toujours la référence originale complète et non un autre *supra* ou *ibid*.

➤ Si la source est identifiée clairement dans le corps du texte (par ex. si le texte indique « la cour d'appel dans *Biorex*[1] »), il n'est pas nécessaire de répéter l'information dans la note (voir note 58).

> [1] *Canada (PG) c Biorex inc*, [1996] RDJ 548 (disponible sur QL) (CA) [*Biorex*] ; voir aussi *Loi sur les jeunes contrevenants*, LRC 1985, c R-1.
>
> [56] *Biorex*, *supra* note 1 à la p 551.
>
> [57] *Ibid* aux pp 552-54. Voir aussi *Loi sur les jeunes contrevenants*, *supra* note 1, art 5.
>
> [58] *Supra* note 43 à la p 120.
>
> [59] Voir aussi *supra* note 24 et texte correspondant.

➤ Pour faire référence à la fois à la note et au corps du texte accompagné par la note, utiliser la formule suivante : *supra* note # et texte correspondant (voir note 59).

➤ Pour faire référence uniquement au texte et non aux notes de bas de page, utiliser ci-dessus (section 1.4.5) et non *supra*.

1.4.4 *Infra*

➤ *Infra* est le mot latin pour « ci-dessous ».

➤ Utiliser *infra* pour indiquer une **note ultérieure**.

➤ L'utilisation d'*infra* est **fortement déconseillée**. Il est préférable de fournir la référence au complet dès la première référence.

➤ Pour faire référence uniquement au texte, utiliser ci-dessous (section 1.4.5) et non *infra*.

1.4.5 Ci-dessus et ci-dessous

➤ Utiliser les expressions ci-dessus et ci-dessous pour renvoyer le lecteur à une **partie du texte** plutôt qu'aux notes de bas de page.

➤ Si le texte n'est pas divisé en parties ou en paragraphes facilement identifiables (par ex. en sous-titres ou en numéros de paragraphes) ou si la pagination finale du

> [1] Voir la partie III-A, ci-dessus, pour l'analyse de cette question.
>
> [2] Voir la discussion plus approfondie de cette cause aux pp 164-70, ci-dessous.
>
> [3] Voir l'analyse de la décision dans l'arrêt *Oakes* au texte correspondant à la note 41.

texte n'est pas définitive au moment de la rédaction, utiliser la formule voir texte correspondant à la note #.

1.5 RÉFÉRENCES AUX SOURCES CITANT OU REPRODUISANT LA SOURCE ORIGINALE

Il est toujours préférable de faire référence à la source originale. Si une source originale se trouve en partie dans une autre source (la source citante), consulter la source originale afin de vérifier le contexte et l'exactitude de la citation.

1.5.1 Source originale difficile à trouver

Tel que cité dans	*Papers Relating to the Commission appointed to enquire into the state and condition of the Indians of the North-West Coast of British Columbia*, British Columbia Sessional Papers, 1888 aux pp 432-33, tel que cité dans Hamar Foster, « Honouring the Queen's Flag: A Legal and Historical Perspective on the Nisga'a Treaty » (1998) 120 BC Studies 11 à la p 13.

➤ Lorsque la source originale est difficile à trouver ou a été détruite, il est possible de faire référence à la source originale telle qu'elle se trouve dans la source citante, en fournissant le plus d'information possible sur la source primaire, suivi de tel que cité dans et de la référence à la source citante.

Reproduit(e) dans	George R au Gouverneur Arthur Phillip, Instruction royale, 25 avril 1787 (27 Geo III), reproduite dans *Historical Documents of New South Wales*, t 1, 2ᵉ partie, Sydney, Government Printer, 1892-1901 à la p 67.

➤ Dans certains cas, la version originale d'un document entièrement réimprimé dans un ouvrage collectif (par ex. les collections reproduisant les débats, les lettres, les traités ou les manuscrits) est uniquement disponible dans les archives. Dans ce cas, fournir le plus d'information possible sur le document original, suivi de reproduit(e) dans et de la référence à la source citante.

✓	*Pacte international relatif aux droits civils et politiques*, 19 décembre 1966, 999 RTNU 171, RT Can 1976 n° 47.
✗	*Pacte international relatif aux droits civils et politiques*, 19 décembre 1966, 999 RTNU 171, RT Can 1976 n° 47, reproduit dans Hugh M Kindred et al, dir, *International Law Chiefly as Interpreted and Applied in Canada : Documentary Supplement*, np, Emond Montgomery, 2000 à la p 87.

➢ Ne pas faire référence aux éditions reproduisant des extraits de sources originales facilement disponibles (par ex. des manuels).

1.5.2 Accent mis sur la source citante

Citant	*Canada (Citoyenneté et Immigration) c Khosa*, 2009 CSC 12, [2009] 1 SCR 339 au para 38, citant Pierre-André Côté, *Interprétation des lois,* 3ᵉ éd, Cowansville (Qc), Yvon Blais, 1999, à la p 91 n 123.

➢ Pour souligner le fait qu'une source citante utilise la source originale (par ex. lorsque la source citante est plus éminente ou a plus de crédibilité), inclure la référence de la source citante, suivie de citant et de la source originale.

1.6   RÈGLES GÉNÉRALES CONCERNANT LES CITATIONS

Ces règles s'appliquent tant au corps du texte qu'aux notes de bas de page.

1.6.1 Emplacement des citations

Il rejette cet argument au motif que, selon lui, il n'existe « aucune contradiction entre le refus de permettre le paiement d'honoraires extrajudiciaires et le droit d'accorder des honoraires spéciaux »[4].

La juge Dutil est également amenée à traiter de l'importance du fait que l'usine s'est établie à cet endroit avant les réclamants. À ce sujet, elle affirme que

[l]a preuve ne démontre pas que les résidents du quartier Villeneuve savaient, à leur arrivée, qu'ils s'exposaient à des inconvénients aussi importants que ceux qu'ils ont vécus. Ils pouvaient s'attendre à certains inconvénients du fait qu'ils étaient voisins d'une cimenterie, cependant, ils s'installaient dans un quartier résidentiel [...][5].

L'art. 32 C.c.Q. accorde à l'enfant un statut qui lui a longtemps été dénigré à travers l'histoire. Il se lit comme suit :

Tout enfant a droit à la protection, à la sécurité et à l'attention que ses parents ou les personnes qui en tiennent lieu peuvent lui donner.

➢ Insérer les citations courtes (de **moins de quatre lignes**) dans le texte entre guillemets. Mettre les citations plus longues (de **quatre lignes ou plus**) en retrait des marges, à simple interligne et sans guillemets. Les dispositions législatives peuvent également être citées en retrait des marges, bien qu'elles aient moins de quatre lignes.

1.6.2 Forme des citations

« [L]'objection identitaire s'avère [...] bien fondée »[32], et représente ainsi un élément important du débat.

Donc, « [c]ette dichotomie découle tout naturellement de *l'impossibilité des juges de se dégager de leurs principes nationaux* » [nos italiques][53].

« L'intérêt d'autrui, auquel l'exercice d'un pouvoir est subordonné, le distingue essentiellement du droit subjectif que son titulaire exerce librement. La poursuite de l'intérêt d'autrui intègre nécessairement au pouvoir un but, dont l'attributaire doit tenir compte dans son exercice » [notes omises].

✓	Il incombe au requérant de démontrer que « [c]ompte tenu des circonstances, il ne pouvait renverser le fardeau de la preuve ».
✗	Il incombe au requérant de démontrer que « [...] compte tenu des circonstances, il ne pouvait renverser le fardeau de la preuve ».

➢ L'orthographe, les majuscules et la ponctuation d'une citation reproduisent la source originale ; toute modification doit être clairement indiquée entre crochets. Si la phrase devient grammaticalement incorrecte, faire un ajustement entre crochets au début de la citation (par ex. changer une majuscule pour une minuscule ou vice-versa).

➢ Utiliser **l'ellipse entre crochets** [...] lorsque la citation est incomplète ou que la phrase citée se poursuit. Omettre les ellipses au début d'une citation.

➢ Lorsque la source originale contient une faute, inclure la correction entre crochets. Ne pas utiliser [*sic*], à moins d'avoir une raison particulière de vouloir signaler l'erreur.

➢ Pour mettre l'accent sur une partie d'une citation, la mettre en italique et ajouter [nos italiques] immédiatement après la citation. Si les italiques étaient déjà indiquées dans la version originale, ajouter [italiques dans l'original]. Lorsque le texte original contient des notes de bas de page et qu'elles ne sont pas reproduites dans la citation, ajouter [notes omises] après la citation. (Cette règle est contraire aux règles de la partie anglaise, selon lesquelles ces expressions sont placées à la fin de la référence et non à la fin de la citation).

1.6.3 Citation d'une source dans une autre langue

➢ Utiliser autant que possible la version française de la source lorsque le texte rédigé est en français et une version anglaise lorsqu'il est rédigé en anglais.

Comme l'indique Robin, « les faits de l'espèce ne permettent pas de conclure à la mauvaise foi » [notre traduction][79].

➢ Le Canada, le Québec, le Manitoba, le Nouveau-Brunswick, l'Ontario, les Territoires du Nord-Ouest et le Yukon adoptent leurs lois en français et en anglais. Cependant, il est possible qu'avant une certaine date, celles-ci n'existent qu'en version anglaise.

> Dans un texte juridique, il n'est pas nécessaire de traduire un passage tiré d'une source dans une autre langue. Toutefois, si cela facilite la compréhension, la référence doit clairement indiquer qui a traduit la citation. Pour une traduction professionnelle, voir la section 6.2.2.5.1. Pour une traduction de l'auteur (vous), indiquer [notre traduction] après la citation.

1.7 RÉDACTION D'UN TEXTE EN LANGUE ÉTRANGÈRE

Puisqu'il s'agit d'un ouvrage intrinsèquement canadien, les règles de ce *Manuel* s'appliquent à la rédaction de textes dans les deux langues officielles. Toutefois, il est possible d'adapter ces règles pour toute autre langue en s'inspirant de la section anglaise **ou** française, selon le degré de maîtrise de l'auteur. Les règles d'or sont l'**uniformité** et la **facilité de retracer une source** pour le lecteur. Les indications suivantes ne sont que des exemples d'adaptation des règles.

> **Traduire les formules** comme « voir », « en accord avec », « tel que cité dans », « nos italiques » ou « avec renvois aux », mais conserver les expressions latines dans la langue d'origine.

> Conserver les règles de **forme** telles quelles, comme l'ordre des éléments et la structure du document.

> Suivre les **règles de ponctuation** de la langue de rédaction. Consulter un ouvrage grammatical si nécessaire. S'assurer que la forme employée soit toujours constante, tant dans les notes de bas de page que dans le corps du texte.

> Pour la **législation**, suivre le modèle de base canadien. Utiliser l'acronyme du recueil et de la législature tel que présenté dans un document officiel de la loi. Inclure une indication géographique.

> Pour la **jurisprudence**, suivre la hiérarchie des sources. Toujours garder en tête le public cible et s'assurer que les lecteurs puissent avoir accès à l'information. Utiliser l'acronyme du recueil tel que présenté dans la source et toujours inclure l'indication géographique et la cour.

> Si l'acronyme d'un **journal** cité ne se trouve pas dans l'**annexe D** du *Manuel*, écrire le nom du journal au complet.

Législation

2   LÉGISLATION

2.1   LOIS

2.1.1   Modèle de base

Titre,	recueil	législature	année,	chapitre	(session ou supplément),	référence précise.
Code criminel,	LR	C	1985,	c C-46,		art 745.
Loi de l'impôt sur le revenu,	LR	C	1985,	c 1	(5e supp),	art 18(1)(m)(iv)(c).
Charte des droits et libertés de la personne,	LR	Q		c C-12,		art 10.

➢ Ne pas mettre d'espace entre le recueil et la législature (LRC ; LRQ).

➢ Pour les lois constitutionnelles, voir la section 2.2.

2.1.2   Sources

➢ Au Canada, la législation se trouve dans des **volumes de lois révisées, refondues** ou **réadoptées**, des **recueils annuels**, des **recueils à feuilles mobiles** ou des **sources électroniques**. Consulter le tableau suivant pour connaître les sources à utiliser pour chacune des juridictions canadiennes.

Législation

Jurisdiction	Ordre des sources à citer
Canada Colombie-Britannique Nouvelle-Écosse Saskatchewan Terre-Neuve-et-Labrador Territoires du Nord-Ouest Yukon	Faire référence aux **lois révisées** imprimées autant que possible. Utiliser les **recueils annuels** imprimés si : → une loi a été adoptée après la publication de la dernière révision ou → l'article pertinent a été ajouté ou modifié depuis la date de révision.
Manitoba	Faire référence aux **lois révisées** et aux **recueils annuels** de la même manière que pour les premières juridictions. Facultatif : faire référence à la ***Codification permanente des lois du Manitoba*** (CPLM) après les recueils annuels (section 2.1.4).
Nouveau-Brunswick	*Avant 2003* : Faire référence aux **lois révisées** et aux **recueils annuels** de la même manière que pour les premières juridictions. -OU- Utiliser la **version électronique officielle** (section 2.1). *Après 2003* : Utiliser la **version électronique officielle** (section 2.1).
Ontario	Faire référence aux **lois révisées** et aux **recueils annuels** de la même manière que pour les premières juridictions. -OU- Utiliser la **version électronique officielle** (e-Laws) (section 2.1.5).
Québec	Faire référence aux **recueils à feuilles mobiles** en premier lieu (section 2.1.4). Si nécessaire, faire référence aux **lois révisées** et aux **recueils annuels** de la même manière que pour les premières juridictions.

2.1.3 Titre

➢ Indiquer le titre de la loi en italique et mettre une virgule non italique après le titre.

> *Loi de 2000 sur la cour d'appel*, LS 2000, c C-42.1, art 11.
>
> *Health Care Protection Act*, SA 2000, c H-3.3.

➢ Utiliser le **titre abrégé officiel** de la loi. Si la loi n'en a pas, indiquer le titre qui se trouve au début de la loi. N'ajouter l'article défini (le, la) que s'il fait partie du titre.

➢ Si le titre de la loi est indiqué dans le corps du texte, ne pas le répéter dans la référence.

➢ Respecter l'usage des majuscules dans le titre de la loi.

> Si l'année fait partie du titre de la loi, elle doit être indiquée comme telle en italique. Inclure l'année après la législature même si l'année fait partie du titre.

N.B. Les lois sont adoptées en français et en anglais dans les juridictions suivantes : Canada, Manitoba, Nouveau-Brunswick, Ontario, Québec, Nunavut, les Territoires du Nord-Ouest et Yukon. Toutefois, il est possible que des lois adoptées avant une certaine date n'existent qu'en anglais.

2.1.4   Lois révisées et recueils annuels

Lois révisées	*Code des droits de la personne*, LRO 1990, c H.19.
	Loi sur les compagnies, LRQ c C-38, art 29.
Recueils annuels	*Protected Areas of British Columbia Act,* SBC 2000, c 17.

> Abréger **Lois révisées**, **Lois refondues** et **Lois réadoptées** par LR. Abréger **Lois** et **Statuts** par L pour les références aux volumes annuels. Abréger *Statutes* par S.

> Utiliser L pour **Lois** (et non O pour **Ordonnances**) pour une référence à un recueil de lois des Territoires du Nord-Ouest ou du Yukon.

N.B. Lorsqu'une loi ne se trouve pas dans les recueils actuels de lois révisées, ne pas présumer que la loi n'existe pas ou qu'elle n'est plus pertinente. Par exemple, la *Loi sur les corporations canadiennes* a été remplacée par la *Loi canadienne sur les sociétés par actions* pour les sociétés à but lucratif, mais elle reste en vigueur pour les sociétés à but non lucratif. La *Loi sur les corporations canadiennes* n'a pas été rapportée dans la révision de 1985 des *Lois révisées du Canada*, mais elle se trouve dans la révision de 1970. Cette version, telle que modifiée, a toujours force de loi.

2.1.5   Recueils à feuilles mobiles

Manitoba	*Code des droits de la personne*, LM 1987-88, c 45, CPLM c H175, art 8.
Québec	*Loi sur la conservation de la faune*, LRQ c C-61, art 89.

> Seules les provinces du Manitoba, du Québec et de la Nouvelle-Écosse publient une version officielle de recueils à feuilles mobiles. Pour le Manitoba, toujours mentionner le recueil annuel avant de faire référence aux recueils à feuilles mobiles.

> Faire référence aux recueils à feuilles mobiles de la Nouvelle-Écosse de la même manière qu'aux lois révisées et recueils annuels (section 2.1.4).

> Ne pas mettre de virgule entre le recueil et le numéro de chapitre (LRQ c B-2).

Législation

2.1.6 Version électronique officielle

Ontario	*Loi sur le Barreau*, LRO 1990, c L.8, art 26.1(1).
Nouveau-Brunswick	*Loi de 2009 sur l'équité salariale*, SNB c P-5.05, art 6(1).

➤ Faire référence à une version électronique officielle de la même manière qu'à une version imprimée (section 2.1.4).

➤ **Nouveau-Brunswick** : Depuis 2003, l'Imprimeur de la Reine du Nouveau-Brunswick ne publie plus les lois sur format papier. Elles se trouvent sur le site du gouvernement (<http://www.gnb.ca/acts>).

➤ **Ontario** : Depuis le 30 novembre 2008, les copies des lois obtenues sur le site Lois-en-ligne (<http://www.e-laws.gov.on.ca>) sont des versions officielles de la loi, à moins qu'elles ne soient accompagnées d'un avertissement avisant qu'il ne s'agit pas d'une copie officielle.

2.1.7 Indication géographique

➤ Inscrire l'indication géographique immédiatement après le recueil.

➤ Voir l'**annexe A-1** pour les abréviations des références législatives.

> *Loi sur les agences de voyages*, LRO 1990, c T.19.
>
> *Workers Compensation Act*, SPEI 1994, c 67.

Abréviations des indications géographiques dans les références législatives :

Alberta	A
Bas-Canada	B-C
Canada	C
Colombie-Britannique	BC
Haut-Canada	UC
Île-du-Prince-Édouard	PEI
Manitoba	M
Nouveau-Brunswick	N-B
Nouvelle-Écosse	NS
Nunavut (à partir du 1er avril 1999)	Nu
Ontario	O
Province du Canada	Prov C
Québec	Q
Saskatchewan	S
Terre-Neuve (Lois et règlements abrogés avant le 6 décembre 2001 / *Gazette* publiée avant le 21 décembre 2001)	N
Terre-Neuve-et-Labrador (Lois et règlements en vigueur à partir du 6 décembre 2001 / *Gazette* publiée à partir du 21 décembre 2001)	NL
Territoires du Nord-Ouest	TN-O
Yukon	Y

Législation

2.1.8   Année, session et supplément

Année	*Loi de 1998 sur l'adoption internationale*, LO 1998, c 29.
Session qui s'étend sur plus d'une année	*Hospital Act*, LY 1989-90, c 13.
Plus d'une session dans une même année	*An Act to Amend the Labour Act*, SPEI 2000 (1re sess), c 7.
Supplément	*Loi sur les douanes*, LRC 1985, c 1 (2e supp).
Année du règne	*An Act respecting the Civilization and Enfranchisement of certain Indians*, S Prov C 1859 (22 Vict), c 9.

➤   Écrire l'année après l'indication géographique, suivie d'une virgule. Si un numéro de session ou de supplément suit l'année, placer la virgule après l'indication de ce numéro ou de ce supplément.

Législation

> Ne pas indiquer l'année pour les recueils à feuilles mobiles du Québec (LRQ) et du Manitoba (CPLM) et ne pas mettre de virgule entre le recueil et le numéro de chapitre (section 2.1.5).

> Lorsqu'une **session s'étend sur plus d'une année**, se référer à toutes les années sur lesquelles s'étend le recueil (par ex. 1980-81).

> Si un **recueil contient les lois de plusieurs sessions**, les chapitres sont numérotés indépendamment pour chaque session. Indiquer entre parenthèses le numéro de la session (1re, 2e, 3e ou 4e), suivi de sess après l'année.

> Faire référence au **supplément** pour les lois et modifications qui ont été adoptées pendant l'année d'une révision ou d'une refonte des lois, mais qui n'ont pas été comprises dans la refonte. Indiquer entre parenthèses le numéro de supplément, suivi de supp après le chapitre.

> Pour les lois fédérales adoptées avant 1867, ainsi que pour les lois provinciales adoptées avant que la province ne se joigne à la confédération, indiquer **l'année du règne** entre parenthèses, à la suite de l'année civile.

Ann	Ann		George	Geo
Edward	Edw		Victoria	Vict
Elizabeth	Eliz		William	Will

2.1.9 Chapitre

> Abréger chapitre par c.

> Écrire la référence numérique ou alphanumérique du chapitre telle qu'indiquée dans le recueil, **incluant les traits d'union et les points**.

> > *Chester Trails Act*, RSNS 2001, c 21.
> >
> > *Loi sur les tribunaux judiciaires*, LRQ c T-16.
> >
> > *Landlord and Tenant (Residential Tenancies) Act, 1973*, SN 1973, no 18.

> N.B. Entre 1934 et 1975-76, les lois des recueils annuels de Terre-Neuve sont désignées par un numéro. Abréger numéro par no.

2.1.10 Référence précise

➢ Pour indiquer un article particulier d'une loi, écrire la référence précise après le chapitre et après une virgule.

➢ Abréger **article(s)** par art (et non "à l'art") dans les notes de bas de page, mais jamais dans le corps du texte.

➢ À l'exception des alinéas non numérotés ou sans désignation alphabétique (voir note 3), les subdivisions plus précises que les articles (par ex. les paragraphes ou sous-paragraphes) sont aussi abrégées par art (voir note 2).

➢ Séparer les **articles consécutifs** par un trait d'union et les articles **non consécutifs** par une virgule (voir note 2).

[1] *Citizens' Representative Act*, SN 2001, C-141, art 41, 46-48.

[2] *Dangerous Goods Transportation and Handling Act*, SA 1998, c D-3, art 3(a)-(d), 6(1)(a), (b).

[3] *Loi de 1999 sur les services gouvernementaux*, LC 1999, c 13, art 2(1), al 4.

[4] *Loi sur les aspects civils de l'enlèvement international et interprovincial d'enfants*, LRQ c A-2301, préambule.

[5] *Loi sur l'assurance-emploi*, LC 1996, c 23, ann II.

➢ Après le numéro de l'article, indiquer chaque alinéa numéroté ou désigné par une lettre entre parenthèses (art 92(1)(a)), et ce, même s'il n'y a pas de parenthèses dans la version officielle de la loi.

➢ Faire référence à un paragraphe non numéroté ou sans désignation alphabétique comme à un alinéa, abrégé al (voir note 3). Ne pas mettre al entre parenthèses.

➢ Ne pas abréger préambule (voir note 4).

➢ Abréger **annexe** par ann (voir note 5).

2.1.11 Modifications, abrogations et remises en vigueur

Modification sous-entendue	*Loi sur les représentations théâtrales*, LRQ 1977, c R-25.
Modification mentionnée	*Loi sur les mesures d'urgence*, LM 1987, c 11, modifiée par LM 1997, c 28.
	Municipal Government Act, RSA 2000, c M-26, art 694(4), mod par *Municipal Government Amendment Act*, SA 2003, c 43, art 4.
Abrogation	*Loi sur les prestations familiales*, LRO 1990, c F2, abrogée par *Loi de 1997 sur la reforme de l'aide sociale*, LO 1997, c 25, art 4(1).
Loi modifiant une loi antérieure	*Loi modifiant la Loi sur les normes du travail*, LTN-O 1999, c 18, modifiant LRTN-O 1988, c L-1.
Loi abrogeant une loi antérieure	*Loi sur la Société de développement autochtone de la Baie James*, LRQ 2000, c S-91, abrogeant *Loi constituant la Société de développement autochtone de la Baie James*, LQ 1978, c 96.

Législation

> Il est sous-entendu que les références se rapportent à la **loi telle que modifiée à la date de publication** du texte de l'auteur.

> **Indiquer que la loi a été modifiée uniquement si cette mention est pertinente** pour la question traitée dans le texte. Lorsqu'il y a une modification, faire référence d'abord à la loi originale, suivie de modifiée par et de la référence à la nouvelle loi.

> Dans le cas d'une loi qui a été **abrogée**, se référer à la loi abrogative en l'introduisant par la formule abrogée par.

> Indiquer modifiant lorsqu'une référence est faite à une **loi qui modifie une loi antérieure** et indiquer abrogeant lorsqu'il s'agit d'une loi qui abroge une loi antérieure.

> Indiquer le **titre de la deuxième loi** (qu'il s'agisse d'une loi modifiée ou abrogée, ou d'une loi modifiant ou abrogeant) uniquement s'il est différent du titre de la première loi ou s'il n'est pas compris dans le titre de celle-ci.

> Si une loi ou une partie d'une loi a été **abrogée et remplacée par une autre**, se référer à la loi originale en premier, suivie de remise en vigueur par et de la référence complète de la nouvelle partie. N'utiliser cette terminologie que lorsque les dispositions abrogées et remplacées se trouvent dans le même article.

2.1.12 Annexes

> Pour les lois paraissant dans une annexe, indiquer la révision ou le volume dont fait partie l'annexe, suivis d'une virgule et du numéro de l'annexe.

> *Déclaration canadienne des droits*, LC 1960, c 44, reproduite dans LRC 1985, ann III.

> Toujours indiquer la référence officielle, suivie de reproduite dans pour introduire la référence à l'annexe.

> Abréger **annexe** par ann.

> Écrire le numéro de l'annexe en chiffres romains.

2.1.13 Loi contenue dans une autre loi

Loi sur la Société d'expansion du Cap-Breton, art 27, constituant la partie II de la *Loi organique de 1987 sur le Canada atlantique*, LC 1988, c 50.

> Faire référence au titre de la loi contenue dans la loi principale en premier lieu, suivi d'une virgule. Écrire ensuite la référence complète de la partie pertinente de la loi principale, introduite par constituant.

> Les références précises à la loi contenue sont indiquées avant la référence à la loi principale (voir l'emplacement de l'art 27 dans l'exemple).

Législation

2.2 LOIS CONSTITUTIONNELLES

Loi constitutionnelle de 1867	*Loi constitutionnelle de 1867* (R-U), 30 & 31 Vict, c 3, reproduite dans LRC 1985, ann II, n° 5.
Loi de 1982 sur le Canada	*Loi de 1982 sur le Canada* (R-U), 1982, c 11.
Loi constitutionnelle de 1982	*Loi constitutionnelle de 1982*, constituant l'annexe B de la *Loi de 1982 sur le Canada* (R-U), 1982, c 11.
Charte	*Charte canadienne des droits et libertés*, partie I de la *Loi constitutionnelle de 1982*, constituant l'annexe B de la *Loi de 1982 sur le Canada* (R-U), 1982, c 11.
Autres lois constitutionnelles	*Acte de Québec de 1774* (R-U), 14 Geo III, c 83, art 3, reproduit dans LRC 1985, ann II, n° 2.

➢ Beaucoup de lois constitutionnelles ont été adoptées sous des noms différents de ceux couramment utilisés ; il faut utiliser le **nouveau titre**. Consulter l'annexe de la *Loi constitutionnelle de 1982* pour trouver le nouveau titre de la loi. Si l'ancien titre est pertinent, l'indiquer entre parenthèses à la fin de la référence.

➢ La *Loi de 1982 sur le Canada* est une loi du Royaume-Uni. Sa référence doit donc se conformer aux règles concernant les lois du Royaume-Uni (section 7.1.1).

➢ Puisque la *Charte* n'a pas été promulguée indépendamment, faire référence à la partie I de la *Loi constitutionnelle de 1982*.

➢ Au besoin, inclure une référence à l'**annexe II des LRC 1985** après la référence officielle, puisque la plupart des lois constitutionnelles canadiennes s'y trouvent.

2.2.1 Référence précise

Loi constitutionnelle de 1867	*Loi constitutionnelle de 1867* (R-U), 30 & 31 Vict, c 3, art 91, reproduit dans LRC 1985, ann II, n° 5.
Loi de 1982 sur le Canada	*Loi de 1982 sur le Canada* (R-U), 1982, c 11, art 1.
Loi constitutionnelle de 1982	*Loi constitutionnelle de 1982*, art 35, constituant l'annexe B de la *Loi de 1982 sur le Canada* (R-U), 1982, c 11.
Charte	*Charte canadienne des droits et libertés*, art 7, partie I de la *Loi constitutionnelle de 1982*, constituant l'annexe B de la *Loi de 1982 sur le Canada* (R-U), 1982, c 11.
Autres lois constitutionnelles	*Acte de Québec de 1774* (R-U), 14 Geo III, c 83, art 3, reproduit dans LRC 1985, ann II, n° 2.

➢ Indiquer les références précises (section 2.1.10) aux articles de la *Charte* et de la *Loi constitutionnelle de 1982* immédiatement après le titre.

➢ Indiquer les références précises aux autres lois constitutionnelles après le numéro du chapitre.

2.3 CODES

Code civil du Québec	Art 1457 CcQ
Code civil du Québec (1980)	Art 441 CcQ (1980)
Code civil du Bas Canada	Art 838 CcBC
Code de procédure civile	Art 20 Cpc
Code de procédure pénale	Art 104 Cpp

➢ **Ne jamais fournir la référence complète pour désigner un code**.

➢ Pour un code mentionné ci-contre, utiliser le nom abrégé dès la première référence.

➢ Pour un code qui n'est pas dans la liste, écrire le nom du code au complet dans la première référence et créer une version abrégée si nécessaire (art 1 *Code des professions* [C prof]).

➢ Faire référence à un paragraphe non numéroté ou sans désignation alphabétique comme à un alinéa, abrégé al (art 1457, al 2 CcQ).

N.B. Pour les **commentaires du ministre**, voir la section 4.2.1.

N.B. Le **CcQ (1980)** se réfère à une série de dispositions concernant le droit de la famille promulguées en 1980 : la *Loi instituant un nouveau Code civil et portant réforme du droit de la famille*, LQ 1980, c 39. Ne pas confondre cette loi avec le *Code civil du Québec*, LQ 1991, c 64 (CcQ), en vigueur depuis le 1er janvier 1994 et remplaçant le *Code civil du Bas Canada* de 1866.

2.4 NUNAVUT

L'Imprimeur du territoire ne publie pas de lois reliées. Des versions non officielles des lois sont disponibles sur le site Internet du ministère de la Justice du Nunavut (<http://www.justice.gov.nu.ca>).

2.4.1 Lois adoptées par le Nunavut

➢ Pour les lois adoptées par le Nunavut après le 1er avril 1999, fournir la référence traditionnelle (section 2.1.1).

Loi sur le drapeau du Nunavut, L Nu 1999, c 1.

2.4.2   Lois adoptées par les Territoires du Nord-Ouest pour le Nunavut

➢ Pour les lois adoptées par les Territoires du Nord-Ouest pour le Nunavut avant le 1er avril 1999 et qui ne s'appliquent qu'au Nunavut, fournir la référence traditionnelle, suivie de : telle qu'adoptée pour le Nunavut, conformément à la *Loi sur le Nunavut*, LC 1993, c 28.

> *Nunavut Judicial System Implementation Act*, LTN-O 1998, c 34, telle qu'adoptée pour le Nunavut, conformément à la *Loi sur le Nunavut*, LC 1993, c 28.

2.4.3   Lois reproduites par le Canada pour le Nunavut

> *Loi sur les langues officielles*, LRTN-O 1998, c O-1, reproduite pour le Nunavut par l'art 29 de la *Loi sur le Nunavut*, LC 1993, c 28.

➢ En vertu de l'article 29 de la *Loi sur le Nunavut*, LC 1993, c 28, les lois des Territoires du Nord-Ouest ont été reproduites pour le Nunavut et sont entrées en vigueur le 1er avril 1999 (dans la mesure où elles s'appliquent au Nunavut).

➢ Fournir la référence traditionnelle suivie de : reproduite pour le Nunavut par l'art 29 de la *Loi sur le Nunavut*, LC 1993, c 28.

2.5   PROJETS DE LOI

	Numéro,	*titre,*	session,	législature,	indication géographique,	année,	référence précise	(renseignements supplémentaires) (facultatif).
Canada	PL C-7,	Loi concernant l'Agence des services frontaliers du Canada,	1re sess,	37e parl,		2005,	art 5(1)(e)	(adopté par la Chambre des communes le 13 juin 2005).
	PL S-1,	Loi concernant les chemins de fer,	2e sess,	40e lég,		2009,	art 1	(première lecture le 26 janvier 2009).
Provinces et territoires	PL 161,	Loi concernant le cadre juridique de technologies de l'information,	2e sess,	36e lég,	Québec,	2001		(sanctionné le 21 juin 2001), LQ 2001, c 32.

Législation

> ➤ Le numéro des projets de loi de la Chambre des communes est précédé par C-, et le numéro des projets de loi du Sénat par S-.

> ➤ Indiquer le **titre non abrégé** du projet de loi. Mettre le titre en italique et respecter l'usage des majuscules.

> ➤ Pour une référence à un projet de loi provincial, mentionner l'indication géographique.

> ➤ Ne pas indiquer l'année du règne.

> ➤ Diviser les projets de loi en **articles** (art).

> ➤ Indiquer les renseignements supplémentaires (par ex. la date d'une des lectures ou l'étape franchie dans l'adoption du projet de loi) entre parenthèses à la fin de la référence, s'il y a lieu.

> ➤ Si possible, indiquer le numéro de chapitre de la future loi en tant que renseignement supplémentaire (par ex. (sanctionné le 21 juin 2001), LQ 2001, c 32)).

2.6   RÈGLEMENTS

Indication géographique	Non refondus	Refondus ou réadoptés
Canada	DORS/2000-111, art 4.	CRC, c 1180, art 3 (1978).
Alberta	Alta Reg 184/2001, art 2.	--
Colombie-Britannique	BC Reg 362/2000, art 4.	--
Île-du-Prince-Édouard	PEI Reg EC1999-598, art 3.	--
Manitoba	Règl du Man 155/2001, art 3.	Règl du Man 368/97R, art 2.
Nouveau-Brunswick	Règl du N-B 2000-8, art 11.	--
Nouvelle-Écosse	NS Reg 24/2000, art 8.	--
Nunavut	Nu Reg 045-99, art 2.	--
Ontario	Règl de l'Ont 426/00, art 2.	RRO 1990, Reg 1015, art 3.
Québec	D 1240-2000, 25 octobre 2000, GOQ 2000II6817, art 2.	RRQ 1981, c C-11, r 9, art 10.
Saskatchewan	Sask Reg 67/2001, art 3.	RRS, c C-502, Reg 21, OC 359/2000, art 6.
Terre-Neuve	Nfld Reg 78/99, art 4.	--
Terre-Neuve-et-Labrador	NLR 08/02, art 2.	CNLR 1151/96, art 6.
Territoires du Nord-Ouest	TN-O Reg 253-77, art 3.	RRTN-O 1990, c E-27, art 16.
Yukon	YD 2000/130, art 9.	--

2.6.1 Règlements fédéraux

2.6.1.1 Règlements refondus

➢ Abréger **Codification des règlements du Canada** par CRC.

Titre,	CRC,	chapitre,	référence précise	(année) (facultatif).
Règlement sur le fil de fer barbelé,	CRC,	c 1180,	art 3	(1978).

➢ L'indication de l'année de la révision des règlements est facultative. À moins qu'une année ne soit spécifiée, il est sous-entendu que les références concernent à la dernière révision.

2.6.1.2 Règlements non refondus

Titre (facultatif),	DORS/	année-numéro du règlement,	référence précise.
Règlement canadien sur la sûreté aérienne,	DORS/	2000-111,	art 4.

➢ Les règlements fédéraux promulgués après la codification se trouvent dans la **partie II de la *Gazette du Canada***. Il n'est pas nécessaire de faire référence à la *Gazette*.

➢ L'indication du titre du règlement est facultative.

➢ Abréger **Décrets, ordonnances et règlements** par DORS.

➢ Pour faire référence aux règlements avant l'année 2000, utiliser les deux derniers chiffres de l'année (98 et non 1998).

2.6.2 Règlements provinciaux et territoriaux

➢ L'indication du titre du règlement au début de la référence (en italique et suivi d'une virgule) est facultative.

➢ Certaines juridictions utilisent tous les chiffres de l'année à partir de l'an 2000, alors que d'autres n'utilisent que les deux derniers chiffres.

N.B. L'Alberta, la Colombie-Britannique, l'Île-du-Prince-Édouard, le Nouveau-Brunswick, Terre-Neuve-et-Labrador, le Nunavut, la Nouvelle-Écosse et le Yukon ne publient pas de version révisée de leurs règlements.

2.6.2.1 Alberta, Colombie-Britannique

Indication géographique	Reg	numéro/année,	référence précise.
Alta	Reg	184/2001,	art 2.
BC	Reg	362/2000,	art 4.

➢ Faire référence aux règlements consolidés sur feuilles mobiles de l'Alberta et de la Colombie-Britannique de la même façon qu'aux règlements non révisés (section 2.6).

2.6.2.2 Manitoba

	Règl du	Indication géographique	année-numéro,	référence précise.
Non réadopté	Règl du	Man	155/2001,	art 3.
Réadopté	Règl du	Man	468/88R,	art 2.

➢ La plupart des règlements manitobains ont été réadoptés en anglais et en français en **1987** et en **1988**.

➢ Pour les règlements manitobains réadoptés, ajouter un R immédiatement après les deux derniers chiffres de l'année.

2.6.2.3 Nouveau-Brunswick

Règl du	indication géographique	année-numéro,	référence précise.
Règl du	N-B	2000-8,	art 11.

➢ Les règlements du Nouveau-Brunswick ont été refondus en **1963**.

➢ Le recueil à feuilles mobiles des règlements du Nouveau-Brunswick n'est pas une refonte officielle.

2.6.2.4 Terre-Neuve-et-Labrador

➢ Toutes les références à « Newfoundland » ont été changées pour « Newfoundland and Labrador ». Pour les règlements qui ont été abrogés avant le 6 décembre 2001, indiquer seulement Newfoundland.

2.6.2.4.1 Non refondus

➢ Pour les règlements abrogés avant le 6 décembre 2001, écrire Nfld Reg. Pour les autres règlements, écrire NL.

Indication géographique	R	numéro/deux derniers chiffres de l'année,	référence précise.
NL	R	8/02,	art 2.

2.6.2.4.2 Refondus

➢ Les règlements de Terre-Neuve-et-Labrador ont été refondus en 1996. Utiliser CNLR pour indiquer *Consolidated Newfoundland and Labrador Regulation*.

CNLR	numéro/ l'année de codification,	référence précise.
CNLR	1151/96,	art 6.

➢ Pour les règlements qui ont été abrogés avant le 6 décembre 2001, faire référence à CNR pour indiquer *Consolidated Newfoundland Regulation*.

2.6.2.5 *Territoires du Nord-Ouest*

2.6.2.5.1 Non refondus

Règl des	indication géographique	numéro-deux derniers chiffres de l'année,	référence précise.
Règl des	TN-O	253-77,	art 3.

2.6.2.5.2 Refondus

RRTN-O	année de refonte,	chapitre,	référence précise.
RRTN-O	1990,	c E-27,	art 16.

2.6.2.6 *Nouvelle-Écosse*

Indication géographique	Reg	numéro/année,	référence précise.
NS	Reg	24/2000,	art 8.

2.6.2.7 *Nunavut*

Règl du	indication géographique	numéro-deux derniers chiffres de l'année,	référence précise.
Règl du	Nu	045-99,	art 2.

➢ Consulter la *Gazette du Nunavut* pour tous les règlements **à partir du 1er avril 1999**.

➢ Pour tous les règlements **avant le 1ᵉʳ avril 1999**, consulter les *Règlements révisés des Territoires du Nord-Ouest* (1990), ainsi que la *Gazette des Territoires du Nord-Ouest*, IIᵉ partie.

➢ Aucune version révisée officielle des règlements du Nunavut n'a été publiée.

2.6.2.8 Ontario

2.6.2.8.1 Non refondus

Règl du	indication géographique	numéro-deux derniers chiffres de l'année,	référence précise.
Règl de	l'Ont	426/00,	art 2.

2.6.2.8.2 Refondus

RRO	année de refonte,	Reg	numéro,	référence précise.
RRO	1990,	Reg	1015,	art 3.

2.6.2.9 Île-du-Prince-Édouard

Indication géographique	Reg	ECannée-numéro,	référence précise.
PEI	Reg	EC1999-598,	art 3.

➢ Dans le numéro du règlement, EC est l'abréviation de ***Executive Council***. Il n'y a pas d'espace entre EC et année-numéro.

2.6.2.10 Québec

2.6.2.10.1 Non refondus

D	numéro-année,	référence à la Gazette,	référence précise.
D	1240-2000,	(2000) GOQ II, 6817,	art 2.

➢ Abréger **Décret** par D.

➢ Pour les références à la *Gazette officielle du Québec*, voir la section 2.7.1.

2.6.2.10.2 Refondus

RRQ 1981,	chapitre,	numéro du règlement,	référence.
RRQ 1981,	c C-11,	r 9,	art 10.

2.6.2.11 Saskatchewan

2.6.2.11.1 Non refondus

Indication géographique	Reg	numéro/année,	référence précise.
Sask	Reg	67/2001,	art 3.

2.6.2.11.2 Refondus

RRS,	chapitre,	numéro,	OC numéro/année (s'il y a lieu),	référence précise.
RRS,	c C-50.2,	Reg 21,	OC 359/2000,	art 6.

2.6.2.12 Yukon

Indication géographique	D	année/ numéro,	référence précise,	référence précise.
Y	D	2000/130,	art 9,	art 6.

➤ Abréger **Décret** par D.

2.7 AUTRES INFORMATIONS PUBLIÉES DANS LES *GAZETTES*

2.7.1 Modèle de base

Titre (information supplémentaire),	(année)	abréviation de la *Gazette*	partie de la *Gazette*,	page	(renseignements supplémentaires) (facultatif).
Ministerial Order 36/91,	(1991)	A Gaz	I,	1609.	
Avis (Banque du Canada),	(1995)	Gaz C	I,	4412.	
D309/2001,	(2001)	A Gaz	I,	1752	(*Provincial Parks Act*).

Législation

➤ Placer un espace entre l'abréviation de la *Gazette* et la partie de la *Gazette* (A Gaz I).

➤ Indiquer le titre du document s'il y a lieu. Si le document est numéroté, inclure le numéro avec le titre, tel qu'indiqué dans la *Gazette*. Inclure le numéro du texte réglementaire (TR) après l'abréviation s'il y en a un. Le nom de la personne ou de la partie concernée par un avis peut être inclus entre parenthèses après le titre (Avis (Banque du Canada)).

➤ Indiquer la partie de la *Gazette* après l'abréviation. Si la *Gazette* n'est pas publiée en plusieurs parties, indiquer la page immédiatement après le point suivant l'année (GOQ, 74).

➤ Inclure des renseignements supplémentaires nécessaires, comme le nom de la loi en vertu de laquelle un décret est promulgué (voir *Provincial Parks Act*).

Abréviations des Gazettes :

The Alberta Gazette	A Gaz
The British Columbia Gazette	BC Gaz
La Gazette de l'Ontario	Gaz O
Gazette des Territoires du Nord-Ouest	Gaz TN-O
Gazette du Canada	Gaz C
Gazette du Manitoba	Gaz M
Nouveau-Brunswick : *Gazette royale*	Gaz N-B
La Gazette du Yukon	Gaz Y
Gazette officielle du Québec	GOQ
The Newfoundland Gazette (avant le 21 décembre 2001)	N Gaz
The Newfoundland and Labrador Gazette (du 21 décembre 2001 à aujourd'hui)	NL Gaz
Nouvelle-Écosse : *Royal Gazette*	NS Gaz
Gazette du Nunavut	Gaz Nu
Île-du-Prince-Édouard : *Royal Gazette*	PEI Gaz
The Saskatchewan Gazette	S Gaz

N.B. La version PDF de la *Gazette du Canada* est officielle depuis le 1er avril 2003 sur le site <http://canadagazette.gc.ca>.

2.7.2 Décrets

Un décret est un instrument du pouvoir exécutif mettant en œuvre une décision du gouvernement (par ex. la création d'un règlement).

2.7.2.1 Fédéral

Titre (s'il y a lieu),	CP année-numéro ou numéro du texte réglementaire,	référence à la *Gazette,*	(renseignements supplémentaires) (facultatif).
	CP 1997-627,	(1997) Gaz C II,1381.	
Décret refusant d'annuler ou de référer au CRTC une décision concernant CFJO-FM,	TR/97-51,	(1997) Gaz C II, 1523.	

> Inclure le titre en italique s'il y en a un.

> Abréger **Conseil Privé** par CP.

> Inscrire le numéro du texte réglementaire (TR), s'il y a lieu.

> Inclure des renseignements supplémentaires entre parenthèses à la fin de la référence (par ex. le titre de la loi en vertu de laquelle le décret a été promulgué) s'il y a lieu.

2.7.2.2 Provincial et territorial

Titre (s'il y a lieu),	numéro du décret,	référence à la Gazette	(renseignements supplémentaires) (facultatif).
	D 1989/19,	(1989) Gaz Y II, 57.	
Town of Paradise Order,	OC 99-529,	(1999) N Gaz II, 451	*(Municipalities Act).*
Règlement sur la levée de la suspension et sur l'application de l'article 411 de la Loi sur les normes du travail à l'égard de certains salariés,	D 570-93,	(1993) GOQ II, 3309.	

> Inclure le titre en italique, s'il y a lieu.

> Pour *Order in Council*, utiliser l'abréviation telle qu'elle paraît dans la Gazette. Utiliser D pour **Décret**.

> Fournir le numéro tel qu'il paraît dans la Gazette. Ce numéro comprend parfois l'année ou les deux derniers chiffres de l'année.

> ➤ Inclure des renseignements supplémentaires entre parenthèses à la fin de la référence si nécessaire (par ex. le titre de la loi en vertu de laquelle le décret est promulgué).

2.7.3   Proclamations et instructions royales

Référence à la loi entrée en vigueur ou émetteur de la Proclamation ou de l'Instruction,	type de document,	date,	numéro du texte réglementaire,	référence.
Loi sur l'Agence spatiale canadienne, LC 1990, c 13,		entrée en vigueur le 14 décembre 1990,	TR/91-5,	(1991) Gaz C I, 74.
	Proclamation,	1er avril 1991,		(1991) S Gaz I, 1174.
George R,	Proclamation,	7 octobre 1763 (3 Geo III),		reproduite dans LRC 1985, ann II, no 1.
George R au Gouverneur Arthur Phillip,	Instruction royale,	25 avril 1787 (27 Geo III),		reproduite dans *Historical Documents of New South Wales*, t 1, 2e partie, Sydney, Government Printer, 1892-1901 à la p 67.

> ➤ Inclure Proclamation et Instruction royale si le contexte l'exige.

> ➤ Indiquer la date, suivie de la *Gazette* ou autre référence.

> ➤ Pour les proclamations fédérales de 1972 à aujourd'hui, indiquer le numéro du texte réglementaire (TR).

2.8   RÈGLEMENTS MUNICIPAUX

	Ville,	Règlement ou Règlement refondu	numéro,	*titre*	(date),	référence precise.
Non refondus	Ville de Blainville,	Règlement	n° 955-43,	*Règlement de zonage*	(10 janvier 1994),	art 2366.
Refondus	Ville de Montréal,	Règlement refondu	c S-011,	*Règlement sur les services de collecte*		art 5.

> ➤ Indiquer le numéro du règlement municipal et le titre complet s'il n'existe pas de titre abrégé.

2.9 RÈGLES DE PRATIQUE

Indication géographique (s'il y a lieu),	organisme (s'il y a lieu),	titre,	référence précise.
		Règles de la Cour suprême du Canada,	r 16.
Terre-Neuve-et-Labrador,		Rules of the Supreme Court,	r 16.01(2).
	Commission québécoise des libérations conditionnelles,	Règles de pratique,	r 10(4).

➤ Les règles de pratique (ou règles de procédure) balisent et régissent le fonctionnement des organes ou organismes judiciaires et administratifs.

➤ Écrire l'indication géographique et l'organisme à moins que l'information ne fasse partie du titre des règles.

➤ Ne pas écrire Canada pour les règles de la Cour suprême du Canada, ni pour les règles de la Cour fédérale.

➤ Abréger **règle** par r.

➤ Pour faire référence au *Code de procédure civile* et au *Code de procédure pénale* du Québec, voir la section 2.3.

2.10 COMMISSIONS DE VALEURS MOBILIÈRES

Titre,	commission	document	bulletin (s'il y a lieu)	(date),	référence précise.
Mutual Reliance Review System for Exemptive Relief Applications,	OSC	NP 12-201		(26 août 2005).	
Proposed Amendments to Multilateral Instrument 52-109 Certification of Disclosure in Issuers' Annual and Interim Filings and Companion Policy 52-109CP,	MSC	Notice 2005-19		(1er avril 2005).	
Règlement 62-104 sur les offres publiques d'achat et de rachat,	AMF	Consultation,	(2006) 3 : 20 BAMF : Valeurs mobilières 1		à la p 2.

Législation

> Pour les **instructions canadiennes**, les **normes canadiennes** et d'autres documents de valeurs mobilières, faire référence aux **commissions de valeurs mobilières provinciales**.

> Abréger **Instruction canadienne** par IC et **Norme canadienne** par NC.

> Pour les **modifications**, les **règlements en consultation**, les **avis du personnel** et d'autres textes de commission, faire référence au **Bulletin de commission** ou à une autre publication similaire.

> Abréger *Bulletin de l'Autorité des marchés financiers : section Valeurs mobilières* par BAMF : Valeurs mobilières.

> Si des règlements ou des textes sont uniquement publiés en anglais, indiquer le nom de la commission et du document en anglais.

Jurisprudence

3   JURISPRUDENCE

3.1 SOURCES

Ordre hiérarchique des sources :

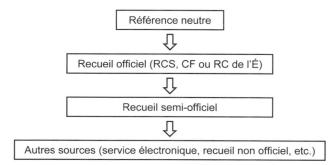

> Pour faire référence à de la jurisprudence, toujours citer **au moins deux** sources pour que l'information soit **bien identifiée** et **accessible**. Inclure plus de références si nécessaire.

> **Avant de faire référence aux sources moins officielles, s'assurer que les sources faisant le plus autorité ne sont pas disponibles** (par ex. ne pas citer de service électronique avant de citer un recueil officiel).

   → Toujours indiquer la **référence neutre** si elle existe.

   → Après la référence neutre, faire référence aux **recueils officiels** (RCS, CF ou RC de l'É).

   → Si la référence neutre et/ou les recueils officiels ne sont pas disponibles, faire référence aux **recueils semi-officiels**.

   → En dernier lieu, utiliser **d'autres sources** (service électronique, recueil non officiel, etc.).

> Choisir les **autres sources** avec soin en gardant en tête le lectorat visé.

   → Préférer les recueils imprimés **facilement disponibles**, **généraux** et couvrant un **vaste territoire** (section 3.7.2).

   → Préférer les services électroniques **facilement accessibles** (section 3.8).

> Consulter le tableau ci-après pour les sources à citer selon les références disponibles.

Source(s) disponible(s)	Règle	Exemple
Référence neutre uniquement	Indiquer la référence neutre et le service électronique utilisé entre parenthèses	*Burke c MNR*, 2008 CCI 680 (disponible sur QL).
Référence neutre et recueil(s) imprimé(s)	Inclure la référence neutre et faire ensuite référence au recueil faisant le plus autorité	*R c Latimer*, 2001 CSC 1, [2001] 1 RCS 3.
Recueil officiel et autre(s) recueil(s)	Indiquer le recueil officiel et utiliser le recueil faisant le plus autorité comme référence parallèle	*Baker c Canada (Ministre de la Citoyenneté et de l'Immigration)*, [1999] 2 RCS 817, 174 DLR (4e) 193.
Recueil(s) imprimé(s) non officiel(s) et/ou service(s) électronique(s)	Faire référence aux deux sources les plus accessibles. Indiquer un recueil papier avant un service électronique	*Coldmatic Refrigeration of Canada Ltd v Leveltek Processing LLC* (2005), 70 OR (3e) 758 (disponible sur CanLII) (Ont CA).
Aucune source disponible	Suivre les règles pour les décisions non publiées (section 3.12)	*Commission des droits de la personne du Québec c Brasserie O'Keefe* (13 septembre 1990), Montréal 500-05-005826-873 (CS).

3.2   MODÈLE DE BASE

3.2.1   Référence neutre disponible

Intitulé,	référence neutre	référence précise,	autre référence,	juge (facultatif)	[*titre abrégé*].
Dunsmuir c Nouveau-Brunswick,	2008 CSC 9	au para 122,	[2008] 1 RCS 190,	juge Binnie	[*Dunsmuir*].
Lemay c Castiglia,	2008 QCCQ 4979	aux para 22-26	(disponible sur WL Can),		[*Lemay*].

3.2.2 Référence neutre non disponible

Intitulé,	(année de la décision) (si nécessaire),	recueil	référence précise,	autre référence	(indication géographique et/ou **cour**) (si nécessaire)	juge (facultatif)	[*titre abrégé*].
R c S (RD),		[1997] 3 RCS 484	au para 16,	161 NSR (2e) 241		juge Major, dissident	[R c S].
R c Caouette	(1998),	149 CCC (3e) 310		(disponible sur QL)	(CS Qc)		[*Caouette*].

3.3 INTITULÉ

➢ L'intitulé est le titre abrégé d'une décision et permet de s'y référer de manière informelle.

➢ **Lorsque l'intitulé est indiqué dans le recueil, utiliser cet intitulé tel quel**. Si la décision ne fournit pas d'intitulé, voir les sections 3.3.1 à 3.3.18.

➢ Ne pas répéter l'intitulé dans la note de bas de page s'il est déjà mentionné dans le texte.

➢ Mettre en italique le nom des parties et le *c* ou le *v* qui sépare le nom des parties.

➢ L'utilisation du *c* ou du *v* dans l'intitulé indique la langue dans laquelle la décision est rendue. Si la décision est rendue en anglais, utiliser le *v*. Si la décision est rendue en français, utiliser le *c*. Pour les décisions bilingues, utilisez le *c* pour la rédaction d'un texte en français.

Décision rendue en français	*Traverse Trois-Pistoles Escoumins Ltée c Québec (Commission des transports)*
Décision rendue en anglais	*Pacific Developments Ltd v Calgary (Ville de)*
Décision bilingue	*Comité pour le traitement égal des actionnaires minoritaires de la Société Asbestos Ltée c Ontario (Commission des valeurs mobilières)*

3.3.1   Nom des parties

✓	*Blackburn-Moreault c Moreault* *Marcil c Hétu*
✗	*Rolande Blackburn-Moreault c Henri Moreault* *Marcil c Hétu et Hurtubise*

➢ N'utiliser que les noms de famille. Omettre les prénoms et les initiales.

➢ Lorsqu'il y a jonction de plusieurs instances, ne mentionner que la première instance.

➢ Omettre toute expression telle que et al, qui indique qu'il y a plusieurs parties.

➢ Mettre en majuscule la première lettre du nom de chaque partie, ainsi que la première lettre des noms propres. Ne pas mettre en majuscule les prépositions, les conjonctions et les autres mots faisant partie des expressions procédurales.

➢ Traduire en anglais les descriptions telles que Ville de, mais ne traduire ni les mots qui appartiennent au nom d'une partie (par ex. Université), ni les abréviations (par ex. Ltée ou srl).

➢ Ne pas inclure Le, La, L', Les ou The s'il s'agit du premier mot du nom d'une partie, même s'il s'agit du nom d'une raison sociale. Toutefois, indiquer l'article défini s'il fait partie du nom d'une chose poursuivie *in rem* (tel qu'un navire ou un avion, par ex. *Le Mihalis Angelos*).

3.3.2   Personne représentée par un tuteur

Dobson (Tuteur à l'instance) c Dobson

3.3.3   Noms corporatifs et de sociétés

➢ Toujours inclure Ltd, Ltée, srl ou LLP. Ne pas traduire ces expressions ou abréviations.

➢ Si le nom de la compagnie indique clairement son statut corporatif, omettre les expressions telles que inc ou Co. Toutefois, si le nom n'indique pas ce statut ou si les termes ne sont pas à la fin du nom de l'entreprise, utiliser ces expressions pour identifier le statut corporatif des parties.

✓	*Pelletier c Madawaska Co Ltée* *JJ Joubert Ltée c Lapierre* *KPMG srl c Lachance* *Lemieux c Société Radio-Canada*
✗	*Pelletier c Madawaska Co* *Joubert Ltée c Lapierre* *Lemieux c Radio-Canada*
Société	*Astier, Favrot c Mendelsohn*

➢ Indiquer les prénoms et les initiales qui font partie de la raison sociale.

> Indiquer les noms de tous les partenaires d'une société.

> Lorsqu'une compagnie a un nom bilingue, utiliser le nom de la compagnie dans la langue de la décision de référence. Si la décision est bilingue, utiliser le nom dans la langue du texte rédigé.

3.3.4 Pays, unités fédérales, provinces et municipalités

Pays	✓	*États-Unis c Shulman*
	✗	*Les États-Unis d'Amérique c Shulman*
Province, État		*Québec (PG) c Auger*
Municipalités		*Laurentide Motels Ltd c Beauport (Ville de)*
		Charlesbourg-Est (Municipalité de) c Asselin
		Vigi Santé Ltée c Montréal (Communauté urbaine de)

> Indiquer le nom français du pays communément utilisé et non son nom officiel ou son abréviation.

> Omettre Province de, État de, Peuple de ou tout autre identificateur du genre.

> Placer les identificateurs, comme Ville de, Communauté urbaine de, Comté de, District de ou Municipalité de entre parenthèses après le nom du lieu.

3.3.5 Testaments et successions

> Ne pas indiquer le nom des exécuteurs testamentaires.

Nom de la succession	*Tremblay c Trudel, succession*
Nom de la succession (lorsque ni le demandeur, ni le défendeur ne sont inclus dans l'intitulé)	*Re Succession Eurig*

3.3.6 Faillites et mises sous séquestre

> Indiquer le nom du failli ou de la compagnie mise sous séquestre suivi de syndic de, séquestre de ou liquidateur de entre parenthèses.

Chablis Textiles (Syndic de) c London Life Insurance

Lasalle Land Co (Liquidateur de) c Alepin

Jurisprudence

3.3.7 Titres de lois

Si le nom de la loi indique clairement l'indication géographique	*Re Code canadien du travail*
Si l'indication géographique ne peut être déduite du nom de la loi	*Renvoi relatif à la Loi sur l'instruction publique (Québec)*

3.3.8 La Couronne : affaires pénales

➤ Utiliser R pour identifier la Couronne dans les causes pénales et pour remplacer les expressions telles que La Reine, Régina, La Couronne, La Reine du chef de ou tout terme semblable qui sert à identifier la Couronne.

R c Blondin

3.3.9 La Couronne : affaires civiles

Procureur général (PG)		*Schreiber c Canada (PG)*
Ministre du Revenu national (MRN)		*Savard c MRN*
Autres organismes gouvernementaux		*Chagnon c Québec (Commission d'accès à l'information)*
Ne pas répéter le nom de l'indication géographique	✓	*Banque Laurentienne du Canada c Canada (Commission des droits de la personne)*
	✗	*Banque Laurentienne du Canada c Canada (Commission canadienne des droits de la personne)*
Ne pas inclure le nom d'un individu représentant un organisme gouvernemental	✓	*Canada (Ministre de l'Emploi et de l'Immigration) c Jiminez-Perez*
	✗	*Jean Boisvert (Directeur du centre d'Immigration Canada de Winnipeg) c Jiminez-Perez*

➤ Dans les affaires civiles, **identifier la juridiction** pour indiquer la Reine du chef du Canada ou de la province.

➤ Utiliser le nom de l'indication géographique, suivi du nom de l'organisme gouvernemental (tel qu'une commission, un ministère ou un département) entre parenthèses.

➤ Abréger **Ministre du Revenu national** par MRN et **Sous-ministre du Revenu national** par Sous-MRN.

➤ Écrire l'abréviation PG pour désigner **Procureur général**.

> Pour faire référence à un **tribunal administratif fédéral ou provincial**, suivre les règles énoncées à la section 3.13.

> Ne pas inclure le nom d'un individu représentant un organisme gouvernemental.

3.3.10 Sociétés d'État

Westaim Corp c Monnaie royale canadienne

> Ne pas indiquer le nom de l'indication géographique avant le nom de la société d'État.

3.3.11 Conseils et organismes municipaux

Québec (PG) c Montréal (Communauté urbaine) Service de police

3.3.12 Conseils scolaires

> Omettre les termes tels que Conseil scolaire et Conseil d'administration; 'indiquer que le nom de l'institution.

✓	*Ross c District n° 15 du Nouveau-Brunswick*
✗	*Ross c Conseil scolaire du district n° 15 du Nouveau-Brunswick*

3.3.13 Syndicats

✓	*Lavigne c Syndicat des employés de la Fonction publique de l'Ontario*
✗	*Lavigne c SEFPO*

> Ne pas abréger le nom des syndicats car de telles abréviations varient d'un cas à l'autre.

3.3.14 Agences d'aide sociale

Doe c Metropolitan Toronto Child and Family Services

Manitoba (Directeur de la protection de l'enfance) c Y

> Inclure le nom de la communauté d'où provient l'agence, sauf si le nom de la communauté fait partie du nom de l'agence.

Jurisprudence

3.3.15 Noms de parties protégées

| DP c S |
| Droit de la famille - 1763 |

➤ Si les noms des parties ne sont pas divulgués, utiliser les initiales disponibles ou le titre et la description numérique fournis dans le recueil.

3.3.16 Intitulés différents pour une même cause : *sub nom*

Compagnie des chemins de fer nationaux du Canada c Canada (Commission des droits de la personne), [1987] 1 RCS 1114, (*sub nom Action Travail des Femmes* c *Canadian National Railways Co*) 40 DLR (4ᵉ) 193.

➤ Débuter toute référence par les noms des parties tels qu'ils paraissent dans le premier recueil.

➤ Si un autre recueil fait référence aux mêmes parties sous des noms différents, indiquer *sub nom*, suivi de l'intitulé entre parenthèses immédiatement avant la référence en question.

➤ *Sub nom* est l'abréviation de *sub nomine*, soit « sous le nom de » en latin.

3.3.17 Tierce partie agissant pour une des parties : *ex rel*

| *Ryel c Québec (PG) ex rel* |
| *Société immobilière du Québec* |

➤ Utiliser l'expression *ex rel* pour indiquer qu'une tierce partie agit au nom d'une autre partie.

➤ *Ex rel* est l'abréviation d'*ex relatione*, qui signifie « à cause de la relation ou de l'information » en latin.

3.3.18 Expressions procédurales et renvois constitutionnels

Constitutionnel	*Renvoi relatif à la Loi sur les armes à feu*
Autre	*Re Denis*
	Ex parte Royal Dress Co : Re Hudson Fashion Shoppe Ltd

➤ L'expression Renvoi relatif à n'est utilisée que pour les renvois constitutionnels. Dans tous les autres cas, écrire *Re*.

➤ Remplacer *In re*, Dans l'affaire de et *In the matter of* par *Re*.

➤ Dans l'intitulé d'une décision, l'expression *ex parte* signifie que la partie nommée après la mention a demandé l'action.

Jurisprudence

3.4   ANNÉE DE LA DÉCISION

Lorsqu'une décision comporte une référence neutre, ne pas indiquer l'année entre parenthèses après l'intitulé. **Appliquer les règles suivantes s'il n'y a pas de référence neutre** :

L'année du recueil n'est pas mentionnée	Fournir l'année de la décision entre parenthèses	*R v Borden* (1993), 24 CR (4e) 184 (NSCA).
L'année du recueil et l'année de la décision sont différentes	Fournir les deux années	*Joyal c Hôpital du Christ-Roi* (1996), [1997] RJQ 38 (CA).
L'année du recueil et l'année de la décision sont les mêmes	Fournir l'année du recueil	*Cadbury Schweppes c Aliments FBI Ltée*, [1999] 1 RCS 142. ✗ *Cadbury Schweppes c Aliments FBI Ltée* (1999), [1999] 1 RCS 142.

➢ Les **parenthèses** sont utilisées pour **l'année de la décision** et sont suivies d'une virgule.

➢ Les **crochets** sont utilisés pour **l'année du recueil** et sont précédés d'une virgule.

3.5   RÉFÉRENCE NEUTRE

Les références neutres émanent directement de la cour où une décision est prise, et seule la désignation officielle doit être utilisée. Toutes les cours canadiennes et un nombre croissant de tribunaux administratifs ont adopté la référence neutre. Pour connaître leur date d'adoption, voir l'**annexe B-3**.

La référence neutre permet l'identification d'une cause indépendamment du service électronique ou des recueils imprimés dans lesquels elle est publiée. Toutefois, une décision devrait toujours être suivie d'une référence à un recueil, puisque la référence neutre ne permet pas au lecteur de savoir où trouver la cause.

Pour plus d'information sur la norme de référence neutre, consulter le document du Comité canadien de la référence intitulé *La préparation, la référence et la distribution des décisions canadiennes*, disponible sur <http://lexum.org/ccc-ccr/preparation/fr/>.

Jurisprudence

Intitulé,	référence neutre			référence traditionnelle,	renseignements facultatifs.	
	année	identifiant du tribunal	numéro de la décision,		numéro de paragraphe	note.
R c Law,	2002	CSC	10,	[2002] 1 RCS 227.		
R v Senko,	2004	ABQB	60,	352 AR 235,	au para 12.	
Ordre des arpenteurs-géomètres du Québec c Tremblay,	2001	QCTP	24,			à la n 14.
Effigi Inc c Canada (Procureur général),	2004	CF	1000,		¶ 34-35, 40.	

➢ La référence est assignée par la cour et ne doit pas être modifiée.

➢ L'indication géographique et le niveau de la cour sont identifiés dans la référence neutre elle-même. Ne pas ajouter d'abréviation ou d'indication géographique additionnelles.

➢ Si le public visé par le texte risque de ne pas reconnaître la provenance de la référence neutre, ajouter avant la référence neutre le code de pays de trois lettres établi par la norme internationale **ISO 3166-1 alpha-3** (par ex. *R c Law*, CAN 2002 SCC 10). Le code est GBR pour le Royaume-Uni, FRA pour la France, AUS pour l'Australie, NZL pour la Nouvelle-Zélande, SGP pour le Singapour et ZAF pour l'Afrique du Sud.

➢ Porter une attention particulière aux services de banques de données électroniques qui utilisent des codes de désignation qui ressemblent à la référence neutre (par ex. Quicklaw).

3.5.1 Année

L'année est celle de la décision rendue par la cour. Si la date de la décision est fixée plus tard, l'année peut être celle de l'entrée de la cause dans le registre de la cour.

3.5.2 Identifiant du tribunal

Le code de désignation du tribunal est assigné par la cour et peut contenir jusqu'à huit caractères. Le code de désignation débute par un préfixe de deux caractères qui, à l'exception des Territoires du Nord-Ouest, correspond au code de l'indication géographique traditionnelle de deux lettres (celles-ci sont les mêmes en anglais et en français).

Alberta	AB
Colombie-Britannique	BC
Île-du-Prince-Édouard	PE
Manitoba	MB
Nouveau-Brunswick	NB
Nouvelle-Écosse	NS
Nunavut	NU
Ontario	ON
Québec	QC
Saskatchewan	SK
Terre-Neuve-et-Labrador	NL (NF avant 2002)
Territoires du Nord-Ouest	NWT or NT
Yukon	YK

➤ Suite à ce préfixe, indiquer **l'acronyme habituel du tribunal ou de la cour**, mais omettre la réintroduction de toute lettre représentant l'indication géographique (par ex. le Tribunal des professions du Québec est QCTP et non QCTPQ).

3.5.3 Numéro de la décision

➤ Le numéro de séquence est assigné par la cour. Ce numéro revient à « 1 » le 1er janvier de chaque année.

3.6   RÉFÉRENCE PRÉCISE

3.6.1 Modèle de base

> *R c Latimer*, 2001 CSC 1 au para 27, [2001] 1 RCS 3.
>
> *Bagagerie SA c Bagagerie Willy* (1992), 45 CPR (3e) 503 à la p 507 (CAF).
>
> *Québec (PG) c Germain*, [1995] RJQ 2313 à la p 2320 et s (CA).
>
> *Canadien Pacifique c Bande indienne de Matsqui*, [1995] 1 RCS 3 aux para 40, 49, 122 DLR (4e) 129.
>
> *Madden c Demers* (1920), 29 BR 505 aux pp 510-12.

➤ Indiquer la référence précise **après la référence neutre**. S'il n'y a pas de référence neutre, indiquer la référence après la première page du jugement.

➤ **Toujours indiquer le paragraphe lorsqu'il y a une référence neutre**. S'il n'y a pas de référence neutre, indiquer le numéro de page ou du paragraphe et identifier le recueil auquel les références sont faites (section 3.6.2). Lorsque les paragraphes sont numérotés, y faire référence en écrivant au para ou en utilisant le symbole ¶. Pour se référer à une page, utiliser à la p et pour plusieurs pages, utiliser aux pp.

➢ Ne pas mettre de virgule avant la référence précise.

➢ Pour indiquer une **partie générale**, écrire et s (abréviation de « et suivantes »)
immédiatement après le numéro. Il est toutefois préférable de se référer aux pages
ou aux paragraphes précis.

➢ Séparer **les pages ou paragraphes consécutifs** par un trait d'union. Retenir au
moins les deux derniers chiffres des nombres (par ex. aux pp 32-35 et non aux pp
32-5).

➢ Séparer **les pages ou paragraphes non consécutifs** par une virgule (par ex. aux
pp 40, 49).

3.6.2   Recueil auquel les références sont faites

R v Sharpe, 2007 BCCA 191, 219 CCC (3e) 187 [*Sharpe*].

Delgamuukw v British Columbia (1991), 79 DLR (4e) 185, [1991] 3 WWR 97 (BCSC)
[*Delgamuukw* avec renvois aux DLR].

Université du Québec à Trois-Rivières c Larocque, [1993] 1 RCS 471 à la p 473, 101 DLR (4e)
494 [*Larocque*].

➢ Ne pas spécifier la source de la référence précise lorsqu'il y a une référence neutre
(voir *Sharpe*). Dans ce cas, les numéros des paragraphes sont établis par la cour et
non par l'éditeur individuel.

➢ Ne pas spécifier la source de la référence précise lorsqu'il y a une référence
précise lors de la première mention d'un cas (voir *Laroque*). Cela sous-entend
que les références subséquentes suivront le même modèle et feront référence au
même recueil.

➢ La référence précise se fait autant que possible **au recueil imprimé le plus
officiel, mentionné en premier lieu**. Pour des références subséquentes, utiliser
le même recueil.

➢ Après le titre abrégé, ajouter avec renvois au(x), suivi du nom du recueil (voir
Delgamuukw).

3.7   RECUEIL IMPRIMÉ

3.7.1 Année du recueil

Recueil classé par année	un volume publié par année	*Hébert c Giguère*, [2003] RJQ 89 (CS).
	plusieurs volumes publiés par année	*Renvoi relatif à la sécession du Québec*, [1998] 2 RCS 217.
Recueil dont les volumes sont classés par série		*R v Borden* (1993), 24 CR (4ᵉ) 184 (NSCA).

> ➤ Les recueils sont publiés en volumes classés par année de parution (par ex. RCS ; RJQ) ou en volumes classés par série (par ex. DLR ; CCC).

>> → Si les volumes sont classés par **année de parution**, l'année est nécessaire à l'identification du volume. Fournir l'année du recueil entre crochets.

>> → Certains recueils classés par année de parution publient **plusieurs volumes à chaque année** (par ex. RCS). Indiquer l'année entre crochets, suivie du numéro du volume.

>> → Si les volumes sont classés par **série**, ne pas indiquer l'année pour identifier le volume.

> ➤ Noter aussi que **certains recueils ont changé leur mode de classification des volumes**.

>> → Entre les années 1877 et 1923, les ***Supreme Court Reports*** ont été classés par volume (par ex. 27 CSC). Entre 1923 et 1974, le recueil a été classé par année (par ex. [1950] CSC). Depuis 1975, plusieurs volumes sont publiés par année (par ex. [1982] 2 CSC).

>> → Avant 1974, les ***Ontario Reports*** étaient classés par année de parution (par ex. [1973] OR). À partir de 1974, ils ont été organisés par série (par ex. 20 OR). Si les volumes sont classés par série, ne pas indiquer l'année pour identifier le volume.

3.7.2 Recueil

Indiquer l'abréviation du nom du recueil selon la liste des abréviations de recueils à l'**annexe C**.

Forbes c Desaulniers (1991), [1992] RL 250 (CA).

3.7.2.1 Recueils officiels

> ➤ Les recueils officiels sont publiés par l'Imprimeur de la Reine.

> ➤ S'il existe des différences entre deux versions du même jugement, la version publiée dans les recueils officiels a préséance.

Jurisprudence

Recueils officiels :

Recueils de la Cour suprême (1970 à aujourd'hui) *Canada Law Reports : Supreme Court of Canada* (1923-1969) *Canada Supreme Court Reports* (1876-1922)	RCS
Recueils des décisions des Cour fédérales (1971 à aujourd'hui)	RCF
Recueils de jurisprudence de la Cour de l'Échiquier (1923-1970) *Exchequer Court of Canada Reports* (1875-1922)	RC de l'É

3.7.2.2 Recueils semi-officiels

> Les recueils semi-officiels sont publiés sous l'égide du barreau d'une province ou d'un territoire.

Recueils semi-officiels publiés (à jour en 2009) :

Alberta	*Alberta Reports* (1976 à aujourd'hui) NB : les *Alberta Law Reports* (5e) (Alta LR (5e)) ne sont pas officiels	AR
Colombie-Britannique	Aucun recueil semi-officiel publié	
Manitoba	Aucun recueil semi-officiel publié	
Nouveau-Brunswick	*New Brunswick Reports* (2e) (1968 à aujourd'hui)	NBR (2e)
Nouvelle-Écosse	*Nova Scotia Reports* (2e) (1969 à aujourd'hui)	NSR (2e)
Nunavut	Aucun recueil semi-officiel publié	
Ontario	*Ontario Reports* (3e) (1991 à aujourd'hui)	OR
Québec	*Recueils de jurisprudence du Québec* (1986 à aujourd'hui)	RJQ
Saskatchewan	Aucun recueil semi-officiel publié	
Terre-Neuve et Île-du-Prince-Édouard	Newfoundland & Prince Edward Island Reports (1971 à aujourd'hui)	Nfld & PEIR
Territoires du Nord-Ouest	Aucun recueil semi-officiel publié	NWTR
Yukon	Aucun recueil semi-officiel publié	

Pour une liste complète des recueils semi-officiels (incluant ceux qui ne sont plus publiés en 2009), voir l'**annexe C-2**.

3.7.2.3 Recueils non officiels

➢ Pour choisir le recueil approprié, respecter les directives suivantes :

→ Les recueils **généraux** (par ex. les *Western Weekly Reports*) sont préférés aux recueils spécialisés (par ex. les *Canadian Criminal Cases*) ;

→ Les recueils couvrant un **grand territoire géographique** (par ex. les *Dominion Law Reports*) sont préférés aux recueils couvrant un territoire géographique plus limité (par ex. les *Saskatchewan Reports*) ;

→ Les recueils **facilement disponibles** (par ex. les *Dominion Law Reports*) sont préférés aux recueils moins accessibles.

Voir la liste des recueils non officiels à l'**annexe C-3**.

3.7.3 Série

Numéro de série	*Newell v Royal Bank of Canada* (1997), 156 NSR (2ᵉ) 347 (CA).
Nouvelle série	*Re Cameron* (1974), 18 CBR (ns) 99 (CS Qué).

➢ Si le recueil a été publié en plusieurs séries, indiquer la série entre parenthèses, entre l'abréviation du recueil et la première page du jugement.

➢ Remplacer **nouvelle série** ou *New Series* par ns.

➢ Indiquer le numéro de série en français ((4ᵉ) et non (4th)).

N.B. Certains services électroniques ne reconnaissent pas les numéros de série français lorsque la décision est publiée en anglais uniquement. Adapter la recherche en conséquence.

3.7.4 Première page

Ford c Québec (PG), [1988] 2 RCS 712.

➢ Indiquer le numéro de la première page du jugement après le recueil.

3.8 SERVICES ÉLECTRONIQUES

➢ Avant de faire référence à un service électronique, s'assurer qu'il s'agit bien de la source la plus appropriée (section 3.1).

➢ Éviter de faire référence à un service électronique auquel la majorité des lecteurs ne pourra accéder (par ex. éviter Azimut si l'auditoire ciblé n'est pas au Québec).

> Inclure le numéro de paragraphe comme référence précise. **Ne pas faire référence aux numéros de page** fournis par le service électronique, puisque la numérotation peut changer d'un format électronique à un autre (par ex. txt, html).

> Utiliser les abréviations des noms des services électroniques à l'**annexe E**.

3.8.1 Jugements publiés et jugements possédant une référence neutre

Référence au recueil imprimé ou référence neutre	(disponible sur	nom du service électronique).
Desputeaux c Éditions Chouette (1987) Inc, [2001] RJQ 945	(disponible sur	Azimut).
R v Wilkening, 2009 ABCA 9	(disponible sur	WL Can).

> Lorsqu'un jugement **est publié dans un recueil imprimé ou possède une référence neutre**, écrire la référence neutre ou le recueil imprimé, puis ajouter disponible sur entre parenthèses, suivi du nom du service électronique.

3.8.2 Jugements non publiés et ne possédant pas de référence neutre

3.8.2.1 CanLII

Intitulé,	code de désignation fourni par le service	référence précise	(indication géographique et/ou **cour**) (si possible).
R v Veeve,	1999 CanLII 1451	au para 39	(Nu CJ).

> L'Institut canadien d'information juridique (CanLII) est un service gratuit et accessible à tous sur <http://www.canlii.org>.

> L'acronyme IIJCan a été abandonné en mars 2007. Utiliser plutôt CanLII.

3.8.2.2 Quicklaw

Intitulé,	code de désignation fourni par le service	référence précise	(indication géographique et/ou **cour**) (si possible)	(QL).
Fuentes v Canada (Minister of Citizenship and Immigration),	[1995] FCJ no 206	au para 10	(FCTD)	(QL).

> Trouver le code de désignation Quicklaw sous l'intitulé. Ne pas le confondre avec des recueils imprimés (par ex. AJ pour Alberta Judgments, BCJ pour British Columbia Judgments et OJ pour Ontario Judgments).

> Vérifier si le jugement a été publié ailleurs dans la banque de données QuickCITE, qui donne une liste de toutes les sources disponibles du jugement.

3.8.2.3 *Westlaw Canada*

Intitulé,	code de désignation fourni par le service	référence précise	(indication géographique et/ou cour) (si possible)	(WL Can).
Underwood v Underwood,	1995 CarswellOnt 88		(Ont Gen Div)	(WL Can).

> En juin 2009, le service Westlaw*e*Carswell a été renommé Westlaw Canada.

> Si le seul code de désignation est celui fourni par Westlaw Canada, le jugement n'est pas publié ailleurs.

3.8.2.4 *Azimut*

Intitulé,	(année),	code de désignation fourni par le service	(Azimut)	référence précise	(indication géographique et/ou cour) (si possible).
Desputeaux c Éditions Chouette,	(2001),	AZ-50085400	(Azimut)	au para 19	(Qc CA).

> Azimut est une banque de données créée par la Société québécoise d'information juridique (SOQUIJ). Si les lecteurs visés ne se trouvent pas uniquement au Québec, éviter de faire référence à Azimut.

3.8.2.5 *Lexis*

Intitulé,	code de désignation fourni par le service	référence précise	(indication géographique et/ou cour) (s'il y a lieu).
Davies v MNR,	1997 Can Tax Ct LEXIS 5874	at 5.	

> Si le seul code de désignation est celui fourni par Lexis, le jugement n'est pas publié ailleurs.

3.8.2.6 *Westlaw*

Intitulé,	code de désignation fourni par le service	référence précise	(indication géographique et/ou cour) (s'il y a lieu).
Fincher v Baker,	1997 WL 675447	à la p 2	(Ala Civ App).

> Si le seul code de désignation est celui fourni par Westlaw, le jugement n'est pas publié ailleurs.

3.8.2.7 BAILII

Intitulé	code de désignation fourni par le service,	(BAILII)	référence précise	(indication géographique et/ou cour) (s'il y a lieu).
London Borough of Harrow v Johnstone,	[1997] UKHL 9,	(BAILII)	au para 6.	

> Ne pas confondre le code de désignation fourni par BAILII avec la référence neutre. Ajouter (BAILII) après le code de désignation pour éviter toute confusion.

3.8.2.8 Lawnet

Intitulé	(année),	code de désignation fourni par le service	(Lawnet)	référence précise	(indication géographique et/ou cour) (si possible).
Beryl Claire Clarke and Others v Silkair (Singapore) Pte Ltd	(2001),	Suit Nos 1746, 1748-1752 de 1999	(Lawnet)	au para 10	(Sing HC).

3.8.2.9 Autres services

Faire référence aux services électroniques ayant à la fois une table des matières claire, des engins de recherche et des rédacteurs professionnels.

3.8.2.9.1   Code de désignation propre au service

Intitulé,	(année) (s'il y a lieu),	code de désignation fourni par le service	(nom du service) (s'il y a lieu)	référence précise	(indication géographique et/ou cour) (si possible).
Abitibi-Consolidated Inc c Doughan,		EYB 2008-139174	(REJB)	au para 23	(CS Qc).

> Ajouter l'année et le nom du service uniquement si l'information n'est pas déjà fournie à l'intérieur du code de désignation.

> Si l'abréviation du service électronique ne se trouve pas dans l'**annexe E** du *Manuel*, utiliser le nom le plus communément utilisé (par ex. écrire REJB et non Répertoire électronique de jurisprudence du Barreau).

3.8.2.9.2   Aucun code de désignation propre au service

Intitulé,	(année)	référence précise	(indication géographique et/ou cour) (si possible)	(disponible sur	nom du service électronique).
R v Woollin,	(1998)	au para 23	(HL)	(disponible sur	Justis).

3.9   INDICATION GÉOGRAPHIQUE ET COUR

> *Beauchemin c Blainville (Ville de)* (2001), 202 DLR (4ᵉ) 147 (CS Qc).
>
> *Re McEachern* (1996), 147 Nfld & PEIR 146 (PEISC (TD)).
>
> *Rempel v Reynolds* (1991), 94 Sask R 299 (QB).
>
> *Air Canada c Joyal*, [1982] CA 39 (Qc).
>
> *Miller c Monit International*, 2001 CSC 13, [2001] 1 RCS 432.

➢ Fournir l'indication géographique et le niveau de la cour :

→ s'il n'y a **pas de référence neutre** (comportant l'indication géographique et la cour) ; **et**

→ si ces **informations ne peuvent être déduites** du nom du recueil.

➢ Fournir l'indication géographique et la cour entre parenthèses après le numéro de page ou la référence précise, ainsi qu'après toutes les références parallèles.

➢ Utiliser les abréviations françaises des indications géographiques et des cours lorsque le lieu en question est bilingue (par ex. BR Man plutôt que Man QB) ; si la cour ne rend que des jugements en anglais, utiliser l'abréviation anglaise (par ex. Sask QB).

➢ Ne pas ajouter d'espace entre les lettres majuscules des abréviations des cours. Toutefois, inclure un espace quand l'abréviation est formée de majuscules et de minuscules (par ex. CQ ; BCCA ; Div gén Ont ; CQ crim & pén).

Voir les abréviations des indications géographiques à l'**annexe A-1** et les abréviations des cours à l'**annexe B**.

3.10 JUGE

> *R c Sharpe*, 2001 CSC 2, [2001] 1 RCS 45 au para 14, juge en chef McLachlin.
>
> *Gosselin c Québec (PG)*, [1999] RJQ 1033 (CA), juge Robert, dissident.

➢ Indiquer le nom du juge à la fin de la référence s'il est pertinent. Ajouter dissident(e) s'il s'agit d'une dissidence.

3.11 ÉTAPES SUCCESSIVES D'UNE CAUSE

3.11.1 Étapes antérieures

Confirmant	*Law c Canada (Ministre de l'Emploi et de l'Immigration)*, [1999] 1 RCS 497, confirmant (1996), 135 DLR (4ᵉ) 293 (CFA).
Infirmant	*Wilson & Lafleur Ltée c Société québécoise d'information juridique*, [2000] RJQ 1086 (CA), infirmant [1998] RJQ 2489 (CS).

➤ Indiquer les étapes antérieures d'une cause à la fin de la référence si elles sont pertinentes.

➤ Séparer les décisions par une virgule.

➤ Les expressions confirmant et infirmant se rapportent à la première référence.

➤ Si la décision confirme ou infirme une décision antérieure pour des motifs autres que ceux discutés, utiliser confirmant pour d'autres motifs ou infirmant pour d'autres motifs.

3.11.2 Étapes postérieures

Décision confirmée	*Granovsky c Canada (Ministre de l'Emploi et de l'Immigration)*, [1998] 3 FC 175 (CA), conf par 2000 CSC 28, [2000] 1 RCS 703.
Décision infirmée	*Ontario English Catholic Teachers' Association c Ontario (PG)* (1998), 162 DLR (4ᵉ) 257 (Div gén Ont), inf par (1999), 172 DLR (4ᵉ) 193 (CA Ont), inf par 2001 CSC 15, [2001] 1 RCS 470.

➤ Indiquer les étapes postérieures d'une cause si celle-ci a été jugée postérieurement par d'autres cours.

➤ Les étapes postérieures d'une cause figurent à la fin de la référence.

➤ Les différentes décisions sont séparées par des virgules.

➤ Utiliser conf par pour abréger **confirmé par** et inf par pour abréger **infirmé par**.

➤ Si la décision a été confirmée ou infirmée pour des motifs autres que ceux discutés, utiliser conf pour d'autres motifs par ou inf pour d'autres motifs par.

➤ Les expressions conf par et inf par se rapportent à la première référence. Ainsi, dans l'exemple *Ontario English Catholic Teachers' Association*, l'expression inf par qui précède la décision de la Cour suprême indique que la Cour suprême a infirmé la décision de la division générale de la Cour de justice de l'Ontario, et non la décision de la Cour d'appel de l'Ontario.

3.11.3 Étapes antérieures et postérieures

Décision confirmée	*Ardoch Algonquin First Nation v Ontario* (1997), 148 DLR (4e) 126 (CA Ont), infirmant [1997] 1 CNLR 66 (Div gén Ont), conf par 2000 CSC 37, [2000] 1 RCS 950 [*Ardoch*].
Décision infirmée	*Canada c Canderel Ltée*, [1995] 2 CF 232 (CA), infirmant [1994] 1 CTC 2336 (CCI), inf par [1998] 1 RCS 147 [*Canderel Ltée*].

➤ Suivre les règles pour les étapes antérieures et postérieures des sections ci-dessus.

➤ Toute décision confirmative ou infirmative renvoie à la première référence :

→ Dans *Ardoch*, la Cour d'appel de l'Ontario a infirmé la décision de la Cour de justice de l'Ontario, et cette décision de la Cour d'appel a été confirmée par la Cour suprême du Canada.

→ Dans *Canderel Ltée*, la Cour fédérale d'appel a infirmé la décision de la Cour canadienne de l'impôt, mais sa propre décision a été infirmée par la Cour suprême du Canada (c'est-à-dire que la Cour suprême du Canada a confirmé la décision de la cour de l'impôt).

➤ Indiquer les étapes antérieures avant les étapes postérieures.

3.11.4 Autorisation de pourvoi

	Référence à la décision dont l'autorisation de pourvoi est demandée,	cour,	référence au recueil ou numéro de greffe (date).
Pourvoi demandé	*White Resource Management Ltd v Durish* (1992), 131 AR 273 (CA),	autorisation de pourvoi à la CSC demandée.	
Pourvoi accordé	*Westec Aerospace v Raytheon Aircraft* (1999), 173 DLR (4e) 498 (BCCA),	autorisation de pourvoi à la CSC accordée,	[2000] 1 RCS xxii.
Pourvoi refusé	*Cie pharmaceutique Procter & Gamble Canada, Inc c Canada (Ministre de la Santé)*, 2004 CAF 393,	autorisation de pourvoi à la CSC refusée,	30714 (21 avril 2005).
Pourvoi de plein droit	*Whiten v Pilot Insurance* (1996), 132 DLR (4e) 568 (Div gén Ont),	pourvoi de plein droit à la CA.	

➤ La liste des décisions d'autorisation de pourvoi à la **Cour suprême du Canada** se trouve au début des RCS. Les décisions elles-mêmes sont disponibles sur CanLII depuis 2005.

➤ Les décisions de **cours d'appel** concernant l'autorisation de pourvoi se trouvent parfois dans les recueils de jurisprudence et dans les services électroniques.

➤ Inclure la référence à la décision pour laquelle l'autorisation de pourvoi est demandée.

Jurisprudence

> Indiquer la cour devant laquelle la demande de pourvoi a été faite. Si possible, indiquer si le pourvoi a été autorisé ou refusé et faire référence à cette décision.

> Pour une requête, faire référence à un recueil imprimé. Si la décision n'a pas été publiée, ou si l'auteur n'a pas accès au recueil imprimé, indiquer le **numéro de greffe** et la date entre parenthèses.

3.12 JUGEMENTS NON PUBLIÉS ET SANS RÉFÉRENCE NEUTRE

Intitulé	(date),	district judiciaire	numéro de greffe	référence à *Jurisprudence Express* (Québec) (s'il y a lieu)	(indication géographique et cour).
R c Crète	(18 avril 1991),	Ottawa	97/03674		(Ont CP).
Commission des normes du travail c Mercier	(13 novembre 2000),	Québec	200-22-010758-993	JE 2000-2257	(CQ).

> Indiquer l'intitulé et la date de la décision entre parenthèses, suivis d'une virgule, du district judiciaire et du numéro de greffe, ainsi que de l'indication géographique et de la cour entre parenthèses.

> Pour les **causes provenant du Québec**, fournir la référence à *Jurisprudence Express* (JE) après le numéro de greffe si possible.

3.13 ORGANES ET TRIBUNAUX ADMINISTRATIFS

3.13.1 Références aux recueils imprimés

Contradictoire	*Médecins (Ordre professionnel des) c Latulippe (CD Méd)*, [1997] DDOP 89 (TP).
Non contradictoire	*Re Citric Acid and Sodium Citrate* (1985), 10 CER 88 (Tribunal canadien des importations).

> Indiquer l'intitulé de la décision tel qu'il apparaît dans le recueil, que le processus soit contradictoire ou non. Lorsqu'il n'y a pas d'intitulé, indiquer le numéro de la décision.

> Indiquer l'abréviation employée par l'organe ou le tribunal administratif entre parenthèses à la fin de la référence s'il est impossible de le déduire du titre du recueil (utiliser le nom si aucune abréviation n'est trouvée).

> Utiliser une abréviation courte pour les provinces et les territoires (par ex. la Commission des valeurs mobilières du Québec est abrégée CVMQ, la Commission des valeurs mobilières de l'Ontario est abrégée CMVO et la Newfoundland and Labrador Human Rights Commission est abrégée NLHRC). À noter que les abréviations d'un recueil imprimé peuvent être différentes de celle d'un organisme administratif (par ex. OSC ; OSCB).

3.13.2 Décisions en ligne

Intitulé	(date),	numéro de la décision (s'il y a lieu),	en ligne :	organe ou tribunal administratif	<adresse>.
Réexamen de la décision de radiodiffusion 2008-222 conformément aux décrets CP 2008-1769 et CP 2008-1770	(11 août 2009),	CRTC 2009-481,	en ligne :	CRTC	<http://www.crtc.gc.ca>.
La commissaire de la concurrence c Phonetime Inc	(5 novembre 2009),	CT-2009-017,	en ligne :	Tribunal de la concurrence	<http://www.ct-tc.gc.ca>.
Autorité des marchés financiers c Jean-Yves Mulet	(9 septembre 2009,	2009-019,	en ligne :	BDRVM	<http://www.bdrvm.com>.

> Indiquer la date précise de la décision entre parenthèses après l'intitulé, et suivie d'une virgule.

> Indiquer le numéro de la décision (s'il y a lieu), suivi de en ligne : et de l'abréviation utilisée par le tribunal ou l'organe administratif. Utiliser une abréviation courte pour les provinces et les territoires (par ex. la Commission des valeurs mobilières du Québec est abrégée CVMQ, la Commission des valeurs mobilières de l'Ontario est abrégée CVMO et la *Newfoundland and Labrador Human Rights Commission* est abrégée NLHRC).

> Écrire l'adresse web de la page d'accueil du tribunal ou de l'organe administratif. Ne pas indiquer le lien précis de la décision.

3.14 PLAIDOIRIES ET DOCUMENTS À L'AUDIENCE

Mémoire	*Renvoi relatif à la sécession du Québec*, [1998] 2 RCS 217 (mémoire de l'appelant au para 16).
Plaidoiries orales	*Vriend c Alberta*, [1998] 1 RCS 493 (plaidoirie orale de l'appelant).
Règlement hors cour	*Mulroney c Canada (PG)* [Règlement hors cour], [1997] AQ nº 45 (CS Qué) (QL).
Éléments de preuve	*R c Swain*, [1991] 1 RCS 933 (preuve, recommandation du Dr Fleming de remettre l'appelant en liberté).

➢ Pour un **mémoire**, indiquer la référence complète de la cause. Ensuite, écrire entre parenthèses : mémoire de, le nom de la partie (appelant ou intimé) et le numéro de la page ou du paragraphe. Utiliser les références complètes pour les parties. Créer un titre abrégé lors de la première référence au document (par ex. mémoire de l'appelant au para 16 [MA]).

➢ Pour une **plaidoirie orale**, indiquer la référence complète de la décision, suivie de plaidoirie orale de et du nom de la partie, entre parenthèses.

➢ Pour un **règlement public hors cour**, fournir l'intitulé, suivi de Règlement hors cour entre crochets, et des autres éléments de la référence. Si le règlement a été annoncé dans un communiqué de presse, voir la section 6.17.

➢ Pour un **élément de preuve**, indiquer la référence complète de la décision, suivie de preuve et d'une brève description de l'élément entre parenthèses.

➢ Pour une **transcription**, suivre les règles des jugements non publiés à la section 3.12.

4   DOCUMENTS GOUVERNEMENTAUX

4.1   DOCUMENTS PARLEMENTAIRES

Cette section s'applique aux documents publiés directement par un organe parlementaire. Pour tous les documents gouvernementaux fédéraux, n'ajouter l'indication géographique (Canada) que si des références à des documents internationaux dans le texte risquent de confondre le lecteur.

4.1.1   Débats législatifs

Indication géographique,	législature,	*titre,*	numéro de la legislature et session,	volume et/ou numéro	(date)	référence précise	(orateur) (s'il y a lieu).
		Débats de la Chambre des communes,	37e parl, 1re sess,	n° 26	(9 mars 2009)	à la p 1457	(Linda Duncan).
		Débats du Sénat,	39e parl, 2e sess,	n° 44	(1 avril 2008)	à la p 1017	(Noël A Kinsella).
Québec,	Assemblée nationale,	*Journal des débats,*	36e lég, 21e sess,	n° 6	(24 mai 2001)	à la p 12	(M Marsan).
Manitoba,	Legislative Assembly,	*Debates and Proceedings,*	39e lég, 3e sess,	n° 21	(7 avril 2008)	à la p 525	(Ms Oswald).

➢ Écrire l'indication géographique (s'il s'agit d'une province) et la législature, à moins que ces informations ne fassent partie du titre du recueil des débats.

➢ Indiquer le titre du recueil des débats en italique.

➢ Si le recueil est divisé en volumes et/ou en numéros, indiquer ces précisions après la virgule (non italique) suivant le titre.

➢ Indiquer la date complète des débats entre parenthèses, suivie d'une référence précise.

➢ S'il y a lieu, indiquer l'orateur entre parenthèses à la fin de la référence.

4.1.2 Journaux

Indication géographique,	législature,	*titre,*	numéro de la législature et session	volume et/ou numéro	(date)	référence précise	(orateur) (s'il y a lieu).
	Sénat,	*Journaux du Sénat,*	40ᵉ lég, 2ᵉ ses,	no 40	(2 juin 2009).		
	Chambre des communes	*Journaux,*	40ᵉ lég, 2ᵉ ses,	no 36	(30 mars 2009)	à la p 333.	
Québec,	Assemblée nationale,	*Journaux de l'Assemblée nationale du Québec,*	29ᵉ lég, 2ᵉ ses,	vol 106	(23 février 1971)	à la p 23.	
		Journals of the House of Assemby of Lower-Canada,	8ᵉ parl, 2ᵉ ses,	vol 25	(16 janvier 1816)	à la p 15	(Thomas Douglass).

➤ Écrire l'indication géographique (s'il s'agit d'une province) et la législature, à moins que ces informations ne fassent partie du titre des journaux.

➤ Indiquer le titre du recueil des débats en italique.

➤ Si le recueil est divisé en volumes et/ou en numéros, indiquer ces précisions après la virgule non italique suivant le titre.

➤ Indiquer la date complète des débats entre parenthèses, suivie d'une référence précise.

➤ S'il y a lieu, indiquer l'orateur entre parenthèses à la fin de la référence.

4.1.3 Feuilletons

Indication géographique,	législature,	*titre du recueil,*	numéro de la législature et session,	numéro	(date)	référence précise.
	Chambre des Communes,	*Feuilleton,*	39ᵉ lég, 1ʳᵉ ses,	nᵒ 167	(8 juin 2007).	
Québec,	Assemblée nationale,	*Feuilleton et préavis,*	38ᵉ lég, 1ʳᵉ ses,	nᵒ 79	(6 mai 2008).	

➤ Inscrire l'indication géographique s'il s'agit d'une province.

➤ Au fédéral, le **Feuilleton** et le **Feuilleton des avis** sont deux parties d'une seule publication. Indiquer le recueil spécifique comme titre du recueil.

4.1.4 *Sessional Papers*

Indication géographique,	législature,	« titre du rapport »	par	auteur	dans	*titre du recueil,*	numéro	(année)	réfé-rence précise.
	Parlement,	« Report of the Chief Inspector of Dominion Lands Agencies »	par	HG Cuttle	dans	*Sessional Papers,*	nº 25	(1920)	à la p 3.
Ontario,	Assemblée législative,	« Report on Workmen's Compensation for Injuries »	par	James Mavor	dans	*Sessional Papers,*	nº 40	(1900)	à la p 6.

➢ Inscrire l'indication géographique s'il s'agit d'une province.

➢ Fournir le titre du rapport entre guillemets après la mention de la législature.

➢ S'il y a un auteur, indiquer son nom après le titre du rapport, suivi de par.

➢ Si le *Sessional Paper* est numéroté, indiquer le numéro après le titre du recueil et une virgule.

➢ Indiquer l'année et non la date complète entre parenthèses.

4.1.5 Procès-verbaux

Indication géographique,	législature,	*titre du recueil,*	numéro de la législature et session,	volume et/ou numéro	(date)	référence précise.
Québec,	Assemblée nationale,	*Procès-verbal,*	39e lég 1re ses,	nº 48	(18 juin 2009)	à la p 517.
Ontario,	Assemblée législative,	*Procès-verbaux,*	38e lég 2e ses,	nº 34	(14 décembre 2005).	

➢ Écrire l'indication géographique (s'il s'agit d'une province) et la législature, à moins que ces informations ne fassent partie du titre du recueil.

➢ Indiquer en italique le titre du recueil.

➢ Indiquer le numéro de la législature et la session.

➢ Si le recueil est divisé en volumes et/ou en numéros, indiquer ces précisions après la virgule suivant la session.

4.1.6   Rapports publiés dans un journal des débats

Indication géographique,	législature,	organisme,	« titre du rapport »	dans	titre du recueil,	volume, numéro	(date)	référence précise.
Québec,	Assemblée nationale,	Commission permanente de l'éducation,	« Étude détaillée du projet de loi no 12 : Loi sur l'aide financière aux études »	dans	Journal des débats de la Commission permanente de l'Éducation,	vol 37, no 11	(1ᵉʳ juin 2001)	à la p 1.

> ➤   Inscrire l'indication géographique s'il s'agit d'une province.

> ➤   Suivre les règles concernant les débats législatifs à la section 4.1.1 en y ajoutant le nom de l'organisme dont émane le rapport et le titre du rapport après le nom de la législature. Placer le titre du rapport entre guillemets.

> ➤   Fournir le numéro du rapport, s'il y en a un, après le titre du recueil et une virgule.

4.1.7   Rapports publiés séparément

Indication géographique,	législature,	organisme,	titre	(date)	référence précise	(président) (s'il y a lieu).
Québec,	Assemblée nationale,	Commission de l'aménagement et de l'équipement,	La procédure d'évaluation des impacts sur l'environnement : Rapport final	(9 avril 2002)	à la p 10.	

> ➤   Inscrire l'indication géographique s'il s'agit d'une province.

> ➤   Après la législature et le nom de l'organisme, indiquer le titre du rapport en italique.

> ➤   Indiquer entre parenthèses la date complète telle que fournie par le rapport.

> ➤   Si le nom du président est indiqué sur la page couverture, ajouter cette information entre parenthèses (par ex. (président : Rob Anders)).

> ➤   Cette section s'applique aux rapports publiés directement par un organe parlementaire. Si le rapport est publié par tout autre organe, voir la section 4.2 sur les rapports non parlementaires.

4.2   DOCUMENTS NON PARLEMENTAIRES

Cette section s'applique aux documents qui ne sont pas publiés par un organisme législatif.

4.2.1   Modèle de base

Indication géographique,	organisme,	*titre,*	tome et/ou volume,	renseignements sur l'édition	réfé-rence précise	(renseigne-ments additionnels) (facultatif).
Québec,	Ministère de la Justice,	*Commentaires du ministre de la Justice : le Code civil du Québec,*	t 2,	Québec, Publications du Québec, 1993	à la p 5.	
	Conseil de la radiodiffusion et des télécommunica-tions canadiennes,	*Rapport annuel : 1978-79,*		Hull, Approvi-sionnements et Services Canada, 1979	à la p 24.	
Québec,	Vérificateur général,	*Rapport à l'Assemblée nationale pour l'année 2000-2001,*	t 1,	Québec, Publications du Québec, 2001	à la p 169	(Vérificateur général : Guy Breton).

➢ Indiquer l'indication géographique, à moins qu'elle ne fasse partie du nom de l'organisme ou du titre du document.

➢ Indiquer l'organisme responsable à moins qu'il ne fasse partie du titre.

➢ Si le type de document (par ex. Étude; Document de travail ou Guide) est indiqué sur la page titre, fournir ce renseignement entre parenthèses après le titre du document. Par exemple : Commission de la santé et de la sécurité du travail du Québec, *Planification des mesures d'urgence pour assurer la sécurité des travailleurs* (Guide), Québec, CSST, 1999 à la p 53.

➢ Indiquer le tome et/ou le volume après le titre (s'il y a lieu).

➢ Fournir les renseignements sur l'édition selon les règles des sections 6.2.5-6.2.9.

➢ L'indication du nom du commissaire ou du président entre parenthèses à la fin de la référence est facultative.

4.2.2 Bulletins d'interprétation

Ministère,	Bulletin d'interprétation	numéro du bulletin,	« titre »	(date)	référence précise.
Agence du revenu du Canada,	Bulletin d'interprétation	IT-459,	« Projet comportant un risque ou une affaire de caractère commercial »	(8 septembre 1980).	
Agence du revenu du Canada,	Bulletin d'interprétation	IT-525R,	« Artistes de la scène »	(17 août 1995).	
Agence du revenu du Canada,	Bulletin d'interprétation	IT-244R3,	« Dons de polices d'assurance-vie à des œuvres charitables »	(6 septembre 1991)	au para 4.

➢ Les **IT** sont des bulletins d'interprétation courants en matière d'impôt sur le revenu et sont publiés par l'Agence du revenu du Canada.

➢ Faire suivre le numéro de bulletin d'un R s'il a été révisé. Le nombre de révisions est indiqué par le chiffre suivant le R (par ex. R3).

➢ Lorsque les bulletins d'interprétation sont divisés en paragraphes, faire référence au numéro de paragraphe.

4.2.3 Rapports d'enquêtes et de commissions

4.2.3.1 Rapports publiés en un seul volume

Indication géographique,	organisme,	titre,	renseignements sur l'édition	référence précise.
	Commission d'enquête sur le programme de commandites et les activités publicitaires,	Qui est responsable ? Rapport factuel,	Ottawa, Travaux publics et Services gouvernementaux Canada, 2005	à la p 14.

➢ Indiquer l'organisme responsable s'il n'est pas déjà mentionné dans le titre.

4.2.3.2 Rapports publiés en plusieurs volumes

4.2.3.2.1 Volumes portant le même titre

Indication géographique,	organisme,	titre,	livre ou cahier,	renseignements sur l'édition	(président) (s'il y a lieu)	référence précise.
		Rapport de la Commission royale d'enquête sur le bilinguisme et le biculturalisme,	livre 1,	Ottawa, Imprimeur de la Reine, 1967	(présidents : André Laurendeau et A Davidson Dunton)	à la page 68.

> Pour faire référence à un rapport publié des volumes distincts portant le même titre, ajouter les éléments qui permettent de distinguer les différentes parties (tel le numéro de volume) après le titre. Si un mot comme livre ou cahier paraît sur la page titre du document, utiliser cette terminologie plutôt que vol.

> Ne pas indiquer le numéro de volume dans les références ultérieures. Toutefois, pour faire référence à un autre volume du rapport dans une référence ultérieure, indiquer le numéro du volume pour éviter toute confusion (*Rapport sur le bilinguisme*, livre 2, *supra* note 5).

4.2.3.2.2   Volumes portant des titres différents

Référence au premier livre	;	référence au deuxième livre.
Rapport de la Commission d'enquête sur la situation de la langue française et sur les droits linguistiques au Québec : La langue de travail, livre 1, Québec, Éditeur officiel, 1972 aux pp 150, 300	;	*Rapport de la Commission d'enquête sur la situation de la langue française et sur les droits linguistiques au Québec : Les droits linguistiques*, livre 2, Québec, Éditeur officiel, 1972 à la p 38.

> Pour faire référence à un rapport publié dans des volumes distincts portant des titres différents, indiquer la référence complète pour chaque division, séparée d'un point-virgule. Indiquer le titre du volume comme si c'était un sous-titre du document (précédé d'un deux-points).

> Indiquer le volume (ou le livre ou le cahier) après le titre abrégé (par ex. *Rapport sur la langue française*, livre 2, *supra* note 4 à la p 38) dans les références ultérieures.

4.2.4 Rapports annuels et bulletins de diffusion

Organisme,	*titre,*	volume, numéro et/ou **chapitre** (s'il y a lieu),	renseignements sur l'édition,	référence précise.
Statistique Canada,	*Le Quotidien,*		Ottawa, StatCan, 31 juillet 2009	à la p 5.
Santé Canada,	*Bulletin de recherche sur les politiques de santé,*	nº 13,	Ottawa, Santé Canada, 2007	à la p 3.
Bureau du vérificateur général du Canada,	*Rapport du vérificateur général du Canada à la Chambre des communes,*	ch 8,	Ottawa, BVG, 2008	à la p 9.
Énergie atomique du Canada Limitée,	*Rapport annuel,*		Mississauga (Ont), EACL, 2006.	

> Indiquer le volume, le numéro ou le chapitre, selon ce qui est indiqué dans l'édition.

> Écrire la date complète telle qu'elle est fournie.

➤ Si l'organisme et l'éditeur sont une seule et même entité, indiquer l'abréviation officielle dans les renseignements sur l'édition (voir les exemples de Statistique Canada et Énergie atomique du Canada Limitée).

4.2.5 Auteur ou éditeur particulier

Organisme,	*titre*	par	auteur ou éditeur,	renseignements sur l'édition.
Ministère des Relations internationales,	*Des lois et des langues au Québec*	par	Marc Chevrier,	Québec, Ministère des Relations internationales, 1997.

➤ Si le document a été rédigé par un auteur particulier, indiquer son nom après le titre, précédé de par.

4.3   DOCUMENTS DE CONFÉRENCES INTERGOUVERNEMENTALES

Conférence ou comité,	*titre*,	numéro du document,	lieu de la conférence,	date de tenue de la conférence.
Réunion fédérale-provinciale-territoriale des ministres responsables de la justice,	*Groupe de travail fédéral-provincial-territorial sur la provocation, Rapport intérimaire,*	Doc 830-600/020,	Montréal,	4-5 décembre, 1997.
Conférence fédérale-provinciale des Premiers ministres,	*Compte rendu textuel de la Conférence fédérale-provinciale des Premiers ministres sur les questions constitutionnelles intéressant les autochtones,*	Doc 800-18/004,	Ottawa,	8-9 mars 1984.

➤ Indiquer le nom complet de la conférence ou du comité, suivi du titre du document et du numéro du document.

➤ Indiquer le lieu et la date complète de la conférence.

5 Documentation internationale F-81

5   DOCUMENTATION INTERNATIONALE

5.1   TRAITÉS ET DOCUMENTS INTERNATIONAUX

5.1.1   Traités et autres accords internationaux

Titre,	parties (s'il y a lieu),	date de signature,	recueil de traités,	autre source	(autre information) (facultatif).
Traité sur l'extradition,	Espagne et El Salvador,	10 mars 1997,	2010 RTNU 139.		
Convention de sauvegarde des droits de l'homme et des libertés fondamentales,		4 novembre 1950,	213 RTNU 221,	STE 5	[Convention européenne des droits de l'homme].
Pacte international relatif aux droits civils et politiques,		19 décembre 1966,	999 RTNU 171, art 9-14,	RT Can 1976 n° 47, 6 ILM 368	(entrée en vigueur : 23 mars 1976, accession du Canada 19 mai 1976) [PIDCP].
Accord de libre-échange nord-américain entre le gouvernement du Canada, le gouvernement des États-Unis et le gouvernement du Mexique,		17 décembre 1992,	RT Can 1994 n° 2,	32 ILM 289	(entrée en vigueur : 1er janvier 1994) [ALÉNA].
Accord général sur les tarifs douaniers et le commerce,		30 octobre 1947,	58 RTNU 187,	RT Can 1947 n° 27	(entrée en vigueur : 1er janvier 1948) [GATT de 1947].

> Indiquer le titre complet du traité. Si le nom des signataires est inclus dans le titre, raccourcir le nom selon l'usage courant (par ex. Royaume-Uni et non Royaume-Uni de Grande-Bretagne et d'Irlande du Nord), mais sans l'abréger (par ex. R-U).

> Si le nom des parties à un traité bilatéral n'est pas indiqué dans le titre, écrire la version courte (mais non abrégée) du nom des parties après le titre, entre virgules. Inclure le nom des parties à un traité multilatéral à la fin de la référence, si nécessaire.

> Après le titre du traité, fournir la date précise de la première signature ou de la présentation pour la signature.

> Suivre l'ordre des recueils suivant : (1) *Recueil de traités des Nations Unies* [RTNU] ou *Recueil de traités de la Société des Nations* [RTSN] ; (2) recueils de traités officiels des États pertinents (par ex. *Recueil des traités du Canada* [RT Can], *United Kingdom Treaty Series* [UKTS]); (3) autres recueils de traités et accords internationaux (par ex. *International Legal Materials* [ILM]).

➢ Fournir des informations supplémentaires à la fin de la référence si nécessaire (par ex. le nom des parties au traité, la date d'entrée en vigueur, le nombre de ratifications et le statut de certains États).

Recueils de traités et accords internationaux et leurs abréviations:

Air and Aviation Treaties of the World	AATW
Australian Treaty Series	ATS
British and Foreign State Papers	UKFS
Canada Treaty Series	Can TS
Consolidated Treaty Series	Cons TS
Documents juridiques internationaux	DJI
European Treaty Series	Eur TS
International Legal Materials	ILM
Journal officiel	JO
League of Nations Treaty Series	LNTS
Organization of American States Treaty Series	OASTS
Recueil des traités d'alliance, de paix, de trêve, de neutralité, de commerce, de limites, d'échange, et plusieurs autres actes à la connaissance des relations étrangères des puissances et États de l'Europe	Rec TA
Recueil des traités de la Société des Nations	RTSN
Recueil des traités des Nations Unies	RTNU
Recueil des traités du Canada	RT Can
Recueil des traités et accords de la France	RTAF
Recueil général des traités de la France	Rec GTF
Série des traités et conventions européennes	STE
Treaties and other International Agreements of the United States of America 1776-1949	TI Agree (*anciennement USBS*)
United Kingdom Treaty Series	UKTS
United Nations Treaty Series	UNTS
United States Statutes at Large	US Stat
United States Treaties and Other International Acts Series	TIAS
United States Treaties and Other International Agreements	UST

5.1.1.1 Référence neutre des traités australiens

Le gouvernement australien de la Commonwealth a adopté sa propre méthode de référence neutre pour les traités, qui doit accompagner toute référence à un recueil imprimé. Introduire la référence neutre après le titre du traité et la date de signature. Indiquer l'année de publication entre crochets, suivie de l'identificateur du recueil et du numéro de document.

Identificateurs de recueils pour la référence neutre:

Australian Treaty Series	ATS	*Agreement on the Conservation of Albatrosses and Petrels*, 19 juin 2001, [2004] ATS 5.
Australian Treaty National Interest Analysis	ATNIA	
Australian Treaty not yet in force	ATNIF	

5.1.2   Documents des Nations Unies

Chaque document ne contient pas toujours tous les éléments inclus dans les exemples ci-dessous. Adapter les références de manière à ce qu'elles fournissent l'information nécessaire à l'identification du document.

Abréviations du vocabulaire fréquemment utilisé dans les documents des Nations Unies:

Décision	déc		Recommandation	rec
Document	doc		Régulier	rég
Document officiels	doc off		Résolution	rés
Extraordinaire	extra		Session	sess
Miméographié	miméo		Spécial	spéc
Numéro	nº		Supplément	supp
Pléniaire	plén		Urgence	urg

5.1.2.1 Charte des Nations Unies

Une référence complète n'est pas nécessaire pour la *Charte des Nations Unies*. Faire référence à la *Charte* de la façon suivante : *Charte des Nations Unies*, 26 juin 1945, RT Can 1945 nº 7.

5.1.2.2 Documents officiels

➢   Les documents officiels publiés par les organes des Nations Unies se divisent en trois parties, soit les **séances**, les **suppléments** et les **annexes**. Faire référence aux documents officiels en inscrivant Doc off avant l'acronyme de l'organe qui en est responsable.

Abréviations officielles des principaux organes des Nations Unies :

Assemblée générale	AG
Conférence des Nations Unies sur le commerce et le développement	CNUCED
Conseil économique et social	CES
Conseil de sécurité	CS
Conseil de tutelle	CT
Conseil du commerce et du développement	CCED
Première commission, Deuxième commission, etc.	C1, C2, etc.

Fournir le nom complet des organes de l'ONU qui n'ont pas d'acronyme officiel.

5.1.2.2.1   Séances

Doc off et acronyme de l'organe responsable,	numéro de sess ou nombre d'années écoulées depuis la création de l'organe ou année civile,	numéro de séance,	numéro de document de l'ONU et (numéro de vente) (s'il y a lieu)	(année du document) (s'il y a lieu)	référence précise	[provisoire] (s'il y a lieu).
Doc off CCED CNUCED,	23ᵉ sess,	565ᵉ séance,	Doc NU TD/B/SR.565	(1981).		
Doc off CS NU,	53ᵉ année,	3849ᵉ séance,	Doc NU S/ PV.3849	(1998)		[provisoire].
Doc off CES NU,	1984,	23ᵉ séance plén,	Doc NU E/1984/SR.23.			

➢ Indiquer Doc off pour **Documents officiels**, suivi de **l'abréviation de l'organe des Nations Unies** et de la mention NU, sauf si celle-ci fait partie de l'acronyme de l'organe.

➢ Fournir le **numéro de session** après le nom de l'organe ou de la mention NU. Si le numéro n'est pas disponible, indiquer **le nombre d'années écoulées depuis la création de l'organe**. Si ni l'une ni l'autre des informations ne sont disponibles, indiquer **l'année civile**.

➢ Indiquer le **numéro de séance** après le numéro de session.

➢ Indiquer le **numéro de document** après le numéro de séance. Si un document a plusieurs numéros, indiquer chacun d'entre eux, séparés par des virgules. Indiquer le numéro de vente (s'il y a lieu) entre parenthèses après le numéro de document.

➢ Indiquer l'année civile du document entre parenthèses après le numéro de document si elle n'a pas été mentionnée précédemment dans la référence.

➢ Précéder toute référence précise d'une virgule.

➢ Indiquer qu'un document est provisoire en ajoutant [provisoire] à la fin de la référence.

5.1.2.2.2   Suppléments

Les résolutions, les décisions et les rapports de l'ONU paraissent dans des suppléments aux documents officiels.

	Auteur (s'il y a lieu),	titre,	Rés ou Déc et organe et no,	Doc off,	session ou année de l'organe ou année civile,	numéro de supp,	numéro de document de l'ONU	(année civile) (s'il y a lieu)	1ᵉ page et référence précise.
Résolutions		*Déclaration universelle des droits de l'Homme,*	Rés AG 217(III),	Doc off AG NU,	3ᵉ sess,	supp n° 13,	Doc NU A/810	(1948)	71.
Décisions		*Protection of the heritage of indigenous people,*	Déc CES 1998/ 277,	Doc off CES NU,	1998,	supp n° 1,	Doc NU E/1998/98		113 à la p 115.
Rapports		*Rapport du Secrétaire général Boutros-Ghali sur les travaux de l'Organisation,*		Doc off AG NU,	46ᵉ sess,	supp n° 1,	Doc NU A/46/1	(1991).	
	Commission on Crime prevention and Criminal Justice,	*Report on the Ninth Session,*		Doc off CES NU,	2000,	supp n° 10,	Doc NU E/2000/30.		

➢ Indiquer le titre en italique. Pour les rapports, indiquer également l'auteur avant le titre, s'il n'est pas déjà mentionné dans celui-ci.

➢ Pour faire référence à une décision ou une résolution, indiquer le numéro de décision ou de résolution après le titre.

➢ Indiquer Doc off pour **Documents officiels**, suivi de **l'abréviation de l'organe des Nations Unies** et de la mention NU, si celle-ci ne fait pas partie de l'acronyme de l'organe. Pour les résolutions et les décisions, indiquer cette information après le numéro de résolution ou de décision. Pour les rapports, indiquer cette information immédiatement après le titre du rapport.

> Indiquer le **numéro de session**. S'il n'est pas disponible, indiquer **le nombre d'années écoulées depuis la création de l'organe**. Si ni l'une ni l'autre information n'est disponible, indiquer **l'année civile**.

> Après la session, faire référence au **numéro de supplément** et au **numéro de document**.

> Indiquer l'année civile du document entre parenthèses après le numéro de document, si elle n'est pas déjà mentionnée dans la référence.

> Placer ensuite le numéro de la première page du document et la référence précise, s'il y a lieu. Si aucune information n'est indiquée entre le numéro de document et le numéro de page, placer une virgule après le numéro de document afin d'éviter toute confusion.

5.1.2.2.3   Annexes

Titre,	Doc off et acronyme de l'organe responsable	numéro de sess ou année de l'organe ou année civile,	annexe, point numéro,	numéro de document de l'ONU	(année civile) (s'il y a lieu)	1re page et/ou référence précise.
Protectionism and Structural Adjustment,	Doc off CNUCED CCED	32e sess,	annexe, point 6,	Doc NU TD/B/1081	(1986)	23.
URSS : Projet de résolution,	Doc off CES NU	3e année, 7e sess,	annexe, point 7,	Doc NU E/884/Rev.1	(1948)	29 au para 3.

> Indiquer le titre en italique, suivi d'une référence aux documents officiels de l'organe responsable.

> Si **le numéro de session** n'est pas disponible, indiquer **le nombre d'années écoulées depuis la création de l'organe**. Si ni l'une ni l'autre information n'est disponible, indiquer **l'année civile**.

> Indiquer **l'annexe** et le point d'ordre du jour, suivis du numéro de document.

> Si l'année civile n'a pas été précédemment indiquée, l'inscrire entre parenthèses après le numéro de document.

> Placer ensuite le numéro de la première page du document si celui-ci fait partie d'une collection reliée, et une référence précise, s'il y a lieu. Si aucune information n'est indiquée entre le numéro de document et le numéro de page, placer une virgule après le numéro de document afin d'éviter toute confusion.

5.1.2.3 *Documents miméographiés*

CES NU, Commission des Droits de l'Homme, *République-Unie de Tanzanie : Projet de résolution révisé*, 24e sess., Doc NU E/CN.4/L.991/Rev.1 (1968) [Miméo, limité].

➢ La forme miméographique est officielle, mais ne devrait être citée que si le document n'est pas publié dans les documents officiels. Les documents miméographiés sont disponibles sur le site <http://documents.un.org/>.

➢ Suivre les règles concernant les suppléments à la section 5.1.2.2.2. Abréger **miméographie** par miméo entre crochets à la fin de la référence. S'il y a lieu, indiquer limité, restreint ou provisoire entre les mêmes crochets.

5.1.2.4 Périodiques

➢ Pour faire référence à un **périodique publié par l'ONU**, suivre les règles de référence aux périodiques énoncées à la section 6.1. Si le titre n'indique pas que le périodique est

> « Emplois rémunérés dans les activités non agricoles » (1989) 63:9 Bulletin mensuel de statistiques 12 (NU, Département des affaires économiques et sociales internationales).

publié par les Nations Unies, ajouter NU et l'organe responsable de la publication entre parenthèses à la fin de la référence.

5.1.2.5 Annuaires

> « Report of the Commission to the General Assembly on the work of its thirty-ninth Session » (Doc NU A/42/10) dans *Yearbook of the International Law Commission 1987*, vol 2, partie 2, New York, NU, 1989 à la p 50 (Doc NUA/CN.4/SER.A/1987/Add.1).

➢ Pour les **articles d'annuaires des Nations Unies**, suivre les règles des ouvrages collectifs à la section 6.3. Si possible, inclure le numéro de document. Indiquer le nom de l'auteur et du directeur s'ils sont disponibles.

5.1.2.6 Publications de vente

> NU, *Recommandations sur le transport des produits dangereux*, 9ᵉ éd, New York, NU, 1995 à la p 118.

➢ Faire référence aux **publications de vente** en utilisant les mêmes règles que pour les monographies (section 6.2).

5.1.3 Documents de l'Union européenne

Les règlements, les directives, les décisions, les débats et les autres documents sont publiés dans le *Journal officiel de l'Union européenne* (JO). Celui-ci remplace le *Journal officiel des Communautés européennes* depuis le 1ᵉʳ février 2003.

Le JO est publié chaque jour de travail dans les langues officielles de l'Union européenne. Il comprend deux séries (la série L pour **la législation** et la série C pour **l'information et les annonces**), ainsi qu'un supplément (la série S pour **les offres publiques** disponibles en format électronique depuis le 1ᵉʳ juillet 1998).

5.1.3.1 Règlements, directives et décisions

La législation des Communautés européennes comprend des règlements, des directives et des décisions qui sont publiés dans la **série L** (Législation) du *Journal officiel de l'Union européenne*.

➢   Indiquer CE, suivi du titre complet de l'instrument en italique.

➢   Le numéro de l'instrument est inclus dans le titre. **Le numéro des directives** et des décisions est composé des deux derniers chiffres de l'année et d'un numéro séquentiel (98/85).

➢   Le numéro des règlements est composé, à l'inverse, d'un numéro séquentiel suivi des deux derniers chiffres de l'année (par ex. 1149/99).

➢   Pour faire référence au *Journal officiel de l'Union européenne*, indiquer JO, suivi de la série (L). Ajouter le numéro de volume et de la première page de l'instrument, séparés par une barre oblique (/).

	CE,	*titre,*	[année du journal]	JO,	série et numéro de volume/1re page	référence précise.
Règlements	CE,	*Règlement (CE) 218/2005 de la Commission du 10 février 2005 portant ouverture et mode de gestion d'un contingent tarifaire autonome pour l'ail à dater du 1er janvier 2005,*	[2005]	JO,	L 39/5	à la p 6.
Directives	CE,	*Directive 2004/79/CE de la Commission du 4 mars 2004 concernant la fixation des caractères et des conditions minimales pour l'examen des variétés de vigne,*	[2004]	JO,	L 71/22.	
Décisions	CE,	*Décision 98/85/CE de la Commission du 16 janvier 1998 relative à certaines mesures de protection à l'égard des oiseaux vivants originaires de Hong Kong ou de la République populaire de Chine,*	[1998]	JO,	L 15/45	à la p 46.

5.1.3.2 Débats du Parlement européen

CE,	titre ou date de la séance,	[année]	JO	Annexe et numéro de volume/1re page	référence précise.
CE,	*Séance du mercredi 5 mai 1999,*	[1999]	JO	Annexe 4-539/144	à la p 152.

➢   Les débats du Parlement européen sont publiés dans l'annexe au *Journal officiel de l'Union européenne* (JO).

➢   Indiquer CE suivi du titre du document ou de la date de séance.

➢   Indiquer ensuite l'année de publication de la séance entre crochets, suivi de JO ainsi que du numéro d'annexe et de la première page. Une barre oblique (/) sépare le numéro de volume de la première page (par ex. 2-356/1).

5.1.3.3 *Autres documents*

Communications et informations	CE, *Note explicative relative à l'annexe III de l'accord UE-Mexique (décision n°2/2000 du Conseil conjoint UE-Mexique)*, [2004] JO C 40/2.
Publications générales	CE, Commission, *Communication de la Commission au Conseil et au Parlement européen*, Luxembourg, CE, 1995.
Périodiques	CE, *Commerce extérieur : statistiques mensuelles* (1994) n° 1 à la p 16.

➢ Indiquer CE pour désigner les Communautés européennes en tant qu'organe responsable. Fournir des précisions sur l'auteur s'il y a lieu.

➢ Faire référence au *Journal officiel de l'Union européenne : Communications et Informations* (**série C**) de la même manière qu' aud autres sections du journal officiel.

➢ Pour les **publications générales**, suivre les règles du chapitre 6.

➢ Pour les **périodiques**, mettre le titre en italique, suivi de l'année et du numéro du périodique.

5.1.4 Documents du Conseil de l'Europe

Les documents émanant du Conseil de l'Europe se trouvent dans les publications officielles suivantes :

Publications officielles	Abréviations
Bulletin d'information sur les activités juridiques	Bull inf
Comptes rendus des débats	Débats
Documents de séance	Documents
Ordres du jour et procès-verbaux	Ordres
Textes adoptés par l'Assemblée	Textes adoptés

	Conseil de l'Europe,	organe,	information sur la session,	*titre* (s'il y a lieu),	publication officielle	(année)	référence précise.
Débats	Conseil de l'Europe,	AP,	2001 sess ordinaire (1re partie),		Débats, vol 1	(2001)	à la p 67.
Textes adoptés	Conseil de l'Europe,	AC,	21e sess, partie 3,		Textes adoptés, Rec 585	(1970)	à la p 1.
Ordres du jour et procès-verbaux	Conseil de l'Europe,	AC,	21e sess, partie 2,		Ordres, 10e séance	(1969)	à la p 20.
Documents de séance	Conseil de l'Europe,	AP,	38e sess,	*Déclaration écrite n° 150 sur la protection du site archéologique de Pompei,*	Documents, vol 7, Doc 5700	(1987)	à la p 1.
Séries	Conseil de l'Europe,	Comité des Ministres,		*Recommandation R(82)1,*	(1980) 12 Bull inf 58.		

➢ Indiquer Conseil de l'Europe, suivi de l'organe responsable. Abréger **Assemblée parlementaire** par AP et **Assemblée consultative** par AC.

➢ Fournir des renseignements sur la session, suivis du titre du document, s'il y a lieu.

➢ Utiliser l'abréviation de la publication officielle.

➢ Indiquer entre parenthèses l'année de publication après la référence à la publication officielle.

➢ Pour les références aux périodiques (Bull inf), suivre les règles de la section 6.1.

5.1.5 Documents de l'Organisation des États américains

OÉA,	organe,	numéro de session (s'il y a lieu),	*titre,*	numéro de document	(année)	référence précise.
OÉA,	Assemblée générale,	2e sess,	*Draft Standards Regarding the Formulation of Reservations to Multilateral Treaties,*	Doc off OEA/ Ser.P/AG/ Doc.202	(1972).	
OÉA,	Commission interaméricaine des Droits de l'Homme,		*Draft of the Inter-American Declaration on the Rights of Indigenous Peoples,*	Doc off OEA/ Ser.L/V/II.90/ Doc.14, rev 1	(1995)	à la p 1.

➢ Les documents de l'OEA n'ont pas d'auteur. Indiquer l'organe responsable du document, à moins que le nom ne soit indiqué dans le titre du document.

➢ Indiquer le numéro de session ou le numéro de séance après avoir indiqué l'organe responsable du document, s'il y a lieu.

> Fournir le titre officiel du document.

> Écrire Doc off (Documents officiels) devant le numéro du document commençant par OEA. Le numéro du document débute avec les trois lettres OEA (Organización de los Estados Americanos) et non pas OÉA ou OAS.

> Indiquer l'année de publication du document entre parenthèses à la fin de la référence, suivie d'une référence précise, s'il y a lieu.

5.1.6 Documents de l'Organisation mondiale du commerce (OMC) et de l'*Accord général sur les tarifs douaniers et le commerce* (GATT)

	OMC ou GATT,	*titre,*	numéro de Déc, Rec ou Doc,	numéro de session,	IBDD	service électronique (s'il y a lieu).
Décisions et recommandations		*Accession of Guatemala,*	GATT PC Déc L/6824,	47ᵉ sess,	supp n° 38 IBDD (1991) 16.	
		Liberté de contrat en matière d'assurance,	GATT PC Rec du 27 mai 1959,	15ᵉ sess,	supp n° 8 IBDD (1960) 26.	
Rapports	GATT,	*Report of the Panel adopted by the Committee on Anti-Dumping Practices on 30 October 1995,*	GATT Doc ADP/137,		supp n° 42 IBDD (1995) 17.	
	OMC,	*Rapport du groupe de travail sur l'accession de la Bulgarie,*	OMC DocWT/ ACC/BGR/5 (1996),			en ligne : OMC <http:// docsonline. wto.org>.
Réunions	OMC, Conseil général,	*Compte rendu de la réunion* (tenue le 22 novembre 2000),	OMC Doc WT/ GC/M/60,			en ligne : OMC <http:// docsonline. wto.org>.

> **Les décisions et les recommandations n'ont pas d'auteur.** Indiquer le GATT, l'OMC et les organes plus précis comme responsables des rapports, à moins que le nom ne soit indiqué dans le titre du rapport.

> Indiquer le numéro de décision ou de recommandation. S'il n'y a pas de numéro, indiquer la date complète de la décision ou de la recommandation. PC désigne **Parties contractantes**, Déc désigne **Décision** et Rec désigne **Recommandation**.

> Si possible, se référer aux Instruments de base et documents divers (IBDD) du GATT. Indiquer l'année entre parenthèses et la première page du document.

> Si un rapport est publié indépendamment, sans numéro de document, suivre les règles pour les monographies (section 6.2) (par ex. GATT, *Les marchés internationaux de la viande : 1990/91*, Genève, GATT, 1991).

5.1.7 Documents de l'Organisation de coopération et de développement économiques

	OCDE, organe (s'il y a lieu),	titre,	titre de la série,	numéro du document de travail,	numéro du document	(renseignements sur l'édition).
Série	OCDE,	Japon (n° 34),	Examens en matière de coopération pour le développement,			Paris, ODCE, 1999.
Documents de travail	OCDE, Département économique,	Pour une croissance écologiquement durable en Australie,		Document de travail n° 309,	n° de doc ECO/ WKP(2001) 35	(2001).
Périodiques	OCDE,	Données OCDE sur l'environ-nement : Compendium 1995,				(1995).

➢   Indiquer OCDE et l'organe particulier, suivi du titre en italique.

➢   Si le document fait partie d'une série, fournir le titre de la série.

➢   Si le document est un document de travail, fournir le numéro du document de travail (s'il y a lieu) ainsi que le numéro du document de l'OCDE. Noter que le numéro de document débute avec OCDE en français et en anglais.

➢   Indiquer les renseignements sur l'édition. Si la seule information disponible est la date, mettre cette date entre parenthèses. Dans le cas d'un périodique, indiquer la date la plus précise possible.

5.2   JURISPRUDENCE

Voir l'annexe A-5 pour une liste des abréviations des organismes internationaux et de leurs recueils.

5.2.1 Cour permanente de Justice internationale (1922-1946)

Faire référence aux lois et aux règles de la CPJI par titre, numéro de recueil et nom de l'édition, suivis de la première page ou du numéro de document (par ex. *Revised Rules of the Court* (1926), CPJI 33 (sér D) n° 1).

5.2.1.1 Jugements, ordonnances et avis consultatifs

	Intitulé (*nom des parties*)	(année),	type de décision,	recueil	numéro de la décision	référence précise.
Jugements	Affaire des zones franches de la Haute-Savoie et du pays de Gex (*France c Suisse*)	(1932),		CPJI (sér A/B)	n° 46	à la p 167.
Avis consultatifs	Trafic ferroviaire entre la Lituanie et la Pologne	(1931),	Avis consultatif,	CPJI (sér A/B)	n° 41	à la p 3.
Ordonnances	Chemin de fer Panevezys-Saldutiskis (*Estonie c Lituanie*),		Ordonnance du 30 juin 1938,	CPJI (sér A/B)	n° 75	à la p 8.

➤ Fournir l'intitulé et le nom des parties entre parenthèses. Ne pas indiquer le nom des parties pour les avis consultatifs.

➤ Pour les jugements et les avis consultatifs, indiquer l'année de la décision entre parenthèses après l'intitulé.

➤ Préciser s'il s'agit d'une ordonnance ou d'un avis consultatif. Fournir la date complète lorsqu'il s'agit d'une ordonnance.

➤ Faire référence à une série de la CPJI et indiquer le numéro de la décision. **Les jugements de la CPJI** sont publiés dans la *Série A : Recueil des arrêts* (CPJI (Sér A)) et dans la *Série A/B : Arrêts, ordonnances et avis consultatifs* (CPJI (Sér A/B)). **Les ordonnances** et **les avis consultatifs** sont publiés dans la *Série B : Recueil des avis consultatifs* (CPJI (Ser B)) et dans la *Série A/B : Arrêts, ordonnances et avis consultatifs* (CPJI (Sér A/B)).

5.2.1.2 Plaidoiries, exposés oraux et autres documents

Intitulé (*nom des parties*),	« titre du document précis »	(date du document),	recueil	numéro de décision,	1ʳᵉ page	référence précise.
Affaire franco-hellenique des phares (*France c Grèce*),	« Exposé oral de M le professeur Basdevant »	(5 février 1934),	CPJI (sér C)	n° 74,	222	à la p 227.
Affaire Pajzs, Csáky, Esterházy (*Hongrie c Yougoslavie*),	« Requête introductive d'instance »	(1ᵉʳ décembre 1935),	CPJI (sér C)	n° 79,	10	à la p 12.

➤ Fournir l'intitulé et, entre parenthèses, le nom des parties.

➤ Indiquer le titre officiel du document précis entre guillemets, suivi de la date complète entre parenthèses.

➤ Faire référence à la série CPJI et indiquer le numéro de la décision. **Les plaidoiries**, **les exposés oraux** et **les autres documents avant 1931** sont publiés dans la *Série C : Actes et documents relatifs aux arrêts et aux avis consultatifs de la cour* (CPJI (Sér C)), et **les documents datant d'après 1931** dans la *Série C :*

Plaidoiries, exposés oraux et documents (CPJI (Sér. C)). **Les documents de base, les annuaires** et **les indices** paraissent dans les séries D à F.

5.2.2   Cour internationale de Justice (1946 à aujourd'hui)

Faire référence aux lois et aux règles de la CIJ par titre, numéro de recueil et nom de l'édition, suivis de la première page ou du numéro de document (par ex. *Travel and Subsistence Regulations of the International Court of Justice*, [1947] CIJ Acts & Doc 94).

5.2.2.1 Jugements, ordonnances et avis consultatifs

Les jugements, opinions et ordres de la CIJ qui ne sont pas encore publiés sont disponibles sur le site Internet de la CIJ <www.icj-cij.org>. Suivre les règles de la référence en ligne pour la jurisprudence (section 5.3).

	Intitulé (*nom des parties*),	type de décision,	[année du recueil]	recueil	1re page	référence précise.
Jugements	*Affaire relative au Timor oriental (Portugal c Australie),*		[1995]	CIJ rec	90	à la p 103.
Ordonnances	*Compétence en matière de pêcheries (Espagne c Canada),*	Ordonnance du 8 mai 1996,	[1996]	CIJ rec	58.	
Avis consultatifs	*Licéité de l'utilisation des armes nucléaires par un État dans un conflit armé,*	Avis consultatif,	[1996]	CIJ rec	226	à la p 230.

➢ Indiquer l'intitulé officiel et, entre parenthèses, le nom des parties. Bien que le CIJ Rec sépare parfois le nom des parties par une barre oblique (*El Salvador/ Honduras*), remplacer la barre oblique par un *c* (*Portugal c Australie*). Ne pas indiquer le nom des parties dans le cas des avis consultatifs.

➢ Après l'intitulé, préciser s'il s'agit d'une ordonnance ou d'un avis consultatif. Fournir la date complète lorsqu'il s'agit d'une ordonnance.

➢ Faire référence au recueil de la CIJ et indiquer la première page de la décision. Les jugements, les ordonnances et les avis consultatifs de la Cour internationale de Justice sont publiés dans le recueil officiel de la cour : *Recueil des arrêts, avis consultatifs et ordonnances* (CIJ Rec).

5.2.2.2 Mémoires, plaidoiries et documents

Intitulé officiel (nom des parties),	« titre du document précis »	(date du document),	[année du recueil]	recueil et numéro de volume	1re page	référence précise.
Affaire du droit de passage sur le territoire indien (Portugal c Inde),	« Plaidoirie de Shri MC Setalvad »	(23 septembre 1957),	[1960]	CIJ Mémoires (vol 4)	14	à la p 23.
Compétence en matière de pêcheries (Espagne c Canada),	« Requête introductive d'instance par l'Espagne »	(28 mars 1995),		CIJ Mémoires	3.	

➢ Indiquer l'intitulé officiel, ainsi que le nom des parties entre parenthèses.

➢ Fournir le titre officiel du document après l'intitulé, puis indiquer la date précise du document entre parenthèses.

➢ Faire référence à CIJ Mémoires et à la première page du document. La CIJ publie les mémoires et autres documents dans Mémoires, plaidoiries et documents (CIJ Mémoires). S'il y a lieu, inclure un numéro de volume avant l'indication de la première page en chiffres arabes (par ex. 1, 2, 3) et entre parenthèses (CIJ Mémoires (vol 4)).

➢ Après 1981, les mémoires n'indiquent pas la date de publication du recueil. Les volumes sont identifiés à partir du titre de la décision à laquelle le document se rapporte. Les mémoires sont disponibles sur le site Internet de la CIJ : <www. icj-cij.org>.

5.2.3 Cour de Justice des Communautés européennes et Tribunal de première instance

	Intitulé,	numéro de décision,	[année du recueil]	recueil	1re page	référence précise,	autre source.
CJE	Commission c Luxembourg,	C-26/99,	[1999]	ECR	I-8987	à la p I-8995.	
CJ (1re inst)	Kesko c Commission,	T-22/97,	[1999]	ECR	II-3775	à la p II-3822.	

➢ Indiquer l'intitulé en utilisant la forme abrégée du nom des institutions (par ex. Conseil et non Conseil des Communautés européennes).

➢ Écrire le numéro de la décision. Un C- indique les décisions de la **Cour de Justice des Communautés européennes** (CJE) et un T- indique celles du **Tribunal de première instance** (CJ (1re inst)).

➢ Faire référence au Rec CE et indiquer la première page de la décision. Les décisions de la CJE et les décisions de la CJ (1re inst) sont reproduites dans la publication officielle de la Cour, le *Recueil de la jurisprudence de la Cour et du Tribunal de première instance*, couramment appelé Recueil de la Cour européenne (Rec CE).

> Les numéros de page sont précédés par I- s'il s'agit d'une **décision de la CJE** et par II- s'il s'agit du **Tribunal de première instance**.

> Utiliser les comme autre source **Common Market Law Reports** (CMLR) ou les **Common Market Reporter** (CMR) comme autre source.

5.2.4 Cour européenne des Droits de l'Homme et Commission européenne des Droits de l'Homme

5.2.4.1 Avant 1999

Intitulé	(année de la décision),	numéro de volume	recueil	1re page et référence précise,	autre source.
Kurt c Turquie	(1998),	74	CEDH (Sér A)	1152,	27 EHRR 373.
Spencer c Royaume-Uni	(1998),	92A	Comm Eur DHDR	56,	41 YB Eu Conv H.R 72.

> Indiquer l'intitulé, suivi de l'année de la décision entre parenthèses.

> Indiquer le numéro de volume du recueil, suivi du nom du recueil et de la première page de la décision. Renvoyer aux publications officielles de la Cour et de la Commission : Cour européenne des Droits de l'Homme, Série A : Arrêts et décisions (Cour Eur DH (Sér A)) ; Recueil de décisions de la Commission européenne des Droits de l'Homme (Comm Eur DH Rec (de 1960 à 1974)) ; Décisions et rapports de la Commission européenne des Droits de l'Homme (Comm Eur DH DR (de 1975 à 1999)).

> Utiliser **l'Annuaire de la Convention européenne des Droits de l'Homme** (Ann Conv Eur DH) ou les **European Human Rights Reports** (EHRR).

5.2.4.2 À partir de 1999

Le Protocole n° 11 de la *Convention de sauvegarde des Droits de l'Homme et des Libertés fondamentales*, en vigueur depuis le 1er novembre 1998, a remplacé l'ancienne cour et l'ancienne commission par une nouvelle cour permanente.

Intitulé,	numéro de demande,	[année]	numéro de volume	recueil	1re page,	autre source.
Allard c Suède,	n° 35179/97,	[2003]	VII	CEDH	207,	39 EHRR 321.
Chypre c Turquie,	n° 25781/94,	[2001]	IV	CEDH	1,	35 EHRR 731.

> Indiquer [GC] entres crochets après l'intitulé et avant la virgule, si l'arrêt ou la décision ont été rendus par la Grande Chambre de la Cour.

> Indiquer entre parenthèses après l'intitulé et avant la virgule, s'il y a lieu : (déc) pour une **décision sur la recevabilité**, (exceptions préliminaires) pour un arrêt portant uniquement sur des **exceptions préliminaires**, (satisfaction équitable)

pour un arrêt portant uniquement sur la **satisfaction équitable**, (révision) pour un arrêt de **révision**, (interprétation) pour un arrêt d'**interprétation**, (radiation) pour un arrêt **rayant l'affaire du rôle**, ou (règlement amiable) pour un arrêt sur un **règlement amiable**.

➢ S'il existe **plus d'un numéro de demande**, inclure uniquement le premier numéro.

➢ Pour les **décisions non publiées**, indiquer le numéro de demande, suivi de la date du jugement (par ex. *Roche c Royaume-Uni*, n° 32555/96 (19 octobre 2005)).

5.2.5 Cour interaméricaine des Droits de l'Homme

5.2.5.1 Jugements, ordres et avis consultatifs

	Intitulé (nom de l'État impliqué)	(année de la décision),	type de décision et numéro,	recueil	numéro de décision,	réfé- rence précise,	autre source.
Jugements	*Affaire Neira Alegría (Pérou)*	(1996),		Inter-Am Ct HR (Sér C)	n° 29,	au para 55,	*Annual Report of the Inter-American Court of Human Rights: 1996*, OEA/ Ser.L/V/III.19/doc.4 (1997) 179.
Avis consultatifs	*Reports of the Inter-American Commission on Human Rights (Art 51 of the American Convention on Human Rights) (Chili)*	(1997),	Avis consultatif OC-15/97,	Inter-Am Ct HR (Sér A)	n° 15,	au para 53,	*Annual Report of the Inter-American Commission on Human Rights: 1997*, OEA/Ser.L/V/ III.39/doc.5 (1998) 307.

➢ Inscrire l'intitulé, suivi de l'année de la décision entre parenthèses. Si la cause implique un État individuel, indiquer le nom de celui-ci entre parenthèses avant l'année de la décision.

➢ Indiquer si la décision est un avis consultatif et fournir le numéro de la décision.

➢ Indiquer le recueil et le numéro de la décision. La Cour interaméricaine des Droits de l'Homme publie ses **décisions** dans *Inter-American Court of Human Rights Series C: Decisions and Judgments* (Inter-Am Ct HR (Sér C)) et ses **avis consultatifs** dans *Inter-American Court of Human Rights Series A: Judgments and Opinions* (Inter-Am Ct HR (Sér A)).

➢ Utiliser le **rapport annuel de la Cour**, les *International Legal Materials* (ILM) ou les *Inter-American Yearbook on Human Rights*, si possible.

5.2.5.2 Mémoires, plaidoiries et documents

Intitulé (nom de l'État impliqué),	type de décision et numéro,	« titre du document »	(date du document),	recueil et (série)	1re page,	autre source.
Proposed Amendments to the Naturalization Provisions of the Constitution of Costa Rica,	Avis consultatif OC-4/84,	« Verbatim Record of Public Hearing »	(7 septembre 1983),	Inter-Am Ct HR (Sér B)	203.	

> ➢ Inscrire l'intitulé. Si l'information n'est pas déjà présente dans l'intitulé, indiquer le nom de l'État impliqué entre parenthèses.

> ➢ Indiquer si la décision est un **avis consultatif** et fournir le numéro de la décision.

> ➢ Inclure le titre entre guillemets et la date du document entre parenthèses.

> ➢ Indiquer le recueil et la première page de la décision. La Cour interaméricaine des Droits de l'Homme publie les mémoires, les plaidoiries et d'autres documents dans *Inter-American Court of Human Rights Series B: Pleadings, Oral Arguments and Documents* (Inter-Am Ct HR (Sér B)).

5.2.6 Commission interaméricaine des Droits de l'Homme

Intitulé	(année du jugement),	Inter-Am Comm HR,	numéro de la décision,	réfé- rence précise,	rapport annuel,	numéro du document.
Sánchez c Mexico	(1992),	Inter-Am Comm HR,	No 27/92,		*Annual Report of the Inter-American Commission on Human Rights: 1992-93,*	OEA/Ser.L/V/ II.83/ doc.14 104.

> ➢ Inscrire l'intitulé suivi de l'année de la décision entre parenthèses.

> ➢ Inscrire Inter-Am Comm HR suivi du numéro de la décision.

> ➢ Les décisions de la Commission interaméricaine des Droits de l'Homme sont publiées dans ses rapports annuels. Faire référence au recueil annuel de la Commission et indiquer son numéro de document. Le numéro de document des publications de l'Organisation des États américains débute toujours avec OEA (Organización de les Estados Americanos) et non OÉA, quelle que soit la langue du document.

5.2.7 Tribunaux de droit pénal international

> Cette section s'applique aux documents provenant :

> → de la Cour pénale internationale ;
> → du Tribunal pénal international pour l'ex-Yougoslavie ;
> → du Tribunal pénal international pour le Rwanda ;
> → de la Cour spéciale pour la Sierra Leone ; et
> → des Groupes d'enquête sur les crimes graves du Timor oriental.

Intitulé,	numéro de l'affaire,	titre du document (version)	(date du document)	référence précise	(tribunal),	source.
Le Procureur c Zdravko Mucic (Jugement Celebici),	IT-96-21-*Abis*,	Arrêt relatif à la sentence	(8 avril 2003)	au para 8	(Tribunal pénal international pour l'ex-Yougoslavie, Chambre d'appel),	(WL).
Le Procureur c Théoneste Bagosora,	ICTR-98-41-I,	Procès-verbal d'audience	(2 avril 2002)		(Tribunal pénal international pour le Rwanda, Chambre de première instance),	en ligne: TPIR <http://www.ictr.org>.
Deputy General Prosecutor for Serious Crimes v Sito Barros,	01/2004,	Jugement final	(12 mai 2005)	au para 12	(Groupes d'enquête sur les crimes graves (Timor-Leste)),	en ligne: Judicial System Monitoring Program <http://www.jsmp.minihub.org>.

> Indiquer le **prénom** de l'accusé dans l'intitulé, s'il y a lieu.

> S'il y a plus d'un accusé, indiquer uniquement le nom du premier accusé dans l'intitulé.

> Inclure les **désignations informelles** (par ex. *Jugement Celebici*), si désiré, entre parenthèses après le titre.

> Le titre du document indique sa fonction. Noter si le renvoi est la **version publique** du document ou la **version confidentielle** dont l'accès est limité au public.

> Voir la section 5.3 pour une référence à un site Internet. Certains sites Internet officiels des organismes judiciaires ne publient qu'une portion limitée des documents disponibles, alors que d'autres services électroniques commerciaux offrent une sélection de documents plus étendue.

> Si le nom du site Internet est le même que celui du tribunal, indiquer uniquement les initiales pour identifier le site Internet (TPIR).

5.2.8 Groupes spéciaux de l'*Accord général sur les tarifs douaniers et le commerce* (GATT) 1947

Intitulé (*plainte(s)*)	(année du document),	numéro de doc GATT,	numéro IBDD et (année)	1ʳᵉ page et référence précise,	autre source.
République de Corée – Restrictions à l'importation de la viande de bœuf (Plainte de la Nouvelle-Zélande)	(1989),	GATT Doc L/6505,	Supp n° 36 IBDD (1990)	234,	en ligne : OMC <http://www.wto.org >.
États-Unis – Droits compensateurs sur la viande de porc fraîche, réfrigérée et congelée en provenance du Canada (Plainte du Canada)	(1991),	GATT Doc DS7/R,	Supp n° 38 IBDD (1990-91)	30,	en ligne : OMC <http://www.wto.org >.

➢ Fournir l'intitulé suivi du nom de l'État (ou des États) ayant déposé la plainte entre parenthèses.

➢ Indiquer la date de la décision entre parenthèses suivie d'une virgule et du numéro de document GATT.

➢ Se référer aux **IBDD** (Instruments de base et documents divers) du GATT en indiquant le numéro de volume suivi de IBDD, de l'année entre parenthèses et de la première page du document.

➢ Faire référence à la page et au paragraphe précis immédiatement après l'année.

➢ Fournir les références électroniques suivant les règles énoncées à la section 5.3.

5.2.9 Rapports de Groupes spéciaux et de l'Organe d'appel de l'Organisation mondiale du commerce (OMC)

	Intitulé (plainte(s))	(année de la décision),	numéro du document de l'OMC	réfé-rence précise	(type de rapport),	autre source.
Groupe spécial	États-Unis – Articles 301 à 310 de la Loi de 1974 sur le commerce extérieur (Plainte des communautés européennes)	(1999),	OMC Doc WT/DS152/R	au n° 3.1	(Rapport du Groupe spécial),	en ligne : OMC <http://www.wto.org/french/docs_f/docs_f.htm>.
Organe d'appel	Inde – Protection conférée par un brevet pour les produits pharmaceutiques et les produits chimiques pour l'agriculture (Plaintes des États-Unis)	(1997),	OMC Doc WT/DS50/AB/R		(Rapport de l'Organe d'appel),	en ligne : OMC <http://www.wto.org/french/docs_f/docs_f.htm>.

➢ Fournir l'intitulé du rapport, suivi du nom de l'auteur ou des auteurs de la plainte. Si les plaintes sont étudiées dans **un seul rapport**, indiquer le nom de tous les États ayant déposé une plainte après l'intitulé du rapport. Si plusieurs États ont déposé des plaintes **traitées séparément**, indiquer le nom de l'État visé par le rapport. Si plus de trois États ont déposé la plainte, indiquer le nom d'un seul État, suivi de et al.

➢ Après avoir indiqué l'année du rapport, fournir le numéro du document. Un rapport peut avoir plusieurs numéros de document (par ex. WT/DS 8, 10, 11/AB/R). Dans le numéro du document, les lettres WT-DS indiquent un **World Trade Dispute Settlement**, les lettres AB représentent l'abréviation d'*Appellate Body* et la lettre R indique un **rapport**. Si un rapport est destiné à un État particulier parmi plusieurs ayant déposé une plainte, l'abréviation du nom de cet État apparaît dans le numéro de document (par ex. OMC doc WT/DS27/R/USA).

➢ À la suite du numéro de document de l'OMC, indiquer entre parenthèses s'il s'agit d'un rapport d'un Groupe spécial ou d'un Organe d'appel.

➢ Fournir les références électroniques selon les règles énoncées à la section 5.3.

5.2.10 Rapports de Groupes spéciaux de l'Accord de libre-échange canado-américain

	Intitulé	(année de la décision),	numéro de document,	recueil	(Groupe spécial),	autre source.
Publiés	Re Framboises rouges du Canada	(1990),	USA-89-1904-01,	3 TCT 8175	(Groupe spéc c 19),	en ligne : Secrétariat de l'ALÉNA <http://www.nafta-sec-alena.org>.
Non publiés	Re Porc frais, frigorifié et congélé du Canada	(1991),	ECC-91-1904-01 USA,		(Comité cont extr),	en ligne : Secrétariat de l'ALÉNA <http://www.nafta-sec-alena.org>.

➢ À la suite de l'intitulé, indiquer l'année entre parenthèses et le numéro de document. Faire référence à un recueil imprimé si possible.

➢ Abréger les divers groupes spéciaux de la façon suivante : Groupe spéc ch 18 pour **Groupe spécial créé en vertu du chapitre 18**, Groupe spéc ch 19 pour **Groupe spécial créé en vertu du chapitre 19** et Comité pour cont extr pour **Comité pour contestation extraordinaire**.

➢ Fournir les références électroniques selon les règles énoncées à la section 5.3.

5.2.11 Rapports de Groupes spéciaux de l'Accord de libre-échange nord-américain (ALÉNA)

	Intitulé (nom des parties)	(année de la décision),	numéro du document	(groupe spécial),	autre source.
Révision des décisions définitives d'organismes américains	Re Certains produits de bois d'œuvre résineux du Canada (États-Unis c Canada)	(2005),	ECC-2004-1904-01USA	(Comité cont extr),	en ligne : Secrétariat de l'ALÉNA <http://www.nafta-sec-alena.org>.
Révision des décisions définitives de l'organisme mexicain	Re Polystyrène et cristale impacte en provenance des États-Unis d'Amérique (États-Unis c Mexique)	(1995),	MEX-94-1904-03	(Groupe spéc c 19),	en ligne : Secrétariat de l'ALÉNA <http://www.nafta-sec-alena.org>.
Révision des mesures canadiennes	Re Tarifs douaniers appliqués par le Canada sur certains produits agricoles en provenance des États-Unis d'Amérique (États-Unis c Canada)	(1996),	CDA-95-2008-01	(Groupe arb c 20),	en ligne : Secrétariat de l'ALÉNA <http://www.nafta-sec-alena.org>.

➢ Après l'intitulé, indiquer le nom des parties entre parenthèses.

➢ Fournir l'année de la décision entre parenthèses. Inclure le numéro de document et faire référence à un recueil si possible.

➢ Fournir des renseignements sur le chapitre dans lequel la plainte a été soumise. Indiquer Groupe spéc ch 19 pour **Groupe spécial binational Chapitre 19**, Groupe Arb ch 20 pour **Groupe arbitral créé en vertu du chapitre 20**, et Comité cont extr pour **Comité pour contestation extraordinaire**.

➢ Fournir les références électroniques selon les règles énoncées à la section 5.3.

5.2.12 Décisions d'arbitrage international

	Intitulé ou **numéro** de la décision	**(année de la décision),**	**recueil et référence précise**	**(cadre),**	**(arbitres)** (facultatif).
Nom des parties divulgué	*Southern Pacific Properties c Egypt*	(1992),	32 ILM 933 à la p 1008	(International Center for Settlement of Investment Disputes),	(arbitres : Dr Eduardo Jiménez de Aréchaga, Mohamed Amin El Mahdi, Robert F Pietrowski Jr).
Parties anonymes	Déc n° 6248	(1990),	19 YB Comm Arb 124 à la p 129	(International Chamber of Commerce).	

➢ Fournir l'intitulé avec le nom des parties si elles sont divulguées. Si les parties sont anonymes, indiquer le numéro de la décision.

➢ Indiquer l'année de la décision entre parenthèses, suivie de la référence au recueil.

➢ Indiquer l'organisme qui a fourni le cadre ou le mécanisme d'arbitrage.

➢ Indiquer le nom des arbitres entre parenthèses à la fin de la référence (facultatif).

5.2.13 Décisions d'arbitrage de l'Organisation mondiale de la propriété intellectuelle (OMPI)

5.2.13.1 Principes directeurs régissant le règlement uniforme des litiges relatifs aux noms de domaine (UDRP)

Intitulé,	**numéro du litige**	**<nom de domaine>**	**(Centre d'arbitrage et de médiation de l'OMPI (UDRP)).**
CareerBuilder, LLC v Names for sale,	D2005-0186	<careersbuilder.com>	(Centre d'arbitrage et de médiation de l'OMPI (UDRP)).

5.2.14 Décisions de droit international prises devant des cours nationales

Intitulé,	recueil du pays d'origine,	recueil international	(pays et juridiction).
Re Noble and Wolf,	[1949] 4 DLR 375,	[1948] Ann Dig ILC 302	(Can, CA Ont).
Lindon v Commonwealth of Australia (n° 2),	(1996), 136 ALR 251,	118 ILR 338	(Austl, HC).
Institute of Chartered Accountants in England and Wales v Commissioners of Customs and Excise,	[1999] 2 All ER 449,	[1999] 2 CMLR 1333	(R-U, HL).

➤ Si une décision de portée internationale est rendue par une **cour nationale**, fournir une référence à un recueil du pays d'origine. Indiquer une référence à un recueil international tel que l'Annual Digest and Reports of Public International Law Cases (Ann Dig ILC), l'International Law Reports (ILR), les Common Market Law Reports (CMLR) ou le Common Market Reporter (CMR).

➤ Indiquer le pays où la décision a été prise et préciser la cour qui a pris la décision.

5.3 SITES INTERNET

Référence traditionnelle,	en ligne :	nom du site	<adresse universelle>.
US, Commission on Security and Cooperation in Europe, *Presidential Elections and Independence Referendums in the Baltic States, the Soviet Union and Successor States*, Washington (DC), The Commission, 1992 à la p 53,	en ligne :	Commission on Security and Cooperation in Europe	<http://www.csce.gov>.
Convention relative aux droits de l'enfant, 20 novembre 1998, 1577 RTNU 3,	en ligne :	Collection des traités des Nations Unies	<http://untreaty.un.org>.

➤ Fournir la référence traditionnelle, suivie d'une virgule. Écrire en ligne : et le nom du site Internet, suivis de l'adresse universelle (URL).

➤ Faire référence à l'adresse universelle de la page d'accueil du document.

➤ Plusieurs textes en ligne disparaissent après un certain temps. Faire référence à une source en ligne si cette source fournit des documents archivés remontant à quelques années.

➤ Inclure un numéro de paragraphe comme référence précise si possible. Si la numérotation de la page d'une source imprimée est reproduite dans une source électronique, faire référence à la numérotation utilisée par la source imprimée.

Doctrine et autres documents

6   DOCTRINE ET AUTRES DOCUMENTS

6.1   PÉRIODIQUES

6.1.1   Modèle de base

Auteur,	« titre de l'article »	(année)	volume	abréviation du périodique	première page	référence précise	(service électronique) (s'il y a lieu).
Marie-Claude Prémont,	« La fiscalité locale au Québec : de la cohabitation au refuge fiscal »	(2001)	46	RD McGill	713	¶ 4	(QL).

6.1.2   Auteur

6.1.2.1   Un seul auteur

Frédéric Bachand, « L'efficacité en droit québécois d'une convention d'arbritrage ou d'élection de for invoquée à l'encontre d'un appel en garantie » (2004) 83:2 R du B 515.

L'honorable Louis LeBel, « La protection des droits fondamentaux et la responsabilité civile » (2004) 49 RD McGill 231.

➢   Indiquer le nom de l'auteur **tel qu'il paraît sur la page couverture**. Inclure tous les noms et initiales utilisés. Ne pas mettre d'espace entre les initiales. Ne pas inscrire un nom lorsque des initiales sont utilisées et ne pas inclure d'intiales lorsqu'un nom est utilisé.

➢   Si le nom de l'auteur sur la page de couverture est précédé d'un **titre honorifique** tel que l'honorable, Rabbin, Professeur ou Lord, inclure ce titre dans la référence. Ne pas indiquer les diplômes ou autre références.

6.1.2.2   Coauteurs

Murielle Paradelle, Hélène Dumont et Anne-Marie Boisvert, « Quelle justice pour quelle réconciliation ? : Le Tribunal pénal pour le Rwanda et le jugement du génocide » (2005) 50 RD McGill 359.

Armel Huet et al, *Capitalisme et industries culturelles*, Grenoble, Presses Universitaires de Grenoble, 1978.

➢   Ne pas indiquer plus de trois auteurs.

→   S'il y a **deux auteurs**, séparer les noms des auteurs par et.

→   S'il y a **trois auteurs**, séparer les deux premiers noms par une virgule et écrire et avant le dernier nom.

→ S'il y a **plus de trois auteurs**, indiquer le nom du premier auteur, suivi de et al.

→ Pour les autres types de **collaborations** (avec), suivre la formule utilisée sur la page titre.

6.1.3 Titre de l'article

Ghislain Otis, « Les sources des droits ancestraux des peuples autochtones » (1999) 40 C de D 591.

Darcy L MacPherson, « Extending Corporate Criminal Liability?: Some Thoughts on Bill C-45 » (2004) 30 Man LJ 253.

➢ Indiquer le titre de l'article **entre guillemets**.

➢ Ne pas mettre de virgule après le titre.

➢ Séparer un titre d'un sous-titre à l'aide de deux-points (:). Ne pas utiliser de tiret (–).

➢ Respecter les règles des **majuscules** et de la **ponctuation** de la langue du titre. Peu importe la langue du titre, utiliser des guillemets français avant et après le titre (par ex. « Titre »).

➢ Pour plus de détails concernant la langue et la ponctuation des titres, voir la section 6.2.3.

6.1.4 Année de publication

Le périodique est organisé par numéro de volume	Michel Poirier, « La convention d'emphytéose peut-elle être à titre gratuit ? » (1998) 68 R du B 401.
Le périodique est organisé par année de publication	Frédéric Pollaud-Dulian, « À propos de la sécurité juridique » [2001] RTD civ 487.

➢ Si le périodique est divisé en volumes numérotés, indiquer la date de publication entre parenthèses.

➢ Si le périodique **n'est pas divisé en volumes numérotés, mais plutôt en années**, indiquer l'année **entre crochets**.

6.1.5 Volume, numéro et série

Auteur, « titre de l'article » (année de publication)	volume	:	numéro	titre de la revue	série (s'il y a lieu)	première page de l'article
Cédric Milhat, « La représentation juridique de la mémoire. L'exemple fraçais. »	43	:	1	RJT		51.
Damian Powell, « Coke in Context: Early Modern Legal Observation and Sir Edward Coke's Reports » (2000)	21	:	3	Health L Rev		34.
RRA Walker, « The English Property Legislation of 1922-6 » (1928)	10			J Comp Legis & Int'l L	(3ᵉ)	1.

➢ Placer le numéro du volume après l'année de publication, suivi d'un deux-points et du numéro de la revue. **Inclure le numéro si le volume en a plus d'un**, peu importe si la pagination des numéros d'un volume est consécutive ou non.

➢ Si une revue est aussi divisée en **séries**, indiquer le numéro de la série entre parenthèses après le titre de la revue.

6.1.6 Titre du périodique

➢ Abréger le titre du périodique selon la liste des abréviations prévue à l'**annexe D**. Consulter également le *Bieber's Dictionary of Legal Abbreviations*. Si l'abréviation n'y figure pas, écrire le titre complet du périodique.

> Will Kymlicka, « Federalism and Secession: At Home and Abroad » (2000) 13 Can JL & Jur 207.
>
> André Cellard et Gérald Pelletier, « Le Code criminel canadien, 1892-1927 : Étude des acteurs sociaux » (1998) 79 Canadian Historical Review 261.

➢ Ne pas mettre l'abréviation ou le titre du périodique en italique.

6.1.6.1 France

Auteur,	« titre »	renseignements sur l'édition.
Jean-Christophe Galloux,	« La loi du 6 mars 1998 relative à la sécurité et à la promotion d'activités sportives »	(1998) JCP I 1085.

➢ Indiquer le nom et le titre d'articles publiés dans les recueils généraux de France de la manière énoncée aux sections 6.1.2 et 6.1.3. Voir **l'annexe C-3** pour la liste de ces recueils.

➢ Consulter la section 3.7 pour les références aux recueils.

Abréviations des recueils :

Actualité juridique de droit administratif	AJDA
Bulletin de la Cour de cassation, section civile	Bull civ
Gazette du Palais	Gaz Pal
Recueil des décisions du Conseil d'État ou Recueil Lebon	Rec
Recueil Dalloz et Recueil Dalloz et Sirey (1945 – présent)	D
Semaine juridique (1937 – présent)	JCP

6.1.7 Première page de l'article

Marie-Josée Bernardi, « La diversité génétique humaine : Éléments de politique canadienne » (2001) 35 RJT 327.

➢ Indiquer la première page de l'article après le titre de la revue. Ne pas écrire « p » ou « à la p ».

➢ Pour les références précises, voir la section 6.1.8.

6.1.7.1 Articles publiés en parties

Publication dans différents volumes	RA Macdonald, « Enforcing Rights in Corporeal Moveables: Revendication and Its Surrogates » (1986) 31 RD McGill 573 et (1986) 32 RD McGill 1.
Publication dans différentes parties d'un même volume	Roderick A Macdonald, « L'image du Code civil et l'imagination du notaire » (1995) 74 R du B can 97 et 330.

➢ Si les parties de l'article ont été publiées dans **plusieurs volumes**, indiquer l'auteur et le titre, suivis de la référence complète pour chaque partie, réunies par et.

➢ Si les parties de l'article ont été publiées dans **un même volume**, indiquer les premières pages de chaque partie, séparées par et.

6.1.8 Référence précise

Nicholas Kasirer, « Agapè et le devoir juridique de secours : Qui est mon prochain ? » [2001] RIDC 575 aux pp 579-80.

Adrian J Bradbrook, Susan V MacCallum et Anthony P Moore, Australian Real Property Law, 2ᵉ éd, Sydney, Law Book Company, 1997 au para 509.

Louis Beaudoin et Madeleine Mailhot, Expressions juridiques en un clin d'œil, Cowansville (Qc), Yvon Blais, 1997 à la p 55, n 1.

➢ Indiquer la référence précise à la fin de la référence.

➤ Indiquer la page ou le paragraphe. Lorsque les paragraphes sont numérotés, y faire référence à l'aide de au para ou du symbole ¶. Pour faire référence à une page, utiliser à la p et pour plusieurs pages, utiliser aux pp.

➤ Séparer les pages et les paragraphes **consécutifs** par un trait d'union. Pour les nombres de deux chiffres et plus, conserver au moins les deux derniers chiffres (par ex. 158-60 ou 32-35, mais jamais 32-5).

➤ Utiliser une virgule pour séparer les pages et les paragraphes **non consécutifs** (par ex. aux pp 21, 48).

➤ Pour indiquer une **partie générale**, inscrire et s (abréviation de « et suivantes ») immédiatement après le numéro. Il est toutefois préférable de faire référence aux pages ou paragraphes précis.

➤ Pour faire référence à **une note**, indiquer le numéro de la page où se trouve la note ainsi que le numéro de la note (par ex. à la p 99, n 140). Pour faire référence à **plusieurs notes**, indiquer le numéro de la page où se trouvent les notes ainsi que les numéros des notes (par ex. à la p 142, nn 73-75). Toutefois, si le numéro de la page n'est pas disponible, faire référence au numéro de la note uniquement (par ex. n 140).

➤ Utiliser le même format de chiffre que le texte (par ex. 5-6; v-vi).

6.2 MONOGRAPHIES

6.2.1 Modèle de base

Auteur,	*titre*,	édition,	autres éléments	lieu d'édition,	maison d'édition,	année d'édition	référence précise	(service électronique) (si utilisé).
Éric Canal-Forgues,	*Le règlement des différends à l'OMC*,	2e éd,		Bruxelles,	Bruylant,	2004	à la p 53.	
J Anthony VanDuzer,	*The Law of Partnerships and Corporations*,			Toronto,	Irwin Law,	1997	ch 2 (B) (3)	(QL).

➤ D'autres éléments peuvent être indiqués, si nécessaire, dans la section « autre éléments » entre l'édition et le lieu d'édition. Leur ordre de présentation est le suivant : **nom du directeur d'un ouvrage collectif** (section 6.2.2.3) ; **nom du traducteur** (section 6.2.2.5) ; **numéro du volume** (section 6.2.4) ; **titre du volume** ; **titre d'une collection et le numéro du volume dans cette collection** et **feuilles mobiles** (section 6.2.6).

6.2.2 Auteur

6.2.2.1 Un seul auteur

Sylvio Normand, *Introduction au droit des biens*, Montréal, Wilson & Lafleur, 2000.

Jean-Pierre Baud, *L'affaire de la main volée : Une histoire juridique du corps*, Paris, Seuil, 1993 à la p 4.

Lucie Laflamme, *Le partage consécutif à l'indivision*, Montréal, Wilson & Lafleur, 1999.

Lord Denning, *What Next in the Law*, Londres, Butterworths, 1982.

➢ Indiquer le nom de l'auteur **tel qu'il paraît sur la page couverture**. Inclure tous les noms et initiales utilisés. Ne pas mettre d'espace entre les initiales. Ne pas inscrire un nom lorsque des initiales sont utilisées et ne pas inclure d'intiales lorsqu'un nom est utilisé.

➢ Si le nom de l'auteur sur la page de couverture est précédé d'un **titre honorifique** tel que l'honorable, Rabbin, Professeur ou Lord, inclure ce titre dans la référence. Ne pas indiquer les diplômes ou autre références.

6.2.2.2 Coauteurs

---

[1] Jacques Bourdon, Jean-Marie Pontier et Jean-Claude Ricci, *Droit des collectivités territoriales*, Paris, Presses Universitaires de France, 1987.

[9] Joel Bakan et al, *Canadian Constitutional Law*, 3e éd, Toronto, Emond Montgomery, 2003.

[10] Pierre-Gabriel Jobin avec la collaboration de Nathalie Vézina, *Baudouin et Jobin : Les obligations*, 6e éd, Cowansville (Qc), Yvon Blais, 2005.

➢ **Ne pas indiquer plus de trois auteurs**. S'il y en a plus, indiquer le nom du premier auteur, suivi de et al.

➢ Séparer le nom des deux derniers auteurs par et.

➢ Pour les **autres types de collaborations** (par ex. avec la collaboration de), suivre la formule utilisée sur la page titre de la monographie (voir note 10).

6.2.2.3 Directeur d'un ouvrage collectif

➢ Indiquer le nom du directeur avant le titre de l'ouvrage collectif, suivi de dir entre virgules.

➢ **Ne pas indiquer plus de trois directeurs**. S'il y en a plus, indiquer le nom du premier, suivi de et al.

Denis Ferland et Benoît Emery, dir, *Précis de procédure civile du Québec*, 3e éd, Cowansville (Qc), Yvon Blais, 1997.

➢ L'abréviation dir vaut autant pour le singulier que pour le pluriel.

➢ Si la référence concerne un **article en particulier** et non l'ouvrage en général, indiquer le nom de l'auteur et de l'article, suivi de dans avant le nom du directeur (section 6.3).

6.2.2.4 Directeur ou correcteur de l'ouvrage d'un autre auteur

6.2.2.4.1   Le nom de l'auteur original fait partie du titre

Directeur,	dir,	titre,	édition,	renseignements sur l'édition.
M Dupin,	dir,	Oeuvres de Pothier,	2e éd,	Paris, Pichon-Béchet, 1835.

➢ Si le nom de l'auteur fait partie du titre, faire référence au directeur, suivi de dir entre virgules.

6.2.2.4.2   Le nom de l'auteur original ne fait pas partie du titre

Auteur,	titre,	édition	par	directeur,	renseignements sur l'édition.
Aubry et Rau,	Droit civil français,	8e éd	par	André Ponsard et Ibrahim Fadlallah,	Paris, Librairies techniques, 1989.

➢ Si le nom de l'auteur ne fait pas partie du titre, mettre le nom du directeur après la mention de l'édition, et l'introduire avec par.

➢ S'il y a plusieurs éditions, indiquer le numéro (par ex. 8e éd par).

➢ Indiquer le nom du ou des auteurs et celeri du ou des directeurs tels qu'ils apparaissent dans la publication.

6.2.2.5 Traducteur

Traduire les textes en langues étrangères qui pourraient ne pas être connues des lecteurs. Le texte original d'une citation peut être inclus dans la note de bas de page.

6.2.2.5.1   Traduction professionnelle

Auteur,	titre,	traduit par	traducteur,	renseignements sur l'édition	[modifiée par l'auteur] (s'il y a lieu).
Jürgen Habermas,	Droit et démocratie : Entre faits et normes,	traduit par	Rainer Rochlitz et Christian Bouchindhomme,	Paris, Gallimard, 1997.	

➢ Faire référence à une traduction professionnelle en indiquant le nom du traducteur avant les renseignements sur l'édition, introduit par traduit par.

➢ S'il est nécessaire de modifier la traduction d'un passage cité, introduire la modification par [modifiée par l'auteur] après les renseignements sur l'édition.

➢ Toujours inclure l'information sur le directeur ou le correcteur (section 6.2.2.4) avant l'information sur le traducteur (section 6.2.2.5).

6.2.2.5.2   Traduction de l'auteur du texte (vous)

> Comme le dit Kronby, « la cour fut convaincue par la preuve de l'épouse » [notre traduction][28].

➢ L'ajout [notre traduction] se réfère à l'auteur (vous) et non à l'auteur du texte cité.

➢ Dans la mesure du possible, traduire un passage tiré d'une source rédigée dans une autre langue que le français ou l'anglais.

➢ Insérer l'ajout [notre traduction] dans le corps même du texte, après les guillemets de la citation traduite et immédiatement avant l'appel de note.

6.2.3 Titre

> [1] B Lefebvre, *La bonne foi dans la formation du contrat*, **Montréal, Yvon Blais, 1998.**
>
> [2] AH Oosterhoff et EE Gillese, *Text, Commentary and Cases on Trusts*, 5e éd, **Toronto, Carswell, 1998.**
>
> [3] Frédéric Garron, *La caducité du contrat : Étude de droit privé*, **Aix-en-Provence, Presses Universitaires d'Aix-Marseille, 2000.**
>
> [4] Michel Vepreaux, *La naissance du pouvoir réglementaire, 1789-1799*, **Paris, Presses Universitaires de France, 1991.**
>
> [5] Jürgen Schwarze, *Europaïsches Varwaltungsrecht [Droit administratif européen]*, 2e éd, **Bruxelles, Bruylant, 2009.**
>
> [6] Waldo Ansaldi, **dir** *La démocratie en Amérique latine : Un bateau de la dérive* (en espagnol), **Buenos Aires, Fondo de Cultura Económica, 2007.**

➢ Indiquer le titre principal en entier et en italique. Suivre l'orthographe et la ponctuation du titre tel que publié avec les exceptions suivantes :

→ précéder le sous-titre de deux-points (notes 3 et 6) ; et

→ insérer une virgule avant une date comprise à la fin du titre, s'il y a lieu (note 4).

➢ Respecter les règles des majuscules et de la ponctuation de la langue du titre.

➢ Si le titre de l'ouvrage est dans une langue qui n'est pas le français, l'anglais ou une autre langue familière aux lecteurs, suivre **l'une** des règles suivantes :

→ Inscrire le titre original suivi d'une traduction en français (note 5). Ne pas mettre la traduction en italique, mais entre crochets, sans ponctuation entre le titre original et la traduction. Si le titre original n'est pas en lettres latines (par ex. en chinois ou en hébreu), transcrire le titre en écriture romaine (par ex. Menachem Elon, *Ha-Mishpat Ha-Ivri* [Droit juif]).

→ Traduire le titre en français et le mettre en italique suivi de l'indication de la langue originale du texte entre parenthèses (note 6). Ne pas ajouter de ponctuation entre la traduction du titre et les parenthèses.

6.2.3.1 *Procédures publiées d'une conférence ou d'un symposium*

➢ Traiter toute information concernant la conférence ou le symposium comme faisant partie du titre.

Marie-France Bich, « Petits éléments pour une réflexion polémique sur la solidarité en droit du travail » dans *Droits de la personne : Solidarité et bonne foi. Actes des Journées strasbourgeoises de l'Institut canadien d'études juridiques supérieures 2000 tenues du 2 au 8 juillet 2000 à Strasbourg*, Cowansville (Qc), Yvon Blais, 2000.

6.2.4 Numéro de volume

6.2.4.1 *Livres en français*

Auteur,	*titre*,	tome et/ou volume,	édition,	directeur (s'il y a lieu),	renseignements sur l'édition.
Jean Carbonnier,	*Droit civil : Les obligations*,	t 4,	22ᵉ éd,		Paris, Presses universitaires de France, 2000.
Henri Mazeaud et al,	*Leçons de droit civil*,	t 3, vol 1,	7ᵉ éd,	Yves Picod, dir,	Paris, Montchrestien, 1999.

➢ Les ouvrages français peuvent être divisés en tomes et subdivisés en volumes.

➢ Utiliser t pour **tome** et vol pour **volume**.

➢ Indiquer les numéros de tomes et de volumes en chiffres arabes (par ex. 1, 2, 3).

➢ Faire suivre le titre par les indications du tome et du volume et les placer entre virgules.

6.2.4.2 *Livres en anglais*

Auteur,	*titre*,	volume,	renseignements sur l'édition	référence précise.
Anne F Bayefsky,	*Canada's Constitution Act 1982 & Amendments: A Documentary History*,	vol 2,	Toronto, McGraw-Hill, 1989	à la p 669.

6.2.4.2.1   Volumes publiés sous différents titres

➢ Indiquer le numéro du volume avant les renseignements sur l'édition.

➢ Indiquer le numéro du volume en chiffres arabes (par ex. 1, 2, 3), même si l'éditeur utilise des chiffres romains.

6.2.4.2.2   Volumes publiés sous un même titre

Auteur,	*titre*,	directeur (s'il y a lieu),	traduction (s'il y a lieu),	renseigne-ments sur l'édition,	volume	référence précise.
Karl Marx,	*Capital: A Critical Analysis of Capitalist Production*,	Friedrich Engels, dir,	trad par Samuel Moore et Edward Aveling,	Londres, Swan Sonnen-schein, 1908,	vol 1	à la p 15.

➤ Indiquer le numéro du volume après les renseignements sur l'édition.

➤ Indiquer le numéro du volume en chiffres arabes (par ex. 1, 2, 3), même si l'éditeur utilise des chiffres romains.

6.2.5 Édition

Germain Brière, *Le nouveau droit des successions*, 2e éd, Montréal, Wilson & Lafleur, 1997.

Maurice Tancelin, *Des obligations : contrat et responsabilité*, éd révisée, Montréal, Wilson & Lafleur, 1986.

➤ Indiquer le numéro de l'édition (par ex. 2e éd) après le titre.

➤ Abréger édition par éd.

➤ Lorsque l'ouvrage a été révisé mais qu'aucun numéro d'édition n'est précisé, indiquer éd révisée après le titre.

6.2.6 Ouvrage à feuilles mobiles

Auteur,	*titre*,	feuilles mobiles (consultées le	date de consultation),	renseignements sur l'édition,	référence précise.
Georges Audet et al,	*Le congédiement en droit québécois en matière de contrat individuel de travail*,	feuilles mobiles (consultées le	18 avril 2009),	Cowansville (Qc), Yvon Blais, 1991,	ch 5 à la p 71.
Madeleine Lemieux,	*Tribunaux administratifs du Québec : Règles et législation annotées*,	feuilles mobiles (consultées le	28 août 2009),	Cowansville (Qc), Yvon Blais, 2002,	ch R9 à la p 85.
Robert W Hillman,	*Hillman on Lawyer Mobility : The Law and Ethics of Partner Withdrawals and the Law Firm Breakups*,	feuilles mobiles (consultées le	4 octobre 2009),	2e éd, Austin, Wolters Kluwer, 1998,	ch 2 à la p 85.

➤ Les règles de cette section s'appliquent aux ouvrages de doctrine dont le contenu est perpétuellement renouvelé. Pour faire référence à la législation sous forme de recueils à feuilles mobiles, voir la section 2.1.5.

➤ Indiquer feuilles mobiles après le titre, et mettre entre parethèses consultées le suivi de la date de consultation.

> Utiliser la date d'édition qui paraît sur la page où sont indiquées les informations sur les droits d'auteur, même si cette date diffère de la date qui se trouve ailleurs dans le livre.

> Faire référence au chapitre en plus de la page si l'ouvrage est divisé en chapitres.

6.2.7 Lieu d'édition

> Indiquer le lieu d'édition tel qu'il figure au recto ou au verso de la page titre. Utiliser la **version française** du nom de la ville si elle existe (par ex. écrire Londres (R-U) et non London (UK)).

> S'il y a **plus d'un lieu d'édition**, ne mentionner que le premier lieu.

J-L Aubert, *La responsabilité civile des notaires*, 3ᵉ éd, Paris, Defrénois, 1998.
Andrée Lajoie, *Pouvoir disciplinaire et tests de dépistage de drogues en milieu de travail*, Cowansville (Qc), Yvon Blais, 1995.

> Si **aucun lieu d'édition n'est fourni**, écrire aucun lieu.

> Si des renseignements supplémentaires sont requis pour identifier le lieu d'édition (par ex. la province, l'État ou le pays), abréger ces renseignements entre parenthèses après le lieu d'édition (par ex. Cowanswille (Qc)). Si deux villes peuvent être confondues, ajouter les renseignements supplémentaires nécessaires (par ex. London (Ont) et Londres (R-U)).

> Voir les abréviations couramment utilisées des provinces candiennes de l'**annexe A-1** et les abréviations des États américains de l'**annexe A-2**.

6.2.8 Maison d'édition

✓	Mireille D Castelli et Dominique Goubau, *Précis de droit de la famille*, Sainte-Foy (Qc), Presses de l'Université Laval, 2000.
	Pierre-Claude Lafond, *Précis du droit des biens*, Montréal, Thémis, 1999.
✓	Gaëlle Breton-LeGoff, *L'influence des organisations non gouvernementales (ONG) sur la négociation de quelques instruments internationaux* (Cowansville, Qc), Yvon Blais, 2001.
✗	Gaëlle Breton-LeGoff, *L'influence des organisations non gouvernementales (ONG) sur la négociation de quelques instruments internationaux*, (Cowansville, Qc), Les Éditions Yvon Blais inc, 2001.

> Indiquer le nom de la maison d'édition **tel qu'il figure à la page titre**.

> Ne pas abréger le nom de la maison d'édition (par ex. Presses de l'Université Laval et non PUL).

> Omettre l'article défini (le, la, les, l', *the*) même s'il est le premier du nom.

> Omettre les expressions indiquant le statut corporatif (par ex. ltée, inc).

> Écrire « édition(s) », « *Publishing* » ou « *Publishers* » uniquement s'il s'agit d'une partie inséparable du nom (par ex. Éditions de l'Homme). Suivre cette même règle pour les autres langues (par ex. Verlag).

➢ Indiquer Presses en français et *Press* en anglais.

➢ S'il y a **plus d'un éditeur**, fournir les lieux d'édition, les noms des coéditeurs, suivis de l'année. Séparer les lieux d'édition des noms des coéditeurs par un point-virgule. Voir l'exemple ci-dessous.

Premier lieu d'édition,	deuxième lieu d'édition ;	premier coéditeur,	deuxième coéditeur,	année.
Latzville (C-B),	Montreal ;	Oolichan Books,	Institute for Research on Public Policy,	1992.

➢ Si un éditeur travaille pour une **organisation**, indiquer pour avant le nom de l'organisation (par ex. Janet E Gans Epner pour la Commission on Women in the Profession).

➢ Si **aucune maison d'édition** n'est indiquée, écrire aucune maison d'édition.

6.2.9 Année d'édition

➢ Indiquer l'année de **l'édition actuelle**, et non celle de la première édition. En général, utiliser la date la plus récente indiquée sur l'édition, à moins que l'année de publication ne soit présentée de façon explicite.

> Jean Pineau, Danielle Burman et Serge Gaudet, *Théorie des obligations*, 4ᵉ éd, Montréal, Thémis, 2001.

➢ Ne pas indiquer l'année d'impression.

➢ Si **aucune année** n'est indiquée, écrire aucune date.

6.2.10 Référence précise

> Pierre-André Côté, *Interprétation des lois*, 3ᵉ éd, Montréal, Thémis, 1999 à la p 307.
>
> Jean-Louis Baudouin, *La responsabilité civile délictuelle*, 4ᵉ éd, Cowansville (Qc), Yvon Blais, 1994 aux pp 102-08, 121-25.
>
> Ronald Joseph De isle et Don Stuart, *Learning Canadian Criminal Procedure*, 5ᵉ éd, Scarborough, Carswell, 1998, ch 2 à la p 377 et s.
>
> Francis Delpérée, *Le droit constitutionnel de la Belgique*, Belgique, Bruxelles, Bruylant, 2000 au no 257.
>
> Isabelle Schulte-Tenckhoff, *La question des peuples autochtones*, Bruxelles, Bruylant, 1997 à la p 56, n 61.

➢ Indiquer la référence précise après l'information sur la publication.

➢ **Les références aux paragraphes sont préférables à celles aux pages**. Lorsque les paragraphes sont numérotés, indiquer au para ou le symbole ¶. Pour faire référence à une page, utiliser à la p et pour plusieurs pages, utiliser aux pp.

➢ Séparer les pages et les paragraphes **consécutifs** par un trait d'union, en conservant au moins les deux derniers chiffres (par ex. 158-60 ou 32-35, mais jamais 32-5).

➢ Utiliser une virgule pour séparer les numéros **non consécutifs** (aux pp 21, 48).

➢ Pour indiquer une **partie générale**, indiquer et s (abréviation de « et suivantes ») immédiatement après le numéro. De préférence, indiquer les pages et paragraphes précis.

➢ Abréger **chapitre** et **chapitres** par ch. La règle diffère pour la législation (section 2.1.9).

➢ Pour faire référence à une **note de bas de page**, indiquer le numéro de la page où se trouve la note ainsi que le numéro de la note (par ex. à la p 99, n 140). Au pluriel, n devient nn. Si le numéro de la page n'est pas disponible, indiquer le numéro de la note (par ex. n 140) seulement.

➢ Pour les chiffres, utiliser le même format que dans le texte (par ex. 5-6; v-vi).

6.3 ARTICLES PUBLIÉS DANS DES OUVRAGES COLLECTIFS

Auteur de l'article,	« *titre* de l'article »	dans	directeur (s'il y a lieu),	dir,	*titre de l'ouvrage,*	renseignements sur l'édition,	1ʳᵉ page de l'article	référence précise (s'il y a lieu).
Madeleine Cantin Cumyn,	« Le Code civil et la gestion des biens d'autrui »	dans	Jean-Louis Baudouin et Patrice Deslau-riers,	dir,	*La responsabilité civile des courtiers en valeurs mobilières et des gestionnaires de fortune : Aspects nouveaux,*	Montréal, Yvon Blais, 1999,	121	à la p 128.
Daniel Jutras,	« Le code et le ministre, essai sur les commen-taires »	dans			*Mélanges offerts à Paul-André Crépeau,*	Cowansville (Qc), Yvon Blais, 1997,	451	à la p 453.
Jocelyn Maclure,	« Introduc-tion »	dans	Jocelyn Maclure et Alain-G Gagnon,	dir,	*Passages : L'identité, diversité et citoyenneté au Québec,*	Montréal, Québec Amérique, 2001,	xi.	

➢ Indiquer le nom de l'auteur et le titre de l'article suivis de la référence à l'ouvrage collectif.

➢ Indiquer le nom du directeur, suivi de dir entre virgules. Omettre l'identité du directeur si celle-ci n'est pas fournie.

➢ Indiquer le titre de l'ouvrage collectif en italique, suivi des renseignements sur l'édition.

➤ Indiquer la première page de l'article et la référence précise s'il y a lieu.

➤ Si le texte n'est pas un article, utiliser comme titre d'article Avant-propos, Préface, Introduction, Conclusion, ou le titre donné à cette section en suivant les règles qui s'appliquent aux articles (voir l'exemple de Jocelyn Maclure).

6.4 DICTIONNAIRES

Titre,	édition ou année,	sub verbo	« mot cherché ».
Le nouveau petit Robert,	1990,	sub verbo	« amphigourique ».
Black's Law Dictionary,	6ᵉ éd,	sub verbo	« promissory estoppel ».

➤ Indiquer le titre du dictionnaire en italique.

➤ Indiquer l'édition ou l'année.

➤ Écrire sub verbo, signifiant « au mot » en latin.

6.4.1 Dictionnaires spécialisés

Directeur ou auteur,	ed (if applicable),	titre,	édition (s'il y a lieu),	renseignements sur l'édition,	sub verbo	« mot cherché ».
Gérard Cornu,	dir,	Vocabulaire juridique,	7ᵉ éd,	Paris, Presses Universitaires de France, 2005,	sub verbo	« minorité ».
Agathe Van Lang,		Dictionnaire de droit administratif,		Paris, Dalloz, 1999.		
Office québécois de la langue française,		Grand dictionnaire terminologique,			sub verbo	« hypothèque ».

➤ Faire référence au dictionnaire de la même manière qu'à une monographie (section 6.2).

6.5 ENCYCLOPÉDIES

6.5.1 *Canadian Encyclopedic Digest*

➤ Le CED est une encyclopédie publiée en feuilles mobiles donnant de l'information générale sur un sujet particulier du droit. Chacun des volumes est organisé par sujet (par ex. droit criminel, droit de la famille).

CED	(série	édition),	volume,	titre	section.
CED	(Ont	4e),	vol 1,	titre 2	à la s 10.

➢ Écrire CED plutôt que le nom au complet de l'encyclopédie au long.

➢ Indiquer la série sous forme abrégée : **Ontario CED** (Ont) et **Western CED** (West).

6.5.2 Common law

Halsbury's Laws of England, 4e éd, vol 34, Londres, Butterworths, 1980 à la p 60, au para 71.

American Jurisprudence, 2e éd, vol 17A, Rochester (NY), Lawyer's Cooperative, 1991 au titre « Contracts », § 97.

➢ Suivre les règles pour les monographies à la section 6.2 **sans indiquer le nom de l'auteur**.

➢ **Faire référence à des paragraphes** (para). Utiliser le symbole § pour les ouvrages américains.

➢ Indiquer le titre d'une partie entre guillemets, s'il y a lieu, après les renseignements sur l'édition et l'indication au titre (voir *American Jurisprudence*).

6.5.3 France

6.5.3.1 Modèle de base

Titre du répertoire,	édition (s'il y a lieu),	identification de la rubrique	par	auteur de la rubrique	référence précise.
Juris-classeur civil,		art 1354, fasc A	par	Roger Perrot.	
Encyclopédie juridique Dalloz : Répertoire de droit commercial,	2e éd,	« Ventes commerciales »	par	Luc Bihl	au n° 256.

➢ Si possible, se rapporter au *Juris-classeur civil*.

➢ Indiquer l'encyclopédie et le titre du répertoire non abrégé et en italique.

➢ Lorsque **plus d'une édition** a été publiée, indiquer le numéro de l'édition.

Abréviations des principaux répertoires :

Encyclopédie juridique Dalloz : Répertoire de droit administratif	Rép admin
Encyclopédie juridique Dalloz : Répertoire de droit civil	Rép civ
Encyclopédie juridique Dalloz : Répertoire de droit commercial	Rép com
Juris-classeur administratif	J-cl admin
Juris-classeur civil	J-cl Civ
Juris-classeur civil annexe	J-cl civ annexe
Juris-classeur commercial	J-cl Com
Juris-classeur commercial : Banque et crédit	J-cl com Banque et crédit
Juris-classeur répertoire notarial	J-cl rép not

6.5.3.2 Rubriques

Classées par ordre alphabétique	Encyclopédie juridique Dalloz : Répertoire de droit civil, « Personnalité (droits de la) », par D Tallon au n° 153. Juris-classeur civil annexes, « Associations », fasc 1-A, par Robert Brichet.
Classées selon les articles d'un code	Juris-classeur civil, app art 3, fasc 4, par Yves Luchaire. Juris-classeur civil, art 1315-1316, par Daniel Veaux.
Classées par volume	Juris-classeur commercial : Banque et crédit, vol 2, fasc 32, par Jean Stoufflet.

➢ **Classées par ordre alphabétique** : indiquer les mots-clés qui identifient la rubrique entre guillemets. Ajouter fasc et le numéro approprié après le nom de la rubrique, s'il y a lieu.

➢ **Classées selon les articles d'un code** : indiquer le numéro de l'article ou des articles sous lesquels la rubrique est classée. Utiliser la même forme que celle du répertoire. Ajouter fasc après le numéro d'article s'il y a lieu.

➢ **Classées par volume** : indiquer le numéro du volume où se trouve la rubrique.

➢ Peu importe la méthode de classification des rubriques, toujours indiquer le numéro du fascicule après celui du volume.

➢ Ne pas indiquer la date de révision du fascicule.

6.6   CODES DE DÉONTOLOGIE

Organisme,	titre du code,	renseignements sur l'édition,	référence précise.
L'Association du Barreau canadien,	Code de déontologie professionnelle,	Ottawa, ABC, 2006,	ch VI, r 1(a).
Association des infirmières et infirmiers du Canada,	Code de déontologie des infirmières et infirmiers,	Ottawa, AIIC, 2008,	préambule à la p 2.

> Si l'organisme et l'éditeur sont les mêmes, indiquer l'abréviation officielle de l'organisme dans les renseignements sur l'édition (par ex. ABC pour L'Association du Barreau canadien).

> Abréger **règle** par r.

> Certains codes de déontologie sont établis par la législation. Faire référence à ces codes comme à des lois ordinaires (section 2.1) (par ex. *Code des professions*, LRQ c C-26).

6.7   DÉCISIONS D'ARBITRAGE

Pour des décisions d'**arbitrage international**, voir la secion 5.2.12. Pour des décisions de l'**OMPI**, voir la section 5.2.13.

6.7.1   Décisions d'arbitrage publiées

Intitulé ou numéro de la décision	(année de la décision),	recueil	référence précise	(arbitres) (facultatif).
California State University v State Employers Trade Council – United	(2009),	126 Lab Arb (BNA) 613		(arbitre : Bonnie G Bogue).

> Indiquer l'intitulé ou le numéro de la décision, suivi de l'année de la décision entre parenthèses et d'une virgule.

> Si la décision est publiée dans un recueil écrit, faire référence au recueil d'arbitrage comme à tout recueil de jurisprudence (section 3.7).

> Ajouter **le nom de l'arbitre** entre parenthèses (facultatif).

6.7.2   Décisions d'arbitrage non publiées

Intitulé ou numéro de la décision	(année de la décision),	code de désignation fourni par le service	(service) (s'il y a lieu)	réfé-rence précise	(arbitres) (facultatif).
Winona School District ISD 861 Winona v Winona Education Association	(2006),	2006 WL 3876585	(WL Can)		(arbitre : Daniel J Jacobowski).

> Indiquer l'intitulé ou le numéro de la décision, suivi de l'année de la décision entre parenthèses et d'une virgule.

> Si la décision est publiée dans un service électronique, inclure le code de désignation fourni par le service. Ajouter l'abréviation du service entre parenthèses si elle n'est pas déjà mentionnée dans le code de désignation.

> Ajouter **le nom de l'arbitre** entre parenthèses (facultatif).

6.8   RECENSIONS

Auteur,	« *titre* de la recension » (s'il y a lieu),	recension de	*titre de l'ouvrage recensé*	de	auteur ou éditeur de l'ouvrage recensé	renseignements sur l'édition.
Bjarne Melkevik,		recension de	*Démocratie et procéduralisation du droit*	de	Philippe Coppens et Jacques Lenoble	(2001) 42 C de D 337.
Yves-Marie Morissette,		recension de	*L'administration de la preuve*	de	Léo Ducharme	(2001) 46 RD McGill 1179.

➢ Les recensions sont l'équivalent des ***book reviews*** en anglais.

➢ Si la recension porte un titre, indiquer celui-ci après le nom de l'auteur, suivi d'une virgule.

➢ Indiquer recension de avant le titre de l'ouvrage recensé.

➢ Introduire par de le nom de l'auteur après le titre de l'ouvrage recensé.

→ Si le titre de la recension indique **à la fois le titre de l'ouvrage recensé et son auteur**, omettre ces informations dans le reste de la référence.

→ Si le titre de la recension indique **soit le titre de l'ouvrage recensé, soit son auteur**, indiquer cette information après recension de, même si une partie de l'information sera répétée.

➢ Si l'ouvrage recensé possède un éditeur plutôt qu'un auteur, écrire éd après le nom de l'éditeur de l'ouvrage recensé et une virgule (par ex. Ronald E Dimock, éd).

6.9 CHRONIQUES DE JURISPRUDENCE ET DE LÉGISLATION

	Auteur,	« titre » (s'il y a lieu),	type de chronique	de	*intitulé* ou nom de la loi ou du projet de loi,	renseignements sur l'édition.
Commentaire d'arrêt	Léo Ducharme,	« La proclamation de l'existence en droit québécois de la règle de common law de l'engagement implicite de confidentialité : *Lac d'amiante*, une décision judiciaire erronée »,	commentaire	de	*Lac d'amiante du Québec ltée c 2858-0702 Québec inc*,	(2000) 79 R du B can 435.
Chronique de législation	Jean-Pierre Colpron,	« Les nouvelles règles visant à réduire les pertes en capital »,	chronique	de	l'art 1123) de la *Loi de l'impôt sur le revenu*,	(1996) 18 Rev de plan fisc & success 177.

➢ Indiquer le titre du commentaire d'arrêt ou de la chronique de législation entre guillemets, s'il y en a un.

➢ Pour faire référence à **un commentaire d'arrêt**, mentionner commentaire de avant l'intitulé de l'arrêt. Toutefois, si le titre indique déjà le nom de l'arrêt, omettre ces informations du reste de la référence.

➢ Pour faire référence à **une chronique de législation**, la mention chronique de précède le titre de la loi. Toutefois, si le titre indique déjà le nom de la loi pertinente, omettre ces informations du reste de la référence.

6.9.1 France

6.9.1.1 Notes

Auteur,	note sous	nom du tribunal,	date de la décision,	(année de publication)	recueil	*titre* abrégé ou numéro de la partie	première page.
Danielle Corrignan-Carsin,	note sous	Cass soc,	10 mai 1999,	(1999)	JCP	II	1425.

➢ Après le nom de l'auteur et la mention note sous, faire référence à la décision et aux recueils pertinents de la même manière que l'on fait référence à la jurisprudence française (section 7.3.2).

➢ Ajouter un espace entre l'année de publication, le recueil et le titre abrégé ou le numéro de la partie (par ex. (1999) JCP 11 1425).

6.9.1.2 *Chroniques publiées dans les recueils généraux*

Auteur,	« *titre* »	(année de publication)	recueil	*titre* abrégé ou numéro de la partie	première page	référence précise.
Bertrand Mathieu et Michel Verpeaux,	« Jurisprudence constitutionnelle »	(2000)	JCP	I	2178	à la p 2180.
Xavier Labbée,	« Esquisse d'une définition civiliste de l'espèce humaine »	(1999)	D	Chron	437	à la p 440.

➢ Ajouter un espace entre l'année de publication, le recueil et le titre abrégé ou le numéro de la partie (par ex. (1999) D Chron 437 à la p 440).

➢ Indiquer l'information concernant les recueils français selon les règles de la section 7.3.2.

6.10 COMMENTAIRES, REMARQUES ET NOTES

Auteur (s'il y a lieu),	« *titre* » (s'il y a lieu),	genre du texte,	renseignements sur l'édition.
Monroe Leigh,		Commentaire éditorial,	(1996) 90 AJIL 235.
	« What We Talk About When We Talk About Persons: The Language of Legal Fiction »,	Note,	(2001) 114 Harv L Rev 1745.

➢ Inscrire le genre du texte (Commentaire éditorial, Note et Remarque) avant les renseignements sur l'édition.

6.11 DOCUMENTS HISTORIQUES LÉGAUX

6.11.1 Droit romain

Collection	Abréviation	Exemple
Lois des douze tables	XII Tab	XII Tab 82
Institutes de Gaius	G	G 3220 (trad par Julien Reinach)
Code de Théodose	Cod Th	Cod Th 8141
Institutes de Justinien	Inst	Inst 44 pr
Digeste de Justinien	Dig	Dig 47101 (Ulpian)
Codex de Justinien	Cod	Cod 64216
Nouvelles	Nov	Nov 223

> Faire référence à la **division traditionnelle** (généralement un livre, un titre ou une partie) et non au numéro de page de l'édition ou de la traduction. Ne pas ajouter d'espace entre les numéros des différentes parties.

→ L'abréviation pr, précédée d'un espace, signifie « *principium* » ou « début » et fait référence au document non numéroté avant la première section d'un titre.

→ Pour faire référence au *Digeste* **de Justinien**, indiquer (s'il y a lieu) l'auteur du passage entre parenthèses à la fin de la référence.

> Utiliser des chiffres arabes (par ex. 1, 2, 3), suivis de points, pour indiquer les divisions, quelle que soit l'utilisation de l'édition ou de la traduction.

> L'édition ou la traduction utilisée peut être indiquée entre parenthèses à la fin de la référence (par ex. (trad par Julien Reinach)).

6.11.2 Droit canonique

Collection	Abréviation	Exemple
Decretum de Gratien	Decr (facultatif)	1re partie : D 50 c 11 2e partie : C 30 q 4 c 5 2e partie, De poenitentia : De poen D 1 c 75 3e partie : De cons D 1 c 5
Décrétales de Grégoire IX (*Liber extra*)	X	X 5.38.12
Décrétales de Boniface VIII (*Liber sextus*)	VI	VI 5.2.16
Constitutions de Clément V (*Clementinae*)	Clem	Clem 3.7.2
Extravagantes de Jean XXII (*Extravagantes Johannis XXII*)	Extrav Jo XII	Extrav Jo XII 14.2
Extravagantes communes (*Extravagantes communes*)	Extrav Com	Extrav Com 3.2.9
Codex Iuris Canonici (1917)	1917 Code	1917 Code c 88, § 2
Codex Iuris Canonici (1983)	1983 Code	1983 Code c 221, § 1

> Faire référence à la division traditionnelle et non au numéro de page de l'édition ou de la traduction utilisée.

> Indiquer l'édition ou la traduction utilisée entre parenthèses à la fin de la référence.

6.11.3 Droit talmudique

Talmud,	*traité*,	référence précise.
Talmud de Babylone,	*Bava Metzia*,	11b.
Talmud de Jérusalem,	*Sanhédrin*,	Mish 1 Hal 5.

➢ Indiquer le Talmud de Babylone ou le Talmud de Jérusalem.

➢ Mettre le nom du traité en italique.

➢ Pour faire référence au Talmud de Babylone, indiquer la **pagination traditionnelle** (de l'édition Vilna) et non le numéro de page fourni par l'éditeur ou le traducteur. Il est toujours sous-entendu que le texte provient de l'édition Vilna. Cependant, si une édition différente est utilisée (par ex. Warsaw), indiquer le nom de l'édition après la référence précise.

➢ Utiliser des chiffres arabes (par ex. 1, 2, 3) pour le numéro de feuille et les lettres a et b pour indiquer le numéro de page.

➢ Pour faire référence à une **édition** ou à une **traduction particulière**, indiquer le nom de la maison d'édition entre parenthèses suivi d'une référence précise (sections 6.2.2.5.1 et 6.2.5).

➢ S'il y a une traduction, indiquer [notre traduction] ou [traduction par l'auteur] à la fin de la citation, après les guillemets et avant l'appel de note (section 6.2.2.5.2).

➢ Pour faire référence au **Talmud de Jérusalem**, fournir une référence précise correspondant au Mishna (Mish) et au Halacha (Hal) et non à la page. Indiquer une référence précise à une page si tous les renseignements sur l'édition peuvent être fournis entre parenthèses (sections 6.2.6 à 6.2.8).

6.12 MANUSCRITS NON PUBLIÉS

6.12.1 Modèle de base

Auteur,	*titre,*	date	[non publié,	archivé	lieu].
J Tremblay,	« Nouveaux développements en droit du travail »,	mai 1997	[non publié,	archivé	à la *Revue de droit de McGill*].

➢ Faire référence au titre du manuscrit selon son genre. Pour les articles, placer le titre entre guillemets. Pour les monographies, inscrire le titre en italique.

➢ Faire suivre le titre du manuscrit de sa date de création.

➢ Indiquer que le manuscrit n'a pas été publié en mettant [non publié, archivé], ainsi que l'endroit où le manuscrit se trouve.

6.12.2 Manuscrits à paraître

Auteur,	titre,	renseignements sur l'édition	[à paraître en	date de publication prévue].
Gérard Notebaert,	« Faut-il réformer le système de l'arbitrage de griefs au Québec ? »,	53 RD McGill	[à paraître en	2008].
Alain Supiot,	*Le Nouvel âge du droit social*,	Seuil	[à paraître en	octobre 2009].

➢ Faire référence au titre du manuscrit selon son genre. Pour les articles, placer le titre entre guillemets. Pour les monographies, inscrire le titre en italique.

➢ Inscrire les renseignements sur l'édition selon le genre du manuscrit mais ne pas indiquer la date de publication.

➢ Indiquer que le manuscrit n'a pas encore été publié en ajoutant [à paraître] et la date de publication prévue, si disponible.

6.12.3 Thèses et dissertations

Auteur,	titre,	diplôme,	institution,	année	[non publié].
Louise Potvin,	*La personne et la protection de son image*,	thèse de doctorat en droit,	Université McGill,	1989	[non publiée].
C Morneau,	*L'éthique dans les entreprises multinationales : Une étude développementale des codes d'éthique*,	mémoire de M Sc,	HEC Montréal,	2006	[non publié].

➢ Après avoir indiqué l'auteur et le titre du document, inscrire le diplôme dans le cadre duquel il a été écrit. Inclure la **discipline étudiée** (par ex. droit, science politique, économie), si l'on ne peut la déduire du diplôme ou du nom de l'institution.

➢ Après la mention de l'année, écrire [non publié].

➢ Si le manuscrit a été publié, faire référence à la source publiée et non à la thèse ou à la dissertation en soi. Suivre les règles appropriées du *Manuel* pour la source publier.

➢ Faire référence aux thèses publiées sur support de microfiche (par ex. les *University Microfilms International*) de la même manière que sont faites les références aux thèses sur support papier.

6.13 ALLOCUTIONS ET TEXTES PRÉSENTÉS DURANT DES CONFÉRENCES

Conférencier,	« titre » ou allocution,	événement,	présenté(e) à	lieu ou institution,	date	renseignements sur l'édition ou [non publié(e)].
Son excellence John Ralston Saul,	allocution d'ouverture	Conférence d'ouverture de la conférence du Conseil international d'études canadiennes,	présentée à	l'Université d'Ottawa,	18 mai 2000	[non publiée]. en ligne : <http://www.gg.ca>.
Le juge John H Gomery,	« The Pros and Cons of Commission of Inquiry »,	Série de conférences annuelles de la Revue de droit de McGill,	présentée à	la Faculté de droit de McGill,	15 février 2006	(2006) 51 RD McGill 783.

➢ Indiquer le titre de l'allocution, si possible. Si **aucun titre** n'est fourni, utiliser allocution.

➢ Inscrire l'événement dans le cadre duquel l'allocution a été prononcée ou le texte a été présenté.

➢ Indiquer le lieu ou l'institution où l'allocution a été faite.

➢ Inclure les renseignements sur l'édition.

➢ Pour faire référence à une **allocution non publiée**, inscrire [non publié(e)] à la fin de la référence (section 6.12.1).

➢ Pour faire référence à une **allocution publiée dans une collection**, respecter les règles de référence des ouvrages collectifs (section 6.3).

6.14 RECUEILS DE COURS

Professeur,	titre,	type de document (s'il y a lieu),	faculté,	date ou année	référence précise
Lara Khoury et Geneviève Saumier,	Coursepack: Extra-contractual Obligations/ Torts,		Faculté de droit, Université McGill,	2003	à la p 20.
Jean-Sébastien Brière,	Droit des brevets,	recueil de cours,	Faculté de droit, Université de Sherbrooke,	automne 2008	à la p 331.

➢ Indiquer le type de document s'il n'est pas déjà inclus dans le titre :

→ Les **recueils de cours** sont des compilations de textes pour les fins d'un cours particulier. Il est préférable d'indiquer la référence originale.

→   Les **notes de cours** sont rédigées par le professeur pour un cours en particulier. Elles ne possèdent pas de référence originale.

6.15 MAGAZINES

Auteur (s'il y a lieu),	« titre de l'article »,	*titre du magazine*	volume : numéro ou n°	(date)	1re page de l'article	référence précise	source électronique (s'il y a lieu).
Jacques Julliard,	« Requiem pour un "peuple interdit" »,	*Le Nouvel Observateur*	n° 1740	(12 mars 1998)	47	à la p 12.	
Julie Latour,	« Garde partagée, avis partagés »,	*Magazine National [de l'Association du Barreau canadien]*		(mars 2001)			en ligne : <http://abc. cba.org>.
Jean Lozeau et Paul Ryan,	« La faillite et la responsabilité fiscale des administrateurs et des tiers »,	*Le Monde Juridique*	12 : 6,		17	à la p 19.	

➢   Indiquer le nom de l'auteur suivi du titre de l'article entre guillemets.

➢   Indiquer le nom du magazine en italique. Placer tout autre renseignement (par ex. le lieu de publication) à la suite du nom du magazine, entre crochets et en italique.

➢   Indiquer le **volume et le numéro** en séparant ces informations par un deux-points (par ex. 10 : 30). S'il n'y a pas de volume, n'indiquer que le numéro (par ex. n° 20).

➢   Indiquer la **date complète** entre parenthèses. Si la revue indique une période, n'indiquer que la **première journée de cette période** (par ex. 22 novembre et non 22-29 novembre).

6.16 JOURNAUX, FILS DE PRESSE ET AUTRES SOURCES DE NOUVELLES

Auteur (s'il y a lieu),	« titre de l'article »,	*journal [lieu d'édition]* (si nécessaire)	(date)	page	source électronique (s'il y a lieu).
Michel Venne,	« Pour un accès gratuit aux lois sur Internet »,	*Le Devoir* [de *Montréal*]	(28 mai 1997)	A2.	
	« Un organisme d'aide juridique est menacé de fermeture par Québec »,	*La Presse canadienne*	(8 août 2001)		(QL).
Sylvia Zappi,	« La Cour de cassation refuse de faire bénéficier les enfants isolés étrangers du droit des mineurs »,	*Le Monde*	(11 novembre 2001)		en ligne : Le Monde.fr <http://www.lemonde.fr/recherche>.
	« Défaite des fabricants de tabac aux États-Unis »,	*La Presse* [de *Montréal*]	(28 mai 1997)	B10.	
LesAvocats[Pro],	« Vol à l'étalage : combien de temps dure la procédure ? »		(24 septembre 2009)		en ligne : Avocat Droit Criminel Montreal <http://avocatdroitcriminel.blog/ca>.

➢ Indiquer le nom de l'auteur, s'il y a lieu, suivi du titre de l'article entre guillemets.

➢ Indiquer le nom du journal, du fil de presse ou de toute autre source en italique. Tout autre renseignement, tel que le lieu de publication, se place à la suite du titre, entre crochets (par ex. *The [Montreal] Gazette)*.

Journaux :

➢ Indiquer le numéro du cahier si les pages sont numérotées par cahier (par ex. B10).

➢ Pour les références précises, ne pas répéter le numéro de page si l'article ne paraît que sur une seule page.

Fils de presse :

➢ Un fil de presse est un service d'information transmettant les toutes dernières nouvelles par satellite ou tout autre système électronique.

➢ Remplacer le nom du journal par le nom du fil de presse.

➢ Pour plus de renseignements sur la référence aux sources électroniques, voir la section 6.21.

6.16.1 Éditoriaux et lettres à la rédaction

Auteur (s'il y a lieu),	« titre de l'éditorial » (s'il y a lieu),	type de document,	*journal*	(date)	page,	source électronique (s'il y a lieu).
Jean Barrué,		lettre à la rédaction,	*Le Monde diplomatique*	(avril 1997)	2.	
Marie-Andrée Chouinard,	« Coup dur »,	éditorial,	*Le Devoir*	(23 octobre 2009)	A8.	

➢ Indiquer lettre à la rédaction après le nom de l'auteur de la lettre.

➢ Indiquer éditorial après le titre d'un éditorial.

➢ Mettre en italique le nom du journal, de la revue ou de toute autre source. Placer à la suite du titre, entre crochets et en italique, tout autre renseignement tel que le lieu de publication (par ex. *La Presse [de Montréal]*).

6.17 COMMUNIQUÉS DE PRESSE

Organisme responsable,	genre du document	numéro (s'il y a lieu),	« titre » (facultatif)	(date),	source électronique (s'il y a lieu).
Organisation des Nations Unies,	communiqué	CS/2284,	« Le conseil demande le retrait immédiat des troupes israéliennes des villes palestiniennes dont Ramallah et la coopération des parties avec l'Envoyé spécial de Washington »	(29 mars 2002),	en ligne : Recherche de communiqués de presse des Nations Unies <http://www.un.org/french/apps/pressreleases>.
Cabinet du premier ministre du Québec,	communiqué		« Journée internationale des femmes : "Nouvelles réalités, solidarités nouvelles" »	(8 mars 2002),	en ligne : Site officiel du premier ministre du Québec <http://www.premier-ministre.gouv.qc.ca/salle-de-presse>.
Comité permanent de l'accès à l'information, de la protection des renseignements personnels et de l'éthique,	communiqué		« Dépôt du rapport concernant la réforme de la *Loi sur l'accès à l'information* »	(18 juin 2009),	en ligne : Parlement du Canada <http://www.parl.qc.ca>.

➢ Indiquer le genre du document tel qu'énoncé sur le document (communiqué).

➢ Indiquer le **numéro du document** immédiatement après le genre du document, s'il y a lieu.

➢ Si possible, fournir la **date du document** entre parenthèses à la fin de la référence, mais avant la source électronique.

6.18 LETTRES ET ENTREVUES

Lettre ou Entrevue	nom des personnes impliquées,	date	renseignements supplémentaires (archives, sources électroniques ou imprimées).
Lettre de	B Diamond au Premier ministre R Lévesque,	(30 novembre 1982).	
Entrevue de	Edward Beauvais par Douglas Sanderson,	(29 mai 1948)	sur *This Week*, CBC Radio, Toronto, CBC Radio Archives.
Lettre de	PE Moore, Acting Superintendent of Medical Services, Indian Affairs Branch, à Ellen L Fairclough, Minister of Citizenship,	[aucune date]	Hull, Affaires Indiennes et du Nord Canada (6-24-3, vol 2).

➢ Identifier une lettre ou une entrevue en indiquant lettre de ou entrevue de, suivi du nom des parties au début de la référence.

➢ Inclure le nom des parties, suivi de la date à laquelle la lettre a été rédigée. Si aucune date n'est fournie, inscrire [aucune date].

➢ Si le titre d'une personne impliquée n'est pas mentionné dans le texte ou ne peut être déduit, fournir autant de renseignements que possible sur ce titre, précédés d'une virgule (par ex. PE Moore, Acting Superintendent of Medical Services, Indian Affairs Branch).

➢ Fournir le nom de l'intervieweur s'il n'est pas aussi l'auteur.

➢ Si la lettre ou l'entrevue est publiée, disponible en ligne ou archivée, inclure la référence.

6.19 DOCUMENTS ARCHIVÉS

Titre du document et (autre information),	lieu des archives,	nom des archives,	(numéro de classification).
Lettres patentes du roi François 1er nommant Jacques Cartier capitaine général de l'expédition destinée au Canada (17 octobre 1540/Saint-Prix),	Ottawa,	Archives nationales du Canada,	(MG 1-Série C11A).
Chief Andrew Paull à TA Crerar (22 juin,	Ottawa,	Archives nationales du Canada,	(RG 10, vol 6826, file 496-3-2, pt 1).

> Si un document se trouve dans des archives locales, fournir le plus de renseignements possible sur le document selon les règles de références traditionnelles, suivies de l'information des archives.

6.20 PROPRIÉTÉ INTELLECTUELLE

6.20.1 Brevets

« Titre de l'invention »,	Pays	Brevet n°	PCT Brevet n°	(date de dépôt),	référence précise.
« Épaulière pour violon »,	Can	Brevet n° 2414383	PCT Brevet n° PCT/US2001/021243	(29 juin 2001),	rev 10.
« Parallel network processor array »,	É-U	Brevet n° 6854117		(31 octobre 2000),	fig 9.

> Indiquer **le titre de l'invention** entre guillemets.

> Indiquer **l'abréviation du pays** où le brevet a été émis ainsi que le numéro du brevet.

> Si le brevet a été délivré par le biais du **Traité de coopération en matière de brevets** (PCT), utiliser le même modèle de référence (PCT Brevet n°).

> Indiquer **la date de dépôt** entre parenthèses.

> Si nécessaire, indiquer le numéro de brevet du pays et le numéro de brevet PCT séparés par une virgule.

> Faire référence à l'abrégé (abrégé), au numéro de revendication (rev) ou à une figure (fig) en référence précise.

> S'il s'agit d'une **demande de brevet**, écrire demande déposée le avant la date de dépôt (par ex. demande déposée le 30 août 2008).

6.20.2 Marques de commerce

« Marque de commerce »,	propriétaire inscrit,	pays	n° d'enregistrement	(date d'enregistrement),	état.
« Kellog's Cinnamon Mini Buns à la Cannelle »,	Kellog Company,	Can	n° enr LMC424258	(4 mars 1994),	radiée.
"Lego",	Lego Juris A/S,	USA	78882203	(3 juin 2008),	existante.

> Indiquer **la marque de commerce** entre guillemets.

> Indiquer **le propriétaire inscrit** et **l'abréviation du pays** où la marque de commerce a été enregistrée.

> Écrire **le numéro d'enregistrement**. Le format du numéro varie selon le pays.

➢ Indiquer **la date d'enregistrement** entre parenthèses.

➢ Écrire **l'état actuel** de la marque de commerce dans le registre. Pour les marques de commerce des États-Unis, écrire existante pour *live* et non existante pour *dead*. Pour le Canada, écrire enregistrée ou radiée.

6.20.3 Droits d'auteur

« Titre de l'œuvre protégée »	(catégorie)	titulaire du droit d'auteur,	pays	n° d'enregistrement	(date d'enregis-trement),	état.
« Twilight »	(musique)	Mary Chapin Carpentier,	É-U	Pau002997899	(20 décembre 2005).	
« Agrippa – Le livre noir »	(littéraire)	Éditions Michel Quintin,	Can	1056747	(11 mars 2003),	enregistrée.

➢ Indiquer **le titre** de l'œuvre protégée entre guillemets.

➢ Au Canada, **la catégorie de l'œuvre** inclut les œuvres littéraires, artistiques, dramatiques et musicales originales; les prestations d'interprètes, enregistrements sonores et signaux de communication; ainsi que les dispositifs mécaniques.

➢ Indiquer **le titulaire du droit d'auteur** et **l'abréviation du pays** où le droit d'auteur a été enregistré.

➢ Écrire **le numéro d'enregistrement**. Le format du numéro varie selon le pays.

➢ Indiquer **la date d'enregistrement** entre parenthèses.

➢ Écrire **l'état actuel** (enregistré ou radié) du droit d'auteur dans le registre.

6.21 SOURCES ÉLECTRONIQUES

6.21.1 Services électroniques

Référence traditionnelle	(service électronique et banque de données).
Denise Boulet, « Le traitement juridique du mineur suicidaire » (2002) 32 RDUS 317	(QL).
Joseph Eliot Magnet, *Constitutional Law of Canada: Cases, Notes and Materials*, 8ᵉ éd, Kingston (Ont), QL, 2001	(QL).

➢ Fournir la référence complète, suivie du service électronique entre parenthèses.

➢ S'il n'y a pas d'éditeur ou si le texte n'est publié que sur un serveur électronique, identifier le service en ligne comme l'éditeur (par ex. Kingston (Ont), QL, 2001).

> Si possible, ne pas faire référence à un service électronique auquel la majorité des lecteurs ne pourra accéder. Par exemple, ne pas faire référence à Azimut lorsque l'auditoire ciblé n'est pas au Québec.

> Pour une liste des abréviations des services électroniques, voir l'**annexe E**.

6.21.2 Revues en ligne (eJournals)

Référence traditionnelle,	en ligne :	(année)	volume : numéro (s'il y a lieu)	revue	numéro de l'article	réfé- rence précise	<adresse Internet>.
Grant Yang, « Stop the Abuse of Gmail! »,	en ligne :	(2005)		Duke L & Tech Rev	14	au para 5	<http://www.law.duke.edu/journals/dltr>.
Kahikino Noa Dettweiler, « Racial Classification or Cultural Identification?: The Gathering Rights Jurisprudence of Two Twentieth Century Hawaiian Supreme Court Justices »,	en ligne :	(2005)	6 : 1	Asian Pac L & Pol'y J	5		<http://www.hawaii.edu/aplpj>.

> Certaines revues ne sont publiées qu'en ligne et possèdent leur propre système de référence.

> Faire référence à ces revues en suivant ce système de classification interne. Indiquer l'adresse Internet à la fin de la référence.

6.21.3 Sites Internet

Référence traditionnelle,	en ligne :	Nom du site	<adresse universelle>.
Benoît Tabaka, « Internet et la diffusion des sondages électoraux : une réforme législative impossible ? » (7 février 2002),	en ligne :	Juriscom.net	<http://www.juriscom.net>.
Jérôme Dupré, « Espionnage économique et droit : l'inutile création d'un bien informationnel » (été 2001),	en ligne :	Lex Electronica	<http://www.lexelectronica.org>.
Gouvernement du Québec, *Les principes du développement durable : un guide pour l'action*, 2002,	en ligne :	Développement durable, Environnement et Parcs Québec	<http://www.mddep.gouv.qc.ca/developpement/principe.htm>.
« Modifications historiques apportées à la *Loi sur la concurrence* au Canada » (19 mars 2009) (ballado),	en ligne :	Osler	<http://www.osler.com/resources.aspx?id=10366>.

> Fournir la référence traditionnelle, suivie d'une virgule. Écrire en ligne : et le nom du site Internet, suivis de l'adresse universelle (URL).

Doctrine et autres documents

> Faire référence à l'adresse universelle de la **page d'accueil du document**. Si la page spécifique du document a peu de chance d'être déplacée, ou s'il est trop difficile de la trouver à partir de la page d'accueil, inclure l'adresse universelle de la page spécifique (par ex. un fichier PDF).

> Certains sites Internet n'incluent pas le nom de l'auteur et des titres formels. Dans ces cas, inclure une information de base permettant de retracer la source à la place de la référence traditionnelle (voir l'exemple du Gouvernement du Québec).

> Plusieurs textes en ligne disparaissent après un certain temps. Renvoyer à une source en ligne seulement si cette source fournit des documents archivés remontant à quelques années.

> Faire référence à un **balado** (*podcast* en anglais) de la même manière qu' à tout autre site Internet, mais en ajoutant (balado) après la référence traditionnelle (voir l'exemple d'Osler). S'il est fourni, inclure le nom de l'orateur au lieu du nom de l'auteur.

> Inclure un numéro de paragraphe comme référence précise si possible. Si la numérotation de la page d'une source imprimée est reproduite dans une source électronique, se référer à la numérotation utilisée par la source imprimée.

6.21.4 Autres supports numériques

Référence traditionnelle,	type de support numérique :	*Titre du support si différent,*	(renseignements sur l'édition).
PW Hogg et ME Turpel, « Implementing Aboriginal Self-Government: Constitutional and Jurisdictional Issues »,	CD-ROM :	*Pour sept générations : legs documentaire de la Commission royale sur les peuples autochtones,*	Ottawa, Libraxus, 1997.
The Paper Chase, 1973,	DVD :		Beverly Hills (Cal), 20th Century Fox Home Entertainment, 2003.

> Fournir la référence traditionnelle du document, suivie d'une virgule.

> Indiquer le type de support numérique (par ex. CD-ROM, DVD, BluRay, MiniDisc) après la virgule.

> Si le titre du support est différent, ajouter un deux-points et indiquer le titre du disque en italique, suivi d'une virgule.

> Fournir les renseignements sur l'édition du support numérique entre parenthèses en y incluant le lieu d'édition, l'éditeur et l'année d'édition.

Doctrine et autres documents

7   SOURCES ÉTRANGÈRES

Pour faire référence à une source d'un pays qui n'est pas traité dans ce chapitre, adapter les règles canadiennes des chapitres précédents.

7.1   ROYAUME-UNI

Voir notamment *Oxford Standard for Citation of Legal Authorities*.

Pour la jurisprudence, voir Donald Raistrick, *Index to Legal Citations and Abbreviations*, 2ᵉ éd, Londres (R-U), Bowker-Saur, 1993.

7.1.1 Législation

7.1.1.1 Lois

➢ Mettre (R-U) après le titre de la loi pour indiquer son origine.

Avant 1963	*Statute of Westminster, 1931* (R-U), 22 & 23 Geo V, c 4, art 2.
1ᵉʳ janvier 1963 à aujourd'hui	*Terrorism Act 2000* (R-U), c 11, art 129.

➢ **Avant 1963** : Lorsque le titre comprend l'année, mettre une virgule avant l'année. Écrire l'année de règne en chiffres arabes (par ex. 1, 2, 3) et le nombre suivant l'abréviation du monarque en chiffres romains (Geo V).

➢ **Du 1ᵉʳ janvier 1963 à aujourd'hui** : Lorsque le titre inclut l'année, ne pas mettre une virgule avant l'année. Lorsque le titre n'inclut pas l'année, l'indiquer après (R-U), précédée d'une virgule.

7.1.1.1.1   Irlande du Nord

7.1.1.1.1.1   Lois adoptées par le Royaume-Uni

Avant 1963	*Public Health (Ireland) Act, 1878* (R-U), 41 & 42 Vict, c 52.
1ᵉʳ janvier 1963 à aujourd'hui	*Northern Ireland Act 1998* (R-U), 1998, c 47, art 5.

➢ Faire référence à la législation de l'Irlande du Nord adoptée par le Royaume-Uni de la même manière qu'à celle du Royaume-Uni.

7.1.1.1.1.2   Lois adoptées par l'Irlande du Nord

1921-1972	*Criminal Law Amendment (Northern Ireland) Act*, RSNI 1923, c 8.
	National Insurance Act, NI Pub Gen Acts 1946, c 23, art 7.
1999 à aujourd'hui	*Family Law Act (Northern Ireland) 2001*, (IN), 2001, c 12.

> Abréger **Northern Ireland Public General Acts** par NI Pub Gen Acts.

> Abréger **Statutes Revised, Northern Ireland** par RSNI.

> Le Royaume-Uni a adopté les lois pour l'Irlande du Nord de 1972 à 1999. L'Assemblée de l'Irlande du Nord, établie le 19 novembre 1998, a obtenu le pouvoir d'adopter ses propres lois à partir du 2 décembre 1999. Pour les lois adoptées par l'Assemblée après 1999, écrire (IN) après le titre de la loi pour indiquer son origine. À noter que le Royaume-Uni peut encore adopter des lois qui s'appliquent en Irlande du Nord.

N.B. L'Assemblée nord-irlandaise et l'exécutif ont été suspendus depuis le 14 octobre 2002. Le *Secretary of State for Northern Ireland* et le *Northern Ireland Office* sont responsables des ministères de l'Irlande du Nord.

7.1.1.1.2   Écosse

> Avant 1998, faire référence à la législation de l'Écosse de la même manière qu'à celle du Royaume-Uni.

> Les *Acts* adoptés par le Royaume-Uni s'appliquent à l'Écosse si ces lois se rapportent à une question réservée ou non transmise.

Avant 1998	*Contract (Scotland) Act 1997* (R-U), 1997, c 34.
	Scotland Act 1998 (R-U), 1998, c 46, art 4.
1998 à aujourd'hui	*Standards in Scotland's Schools etc Act*, ASP 2000, c 6, art 2.

> Abréger **Acts of Scottish Parliament** par ASP à partir du 19 novembre 1998.

7.1.1.1.3   Pays de Galles

> Le Royaume-Uni adopte la législation relative au Pays de Galles. Suivre le même modèle de référence des lois que pour le Royaume-Uni.

Government of Wales Act 1998 (R-U), 1998, c 38, art 3.

7.1.1.2 Projets de loi

7.1.1.2.1   Royaume-Uni

Numéro du projet de loi,	*titre,*	session,	année,	référence précise	(renseignements supplémentaires) (facultatif).
Bill 4,	*London Olympics Bill,*	sess 2005-2006,	2005,		(1re lecture, 1er juillet 2005).
Bill 40,	*Harbours Bill* [HL],	sess 2005-2006,	2005,	art 2.	

> Inclure [HL] (non italique) après le titre pour les projets de loi qui proviennent de la Chambre des Lords.

7.1.1.2.2   Irlande du Nord

Numéro,	titre,	session,	année,	référence précise	(renseignements supplémentaires) (facultatif).
NIA Bill 15/00,	A Bill to amend the Game Preservation (Northern Ireland) Act 1928,	sess 2001-2002,	2001,	art 2	(Committee Stage Extension 29 octobre 2001).
NIA Bill 17/07,	Child Maintenance Bill,	sess 2007-2008,	2008,	art 12.	

7.1.1.2.3   Écosse

Numéro,	titre,	session,	année,	référence précise	(renseignements supplémentaires) (facultatif).
SP Bill 42,	Human Tissue (Scotland) Bill,	2ᵉ sess,	2005,	art 6	(1ʳᵉ lecture 3 juin 2005).
SP Bill 17,	Climate Change (Scotland) Bill,	3ᵉ sess,	2008,	art 3(2)(b)	(1ʳᵉ étape du débat 6-7 mai 2009).

7.1.1.3 Règlements

7.1.1.3.1   Royaume-Uni

	Titre (facultatif),	SR & O ou SI	année/numéro.
Avant 1948	Public Health (Prevention of Tuberculosis) Regulations 1925,	SR & O	1927/757.
1948 à aujourd'hui	The Welfare Food (Amendment) Regulations 2005,	SI	2005/68844.

> L'indication du titre du règlement est facultative.

> Abréger ***Statutory Rules & Orders*** (avant 1948) par SR & O et ***Statutory Instruments*** (après 1948) par SI.

7.1.1.3.2   Règlements et ordres de l'Irlande du Nord

Titre (facultatif),	SR & O ou SI	année/numéro	(NI numéro).
The Proceeds of Crime (Northern Ireland) Order 1996,	SI	1996/1299	(NI 9).
The Tax Credits 2001 (Miscellaneous Amendments No 8) (Northern Ireland) Regulations,	SI	2001/3086.	
Cheese Regulations (NI) 1970,	SR & O	1970/14.	

➢ L'indication du titre du règlement est facultative.

➢ Les règlements et les ordres adoptés par le Royaume-Uni se trouvent dans les *Statutory Instruments* (SI).

➢ Abréger un règlement adopté par l'Assemblée de l'Irlande du Nord par SR (*Statutory Rule*).

➢ Les règlements de l'Irlande du Nord sont inclus dans les *Statutory Regulations and Orders* (abrégés SR & O) à partir de 1922.

➢ S'il y a un **numéro d'ordre de l'Irlande du Nord**, l'inclure après année/numéro pour indiquer que l'ordre a été promulgué par l'Assemblée de l'Irlande du Nord.

7.1.1.3.3   Écosse

Faire référence aux règlements de l'Écosse de la même manière qu'à ceux du Royaume-Uni (section 7.1.1.3.1).

7.1.1.3.3.1   Règlements adoptés par le Royaume-Uni

Titre (facultatif),	SR & O ou SI	année/numéro.
Employment Tribunals (Constitution and Rules of Procedure) (Scotland) Regulations 2001,	SI	2001/1170.
Local Government Pension Scheme Amendment (Scotland) Regulations 2009,	SI	2009/93.

7.1.1.3.3.2   Règlements adoptés par l'Écosse

Titre (facultatif),	Scot SI	année/numéro.
National Health Service (General Ophthalmic Services) (Scotland) Amendment Regulations 2001,	Scot SI	2001/62.
Plastic Materials and Articles in Contact with Food (Scotland) Regulations 2009,	Scot SI	2009/30.

➢ Abréger *Scottish Statutory Instruments* par Scot SI.

7.1.1.3.4   Pays de Galles

Titre (facultatif),	SR & O ou SI	année/numéro	(W numéro).
Children's Homes Amendment (Wales) Regulations 2001,	SI	2001/140	(W 6).

➢ Après année/numéro, inclure le numéro du règlement du Pays de Galles pour indiquer qu'il a été promulgué par l'Assemblée du Pays de Galles.

Sources étrangères

7.1.2 Jurisprudence

7.1.2.1 Modèle de base

Intitulé	(année de la décision),	[année du recueil]	volume	recueil	page	(cour).
R v Woollin	(1998),	[1999]		AC	82	HL (Eng).
Burgess v Home Office	(2000),	[2001]	1	WLR	93	(CA).

➤ Les *Law Reports* ont préséance sur les *Weekly Law Reports* (WLR) et sur les *All England Law Reports* (All ER).

➤ Voir la liste des recueils de jurisprudence du Royaume-Uni et leurs abréviations à l'**annexe C-3**, et la liste des cours et de leurs abréviations à l'**annexe B**.

7.1.2.2 Référence neutre

➤ Plusieurs tribunaux du Royaume-Uni ont officiellement adopté un système de référence neutre. Suivre les règles de la référence neutre au Canada (section 3.5), à l'exception de l'année, qui est placée entre crochets.

7.1.2.3 Cours d'appel

[1] *Campbell v MGN Limited*, [2004] UKHL 22.

[2] *Copping v Surrey County Council*, [2005] EWCA Civ 1604 ¶ 15.

House of Lords	[année] UKHL numéro
Privy Council	[année] UKPC numéro
England and Wales Court of Appeal (Division civile)	[année] EWCA Civ numéro
England and Wales Court of Appeal (Division criminelle)	[année] EWCA Crim numéro

➤ Les références neutres pour les cours d'appel et de l'*Administrative Court* de la *High Court* sont officielles **depuis le 11 janvier 2001**.

➤ Indiquer l'année de la décision entre crochets, suivie du code de désignation du tribunal et du numéro de la cause.

7.1.2.4 High Court

[Année]	cour	numéro	(division)	paragraphe.
[2005]	EWHC	1974	(Admlty)	¶ 10.
[2005]	EWHC	2995	(Comm).	

➤ Les références neutres pour la *High Court* sont officielles **depuis le 14 janvier 2002**.

> Pour les causes plaidées devant la *High Court*, la division de cette cour est placée entre parenthèses après le numéro de la cause.

> N.B. La référence neutre pour les causes plaidées devant l'*Administrative Court* durant l'année 2001 s'écrit de la façon suivante : [année] EWHC Admin numéro. Ce format est semblable à celui de la Cour d'appel (section 7.1.2.3).

> Faire des références précises aux paragraphes. Utiliser le symbole ¶ ou au para.

Divisions et abréviations de la *High Court* :

Chancery Division	Ch		Commercial Court	Comm
Patents Court	Pat		Admiralty Court	Admlty
Queen's Bench Division	QB		Technology & Construction Court	TCC
Administrative Court	Admin		Family Division	Fam

7.1.2.5 Recueils

7.1.2.5.1   Law Reports

> Les *Law Reports* sont **organisés en séries**. Se référer à la série et non aux *Law Reports*.

> Il n'y a pas de recueil distinct pour la Cour d'appel. Inclure l'abréviation CA pour *Court of Appeal* à la fin de chaque référence à une décision rendue par cette cour.

Les *Law Reports* et leurs abréviations:

Chancery (*Chancery Division* et décisions en appel de la *Court of Appeal*)	Ch
Queen's (King's) Bench (Division du Banc de la Reine (du Roi) et décisions de ces divisions en appel devant la *Court of Appeal*)	QB (KB)
Probate (1891-1971) (*Family Division*, *Probate*, *Divorce* et *Admiralty Division*, décisions en appel de ces divisions et *Ecclesiastical Courts*)	P
Family (1972 à aujourd'hui)	Fam
Industrial Courts Reports (1972-1974) and *Industrial Cases Reports* (1975 à aujourd'hui)	ICR
Law Reports Restrictive Practices (1957-1972) (*National Industrial Relations Court and Restrictive Practices Court*, décisions en appel de cette cour et les décisions de la *High Court* pertinentes aux relations industrielles)	LR RP

7.1.2.5.1.1 Modèle d'une cause de 1875 à 1890

> Indiquer D, l'abréviation de **Division**, après l'abréviation du titre du recueil, afin de distinguer la collection des

Bird v Jones (1845), 7 QBD 742 (CA) [Bird].

recueils datant de 1875 à 1890 de la collection plus récente qui porte le même nom.

7.1.2.5.1.2 Modèle d'une cause de 1865 à 1875

Currie v Misa (1875), LR 10 Ex 153.

> Indiquer LR, l'abréviation de **Law Reports**, avant le volume, afin de distinguer cette collection de recueils de la collection plus récente qui porte le même nom.

7.1.2.5.1.3 Modèle d'une cause de 1537 à 1865

> Si possible, renvoyer au recueil nommé (*nominate reporter*) et fournir une référence parallèle aux **English Reports** si disponible.

Lord Byron v Johnston (1816), 2 Mer 28, 35 ER 851 (Ch).

> Les *English Reports* et les *All England Reports Reprints* sont des réimpressions.

7.1.2.6 Annuaires

Intitulé	(année),	annuaire	trimestre	année du règne	monarque,	numéro du plaidoyer (plea),	numéro du feuillet (folio).
Doige's Case	(1422),	YB	Trin	20	Hen VI,	pl 4,	fol 34.

> Utiliser les abréviations de trimestres suivantes : Mich pour **Michaelmas**, Hil pour **Hilary**, Pach pour **Easter** et Trin pour **Trinity**.

> Indiquer l'année du règne en chiffres arabes.

> Indiquer le monarque en chiffres romains.

> Abréger **plea** par pl.

> Abréger **folio** par fol.

7.1.2.7 Réimpressions

Référence à l'annuaire,	reproduit dans	référence à la réimpression.
Beauver v Abbot of St Albans (1312), YB Mich 6 Edw II,	reproduit dans	(1921) 38 Selden Soc 32.

➤ Pour une réimpression, fournir autant de renseignements que possible sur la première édition de l'annuaire. Faire référence à la source dans laquelle se trouve la réimpression.

7.1.2.8 Écosse, Irlande et Irlande du Nord

Écosse	*M'Courtney v HM Advocate*, [1977] JC 68 (HCJ Scot).
Irlande	*Hardman v Maffet* (1834), 13 LR Ir 499 (ChD).
Irlande du Nord	*R v Crooks*, [1999] NI 226 (CA).

➤ Lorsque le titre du recueil n'indique pas l'indication géographique, indiquer Scot pour *Scotland*, Ir pour *Ireland*, et NI pour *Northern Ireland*, entre parenthèses à la fin de la référence.

➤ Indiquer le nom de la cour, puisque chaque volume est divisé en parties selon la cour et que chaque partie est paginée séparément.

➤ Voir l'**annexe B** pour les abréviations des tribunaux et l'**annexe C** pour celles des recueils.

7.1.2.9 Référence neutre

➤ Les règles concernant les références neutres sont les mêmes pour l'Écosse, l'Irlande et l'Irlande du Nord. Suivre les règles de la référence neutre au Canada (section 3.5), à l'exception de l'année, qui est placée entre crochets.

7.1.2.9.1   Écosse

Smith v Brown, [2005] HCJT 2 (Scot).

Kinross v Dunsmuir, [2005] HCJAC 3 ¶ 12 (Scot).

McBride v MacDuff, [2005] CSOH 4 (Scot).

High Court of Justiciary	[année] HCJT numéro
Court of Criminal Appeal	[année] HCJAC numéro
Court of Session, Outer House	[année] CSOH numéro
Court of Session, Inner House	[année] CSIH numéro

➤ Si la référence neutre ne contient pas d'indication géographique, indiquer Scot entre parenthèses à la fin de la référence.

7.1.2.9.2   Irlande

Smith v Brown, [2005] HCJT 2 (Scot).

Kinross v Dunsmuir, [2005] HCJAC 3 ¶ 12 (Scot).

McBride v MacDuff, [2005] CSOH 4 (Scot).

High Court	[année] IEHC numéro
Supreme Court	[année] IESC numéro
Court of Criminal Appeal	[année] IECCA numéro

7.1.2.9.3   Irlande du Nord

McDonnell v Henry, [2005] NICA 17.

Barkley v Whiteside, [2004] NIQB 12 ¶ 12.

Court of Appeal	[année] NICA numéro
County Court	[année] NICty numéro
Magistrates Court	[année] NIMag numéro

High Court :

Queen's Bench Division	[année] NIQB numéro
Family Division	[année] NIFam numéro
Chancery Division	[année] NICh numéro

7.1.2.10 Juge

Lord Justice	LJ
Lord Justices	LJJ
Master of the Rolls	MR
Lord Chancellor	LC
Vice Chancellor	VC
Baron	B
Chief Baron	CB

7.1.3   Documents gouvernementaux

Indiquer R-U au début de la référence.

7.1.3.1 Débats

7.1.3.1.1   Avant 1803

R-U,	chambre,	*Parliamentary History of England,*	volume,	colonne	(date)	(orateur) (facultatif).
R-U,	HC,	*Parliamentary History of England,*	vol 12,	col 1327	(27 mai 1774).	
R-U,	HL,	*Parliamentary History of England,*	vol 2,	col 791	(24 mai 1641).	

➢ Pour les débats d'avant 1803, se référer au recueil *Parliamentary History of England.*

➢ Abréger ***House of Commons*** par HC et ***House of Lords*** par HL.

➢ Indiquer l'orateur entre parenthèses à la fin de la référence si nécessaire.

7.1.3.1.2   1803 à aujourd'hui

R-U,	chambre,	*titre,*	série,	volume,	colonne	référence précise	(date)	(orateur) (facultatif).
R-U,	HL,	*Parliamentary Debates,*	5ᵉ sér,	vol 442,	col 3	à la col 6	(3 mai 1983)	(Baroness Masham of Ilton).
R-U,	SP,	*Official Report,*	sess 1 (2000),	vol 7, n° 6,	col 634		(22 juin 2000)	(Peter Peacock).
R-U,	NIA,	*Official Report,*				à la p 500	(24 octobre 2000).	
R-U,	NAW,	*Official Record,*				à la p 27	(19 juillet 2001).	

➢ Indiquer l'entre parenthèses à la fin de la référence si nécessaire.

➢ Après R-U, indiquer la chambre.

Abréviations des chambres :

House of Commons	HC
House of Lords	HL
National Assembly for Wales	NAW
Northern Ireland Assembly	NIA
Scottish Parliament	SP

7.1.3.2 Journaux

R-U,	journal,	volume	(date)	référence précise.
R-U,	Journal of the House of Commons,	vol 234	(9 décembre 1977)	à la p 95.
R-U,	Journal of the House of Lords,	vol 22	(10 janvier 1995)	à la p 89.

➢ Ne pas répéter le nom de la chambre, puisqu'il est indiqué dans le titre du journal.

7.1.3.3 Documents parlementaires

R-U,	chambre,	« titre »,	numéro sessionnel ou command number	dans Sessional Papers,	vol	(année)	1ʳᵉ page	référence précise	(président) (s'il y a lieu).
R-U,	HC,	« Report of the Committee on the Law Relating to Rights of Light »,	Cmnd 473	dans Sessional Papers,	vol 17	(1957-58)	955		(président : Sir CE Harman).
R-U,	HC,	« Monopolies and Mergers Commission Report on the Supply in the UK of the Services of Administering Performing Rights and Film Synchronisation Rights »,	Cm 3147	dans Sessional Papers,		(1995-96)	1.		

➢ Indiquer le titre tel qu'il apparaît à la page titre du rapport.

➢ Indiquer le numéro sessionnel ou le numéro du *Command Paper* après le titre.

➢ Faire référence aux **Sessional Papers** de la *House of Commons* à moins que le document n'apparaisse que dans les *Sessional Papers* de la *House of Lords*.

➢ Écrire le numéro du volume (s'il y a lieu) après *Sessional Papers*.

➢ Inscrire le nom du président entre parenthèses à la fin de la référence si cette information est connue.

> ➤ **L'abréviation appropriée du *Command* est essentielle pour identifier le document**. Elle apparaît sur la première page de chaque *Command Paper*.

1833-1869	1ʳᵉ série (1-4222)	c
1870-1899	2ᵉ série (1-9550)	C
1900-1918	3ᵉ série (1-9239)	Cd
1919-1956	4ᵉ série (1-9889)	Cmd
1957-1986	5ᵉ série (1-9927)	Cmnd
1986 à aujourd'hui	6ᵉ série (1-)	Cm

> ➤ Indiquer la première page du document après la date.

> ➤ Utiliser la pagination interne du document pour les références précises.

7.1.3.4 Documents non parlementaires

R-U,	organisme,	*titre,*	(type de document) (s'il y a lieu)	auteur (s'il y a lieu),	renseignements sur l'édition.
R-U,	Royal Commission on Criminal Procedure,	*Police Interrogation: The Psychological Approach,*			Londres, Her Majesty's Stationery Office, 1980.
R-U,	Royal Commission on the Press,	*Studies on the Press,*	(Working Paper nº 3)	par Oliver Boyd-Barret, Colin Seymour-Ure et Jeremy Turnstall,	Londres, Her Majesty's Stationery Office, 1978.
R-U,	Law Commission,	*The Illegality of Defence in Tort,*	(Consultation Paper nº 160)		Londres, Her Majesty's Stationery Office, 2001.
R-U,		*Report of the Committee on Homosexual Offences and Prostitution,*			Londres, Her Majesty's Stationery Office, 1957.

> ➤ Suivre les règles des documents non parlementaires canadiens à la section 4.2.

> ➤ Ne pas indiquer l'organisme s'il est déjà spécifié dans le titre (voir l'exemple *Report of the Committee on Homosexual Offences and Prostitution*).

7.2   ÉTATS-UNIS

> ➤ Tous les éléments de référence à la législation des États-Unis sont en anglais, à l'exception des mentions telles que « codifié à ».

> Voir l'édition la plus récente de ***The Bluebook: A Uniform System of Citation***.

7.2.1 Législation

7.2.1.1 Constitution fédérale et constitutions des États

> Abréger **article** par art, **section** par § et **sections** par §§.

> Un paragraphe qui fait partie d'une section est une **clause**, abrégée cl (au singulier comme au pluriel).

US Const art II, § 2, cl 1.

US Const amend XVIII, § 1.

Fla Const, Part V, § 3(b)(4).

> Abréger **amendement** par amend.

> Abréger **préambule** par pmbl.

> Indiquer les numéros d'article et de modification en chiffres romains majuscules. Les numéros de section et de clause sont indiqués en chiffres arabes.

> Voir l'**annexe A-2** pour la liste des abréviations des États.

7.2.1.2 Lois

Ordre hiérarchique des sources :

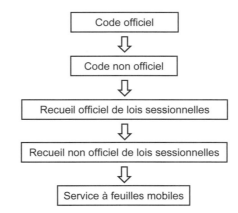

7.2.1.2.1   Codes

> Aux États-Unis, un code constitue le regroupement et la codification par sujet des lois générales et permanentes des États-Unis.

> Un **code officiel** est un code des lois des États-Unis organisé en 50 titres et rédigé sous la surveillance d'une autorité gouvernementale appropriée (par ex. le département de la Justice fédérale).

> Le ***United States Code*** (USC) est le code officiel du gouvernement fédéral.

> ➤ Pour déterminer si un code étatique est officiel ou non, consulter le *Bluebook*.

> ➤ Un **code non officiel** est un code des lois des États-Unis préparé par une maison d'édition. Il existe deux codes non officiels pour les lois fédérales :

> → **le United States Code Service (USCS) et**
> → **le United States Code Annotated (USCA).**

	Titre (exceptionnel-lement),	partie du code (s'il y a lieu)	titre abrégé du code	numéro du titre (s'il y a lieu)	article	(éditeur	supplé-ment (s'il y a lieu)	année).
Codes officiels	*Clayton Act,*	15	USC		§ 3			(1993).
			Minn Stat		§ 169947			(1990).
			IRC		§ 61			(1994).
Codes non officels		18	USCA		§ 351	(West		1997).
			Pa Stat Ann	tit 63	§ 4253	(West	Supp	1986).
			Wis Stat Ann		§ 939645	(West	Supp	1992).

> ➤ Ne pas faire référence au titre original d'une loi codifiée. **N'indiquer le titre que pour des raisons particulières** (par ex. si la loi est normalement connue sous ce nom). Mettre le titre en italique.

> ➤ Si le code est **classé** par titres, chapitres ou volumes distincts et numérotés, indiquer le numéro de cette division. Dans le cas du code fédéral, indiquer la division avant l'abréviation du code.

> ➤ Ne pas mettre le titre abrégé du code en italique. Pour une référence à l'*Internal Revenue Code*, il est possible de remplacer 26 USC par IRC.

> ➤ À moins que le code ne soit publié par un éditeur officiel, indiquer le nom de l'éditeur avant l'année ou avant Supp, selon le cas.

> ➤ Pour indiquer un supplément inséré dans une pochette, écrire Supp avant la mention de l'année qui paraît sur la page titre du supplément.

> ➤ Indiquer l'année de publication du code entre parenthèses à la fin de la référence. Pour un **recueil relié**, fournir l'année qui paraît sur la reliure. Pour un **supplément**, fournir l'année qui figure sur la page titre du supplément.

7.2.1.2.2   Lois sessionnelles

Les lois sessionnelles sont les lois promulguées par une session du Congrès, reliées et organisées par ordre chronologique. Les lois sessionnelles font le suivi d'une loi.

Titre ou date de promulgation,	numéro de la loi ou du chapitre,	partie (s'il y a lieu),	référence au recueil des lois sessionnelles	première page de la loi	référence précise au recueil	(année) (si elle n'est pas dans le titre)	(référence au code) (facultatif).
The Deficit Reduction Act of 1984,	Pub L No 98-369,		98 Stat	494			(codifié tel que modifié au 26 USC § 1-9504 (1988)).
Coastal Zone Protection Act of 1996,	Pub L No 104-150,	§ 7(2),	110 Stat	1380	à la p 1382	(1997).	
Act of 25 April 1978,	c 515,	§ 3,	1978 Ala Acts	569	à la p 569.		

➢ Indiquer le titre de la loi en italique. Si la loi n'a pas de titre, l'identifier par la date de sa promulgation (Act of 25 April 1978). S'il n'y a pas de date de promulgation, identifier la loi par sa date de mise en vigueur (Act effective [date]).

➢ Indiquer le numéro de la loi (*public law number*), introduit par l'abréviation Pub L No ou par le numéro du chapitre précédé de c. Le numéro devant le trait d'union du *public law number* est le numéro de session; le numéro après le trait d'union est le numéro de référence.

➢ Pour faire référence à une **partie particulière**, indiquer le numéro de la partie après le numéro de la loi ou le numéro du chapitre, selon le cas. Indiquer la référence précise au recueil.

➢ Le **recueil officiel** des lois fédérales est le *Statutes at Large*, abrégé Stat. L'abréviation du recueil est précédée par le numéro de volume et suivie par la première page de la loi. Pour déterminer si un recueil de lois sessionnelles étatiques est officiel ou non, consulter le *Bluebook*.

➢ Indiquer la **référence précise** au recueil de lois sessionnelles après la référence à la première page. Inclure une référence précise à la partie après le numéro de la loi ou du chapitre.

➢ Indiquer **l'année de publication** entre parenthèses à la fin de la référence, à moins que l'année ne fasse partie du titre de la loi. Si l'année du titre ne coïncide pas avec l'année de publication de la loi, les deux années doivent être indiquées. Voir l'exemple du *Coastal Zone Protection Act of 1996*.

➢ Fournir les renseignements concernant la **codification de la loi** s'ils sont disponibles. Si une loi est divisée et classée sous plusieurs sections du code, fournir ce renseignement entre parenthèses à la fin de la référence ((codifié tel que modifié dans plusieurs sections du 26 USC) suivi du nom du code).

7.2.1.2.3   Recueil non officiel de lois sessionnelles

Référence à l'annuaire,	reproduit dans	référence à la réimpression.
Beauver v Abbot of St Albans (1312), YB Mich 6 Edw II,	reproduit dans	(1921) 38 Selden Soc 32.

➢ Le recueil de lois sessionnelles fédérales le plus important est le *United States Code Congressional and Administrative News*, abrégé USCCAN.

➢ Pour citer l'USCCAN, indiquer la référence aux *Statutes at Large* (Stat), recueils officiels dans lesquels paraîtra la loi.

7.2.1.3 Uniform Codes, Uniform Acts et Restatements

Titre	partie	(année d'adoption).
UCC	§ 2-012	(1995).
Uniform Adoption Act	§ 10	(1971).
Restatement of Contracts	§ 88	(1932).
Restatement (Second) of the Law of Property	§ 15	(1977).

➢ Les *Uniform Codes* et *Uniform Acts* sont des propositions législatives publiées par la *National Conference of Commissioners of Uniform State Laws*, qui visent l'adoption par tous les congrès d'États, les districts et les protectorats. Les *Restatements* sont des rapports sur l'état de la *common law* américaine qui porte sur tel sujet ou telle interprétation des lois publiques publiées par le *American Law Institute*.

➢ Indiquer le titre en italique, à moins qu'il ne s'agisse d'un code.

➢ Ne pas mettre de virgule après le titre d'un code ou d'un *Restatement*.

➢ Lorsqu'il existe plus d'un *Restatement*, indiquer son numéro entre parenthèses.

➢ Indiquer l'année d'adoption, de promulgation ou de la plus récente modification entre parenthèses à la fin de la référence.

7.2.1.4 Projets de loi et résolutions

7.2.1.4.1   Projets de loi fédéraux

É-U,	Bill	chambre	numéro,	titre,	numéro du Congrès,	année,	référence précise	(état, si promulgué).
É-U,	Bill	HR	6,	Higher Education Amendments of 1988,	105ᵉ Cong,	1997		(promulgué).
É-U,	Bill	S	7,	Educational Excellence for All Learners Act of 2001,	107ᵉ Cong,	2001,	art 103.	

➤ Abréger *House of Representatives* par HR et *Senate* par S.

7.2.1.4.2   Résolutions fédérales

É-U,	résolution	numéro,	titre,	numéro du Congrès,	année	(état, si promulgué).
É-U,	HR Con Res	6,	Expressing the Sense of the Congress Regarding the Need to Pass Legislation to Increase Penalties on Perpetrators of Hate Crimes,	107ᵉ Cong,	2001.	
É-U,	HR Res	31,	Designating Minority Membership on Certain Standing Committees of the House,	104ᵉ Cong,	1995	(promulgué).

Abréviations employées pour les résolutions :

House Concurrent Resolutions	HR Con Res
House Resolutions	HR Res
House Joint Resolutions	HRJ Res
Senate Concurrent Resolutions	S Con Res
Senate Resolutions	S Res
Senate Joint Resolutions	SJ Res

7.2.1.4.3   États

É-U,	catégorie du Bill ou de la résolution	numéro,	*titre,*	année ou numéro de la législature,	numéro ou désignation de la session législative,	État,	année,	réfé- rence précise	(état, si prom- ulgué).
É-U,	AB	31,	*An Act to Add Section 51885 to the Education Code, Relating to Educational Technology,*	1997-98,	Reg Sess,	Cal,	1996,	art 1.	
É-U,	SR	ˊ0,	*Calling for the Establishment of a Delaware State Police Community Relations Task Force,*	141ᵉ Gen Assem,	Reg Sess,	Del,	2001,		(prom- ulgué).

> En plus des *Regular Sessions* (Reg Sess), les législateurs étatiques peuvent tenir des *First, Second* et *Third Extraordinary Sessions*. Abréger ces expressions par 1st Extra Sess, 2d Extra Sess et 3d Extra Sess. Abréger *Special Sessions* par Spec Sess.

> Voir la liste des abréviations des États à l'**annexe A-2**.

7.2.1.5 Règles et règlements

7.2.1.5.1   Code of Federal Regulations

Le *Code of Federal Regulations* regroupe les règlements codifiés des États-Unis, classés selon les 50 mêmes titres que le *United States Code*.

Titre (exceptionellement),	volume	recueil	référence précise	(année).
EPA Effluent Limitations Guidelines,	40	CFR	§ 405.53	(1980).
	47	CFR	§ 73.609	(1994).

> Indiquer le titre de la règle ou du règlement s'il est mieux connu ainsi.

> Pour les règles et les règlements fédéraux, faire référence à la compilation officielle du gouvernement, si possible.

> Le *Code of Federal Regulations*, abrégé CFR, est la compilation officielle du gouvernement fédéral.

> Pour identifier les compilations étatiques officielles, voir le *Bluebook*.

7.2.1.5.2   Registre administratif

Les registres administratifs comprennent entre autres les règlements administratifs mis en application par les autorités gouvernementales.

Titre (s'il y a lieu),	volume	Fed Reg	page	(année)	(information sur la codification	référence précise).
	44	Fed Reg	41629	(1980)	(sera codifié au 12 CFR	§ 201.51-201.53).
Outer Continental Sheld Air Regulation Consistency Update for California,	70	Fed Reg	19472	(2009)	(sera codifié au 40 CFR	§ 55).

➢ Lorsque des règles ou des règlements n'ont pas encore été codifiés, faire référence aux registres administratifs.

➢ Au niveau fédéral, se référer au *Federal Register* (Fed Reg).

➢ Indiquer le numéro du volume, l'abréviation du registre, le numéro de page et l'année.

➢ Si possible, indiquer à quel endroit la règle ou le règlement paraîtra dans le CFR ou autre compilation officielle à la fin de la référence.

➢ Pour identifier les registres administratifs étatiques, voir le *Bluebook*.

7.2.2 Jurisprudence

7.2.2.1 Modèle de base

Intitulé,	vol	recueil	(série)	page	référence précise	(indication géographique et/ou **cour**	année)	(autre information) (s'il y a lieu).
People v Kevorkian,	527	NW	(2d)	714		(Mich	1994).	
Roche Holding Ltd,	113	FTC		1086	aux pp 1087-90		(1990).	
Headquarters Space & Missile,	103	Lab Arb Rep (BNA)		1198			(1995)	(McCurdy, Arb).

➢ Les références aux décisions administratives et à l'arbitrage suivent le même modèle de référence que les autres jugements.

➢ Pour l'arbitrage, fournir le nom de l'arbitre suivi d'une virgule et Arb entre parenthèses à la fin de la référence.

7.2.2.2 Intitulé

✓	*California v United States Larez v Los Angeles (City of)*
✗	*State of California v United States of America Larez v LA*

➤ Indiquer l'intitulé selon les règles de la section 3.3.

➤ Pour un État ou un pays, utiliser le nom couramment utilisé plutôt que la forme descriptive ou l'abréviation.

➤ Si une des parties est une ville dont le nom pourrait être confondu avec celui d'un État, indiquer les renseignements permettant de l'identifier entre parenthèses : New York (City of) ou Washington (DC).

7.2.2.3 Référence neutre

➤ Il n'existe **aucun standard uniforme aux États-Unis pour les références neutres**, toutefois certaines juridictions ont adopté ces références. Pour plus de détails, voir le *Bluebook*.

7.2.2.4 Recueil et série

➤ Après l'intitulé, indiquer le numéro du volume, l'abréviation du recueil, le numéro de la série et la première page de l'arrêt. Il y a toujours un espace entre l'abréviation du recueil et le numéro de la série.

Lotus Development v Borland International, 140 F (3d) 70 (1er Cir 1998) [*Lotus*].
Scott v Sanford, 60 US (19 How) 393 (1857).

➤ **Avant 1875**, les *US Reports* sont aussi numérotés en ordre consécutif selon chaque éditeur. Indiquer ce numéro ainsi que le nom de l'éditeur entre parenthèses après US.

Abréviations d'éditeurs :

Wallace	Wall
Black	Black
Howard	How
Peters	Pet
Wheaton	Wheat
Cranch	Cranch
Dallas	Dal

Sources étrangères

Abréviations des principaux recueils :

Atlantic Reporter	A
California Reporter	Cal
Federal Reporter	F
Federal Supplement	F Supp
Lawyers' Edition	L Ed (2d)
New York Supplement	NYS
North Eastern Reporter	NE
North Western Reporter	NW
Pacific Reporter	P
South Eastern Reporter	SE
South Western Reporter	SW
Southern Reporter	So
Supreme Court Reporter	S Ct
United States Reports	US
United States Law Week	USLW

➢ Pour la Cour suprême des États-Unis, faire référence aux recueils dans l'ordre de préférence suivant : **US → S Ct → L Ed (2d) → USLW**.

➢ Pour les cours fédérales, faire référence à F ou F Supp.

➢ Pour les cours d'États, faire référence au recueil régional plutôt qu'au recueil de l'État.

➢ Pour une liste plus étoffée des recueils et de leurs abréviations, voir l'**annexe C**.

7.2.2.5 *Référence précise*

United States v McVeigh, 153 F (3d) 1166 à la p 1170 (10ᵉ Cir 1998). *McVeigh*, *supra* note 1 à la p 1173.	➢ Indiquer à la p avant la référence précise.

7.2.2.6 Cour

7.2.4.6.1   Cours fédérales

Cour suprême des États-Unis	*Roe v Wade*, 410 US 113 (1973).
	AT&T v Iowa Utilities Board, 66 USLW 3387 (US 17 novembre 1997).
Cours d'appel	*Microsystems v Microsoft*, 188 F3d 1115 (9ᵉ Cir 1999).
Cours de district	*Yniguez v Mofford*, 730 F Supp 309 (D Ariz 1990).

➢ La **Cour suprême des États-Unis** ne requiert pas d'abréviation, à moins de citer au *United States Law Week* (USLW). Pour citer l'USLW, ajouter US ainsi que la date (jour, mois et année) entre parenthèses à la fin de la référence.

➢ Abréger les cours d'appel de chaque circuit en précisant le numéro du circuit.

➢ Utiliser DC Cir pour désigner la **Cour d'appel du circuit du** *District of Columbia* et Fed Cir pour désigner la **Cour du circuit fédéral**.

➢ Pour les cours de district, fournir l'abréviation du nom du district.

7.2.2.6.2   Cours d'États

➢ Indiquer le nom de la cour et l'indication géographique entre parenthèses, en utilisant les abréviations des **annexes A-2** et **B**.

➢ Ne pas inclure le nom de l'État si celui-ci fait partie du titre du recueil.

> *Peevyhouse v Garland Coal & Mining*, 382 P2d 109 (Okla Sup Ct 1963).
>
> *Truman v Thomas*, 165 Cal Rptr 308 (Sup Ct 1980).
>
> *Hinterlong v Baldwin*, 308 Ill App (3d) 441 (App Ct 1999).

➢ Ne pas inclure le nom de la cour s'il s'agit du plus haut tribunal de l'État.

7.2.2.7 Année de la décision

➢ Fournir l'année de la décision entre parenthèses à la fin de la référence. S'il y a une abréviation d'un tribunal, inclure l'année au sein des mêmes parenthèses ((App Ct 1999)).

7.2.3 Documents gouvernementaux

Indiquer É-U au début de la référence.

7.2.3.1 Débats

É-U,	*Cong Rec,*	édition,	tome,	partie,	référence précise	(date)	(orateur) (facultatif).
É-U,	Cong Rec,		t 125,	15,	à la p 18691	(1979).	
É-U,	Cong Rec,	daily ed,	t 143,	69,	à la p H3176	(22 May 1977)	(Rep Portman).

> Faire référence au ***Congressional Record*** (Cong Rec) pour les débats du Congrès qui ont eu lieu après 1873.

> Pour faire référence aux débats plus anciens du Congrès, consulter le *Bluebook*.

> Utiliser **l'édition quotidienne** seulement si le débat ne se trouve pas encore dans l'édition reliée.

7.2.3.2 Sessions de comités

7.2.3.2.1 Fédéral

É-U,	*titre,*	numéro du Congrès,	renseignements sur l'édition	référence précise	(orateur) (facultatif).
É-U,	*Federal Property Campaign Fundraising Reform Act of 2000 : Hearing on HR 4845 Before the House Committee of the Judiciary,*	106ᵉ Cong,	2000	aux pp 2-3.	
É-U,	*Assisted Suicide : Legal, Medical, Ethical and Social Issues : Hearing Before the Subcommittee on Health and Environment of the House Committee on Commerce,*	105ᵉ Cong,	Washington, DC, United States Government Printing Office, 1997	à la p 2	(Dr C Everett Koop).

> Toujours indiquer l'année de publication. Outre l'année, fournir le plus de renseignements possible sur l'édition.

7.2.3.2.2 État

É-U,	*titre,*	numéro du corps législatif ou année,	numéro ou désignation de la session législative,	état	(renseigne-ments sur l'édition)	réfé-rence précise	(orateur) (faculta-tif).
É-U,	*Rico Litigation: Hearing on S 1197 Before the Senate Comm on Commerce and Econ Dev,*	41ᵉ légis,	1ʳᵉ sess rég 5,	Ariz	(1993)		(affirmé par Barry Wong, analyste politique).

> Voir la liste d'abréviations des États à l'**annexe A-2**.

➢ Toujours indiquer l'année de publication et fournir le plus de renseignements possible sur l'édition.

7.2.3.3 Rapports et documents

7.2.3.3.1   Fédéral

7.2.3.3.1.1   Documents et rapports numérotés

É-U,	organisme,	titre	(numéro),	renseignements sur l'édition	référence précise.
É-U,		Secrecy: Report of the Commission on Protecting and Reducing Government Secrecy: Pursuant to Public Law 236, 103rd Congress	(S Doc n° 105-2),	Washington, DC, US Government Printing Office, 1997	à la p 3.
É-U,	Senate Committee on the Budget, 111ᵉ Cong,	Concurrent Resolution on the Budget FY 2010,		Washington, DC, US Government Printing Office, 2009	à la p 213.

➢ Indiquer l'organisme responsable, à moins qu'il ne soit mentionné dans le titre.

➢ Toujours indiquer l'année de publication et fournir le plus de renseignements possible sur l'édition.

Abréviations des numéros :

Documents	Rapports
HR Doc n°	HR Rep n°
HR Misc Doc n°	HR Conf Rep n°
S Doc n°	S Rep n°
S Exec Doc n°	

7.2.3.3.1.2   Documents non numérotés et *Committee Prints*

É-U,	organisme,	*titre,*	Committee Print (si pertinent),	renseignements sur l'édition	référence précise.
É-U,	Staff of House Committee on Veterans' Affairs, 105th Cong,	*Persian Gulf Illnesses: An Overview,*	Committee Print,	1998	à la p 15.
É-U,	National Commission on Children,	*Beyond Rhetoric: A New American Agenda for Children and Families,*		Washington (DC), The Commission, 1991	à la p 41.

➢   Indiquer le numéro du congrès avec l'organisme si pertinent.

➢   Toujours indiquer l'année de publication et fournir le plus de renseignements possible sur l'édition.

7.2.3.3.2   État

	É-U,	organisme,	titre	(numéro) (si pertinent),	renseignements sur l'édition	référence précise.
Documents et rapports numérotés	É-U,	California Energy Commission	*Existing Renewable Resources Account,* vol 1	(500-01-014V1),	2001.	
Documents et rapports non numérotés	É-U,	Washington State Transport Commission,	*Washington's Transportation Plan 2003-2022,*		Washington State Department of Transportation, 2002.	

➢   Fournir le numéro du document, s'il y a lieu.

➢   Toujours indiquer l'année de publication et fournir le plus de renseignements possible sur l'édition.

7.3   FRANCE

7.3.1   Législation

7.3.1.1 Lois et autres instruments législatifs

Titre,	JO,	date de publication,	(NC) (s'il y a lieu),	page,	autre source.
Loi n° 99-493 du 15 juin 1999,	JO,	16 juin 1999,		8759,	(1999) D Lég 3.7.
Ordonnance n° 2001-766 du 29 août 2001,	JO,	31 août 2001,		13946,	(2001) D Lég 2564.
Décret du 5 décembre 1978 portant classement d'un site pittoresque,	JO,	6 décembre 1978	(NC),	9250.	

> Inclure le titre si l'instrument législatif n'est pas numéroté. S'il est numéroté, l'inclusion du titre est facultative.

> Toujours faire référence au ***Journal officiel de la République française*** en premier lieu, abrégé JO, suivi de la date de publication et du numéro de page. Pour une liste des titres des anciens journaux officiels, voir la section 7.3.3.2. Pour les suppléments du JO, indiquer (NC) pour **numéro complémentaire** après la date de publication.

> Si possible, indiquer une référence à un recueil général français, selon les règles à la section 7.3.2.10.

7.3.1.2 Codes

Code civil des Français (1804-1807)	art 9 CcF
Code Napoléon (1807-1814)	art 9 CN
Code civil (1815-)	art 2203 C civ
Code pénal	art 113-10 C pén
Code de propriété intellectuelle	art 123(8) CPI
Nouveau Code de procédure civile	art 1435 NC proc civ
Code de procédure pénale	art 144(2) C proc pén

> Ne jamais fournir une référence complète pour se rapporter à un code.

> Pour faire référence aux codes mentionnés ci-dessus, utiliser le titre abrégé dès la première référence.

> Pour faire référence à un code qui n'est pas dans la liste, écrire le nom du code au complet dans la première référence et créer un abrégé si nécessaire (art 1 Code de la consommation [C conso]).

7.3.2   Jurisprudence

➢   Toujours indiquer **la pagination en haut** des pages de *La semaine juridique* et non celle du bas.

7.3.2.1 *Modèle de base*

	Tribunal ou chambre (s'il y a lieu)	ville (s'il y a lieu),	date,	*intitulé* (s'il y a lieu),	(année du recueil)	recueil	partie du recueil (s'il y a lieu)	page et/ou numéro de la décision	(note) (s'il y a lieu).
Cour de cassation	Cass civ 2ᵉ,		14 juin 2001,		(2001)	D	Jur	3075	(annotation Didier Cholet).
Cour d'appel	CA	Paris,	12 janvier 2000,		(2000)	JCP	II	10433	(annotation Philippe Pierre).
Cour de première instance	Trib gr inst	Mans,	7 septembre 1999,		(2000)	JCP	II	10258	(annotation Colette Saujot).

7.3.2.2 *Cour*

7.3.2.2.1   Tribunaux de première instance

Tribunal	ville,	date,	*intitulé* (s'il y a lieu),	(année de publication du recueil	semestre) (s'il y a lieu)	recueil	partie du recueil	page	(note) (s'il y a lieu).
Trib admin	Nantes,	27 novembre 1981,	*Mme Robin*,	(1981)		Rec		544.	
Trib gr inst	Paris,	10 septembre 1998,		(1999	1ᵉʳ sem)	Gaz Pal	Jur	37.	

➢   Indiquer la ville où le tribunal siège après le nom du tribunal.

Abréviations des tribunaux:

Tribunal administratif	Trib admin
Tribunal civil ou Tribunal de première instance (Tribunal civil de droit commun avant 1958)	Trib civ
Tribunal commercial	Trib com
Tribunal correctionnel	Trib corr
Tribunal de grande instance (Tribunal civil de droit commun après 1958)	Trib gr inst
Tribunal d'instance (Tribunal civil de droit commun pour les petites créances après 1958)	Trib inst

Pour une liste plus complète des cours et tribunaux, voir l'**annexe B**.

7.3.2.2.2   Cour d'appel

CA	ville,	date,	*intitulé* (s'il y a lieu),	(année de publica- tion	semestre) (s'il y a lieu)	recueil	partie du recueil	page,	numéro de décision,	(annota- tion).
CA	Orléans,	23 octobre 1997,		(1999	1er sem)	Gaz Pal	Jur	217	n° 94/002561	(annota- tion Benoît de Roque- feuil).
CA	Paris,	21 mai 2008,	*K c E et Sté nationale de télévision France 2,*	(2008)		JCP	Jur	390	n° 06/07678.	

7.3.2.2.3   Cour de cassation

Chambre,	date,	(année de publication)	recueil	section,	page,	numéro de décision (s'il y a lieu).
Cass civ 1re,	30 mars 1999,	(1999)	Bull civ	I,	77,	n° 118.
Cass crim,	24 février 2009,	(2009)	D Jur		951,	n° 08-87.409.

Abréviations des cours et des chambres :

Chambre civile	Cass civ 1re
	Cass civ 2e
	Cass civ 3e
Chambre commerciale	Cass com
Chambre sociale	Cass soc
Chambre criminelle	Cass crim
Chambre des requêtes	Cass req
Chambres réunies (avant 1967)	Cass Ch réun
Assemblée plénière (après 1967)	Cass Ass plén
Chambre mixte	Cass mixte

7.3.2.2.4   Conseil d'État

Cour,	date,	*intitulé,*	année de publication	recueil	page.
CE,	27 janvier 1984,	Ordre des avocats de la Polynésie française,	(1984)	Rec	20.

➢   Abréger Conseil d'État par CE.

7.3.2.2.5   Conseil constitutionnel

Cour,	date,	*intitulé,*	(année de publication)	recueil	page,	numéro de la décision.
Cons const,	25 juin 1986,	*Privatisations,*	(1986)	Rec	61,	86-207 DC.
Cons const,	19 juin 2008,		(2008)	JCP Jur	449,	2008-564 DC.

➢ Abréger **Conseil constitutionnel** par Cons const.

➢ Indiquer le numéro de la décision à la fin de la référence.

7.3.2.3 Intitulé

Cass com, 22 janvier 1991, *Ouest Abri*, (1991) D Jur 175.

➢ **L'intitulé des causes françaises n'est habituellement pas indiqué, sauf** :

→ pour faire référence à une décision d'un tribunal administratif ou du Conseil d'État (mais pas dans tous les cas) ;

→ pour faire référence à un jugement non publié ou à un jugement résumé dans la partie « Sommaire » d'un recueil ;

→ pour éviter la confusion (par ex. lorsqu'un tribunal a rendu deux décisions un même jour) ; et

→ lorsque la cause est mieux connue sous le nom des parties que selon les renseignements habituels.

➢ Mettre l'intitulé en italique, entre virgules, après la date à laquelle la décision a été rendue.

7.3.2.4 Année

Paris, 5 février 1999, (1999 2ᵉ sem) Gaz Pal Jur 452.

➢ Indiquer l'année de publication du volume avant l'abréviation du recueil.

7.3.2.5 Semestre

➢ Pour faire référence à la *Gazette du Palais* (Gaz Pal), indiquer le numéro du semestre après l'année de publication, dans les parenthèses.

7.3.2.6 Recueil

Cour,	date,	(année de publication du recueil	semestre) (s'il y a lieu)	recueil	partie du recueil	page et/ou numéro de décision.
Cass civ 3ᵉ,	23 juin 1999,	(2000)		JCP	II	10333.
Cass soc,	3 février 1998,	(1998	1ᵉʳ sem)	Gaz Pal	Jur	176.

> ➢   Il y a un espace entre chaque information (par ex. (1998 1ᵉʳ sem) Gaz Pal Jur 176).

Liste des recueils les plus courants :

Recueil Dalloz *Recueil Dalloz et Sirey* (de 1945 à aujourd'hui)	D
Gazette du Palais	Gaz Pal
Bulletin de la Cour de cassation, section civile	Bull civ
Semaine Juridique (de 1937 à aujourd'hui)	JCP
Recueil des décisions du Conseil d'État ou *Recueil Lebon*	RCE ou Rec
Actualité juridique de droit administratif	AJDA

Voir l'**annexe C** pour une liste plus complète des abréviations des titres des recueils.

7.3.2.7 Partie du recueil

> ➢   Lorsque la partie du recueil est numérotée, indiquer le numéro de la partie en chiffres romains après l'année de publication.

> ➢   Lorsque la partie du recueil n'est pas numérotée, indiquer l'abréviation du titre de la partie.

> ➢   Ne pas inclure la partie du recueil dans le cas du ***Recueil Lebon*** (Rec) ou de l'***Actualité juridique de droit administratif*** (AJDA).

Abréviation des titres des parties des recueils :

Assemblée plénière	Ass plén
Chambre mixte	Ch mixte
Chambres des requêtes	Req
Chambres réunies	Ch réun
Chroniques	Chron
Doctrine	Doctr
Informations rapides	Inf
Jurisprudence	Jur
Législation, Lois et décrets, Textes de lois, etc.	Lég
Panorama de jurisprudence	Pan
Sommaire	Somm

7.3.2.8 Page et numéro de la décision

Semaine juridique	Ass plén, 6 novembre 1998, (1999) JCP II 10000 bis.
Bulletin de la Cour de cassation	Cass civ 2e, 7 juin 2001, (2001) Bull civ II 75, no 110.

➢ Indiquer la première page de la décision après la partie du recueil ou son année de publication.

➢ Pour la *Semaine juridique*, indiquer le numéro de la décision (par ex.10000 bis).

➢ Pour les *Bulletin de la Cour de cassation*, mentionner le numéro de page et le numéro de la décision, séparés par une virgule et un espace.

7.3.2.9 Référence précise

Trib gr inst Narbonne, 12 mars 1999, (1999 1er sem) Gaz Pal Jur 405 à la p 406.

➢ Étant donné la brièveté de la plupart des jugements, les références précises sont rarement utilisées. Le cas échéant, indiquer la référence précise après le numéro de la première page, précédée de à la p.

7.3.2.10   Autres sources

Première référence,	autre source.
Cass civ 1re, 26 mai 1999, (1999) Bull civ I 115, no 175,	(1999) JCP II 10112.
Cass crim, 21 janvier 2009, (2009) Bull crim 74, no 08-83.492,	(2009) D Jur 374.

Sources étrangères

7.3.2.11 Notes, rapports et conclusions

Cass civ 1re, 6 juillet 1999, (1999) JCP II 10217 (note Thierry Garé).

➤ Si la décision est suivie d'une note, d'un rapport ou d'une conclusion, ajouter cette information à la fin de la référence.

➤ Inscrire, entre parenthèses, l'information suivante : note, rapport ou conclusion, suivi du nom de l'auteur.

7.3.3 Documents gouvernementaux

Indiquer France au début de chaque référence à des documents gouvernementaux.

7.3.3.1 Débats

7.3.3.1.1 De 1787 à 1860

France,	*Archives parlementaires,*	série,	tome,	date,	référence précise	(orateur) (facultatif).
France,	*Archives parlementaires,*	1re série,	t 83,	5 janvier 1794,	s 3.	

➤ Abréger *Archives parlementaires : Recueil complet des débats législatifs et politiques des chambres françaises* par *Archives parlementaires*.

➤ Indiquer la série après le titre. La première série couvre les années 1787-1799, alors que la deuxième série couvre les années 1800-1860.

➤ Les références précises se font aux sections et non pas aux articles.

➤ Le nom de l'orateur peut être ajouté entre parenthèses à la fin de la référence.

7.3.3.1.2 De 1871 à aujourd'hui

France,	*journal,*	chambre,	Débats parlementaires,	division,	numéro et date,	référence précise	(orateur) (facultatif).
France,	*JO,*	Assemblée nationale,	Débats parlementaires,	Compte rendu intégral,	1re séance du 23 janvier 2001,	à la p 635	(Gilbert Maurel).
France,	*JO,*	Sénat,	Débats parlementaires,	Compte rendu intégral,	séance du 3 avril 2001.		

➤ À partir de 1871, les débats parlementaires sont publiés dans le ***Journal officiel de la République française***, abrégé *JO*.

➤ Indiquer la chambre, suivie de Débats parlementaires.

→ 1871-1880 : omettre la chambre et Débats parlementaires.

→ 1943-1945; 1945-1946; 1947-1958 : indiquer seulement Débats de [nom de la chambre].

Noms des chambres selon les époques :

1881-1940	Chambre des députés	1880-1940	Sénat
1943-1945	Assemblée consultative provisoire		
1945-1946	Assemblée constituante		
1947-1958	Assemblée de l'Union française	1946-1958	Conseil de la République
1958 à aujourd'hui	Assemblée nationale	1958 à aujourd'hui	Sénat

➤ La division ne doit être indiquée qu'à partir de 1980 pour l'Assemblée nationale et à partir de 1983 pour le Sénat. Dans le cas de l'Assemblée nationale, les débats parlementaires se scindent en deux : Compte rendu intégral et Questions écrites remises à la Présidence de l'Assemblée nationale et réponses des ministres. Il existe également deux divisions pour le Sénat : Compte rendu intégral et Questions remises à la Présidence du Sénat et réponses des ministres aux questions écrites.

➤ Terminer par le numéro (s'il y a lieu) et la date de la séance, puis par la référence précise à la page consultée.

➤ Si nécessaire, ajouter le nom de l'orateur entre parenthèses à la fin de la référence.

7.3.3.2 Anciens Journaux officiels

France,	titre,	année ou date de publication,	tome ou volume	référence précise.
France,	Journal officiel de l'Empire français,	1868,	t 1	à la p 14.
France,	Gazette nationale, ou le Moniteur universel,	1er juillet 1791,	t 9	à la p 3.

➤ Les débats parlementaires, les documents parlementaires et les documents non parlementaires **précédant l'année 1871** sont généralement publiés à l'intérieur d'anciennes versions du Journal officiel de la République française.

1787-1810	Gazette nationale, ou le Moniteur universel
1811-1848	Moniteur universel
1848-1852	Moniteur universel, Journal officiel de la République
1852-1870	Journal officiel de l'Empire français

> Le mode de référence peut varier selon l'organisation du journal. Généralement, la référence devrait au moins inclure le titre du journal, l'année de référence ou la date de publication, le tome ou le volume (s'il y a lieu), ainsi que le numéro de la page consultée.

7.3.3.3 Documents parlementaires

7.3.3.3.1   Travaux et réunions parlementaires

France,	chambre,	organisme,	« titre des travaux »,	Compte rendu ou Bulletin	(date)	(président) (facultatif).
France,	Assemblée nationale,	Délégation aux droits des femmes,	« Auditions sur le suivi de l'application des lois relatives à l'IVG et à la contraception »,	Compte rendu n° 4	(6 novembre 2001)	(présidente : Martine Lignières-Cassou).
France,	Sénat,	Commission des affaires culturelles,	« Auditions de M Jack Lang, ministre de l'éducation nationale »,	Bulletin du 11 juin 2001	(13 juin 2001)	(président : Adrien Gouteyron).

> Indiquer le titre des travaux, puis le numéro du compte rendu ou du bulletin correspondant. Les **Comptes rendus** sont utilisés pour les travaux de l'Assemblée nationale, alors que les **Bulletins** sont utilisés pour les travaux du Sénat. Contrairement au terme Compte rendu, le terme Bulletin est en italique.

> Terminer par la date, le président des travaux (facultatif) et la référence précise.

7.3.3.3.2   Rapports d'information

France,	chambre,	organisme (s'il y a lieu),	titre du rapport,	par auteur(s),	numéro du rapport	(date)	référence précise.
France,	Sénat,	Délégation pour l'Union européenne,	Le projet de traité établissant une Constitution pour l'Europe,	par Hubert Haenel,	rapport n° 3	(1er octobre 2003)	à la p 4.
France,	Assemblée nationale,		Rapport d'information déposé en application de l'article 145 du Règlement par la mission d'information commune sur le prix des carburants dans les départements d'outre-mer,	par Jacques Le Guen et Jérôme Cahuzac,	rapport n° 1885	(23 juillet 2009)	à la p 63.

7.3.3.4 Documents non parlementaires

France,	organisme,	titre,	numéro, tome ou volume,	renseignements sur l'édition	référence précise	(renseignements additionnels) (facultatif).
France,		Commission d'enquête sur la sécurité du transport maritime des produits dangereux ou polluants,	Rapport n° 2535, t 1			(5 juillet 2000 ; président : Daniel Paul).
France,	Conseil économique et social,	La conjoncture économique et sociale en 2005,		Avis et rapports du Conseil économique et social, JO, n° 2005-09	à la p I-4	(1er juin 2005 ; rapport présenté par Luc Guyau).
France,	Ministère de la justice,	Bulletin officiel,	n° 82		à la p 3	(1er avril-30 juin 2001).

➢ La référence aux documents non parlementaires de France suit le même modèle de référence que les documents non parlementaires canadiens à la section 4.2.

7.4   AUSTRALIE

7.4.1 Législation

7.4.1.1 Lois

Titre	(indication géographique),	référence précise.
Corporations Act 2001	(Cth).	
Electricity Reform Act 2001	(NT).	
Marine Pollution Act 1987	(NSW),	art 53(1)(d).

➢ Écrire le titre abrégé officiel de la loi en italique. Inclure l'année dans le titre.

➢ Indiquer l'abréviation de l'indication géographique immédiatement après le titre, entre parenthèses.

Abréviations des indications géographiques :

Commonwealth	Cth
Territoire de la capitale australienne	ACT
Nouvelle-Galles-du Sud	NSW
Territoire du Nord	NT
Queensland	Qld
Australie méridionale	SA
Tasmanie	Tas
Victoria	Vic
Australie occidentale	WA

Compilations statutaires :

Acts of Parliament of the Commonwealth of Australia
Laws of the Australian Capital Territory, Acts
Statutes of New South Wales
Northern Territory of Australia Laws
Laws of the Northern Territory of Australia
Queensland Acts

Queensland Statutes
South Australia Statutes
Tasmanian Statutes
Acts of the Victorian Parliament
Victorian Statutes
Statutes of Western Australia

7.4.1.2 Législation déléguée (règlements)

Titre	(indication géographique),	référence précise.
Admiralty Rules 2002	(Cth),	art 5(b).
Income Tax Regulations (Amendment) 1996	(Cth).	
Education Regulation 2005	(ACT),	art 5.

➢ La référence aux règlements et aux règles suit le modèle des lois (section 7.4.1.1).

Compilations des règlements :

Commonwealth Statutory Rules
Laws of the Australian Capital Territory, Subordinate Legislation
New South Wales Rules, Regulations, and By-Laws
Queensland Subordinate Legislation
Tasmanian Statutory Rules
Victorian Statutory Rules, Regulations, and By-Laws
Western Australia Subsidiary Legislation

7.4.2   Jurisprudence

7.4.2.1 Modèle de base

Intitulé	(année),	référence neutre	[année du recueil]	volume	recueil	page	(indication géographique et/ ou **cour**) (s'il y a lieu).
Neilson v Overseas Projects Corporation of Victoria Ltd,		[2005] HCA 54.					
Macleod v Australian Securities and Investment Commission,		[2002] HCA 37,		211	CLR	287.	
Standard Portland Cement Company Pty Ltd v Good	(1983),			57	ALJR	151	(PC).
Thwaites v Ryan	(1983),		[1984]		VR	65	(SC).

7.4.2.2 Référence neutre

➢ Plusieurs tribunaux australiens ont adopté un système de référence neutre. Suivre les règles de la référence neutre au Canada (section 3.5), à l'exception de l'année, qui est placée entre crochets.

[année]	cour	numéro	paragraphe.
[2005]	HCA	54	¶ 26.

7.4.2.3 Recueil

7.4.2.3.1   Law Reports

Abréviations des recueils des Law Reports :

Commonwealth Law Reports (de 1903 à aujourd'hui) : Officiel	CLR
Australian Law Reports (de 1973 à aujourd'hui)	ALR
Federal Court Reports (de 1984 à aujourd'hui) : Officiel	FCR
Australian Law Journal Reports (de 1958 à aujourd'hui)	ALJR
Federal Law Reports (de 1956 à aujourd'hui)	FLR
New South Wales Law Reports (de 1971 à aujourd'hui) : Officiel	NSWLR
Queensland State Reports (1902-1957) : Officiel	Qd SR
Queensland Reports (de 1958 à aujourd'hui) : Officiel	Qd R
South Australia State Reports (de 1922 à aujourd'hui) : Officiel	SASR
Tasmanian Law Reports (1896-1940) : Officiel	Tas LR
Tasmanian State Reports (1941-1978)	Tas R
Tasmanian Reports (de 1979 à aujourd'hui) : Officiel	Tas R
Victorian Law Reports (1875-1956)	VLR
Victorian Reports (de 1957 à aujourd'hui) : Officiel	VR
Western Australia Law Reports (1899-1959)	WALR
Western Australia Law Reports (de 1960 à aujourd'hui) : Officiel	WAR
Australian Capital Territory Reports (de 1973 à aujourd'hui)	ACTR
Northern Territory Reports (de 1978 à aujourd'hui)	NTR
Northern Territory Law Reports (de 1992 à aujourd'hui)	NTLR

➤ Pour les décisions du **Privy Council** (PC) et de la **High Court of Australia** (HCA), faire référence aux CLR et au ALR dans cet ordre de préférence.

➤ Pour les autres décisions de cours générales, utiliser de préférence le FC.

➤ Pour les États et territoires australiens, privilégier le recueil étatique ou territorial officiel.

7.4.2.4 Cour

Abréviations des cours :

Cour	Abbreviation and identifiers
Privy Council (Australia)	PC
High Court of Australia	HCA
Federal Court of Australia	FCA
Supreme Court of Queensland—Court of Appeal	QCA
Supreme Court of Queensland	QSC
Supreme Court of the Australian Capital Territory	ACTSC
Supreme Court of New South Wales	NSWSC
Supreme Court of New South Wales—Court of Appeal	NSWCA
Supreme Court of Tasmania	TASSC
Supreme Court of Victoria—Court of Appeal	VSCA
Supreme Court of Victoria	VSC
Supreme Court of Southern Australia	SASC
District Court of Southern Australia	SADC
Supreme Court of Western Australia	WASC
Supreme Court of Western Australia—Court of Appeal	WASCA
Supreme Court of the Northern Territory	NTSC

➢ Si l'indication géographique des tribunaux étatiques et territoriaux est évidente, n'indiquer que l'instance de la cour.

7.4.3 Documents gouvernementaux

Indiquer Austl au début de la référence.

Sources étrangères

7.4.3.1 Débats

Austl,	indication géographique,	chambre,	Parliamentary Debates	(date)	référence précise	(orateur) (facultatif).
Austl,	Commonwealth	House of Representatives,	Parliamentary Debates	(17 septembre 2001)	à la p 30739	(M Howard, premier ministre).
Austl,	Victoria,	Legislative Assembly,	Parliamentary Debates	(23 octobre 1968)	à la p 1197.	

> ➤ Après Austl, inscrire l'indication géographique. Voir l'**annexe A-3** pour les abréviations australiennes.

> ➤ Toujours utiliser les *Parliamentary Debates* en tant que recueil.

7.4.3.2 Rapports parlementaires

Austl,	indication géographique,	*titre*,	numéro	(année)	référence précise.
Austl,	Commonwealth,	*Department of Foreign Affairs Annual Report 1975*,	Parl Paper n° 142	(1976)	à la p 5.

> ➤ Écrire Parl Paper n° avant le numéro.

7.4.3.3 Rapports non parlementaires

Austl,	indication géographique,	organisme,	titre	(type de document)	par auteur(s) (s'il y a lieu),	renseignements sur l'édition	référence précise.
Austl,	Common-wealth,	Royal Commission into Aboriginal Deaths in Custody,	Report of the Inquiry into the Death of Stanley John Gollan		par Commissioner Elliott Johnston, QC,	Canberra, Australian Government Publishing Service, 1990	à la p 31.
Austl,	Common-wealth,	Law Reform Commission,	Annual Report 1998	(Rapport n° 49),		Canberra, Australian Government Publishing Service, 1988.	

7.4.3.4 Documents des ministères

Auteur,	indication géographique,	*titre*,	service du document,	numéro	(date)	référence précise.
Paul Keating,	Commonwealth (Austl),	*Opening of the Global Cultural Diversity Conference*,	Ministerial Document Service,	n° 172/ 94-95	(27 avril 1995)	à la p 5977.

> ➤ Si des renseignements supplémentaires sont nécessaires pour identifier précisément l'indication géographique à l'intérieur de l'Australie, fournir l'indication géographique suivie de Austl entre parenthèses et avant la virgule précédant le titre.

7.5   NOUVELLE-ZÉLANDE

7.5.1 Législation

7.5.1.1 Lois

Titre	(N-Z),	année/numéro,	volume RS	première page.
Abolition of the Death Penalty Act 1989	(N-Z),	1989/119,	41 RS	1.
Kiwifruit Industry Restructuring Act 1999	(N-Z),	1999/95.		

> ➤ Fournir le numéro du volume, suivi de RS (l'abréviation de *Reprint Series*).

7.5.1.2 Législation déléguée (règlements)

Titre	(N-Z),	année/numéro ou *Gazette* année,	page de la *Gazette*	vol RS	première page.
Kiwifruit Export Regulations 1999	(N-Z),	1999/310.			
Ticketing of Meat Notice 1979	(N-Z),	*Gazette* 1979,	2030.		
High Court Amendment Rules (No 2) 1987	(N-Z),	1987/169,		40 RS	904.

> ➤ Fournir le numéro du volume, suivi de RS (l'abréviation de *Reprint Series*).

7.5.2   Jurisprudence

7.5.2.1 Modèle de base

Intitulé,	(année de la décision),	référence neutre	[année du recueil]	volume	recueil	page	(indication géographique et/ou cour) (s'il y a lieu).
R v Clarke,		[2005] NZSC 60.					
Pfizer v Commissioner of Patents,			[2005]	1	NZLR	362	(HC).

7.5.2.2 Référence neutre

> La Cour suprême de Nouvelle-Zélande a officiellement adopté un système de référence neutre pour

[Année]	cour	numéro	paragraphe.
[2005]	NZSC	46	¶ 4.

les jugements qui ont été rendus pendant ou après l'année 2005. Suivre les règles de la référence neutre au Canada (section 3.5), à l'exception de l'année, qui est placée entre crochets.

7.5.2.3 Recueil

7.5.2.3.1   Law Reports

> Les *Law Reports* sont divisés en séries. **Faire référence aux séries plutôt qu'aux Law Reports**.

> Puisqu'il n'y a pas de recueil particulier pour le ***Judicial Committee of the Privy Council*** (après 1932), la ***Court of Appeal*** ou la ***High Court***, inclure PC, CA, ou HC à la fin de chaque référence à une décision d'une de ces cours.

Sources étrangères

Abréviations des séries des *Law Reports* :

New Zealand Law Reports (1883 à aujourd'hui) (Privy Council, Supreme Court of New Zealand, Court of Appeal, High Court)	NZLR
New Zealand Privy Council Cases (1840-1932)	NZPCC
Gazette Law Reports (1898-1953) (Court of Appeal, Supreme Court (High Court), Court of Arbitration)	GLR
District Court Reports (1980 à aujourd'hui)	NZDCR
Magistrates' Court Decisions (1939-1979)	MCD
Magistrates' Court Reports (1906-1953)	MCR
Book of Awards (1894-1991) (Arbitration Court, Court of Appeal)	BA
Employment Reports of New Zealand (1991 à aujourd'hui) (Court of Appeal, Labour Court, Aircrew Industrial Tribunal)	ERNZ
New Zealand Industrial Law Reports (1987-1990) (Labour Court, Court of Appeal, Aircrew Industrial Tribunal)	NZILR
Judgments of the Arbitration Court of New Zealand (1979-1986) (Arbitration Court, Court of Appeal)	NZAC
New Zealand Family Law Reports (1981 à aujourd'hui) (Privy Council, Court of Appeal, High Court, Family Court, Youth Court, District Court)	NZFLR
Criminal Reports of New Zealand (1993 à aujourd'hui) (Court of Appeal, High Court)	CRNZ

7.5.2.4 Cour

Privy Council (Nouvelle-Zélande)	PC
New Zealand Supreme Court – établie en 2004	NZSC
New Zealand Court of Appeal	NZCA
New Zealand High Court	NZHC
District Court of New Zealand	DCNZ
Magistrates' Court of New Zealand	Mag Ct NZ
Coroners Court	Cor Ct
New Zealand Employment Court	NZ Empl Ct
Environment Court	Env Ct
Family Court of New Zealand	Fam Ct NZ
Maori Land Court / Te Kooti Whenua Maori	Maori Land Ct
Maori Appellate Court	Maori AC
New Zealand Youth Court	NZYC
Waitangi Tribunal / Te Rōpū Whakamana i te Tiriti o Waitangi	Waitangi Trib

N.B. Le *Supreme Court Act 2003* a créé la Cour suprême de Nouvelle-Zélande et a aboli les appels au *Privy Council*.

7.5.3 Documents gouvernementaux

Indiquer NZ au début de la référence.

7.5.3.1 Débats

N-Z,	*Hansard,*	étape : sujet	(numéro de la question)	date	(orateur) (facultatif).
N-Z,	*Hansard,*	Questions to Ministers : Biosecurity Risk-Motor Vehicle and Equipment Imports	(n° 3)	1er mars 2000	(Ian Ewen-Street).

> ➢ **Hansard** fournit le type d'étape : *Questions to Ministers* ; *Debate-General* ; *Report of [nom] Committee* ou *Miscellaneous*.

> ➢ Indiquer le titre du débat en tant que sujet (Labour, Associate Minister-Accountability). Ne pas répéter l'information si l'étape et le sujet sont les mêmes.

7.5.3.2 Documents parlementaires

N-Z,	« titre »,	date,	session	(président) (facultatif)	préfixe et numéro.
N-Z,	« Report of the Government Administration Committee, Inquiry into New Zealand's Adoption Laws »,	août 2001,	46e parlement	(présidente : Dianne Yates)	
N-Z,	« Report of the Game Bird Habitat Trust Board for the year ended 31 August 1999 »,	février 2000,			C.22.

> ➢ Ne pas mettre d'espace entre le préfixe et le numéro. La lettre qui précède le numéro (le préfixe) indique le sujet sur lequel porte le rapport.

Préfixe
A. Affaires politiques et étrangères
B. Finance et revenu
C. Environnement
D. Énergie et travaux
E. Bien-être et justice
F. Communications
G. Général
H. Commissions, Royal Commissions

7.6 SINGAPOUR

7.6.1 Législation

N.B. Si aucune autre information n'indique que le document législatif provient du Singapour, écrire Rev Ed Sing.

7.6.1.1 Documents constitutionnels

➢ Faire référence aux modifications constitutionnelles de la même manière qu'à toute autre forme de législation.

➢ Abréger *Revised Edition* par Rev Ed.

> *Constitution of the Republic of Singapore* (1999 Rev Ed), art 12(1).
>
> *Independence of Singapore Agreement 1965* (1985 Rev Ed).
>
> *Republic of Singapore Independence Act* (1985 Rev Ed), n° 9 de 1965, art 2.

7.6.1.2 Lois

Lois incluses dans l'édition refondue	*Penal Code* (Cap 224, 1985 Rev Ed Sing), art 34.
Lois qui n'ont pas encore un chapitre assigné dans l'édition refondue	*United Nations Act 2001* (n° 44 de 2001, Sing), art 2.

➢ Abréger l'édition refondue des lois de la République de Singapour par Rev Ed Sing.

➢ Abréger chapitre par Cap. Pour les lois récentes qui n'ont pas un chapitre assigné dans l'édition refondue, utiliser le numéro de la loi tel qu'indiqué dans l'exemple ci-dessus. Ne pas confondre le numéro de la loi avec le numéro du supplément de la loi (*Acts Supplement*), un numéro attribué à chaque supplément de la *Government Gazette* publiant les amendements subséquents de la loi.

➢ Pour la législation **précédant le 15 août 1945**, ajouter les abréviations suivantes après le titre de la loi :

→ pour la législation promulguée de la période de Straits Settlements (du 1er avril 1867 au 15 février 1942), utiliser SS.

→ pour la législation promulguée sous l'administration militaire japonaise lors de l'occupation de Singapour (du 15 février 1942 au 15 août 1945), utiliser JMA pour Japanese Military Administration.

➢ Pour la législation promulguée **après le 15 août 1945**, utiliser Sing pour se référer à la législation promulguée pendant les périodes suivantes :

→ Administration militaire britannique (British Military Administration) ;

→   Colonie de Singapour (Colony of Singapore) ;

→   État de Singapour (State of Singapore) avant et pendant la fédération avec la Malaisie ;

→   République de Singapour (Republic of Singapore).

7.6.1.3 Modifications et abrogations

> *Penal Code* (Cap 224, 1985 Rev Ed Sing), art 73, mod par *Penal Code (Amendment) Act*, n° 18 de 1998, art 2.
>
> *Control of Imports and Exports Act* (cap 56, 1985 Ref Ed Sing), mod par *Regulation of Imports and Exports Act 1995* (No 24 of 1995).

➤   Pour plus de détails, voir la section 2.1.11.

7.6.1.4 Lois anglaises applicables à Singapour

➤   Faire référence aux lois anglaises applicables à Singapour en vertu du *Application of English Law Act* (Cap 7A, 1994 Rev Ed

> *Misrepresentation Act* (Cap 390, 1994 Rev Ed Sing), art 2.
>
> *Hire-Purchase Act* (Cap 125, 1999 Rev Ed), art 5.

Sing) en utilisant l'édition refondue de Singapour de la même manière que les lois promulguées par Singapour.

7.6.1.5 Législation auxiliaire (Règles, règlements, avis, ordonnances)

7.6.1.5.1   Refondus

Titre	(Cap, type de législation et le numéro, Rev Ed),	référence précise.
Housing and Development Conveyancing Fees Rules	(Cap 129, R 2, 1999 Rev Ed Sing),	r 2.
Telecommunications (Class Licenses) Regulations	(Cap 323, Reg 3, 2000 Rev Ed Sing),	reg 10.

➤   Pour la législation auxiliaire refondue, le numéro Cap est le numéro du chapitre de la loi habilitante.

> *Penal Code* (Cap 224, 1985 Rev Ed Sing), art 73, mod par *Penal Code (Amendment) Act*, n° 18 de 1998, art 2.
>
> *Control of Imports and Exports Act* (cap 56, 1985 Ref Ed Sing), mod par *Regulation of Imports and Exports Act 1995* (No 24 of 1995).

> ➤ Utiliser R pour indiquer **Rule**, Reg pour **Regulation**, N pour **Notification** et O pour **Order**.

> ➤ Indiquer l'année de l'édition refondue de la législation auxiliaire.

> ➤ Abréger **Revised Edition** par Rev Ed.

> ➤ Pour la référence précise, utiliser r pour indiquer **rule**, reg pour **regulation** o pour **order** et n pour **notification**.

> ➤ Le type de la référence précise peut être différent de celui de la législation auxiliaire (par ex. une règle peut contenir des ordonnances).

7.6.1.5.2   Non refondus

Titre	(S numéro/année Sing),	référence précise.
United Nations (Anti-Terrorism Measures) Regulations 2001	(S 561/2001 Sing),	reg 3.
Monetary Authority of Singapore (Merchant Banks – Annual Fees) Notification 2005	(S 405/2005 Sing),	n 2(2).
Payment and Settlement Systems (finality and Netting) (Designated System) Order 2002	(S 620/2002 Sing),	o 3(a).

7.6.2 Jurisprudence

7.6.2.1 Modèle de base

Intitulé	(année de la décision),	référence neutre,	[année du recueil]	volume	recueil	page	(indication géographique et/ou cour) (s'il y a lieu).
Er Joo Nguang v Public Prosecutor,			[2000]	2	SLR	645	(HC).
Firstlink Energy Pte Ltd v Creanovate Pte Ltd,		[2006] SGHC 19.					
Re Ong Yew Teck	(1960),			26	MLJ	67	(Sing HC).

> ➤ Indiquer le nom au complet des parties afin d'identifier la pluralité des pratiques culturelles gouvernantes à Singapour.

> ➤ Inclure l'abréviation Sing, sauf si la référence est au *Singapore Law Reports*.

7.6.2.2 Référence neutre

> ➤ Les tribunaux du Singapour ont officiellement adopté un système de référence neutre.

[Année]	cour	numéro	paragraphe.
[2005]	SGCA	55	[11].

Suivre les règles de l a référence neutre au Canada (section 3.5), à l'exception de l'année, qui est placée entre crochets.

> Indiquer les numéros de paragraphe entre crochets (par ex. [11]).

> La Cour suprême a établi que les références aux Singapore Law Reports ont priorité sur la référence neutre.

7.6.2.3 Recueil

Abréviations des principaux recueils :

Singapore Law Reports	SLR
Singapore Law Reports (Reissue) (1965-2002)	SLR (R)
Malayan Law Journal	MLJ
Criminal Law Aid Scheme News	CLASN
Straits Settlements Law Reports	SSLR

> Les *Singapore Law Reports (Reissue)* entre les années 1965 et 2002 ont modifié les résumés précédents et numéroté les paragraphes. Ils sont tout aussi officiels que les *Singapore Law Reports.*

7.6.2.4 Cours

Abréviations des cours :

Cour	Abréviation	Désignation
Court of Appeal	CA	SGCA
High Court	HC	SGHC
District Court	Dist Ct	SGDC
Magistrates' Court	Mag Ct	SGMC

> Les cours de première instance n'ont pas de subdivisions.

7.6.2.5 Décisions non publiées sans référence neutre

Intitulé	(date),	numéro de la décision	(indication géographique et/ou cour) (s'il y a lieu).
Public Prosecutor v Loh Chai Huat	(31 mai 2001),	DAC No 36923 de 2000	(Sing Dist Ct).

7.6.3   Documents gouvernementaux

7.6.3.1 Débats parlementaires

Parliamentary Debates Singapore: Official Report,	volume,	colonne	(date)	(nom de l'orateur) (facultatif).
Parliamentary Debates Singapore: Official Report,	vol 73,	à la col 2436	(15 octobre 2001)	(Professeur S Jayakumar).
Parliamentary Debates Singapore: Official Report,	vol 80	à la col 2293	(13 février 2006)	(Professeur Ivan Png Paak Liang).

7.6.3.2 Directives de pratique

Les directives de pratique sont publiées par la Cour suprême pour réglementer les litiges. Jusqu'en 1994, elles étaient publiées sous forme de documents distincts. Depuis, elles ont été consolidées dans un document intitulé *Supreme Court Practice Directions*.

7.6.3.2.1 Directives de pratique consolidées

Sing,	The Supreme Court Practice Directions	(année)	partie	article.
Sing,	The Supreme Court Practice Directions	(2007)	partie XV	art 123(1).

7.6.3.2.2 Modifications aux directives de pratique

Sing,	DP de la Cour suprême	numéro	de l'année,	article.
Sing,	DP de la Cour suprême	n° 1	de 2008,	art 7.

> ➤ Abréger **directives de pratique** par DP.

7.7   AFRIQUE DU SUD

7.7.1   Législation

7.7.1.1 Lois

Titre,	(S Afr),	numéro	de l'année,	référence précise.
Constitution of the Republic of South Africa 1996,		n° 108	de 1996.	
Consumer Protection Act	(S Afr),	n° 68	de 2008,	art 33.

7.7.1.2 Modifications et abrogations

> Constitution of the Republic of South Africa, n° 108 de 1996 mod par Constitution of the Republic of South Africa Amendment Act, n° 3 de 1999

➢ Pour plus de détails, voir la section 2.1.11.

7.7.1.3 Projets de loi

Numéro,	titre,	(S Afr),	session,	parlement,	année,	référence précise.
B30-2005,	Precious Metals Bill	(S Afr),	3e sess,	3e Parl,	2005.	
B26-2005,	Nursing Bill	(S Afr),	3e sess,	3e Parl,	2005,	art 17.

7.7.2 Jurisprudence

7.7.2.1 Modèle de base

Intitulé	(année de la décision),	[année du recueil]	volume	recueil	page,	référence précise	(indication géographique et/ou cour) (s'il y a lieu).
Oosthuizen v Stanley,		[1938]		AD	322		(S Afr SC).
Messina Associated Carriers v Kleinhaus,		[2001]	3	S Afr LR	868		(SCA).

➢ Faire référence aux **South African Law Reports** ou aux **Butterworths Constitutional Law Reports** autant que possible.

7.7.2.2 Référence neutre

➢ Certains tribunaux d'Afrique du Sud ont officiellement adopté un système de référence neutre. Suivre les règles de la référence neutre au Canada (section 3.5), à l'exception de l'année, qui est placée entre crochets.

[Année]	cour	numéro	paragraphe.
[2006]	ZACC	25	at para 1.

7.7.2.3 Recueil

Abréviations des principaux recueils :

All South African Law Reports	All SA
Butterworths Constitutional Law Reports	B Const LR
South African Law Reports, Appellate Division (1910-1946)	S Afr LR, AD
South African Law Reports (1947 à aujourd'hui)	S Afr LR

➢ Pour une liste complète des recueils, voir l'**annexe C**.

Sources étrangères

7.7.2.4 Tribunal

Abréviations des tribunaux :

Bophuthatswana High Court	Boph HC
Cape Provincial Division	Cape Prov Div
Ciskei High Court	Ciskei HC
Constitutional Court of South Africa	S Afr Const Ct
Durban and Coast Local Division	D&C Local Div
Eastern Cape Division	E Cape Div
Labour Court of South Africa	S Afr Labour Ct
Labour Court of Appeal of South Africa	S Afr Labour CA
Land Claims Court of South Africa	S Afr Land Claims Ct
Natal Provincial Division	Natal Prov Div
Northern Cape Division	N Cape Div
Orange Free State Provincial Division	OFS Prov Div
South-Eastern Cape Division	SE Cape Div
Supreme Court of Appeal of South Africa	S Afr SC
Transkei High Court	Transkei HC
Transvaal Provincial Division	Transv Prov Div
Witwatersrand Local Division	Wit Local Div
Venda High Court	Venda HC

7.7.3   Documents gouvernementaux

7.7.3.1 Débats

S Afr,	*Hansard,*	chambre,	date	référence précise	(orateur) (facultatif).
S Afr,	*Hansard,*	Assemblée nationale,	9 février 2009,	à la p 1	(MJ Ellis).

7.7.3.2 Rapports, documents de discussion et exposés

Titre,	commission (s'il y a lieu),	numéro de projet (s'il y a lieu)	(date)	référence précise.
Truth and Reconciliation Commission of South Africa Report			(29 octobre 1998)	au ch 1, para 91.
Report on Trafficking in Persons,	South African Law Reform Commission,	projet n° 131	(août 2008)	à la p 23.
Domestic Violence,	South African Law Reform Commission,	projet n° 100	(30 mai 1997)	à la p 14.

➤ Inclure le nom de la commission si elle n'est pas mentionnée dans le titre.

INDEX

APPENDICES

ANNEXES

TABLE OF CONTENTS / TABLE DES MATIÈRES

APPENDIX A / ANNEXE A

A. JURISDICTION ABBREVIATIONS ~ *ABRÉVIATIONS DE JURIDICTIONS*

(A-1) Abbreviations for Canada ~ *Abréviations canadiennes*

Jurisdiction	Statutes and Gazettes	Regulations	Courts and Journals	Neutral Citation	Law Reporters
Alberta *Alberta*	A	Alta	Alta	AB	A or Alta
British Columbia *Colombie-Britannique*	BC	BC	BC	BC	BC
Canada	C	C	C or Can	--	C or Can
Lower Canada *Bas-Canada*	LC	LC	LC	--	LC
Manitoba	M	Man	Man	MB	Man
New Brunswick *Nouveau-Brunswick*	NB	NB	NB	NB	NB
Newfoundland[1] *Terre-Neuve*[2]	N	Nfld	Nfld	NF	Nfld
Newfoundland & Labrador[3] *Terre-Neuve-et-Labrador*[4]	NL	NL	NL	NL (NF – before 19 March 2002 / avant le 19 mars 2002)	Nfld
Northwest Territories *Territoires du Nord-Ouest*	NWT	NWT	NWT	NWT	NWT
Nova Scotia *Nouvelle-Écosse*	NS	NS	NS	NS	NS
Nunavut	Nu	Nu	Nu	NU	Nu
Ontario	O	O	Ont	ON	O
Prince Edward Island *Île-du-Prince-Édouard*	PEI	PEI	PEI	PE	PEI
Province of Canada	Prov C	Prov C	Prov C	--	--
Quebec *Québec*	Q	Q	Q (Journals) or Qc (Courts)	QC	Q
Saskatchewan	S	S	Sask	SK	Sask
Upper Canada *Haut-Canada*	UC	UC	UC	--	UC
Yukon	Y	Y	Y	YK	Y

[1] *Gazette*: before 21 December 2001 / Regulations: before 13 December 2001 / Most other purposes including statutes: before 6 December 2001.
[2] *Gazette*: avant le 21 décembre 2001 / Règlements: avant le 13 décembre 2001 / Pour le reste (incluant les lois) : avant le 6 décembre 2001.
[3] *Gazette*: 21 December 2001 and after / Regulations: 13 December 2001 and after / Most other purposes including statutes: 6 December 2001 and after.
[4] *Gazette*: depuis le 21 décembre 2001 / Règlements : depuis le 13 décembre 2001 / Pour le reste (incluant les lois) : depuis le 6 décembre 2001.

Commonly used Canadian Province Abbreviations / *Abréviations des provinces canadiennes couramment utilisées:*

> The following is a list of commonly used Canadian province abbreviations. Use them when referring to provinces in documents that are not mentioned in the previous table (e.g. "F Allard et al, eds, *Private Law Dictionary of Obligations and Bilingual Lexicons*, (Cowansville, Que: Yvon Blais, 2003)").

> Voici une liste des abréviations des provinces canadiennes couramment utilisées. Utiliser cette liste pour faire référence à des documents qui ne sont pas mentionnés dans le tableau précédent (par ex. « Louis Beaudoin et Madeleine Mailhot, *Expressions juridiques en un clin d'œil*, Cowansville (Qc), Yvon Blais, 1997 »).

Province / Territory	Abbreviation
Alberta	Alta
British Columbia	BC
Manitoba	Man
New Brunswick	NB
Newfoundland and Labrador	NL
Northwest Territories	NWT
Nova Scotia	NS
Nunavut	--
Ontario	Ont
Prince Edward Islanc	PEI
Quebec	Que
Saskatchewan	Sask
Yukon	YT

Province / Territoire	Abréviation
Alberta	Alb
Colombie-Britannique	C-B
Manitoba	Man
Nouveau-Brunswick	N-B
Terre-Neuve-et-Labrador	T-N-L
Territoires du Nord-Ouest	TN-O
Nouvelle-Écosse	N-É
Nunavut	--
Ontario	Ont
Île-du-Prince-Édouard	Î-P-É
Québec	Qc
Saskatchewan	Sask
Yukon	Yn

(A-2) Abbreviations for the United States ~ *Abréviations américaines*

Alabama	Ala		Minnesota	Minn
Alaska	Alaska		Mississippi	Miss
Arizona	Ariz		Missouri	Mo
Arkansas	Ark		Montana	Mont
California	Cal		Nebraska	Neb
Californie	Cal		Nevada	Nev
Caroline du Nord	NC		New Hampshire	NH
Caroline du Sud	SC		New Jersey	NJ
Colorado	Colo		New Mexico	N Mex
Connecticut	Conn		New York	NY
Dakota du Nord	N Dak		North Carolina	NC
Dakota du Sud	S Dak		North Dakota	N Dak
Delaware	Del		Nouveau Mexique	N Mex
District de Colombie	DC		Ohio	Ohio
District of Colombia	DC		Oklahoma	Okla
États-Unis	É-U		Oregon	Or
Florida	Fla		Pennsylvania	Pa
Floride	Fla		Pennsylvanie	Pa
Georgia	Ga		Rhode Island	RI
Géorgie	Ga		South Carolina	SC
Hawaii	Hawaii		South Dakota	S Dak
Idaho	Idaho		Tennessee	Tenn
Illinois	Ill		Texas	Tex
Indiana	Ind		United States	US
Iowa	Iowa		Utah	Utah
Kansas	Kan		Vermont	Vt
Kentucky	Ky		Virginia	Va
Louisiana	La		Virginie	Va
Louisiane	La		Virginie occidentale	W Va
Maine	Me		Washington	Wash
Maryland	Md		West Virginia	W Va
Massachussetts	Mass		Wisconsin	Wis
Michigan	Mich		Wyoming	Wyo

(A-3) Abbreviations for Australia ~ *Abréviations australiennes*

Jurisdiction / *Indication géographique*	Legislation and Courts / *Législation et cours*	Neutral citation / *Référence neutre*
Australia	Austl	--
Commonwealth	Cth	--
Australian Capital Territory *Territoire de la capitale australienne*	ACT	--
New South Wales *Nouvelle-Galles du Sud*	NSW	NSW
Northern Territory *Territoire du Nord*	NT	NT
Queensland	Qld	Q
South Australia *Australie méridionale*	SA	SA
Tasmania *Tasmanie*	Tas	TAS
Victoria	Vic	V
Western Australia *Australie occidentale*	WA	WA

(A-4) Other Jurisdictional Abbreviations ~ *Abréviations d'autres juridictions*

Afrique du sud	Afr du sud		Nouvelle-Zélande	N-Z
Écosse	Écosse		Royaume-Uni	R-U
États-Unis	É-U		Scotland	Scot
European Union	EU		Singapore / *Singapour*	Sing
France	France		South Africa	S Afr
Ireland	I		Union européenne	UE
Irlande du nord	IN		United Kingdom	UK
New Zealand	NZ		United States	US
Northern Ireland	NI			

(A-5) Abbreviations of International Organizations ~ *Abréviations d'organismes internationaux*

Abbreviation / *Abréviation*	Organization / *Organisme*
AC	Assemblée consultative (Conseil de l'Europe)
AG	Assemblée générale (NU)
AIEA	Agence internationale de l'énergie atomique (NU)
AP	Assemblée parlementaire (Conseil de l'Europe)
APEC	Asia Pacific Economic Cooperation
AU	African Union
Bur	Bureau (NU)
C1	Première Commission (NU)
C2	Deuxième Commission (NU)
C3	Troisième Commission (NU)
CA	Consultative Assembly (Council of Europe)
CIJ	Cour internationale de Justice
CJ (1re inst)	Tribunal de première instance (CE)
CJE	Cour de justice des Communautés européennes
CCED	Conseil du commerce et du dévoloppement (NU)
CDH	Commission des droits de l'homme (NU)
CE	Communautés européennes
CES	Conseil économique et social (NU)
CNUCED	Conférence des Nations Unies sur le commerce et le développement
CNUDCI	Commission des Nations Unies pour le droit commercial international
Comm Eur DH	Commission européenne des Droits de l'Homme
Comm Interam DH	Commission interaméricaine des Droits de l'Homme
Conseil de l'Europe	Conseil de l'Europe
Council of Europe	Council of Europe
Cour Eur DH	Cour européenne des Droits de l'Homme
Cour Interam DH	Cour interaméricaine des Droits de l'Homme
CPJI	Cour permanente de justice internationale
CS	Conseil de sécurité (NU)
CT	Conseil de tutelle (NU)
EC	European Communities
ECFI	European Court of First Instance
ECJ	Court of Justice of the European Communities

ESC	Economic and Social Council (UN)
EU	European Union
Eur Comm HR	European Commission of Human Rights
Eur Ct HR	European Court of Human Rights
FMI	Fonds monétaire international (NU)
GA	General Assembly (GA)
GATT	Accord général sur les tarifs douaniers et le commerce General Agreement on Tariffs and Trade
GC	General Committee (UN)
HCDH	Haut-Commissariat aux droits de l'homme (NU)
HCR	Haut-Commissariat des Nations Unies pour les réfugiés
HRC	Human Rights Committee (UN)
IAEA	International Atomic Energy Agency (UN)
ICAO	International Civil Aviation Organization (NU)
ICJ	International Court of Justice
ICTR	International Criminal Tribunal for Rwanda (UN)
ICTY	International Criminal Tribunal for the Former Yugoslavia (UN)
ILO	International Labor Organization (UN)
IMF	International Monetary Fund (UN)
Inter-Am Comm HR	Inter-American Commission on Human Rights
Inter-Am Ct HR	Inter-American Court of Human Rights
NATO	North Atlantic Treaty Organization
NU	Nations Unies
NUCED	Conférence des Nations Unies sur le commerce et le développement
OACI	Organisation de l'aviation civile internationale (NU)
OAS	Organization of American States
OÉA	Organisation des États américains
OIT	Organisation internationale du Travail
OMC	Organisation mondiale du commerce
OMPI	Organisation mondiale de la propriété intellectuelle
OTAN	Organisation du Traité de l'Atlantique Nord
PA	Parliamentary Assembly (Council of Europe)
PCIJ	Permanent Court of International Justice
SC	Security Council
TC	Trusteeship Council
TDB	Trade and Development Board (UN)
TPIR	Tribunal pénal international pour le Rwanda (NU)

TPIY	Tribunal pénal international pour l'ex-Yougoslavie (NU)
UA	Union africaine
UE	Union européenne
UN	United Nations
OHCHR	United Nations High Commissioner for Human Rights, Office of the (UN)
UNHCR	United Nations High Commissioner for Refugees
UNCITRAL	United Nations Commission on International Trade Law
UNCTAD	United Nations Conference on Trade and Development
WBO	Banque mondiale World Bank Organization
WIPO	World Intellectual Property Organization
WTO	World Trade Organization

APPENDIX B / ANNEXE B

B. COURTS AND TRIBUNALS ~ *COURS ET TRIBUNAUX*

(B-1) General Rules ~ *Règles générales*

This appendix contains a list of abbrevations of courts and tribunals, both current and historical. Place the jurisdictional abbreviation before or after the court abbreviation according to the rules below.

➢ Identify a **court** unless it is obvious from the reporter (e.g. SCR). See section 3.9.

➢ Identify the **jurisdiction** unless it is obvious from the name of the court or the reporter (e.g. TAQ).

→ For English abbreviations, the abbreviation for the province, territory, or state normally precedes the abbreviation for the court (e.g. NBCA; Ont Gen Div; Qc Sup Ct).

→ For French abbreviations, provide the abbreviation for the province after the abbreviation of the court for Ontario, New Brunswick and Quebec (Div gén Ont; CAN-B; CS Qc), otherwise follow the English rule.

➢ Identify the **country** if the province, territory or state is unfamiliar to the majority of readers and is not found in this *Guide*. Generally, courts located in a province, territory or state are only identified using the abbreviation of that province, territory, or state. For example, it would be incorrect to write "NSWCA Austl" or "NSCA Can" because it is redundant.

→ Generally, federal, national, and unitary courts are identified by their country unless the country is obvious either from the reporter or from the abbreviation of the court itself. (The jurisdiction is obvious from the court's abbreviation when the name of the jurisdiction is contained in the abbreviation or when no other court shares the abbreviation.)

→ When citing from the Citizenship Appeals Court of Canada, the Court Martial Appeal Court, or the Exchequer Court of Canada, include the abbreviation Can (Cit AC Can). For any other Canadian federal court, the jurisdiction is obvious and Can should not be included.

→ In most cases, the jurisdiction of French courts is obvious from the court abbreviation and the abbreviation Fr should not be included.

→ The country abbreviation normally follows the court abbreviation (e.g. Dist Ct Sing, DCNZ), but there are exceptions, especially if the name of the jurisdiction is part of the name of the court (e.g. NZCA). For Singapore, include the abbreviation Sing unless the citation is to the ***Singapore Law Reports***.

→ In **court acronyms**, there is no space in an abbreviation consisting solely of upper case letters. Leave a space when an abbreviation consists of both upper case letters and lower case letters (e.g. BCCA; Ont Div Ct; NS Co Ct; Alta QB).

➤ Include the abbreviation of the **federal or provincial administrative agency or tribunal** in parentheses at the end of the citation if it is not evident from the title of the cited reporter (if an abbreviation cannot be found, use the full name). Use the abbreviation as it is provided by the administrative body. For further information, see section 3.13.

NB: In English, the abbreviation for Supreme Court of Canada is SCC, and the abbreviation for Superior Court is Sup Ct. In French, Cour suprême du Canada is abbreviated CSC and Cour supérieure is abbreviated CS. Also, note that the American abbreviations are Super Ct for Superior Court and Sup Ct for a state Supreme Court.

Cette annexe comprend une liste des abréviations des cours et des tribunaux, à la fois actuels et historiques. Mettre l'abréviation des indications géographiques avant ou après l'abréviation des cours en respectant les règles ci-dessous.

➤ Identifier **la cour**, à moins que le recueil n'indique l'information (par ex. RCS). Voir section 3.9.

➤ Identifier **la juridiction**, à moins que cette information ne puisse être déduite du nom de la cour ou du recueil (par ex. TAQ).

→ Pour les abréviations en anglais, l'abréviation de la province, du territoire ou de l'État précède normalement l'abréviation de la cour (par ex. NBCA ; Ont Gen Div ; Qc Sup Ct).

→ Pour les abréviations en français, fournir l'abréviation de la province après l'abréviation de la cour pour l'Ontario, le Nouveau-Brunswick et le Québec (Div gén Ont ; CAN-B ; CS Qc). Dans tous les autres cas, respecter la règle d'abréviation en anglais.

➤ Identifier **le pays** si l'abréviation de la province, du territoire ou de l'État risque de ne pas être connue des lecteurs ou n'est pas fournie dans ce *Manuel*. Généralement, les cours siégeant dans une province, un territoire ou un État sont déjà identifiées par l'abréviation de la province, du territoire ou de l'État. Par exemple, il serait redondant d'écrire « NSWCA Austl » ou « NSCA Can ».

→ Les cours fédérale, nationale et unitaire sont identifiées par le nom du pays, à moins que celui-ci ne puisse être déduit du recueil ou de l'abréviation de la cour.

→ Lorsqu'on renvoie à la Cour d'appel de citoyenneté, la Cour d'appel de la cour martiale du Canada, ou la Cour de l'Échiquier, il faut inclure l'abréviation Can (CA cit Can). Pour toute autre cour fédérale, l'indication géographique Can est évidente et ne doit pas être incluse.

→ Dans la plupart des cas, la juridiction des cours en français est évidente et l'abréviation Fr ne doit pas être incluse.

→ L'abréviation du pays suit l'abréviation de la cour (par ex. Dist Ct Sing ; DCNZ), excepté si le nom de la juridiction fait partie du nom de la cour (par ex. NZCA). Pour le Singapour, inclure l'abréviation Sing à moins que la référence ne provienne des ***Singapore Law Reports***.

➢ Pour les **acronymes des cours**, il n'y a pas d'espace entre les lettres majuscules des abréviations. Toutefois, il y a un espace quand l'abréviation est formée de minuscules et/ou de majuscules (par ex. CQ ; BCCA ; Div gén Ont ; CQ crim & pén).

➢ Indiquer l'abréviation de **l'organe ou du tribunal administratif** entre parenthèses à la fin de la référence, s'il est impossible de le déduire du titre du recueil (utiliser le nom au complet si aucune abréviation n'est trouvée). Utiliser l'abréviation utilisée par l'organe administratif. Pour plus d'informations, voir la section 3.13.

N.B. En anglais, l'abréviation de Supreme Court of Canada est SCC et l'abréviation des cours supérieures est Sup Ct. En français, ces abréviations sont inversées : Cour suprême du Canada devient CSC et Cour supérieure devient CS. De plus, noter que les abréviations américaines sont Super Ct pour Superior Court et Sup Ct pour la Cour suprême des États.

(B-2) Abbreviations ~ *Abréviations*

Court or Tribunal / *Cour ou tribunal*	Abbreviation / *Abréviation*
Frequent abbreviations / *Abréviations principales*	
Cour d'appel	CA
Court of Appeal	CA
Court of Justice	Ct J
Cour provinciale	CP
Cour supérieure	CS
Cour suprême du Canada	CSC
Federal Court of Appeal	FCA
High Court	HC
Provincial Court	Prov Ct
Superior Court	Sup Ct
Traffic Court	Traffic Ct
Youth Court	Youth Ct
Canadian Courts / *Cours canadiennes*	
Coroners Court	Cor Ct
Cour canadienne de l'impôt	CCI
Cour d'appel	CA
Cour d'appel fédérale	CAF
Cour de comté	Cc
Cour de l'Ontario, division générale	Div gén Ont
Cour des divorces et des causes matrimoniales	C div & causes mat
Cour des juges de la Cour de comté siégeant au criminel	C j Cc crim
Cour des petites créances	C pet cré
Cour des successions	C succ

Cour divisionnaire	C div
Cour du Banc de la Reine	BR
Cour du Banc de la Reine (Division de la famille)	BR (div fam)
Cour du Banc de la Reine (Division de première instance)	BR (1re inst)
Cour du Québec	CQ
Cour du Québec, Chambre de la jeunesse	CQ jeun
Cour du Québec, Chambre civile	CQ civ
Cour du Québec, Chambre civile (Division des petites créances)	CQ civ (div pet cré)
Cour du Québec, Chambre criminelle et pénale	CQ crim & pén
Cour fédérale, première instance	CF (1re inst)
Cour municipale	CM
Cour provinciale	CP
Cour provinciale (Division civile)	CP Div civ
Cour provinciale (Division criminelle)	CP Div crim
Cour provinciale (Division de la famille)	CP Div fam
Cour supérieure	CS
Cour supérieure (Chambre administrative)	CS adm
Cour supérieure (Chambre civile)	CS civ
Cour supérieure (Chambre criminelle et pénale)	CS crim & pén
Cour supérieure (Chambre de la famille)	CS fam
Cour supérieure (Division des petites créances)	CS pét cré
Cour supérieure (Chambre de la faillite et de l'insolvabilité)	CS fail & ins
Cour suprême (Division de la famille)	C supr fam
Cour suprême (Division d'appel)	C supr A
Cour suprême (Division du Banc de la Reine)	C supr BR
Cour suprême du Canada	CSC
Court Martial Appeal Court	Ct Martial App Ct
Cour d'appel de la cour martiale	CACM
Court of Appeal	CA
Court of Appeal in Equity	CA Eq
Court of Justice (General Division)	Ct J (Gen Div)
Court of Justice (General Division, Small Claims Court)	Ct J (Gen Div Sm Cl Ct)
Court of Justice (General Division, Family Court)	Ct J (Gen Div Fam Ct)
Court of Justice (Provincial Division)	Ct J (Prov Div)
Court of Justice (Provincial Division, Youth Court)	Ct J (Prov Div Youth Ct)
Court of Quebec	CQ
Court of Quebec (Civil Division)	CQ (Civ Div)
Court of Quebec (Civil Division, Small Claims)	CQ (Civ Div Sm Cl)
Court of Quebec (Criminal & Penal Division)	CQ (Crim & Pen Div)
Court of Quebec (Youth Division)	CQ (Youth Div)
Court of Queen's Bench	QB
Court of Queen's Bench (Family Division)	QB (Fam Div)
Court of Queen's Bench (Trial Division)	QB (TD)
Divisional Court	Div Ct

Divorce and Matrimonial Causes Court	Div & Mat Causes Ct
Federal Court of Appeal	FCA
Federal Court (Trial Division)	FCTD
High Court of Justice	H Ct J
Municipal Court	Mun Ct
Probate Court	Prob Ct
Provincial Court (Civil Division)	Prov Ct (Civ Div)
Provincial Court (Civil Division, Small Claims Court)	Prov Ct (Civ Div Sm Cl Ct)
Provincial Court (Criminal Division)	Prov Ct (Crim Div)
Provincial Court (Family Court)	Prov Ct (Fam Ct)
Provincial Court (Family Division)	Prov Ct (Fam Div)
Provincial Court (Juvenile Division)	Prov Ct (Juv Div)
Provincial Court (Small Claims Division)	Prov Ct (Sm Cl Div)
Provincial Court (Youth Court)	Prov Ct (Youth Ct)
Provincial Court (Youth Division)	Prov Ct (Youth Div)
Provincial Offences Court	Prov Off Ct
Small Claims Court	Sm Cl Ct
Superior Court (Canada)	Sup Ct
Superior Court (Administrative Division)	Sup Ct (Adm Div)
Superior Court (Bankruptcy and Insolvency Division)	Sup Ct (Bank & Ins Div)
Superior Court (Civil Division)	Sup Ct (Civ Div)
Superior Court (Criminal and Penal Division)	Sup Ct (Crim & Pen Div)
Superior Court (Family Division)	Sup Ct (Fam Div)
Superior Court (Small Claims Division)	Sup Ct (Sm Cl Div)
Supreme Court of Canada	SCC
Supreme Court (Appellate Division) (Can provincial / Can Provinciale)	SC (AD)
Supreme Court (Family Division)	SC (Fam Div)
Supreme Court (Queen's Bench Division)	SC (QB Div)
Supreme Court (Trial Division)	SC (TD)
Tax Court of Canada	TCC
Tax Review Board	T Rev B
Territorial Court	Terr Ct
Territorial Court (Youth Court)	Terr Ct Youth Ct

UK Courts / *Cours du Royaume-Uni*

Chancery Court	Ch
Court of Justice (Scotland / Écosse)	Ct Just
Court of Sessions (Scotland / Écosse)	Ct Sess
High Court of Admiralty	HC Adm
High Court of Justice	HCJ
High Court: Chancery Division (UK / R-U)	ChD
High Court: Family Division (UK / R-U)	FamD
High Court: Queen's Bench Division (UK / R-U)	QBD
House of Lords (England / Angleterre)	HL (Eng)

House of Lords (Scotland / Écosse)   HL (Scot)
Judicial Committee of the Privy Council (Commonwealth)   PC
Stipendiary Magistrates' Court   Stip Mag Ct

United States Courts / *Cours américaines*
Administrative Court   Admin Ct
Admiralty [Court, Division]   Adm
Alderman's Court   Alder Ct
Appeals Court   App Ct
Appellate Court   App Ct
Appellate Division   App Div
Bankruptcy Appellate Panel   BAP
Bankruptcy [Court, Judge]   Bankr
Board of Tax Appeals (US / É-U)   BTA
Borough Court   [name] Bor Ct
Chancery [Court, Division]   Ch
Children's Court   Child Ct
Circuit Court   Cir Ct
Circuit Court of Appeals (federal, US / *fédéral, É-U*)   Cir
Circuit Court of Appeals (state)   Cir Ct App
Circuit Court and Family Court   Cir Ct & Fam Ct
Citizenship Appeals Court (US / *É-U*)   Cit AC
City Court   [name] City Ct
City and Parish Courts   City & Parish Ct
Civil Appeals   Civ App
Civil Court   Civ Ct
Civil Court of Record   Civ Ct Rec
Civil District Court   Civ Dist Ct
Claims Court   Cl Ct
Commerce Court   Comm Ct
Common Pleas   CP
Commonwealth Court   Commw Ct
Conciliation Court   Concil Ct
Constitutional County Court   Const County Ct
County Court   Co Ct
County Court at Law   County Ct at Law
County Court Judges' Criminal Court   Co Ct J Crim Ct
County Judge's Court   County J Ct
County Recorder's Court   County Rec Ct
Court of Appeals (federal)   Cir
Court of Appeal [s] (state)   Ct App
Court of Chancery   Ct Ch
Court of Civil Appeals   Ct Civ App
Court of Claims   Ct Cl
Court of Common Pleas   Ct Com Pl

Court of Criminal Appeals	Ct Crim App
Court of Customs and Patent Appeals	CCPA
Court of Customs Appeals	Ct Cust App
Court of Errors	Ct Err
Court of Errors and Appeals	Ct Err & App
Court of Federal Claims	Ct Fed Cl
Court of First Instance	Ct First Inst
Court of [General, Special] Sessions	Ct [Gen, Spec] Sess
Court of International Trade	Ct Int'l Trade
Court of Review	Ct Rev
Court of Special Appeals	Ct Spec App
Court of Tax Review	Ct T Rev
Criminal Appeals	Crim App
Criminal District Court	Crim Dist Ct
Customs Court	Cust Ct
District Court (US Federal / É-U fédéral)	D
District Court (US states / États É-U)	Dist Ct
District Court of Appeal [s]	Dist Ct App
District Justice Court	Dist Just Ct
Domestic Relations Court	Dom Rel Ct
Emergency Court of Appeal [s]	Emer Ct App
Environmental Court	Env Ct
Equity [Court, Division]	Eq
Family Court	Fam Ct
General Sessions Court	Gen Sess Ct
High Court	High Ct
Housing Court	Housing Ct
Intermediate Court of Appeals	Intermed Ct App
Justice Court	J Ct
Justice of the Peace's Court	JP Ct
Juvenile Court	Juv Ct
Juvenile Delinquents' Court	Juv Del Ct
Juvenile and Family Court	Juv & Fam Ct
Land Court	Land Ct
Law Court	Law Ct
Magistrate Court	Magis Ct
Magistrate Division	Magis Div
Mayor's Court	Mayor's Ct
Municipal Court	[name] Mun Ct
Municipal Court not of Record	Mun Ct not Rec
Municipal Criminal Court of Record	Mun Crim Ct Rec
Orphans' Court	Orphans' Ct
Parish Court	[name] Parish Ct
Police Justice's Court	Police J Ct
Prerogative Court	Prerog Ct

Probate Court	Prob Ct
Recorder's Court	Rec Ct
Small Claims Court	Small Cl Ct
State Court	State Ct
Superior Court (US / *É-U*)	Super Ct
Supreme Court (federal)	US
Supreme Court (state, US / *État, É-U*)	Sup Ct
Supreme Court, Appellate Division (state, US / *État, É-U*)	Sup Ct App Div
Supreme Court of Appeals	Sup Ct App
Supreme Court of Errors	Sup Ct Err
Supreme Court of the United States	USSC
Supreme Judicial Court	Sup Jud Ct
Surrogate Court	Surr Ct
Tax Appeal Court	Tax App Ct
Tax Court	TC
Teen Court	Teen Ct
Town Court	Town Ct
Traffic Court	Traffic Ct
Tribal Court	[name] Tribal Ct
Unified Family Court	Unif Fam Ct
Water Court	Water Ct
Workers' Compensation Court	Workers' Comp Ct
Youth Court	Youth Ct

French Courts / *Cours françaises*

Conseil constitutionnel (France)	Cons const
Conseil d'État (France)	Cons d'État
Cour de cassation : Assemblée plénière (France)	Cass Ass plén
Cour de cassation : Chambre commerciale (France)	Cass com
Cour de cassation : Chambre criminelle (France)	Cass crim
Cour de cassation : Chambre des requêtes (France)	Cass req
Cour de cassation : Chambre mixte (France)	Cass Ch mixte
Cour de cassation : Chambre sociale (France)	Cass soc
Cour de cassation : Chambres réunies (France)	Cass Ch réun
Cour de cassation : Première chambre civile (France)	Cass civ 1re
Cour de cassation : Deuxième chambre civile (France)	Cass civ 2^{e}
Cour de cassation : Troisième chambre civile (France)	Cass civ 3^{e}
Cour de magistrat	C mag
Cour de révision	C rév
Haute Cour de justice	HCJ
Justice de Paix (before 1958 / *avant 1958*) (France)	JP

Australian & New Zealand Courts / *Cours d'Australie et de Nouvelle-Zélande*

District Court of New Zealand	DCNZ
Environment Court	Env Ct

Family Court	Fam Ct
Federal Court of Australia	FCA
High Court of Australia	HCA
Labour Court	Lab Ct
Magistrates' Court	Mag Ct
Magistrates' Court of New Zealand	Mag Ct NZ
New Zealand Court of Appeal	NZCA
New Zealand High Court	NZHC
New Zealand Employment Court	NZ Empl Ct
New Zealand Youth Court	NZYC

South Africa Courts / *Cours d'Afrique du Sud*

Constitutional Court of South Africa	S Afr Const Ct
Labour Court of South Africa	S Afr Labour Ct
Labour Court of Appeal of South Africa	S Afr Labour CA

(B-3) Neutral citation ~ *Référence neutre*

Below are the **dates of implementation** and the **abbreviations** of the neutral citation in Canadian courts. Before these dates, the neutral citation was not officially used and must not be cited for any given court.

Jurisdiction	Name of the court	Abbreviation	Implementation
Canada	Supreme Court of Canada	SCC	January 2000
	Federal Court	FC	February 2001
	Federal Court of Appeal	FCA	February 2001
	Tax Court of Canada	TCC	January 2003
	Court Martial Appeal Court of Canada	CMAC	October 2001
	Competition Tribunal of Canada	Comp Trib	January 2001
	Canadian Human Rights Tribunal	CHRT	January 2003
	Public Service Labour Relations Board	PSSRB	January 2000
Alberta	Court of Appeal	ABCA	January 1998
	Court of Queen's Bench	ABQB	January 1998
	Provincial Court	ABPC	January 1998
	Alberta Securities Commission	ABASC	June 2004
British Columbia	Court of Appeal	BCCA	January 1999
	Supreme Court of British Columbia	BCSC	January 2000
	Provincial Court of British Columbia	BCPC	February 1999
	British Columbia Human Rights Tribunal	BCHRT	January 2000
	British Columbia Securities Commission	BCSECCOM	January 2000
Manitoba	Court of Appeal	MBCA	March 2000
	Court of Queen's Bench of Manitoba	MBQB	April 2000
	Provincial Court of Manitoba	MBPC	January 2007
New Brunswick	Court of Appeal of New Brunswick	NBCA	May 2001
	Court of Queen's Bench of New Brunswick	NBQB	January 2002
	Provincial Court	NBPC	December 2002
Newfoundland and Labrador	Supreme Court of Newfoundland and Labrador, Court of Appeal	NFCA	January 2001
	Supreme Court of Newfoundland and Labrador, Trial Division	NLSCTD	July 2003
Northwest Territories	Court of Appeal for the Northwest Territories	NWTCA	December 1999
	Supreme Court of the Northwest Territories	NWTSC	October 1999
	Territorial Court of the Northwest Territories	NWTTC	October 1999
Nova Scotia	Nova Scotia Court of Appeal	NSCA	September 1999
	Supreme Court of Nova Scotia	NSSC	December 2000
	Supreme Court of Nova Scotia, Family Division	NSSF	January 2001
	Provincial Court of Nova Scotia	NSPC	March 2001
	Nova Scotia Utility and Review Board	NSUARB	January 1997
	Nova Scotia Barristers' Society Hearing Panel	NSBS	January 2004

Nunavut	Nunavut Court of Justice	NUCJ	January 2001
	Court of Appeal of Nunavut	NUCA	May 2006
Ontario	Ontario Court of Appeal	ONCA	January 2007
	Ontario Superior Court	ONSC	January 2010
	Ontario Court of Justice	ONCJ	January 2004
	Workplace Safety and Insurance Appeals Tribunal	ONWSIAT	January 2000
	Law Society Appeal Panel	ONLSAP	February 2004
	Law Society Hearing Panel	ONLSHP	January 2004
Prince Edward Island	Supreme Court, Appeal Division	PESCAD	January 2000
	Supreme Court, Trial Division	PESCTD	January 2000
Quebec	Court of Appeal of Québec	QCCA	January 2005
	Superior Court of Québec	QCCS	January 2006
	Court of Québec	QCCP	January 2006
	Tribunal des professions du Québec	QCTP	January 1999
	Conseil de la magistrature du Québec	CMQC	November 2000
	Commission des relations du travail	QCCRT	November 2002
Saskatchewan	Court of Appeal for Saskatchewan	SKCA	January 2000
	Court of Queen's Bench	SKQB	January 1999
	Provincial Court	SKPC	January 2002
	Automobile Injury Appeal Commission	SKAIA	July 2003
Yukon	Court of Appeal	YKCA	March 2000
	Supreme Court of the Yukon Territory	YKSC	March 2000
	Territorial Court of Yukon	YKTC	December 1999
	Small Claims Court	YKSM	May 2004
	Youth Court	YKYC	January 2001

Le tableau ci-dessous expose les **dates d'implémentation** et les **abréviations** de la référence neutre pour les cours canadiennes. Avant ces dates, la référence neutre n'était pas officiellement en vigueur et ne peut être citée pour une cour.

Juridiction	Nom de la cour	Abréviation	Implémentation
Canada	Cour suprême du Canada	CSC	janvier 2000
	Cour fédérale	CF	février 2001
	Cour d'appel fédérale	CAF	février 2001
	Cour canadienne de l'impôt	CCI	janvier 2003
	Cour d'appel de la cour martiale du Canada	CAMC	octobre 2001
	Tribunal de la concurrence du Canada	Trib conc	janvier 2001
	Tribunal canadien des droits de la personne	TCDP	janvier 2003
	Commission des relations de travail dans la fonction publique	PSSRB	janvier 2000

Alberta	Court of Appeal	ABCA	janvier 1998
	Court of Queen's Bench	ABQB	janvier 1998
	Provincial Court	ABPC	janvier 1998
	Alberta Securities Commission	ABASC	juin 2004
Colombie-Britannique	Court of Appeal	BCCA	janvier 1999
	Supreme Court of British Columbia	BCSC	janvier 2000
	Provincial Court of British Columbia	BCPC	février 1999
	British Columbia Human Rights Tribunal	BCHRT	janvier 2000
	British Columbia Securities Commission	BCSECCOM	janvier 2000
Île-du-Prince-Édouard	Supreme Court, Appeal Division	PESCAD	janvier 2000
	Supreme Court, Trial Division	PESCTD	janvier 2000
Manitoba	Cour d'appel	MBCA	mars 2000
	Cour du Banc de la Reine du Manitoba	MBQB	avril 2000
	Cour provinciale du Manitoba	MBPC	janvier 2007
Nouveau-Brunswick	Cour d'appel du Nouveau-Brunswick	NBCA	mai 2001
	Cour du banc de la Reine du Nouveau-Brunswick	NBQB	janvier 2002
	Cour provinciale	NBPC	décembre 2002
Nouvelle-Écosse	Nova Scotia Court of Appeal	NSSC	septembre 1999
	Supreme Court of Nova Scotia	NSPC	décembre 2000
	Supreme Court of Nova Scotia, Family Division	NSSF	janvier 2001
	Provincial Court of Nova Scotia	NSPC	mars 2001
	Nova Scotia Utility and Review Board	NSUARB	janvier 1997
	Nova Scotia Barristers' Society Hearing Panel	NSBS	janvier 2004
Nunavut	Cour de justice du Nunavut	NUCJ	janvier 2001
	Cour d'appel du Nunavut	NUCA	mai 2006
Ontario	Cour d'appel de l'Ontario	ONCA	janvier 2007
	Cour supérieure de l'Ontario	ONSC	janvier 2010
	Cour de justice de l'Ontario	ONCJ	janvier 2004
	Tribunal d'appel de la sécurité professionnelle et de l'assurance contre les accidents de travail	ONWSIAT	janvier 2000
	Comité d'appel du Barreau	ONLSAP	février 2004
	Comité d'audition du Barreau	ONLSHP	janvier 2004
Québec	Court of Appeal of Québec Cour d'appel du Québec	QCCA	janvier 2005
	Cour supérieure du Québec	QCCS	janvier 2006
	Cour du Québec	QCCP	janvier 2006
	Tribunal des professions du Québec	QCTP	janvier 1999
	Conseil de la magistrature du Québec	CMQC	novembre 2000
	Commission des relations du travail	QCCRT	novembre 2002

Saskatchewan	Court of Appeal for Saskatchewan	SKCA	janvier 2000
	Court of Queen's Bench	SKQB	janvier 1999
	Provincial Court	SKPC	janvier 2002
	Automobile Injury Appeal Commission	SKAIA	juillet 2003
Terre-Neuve-et-Labrador	Supreme Court of Newfoundland and Labrador, Court of Appeal	NFCA	janvier 2001
	Supreme Court of Newfoundland and Labrador, Trial Division	NLSCTD	juillet 2003
Territoires du Nord-Ouest	Cour d'appel des territoires du Nord-Ouest	NWTCA	décembre 1999
	Cour suprême des territoires du Nord-Ouest	NWTSC	octobre 1999
	Cour territoriale des territoires du Nord-Ouest	NWTTC	octobre 1999
Yukon	Cour d'appel	YKCA	mars 2000
	Cour suprême du territoire du Yukon	YKSC	mars 2000
	Cour territoriale du Yukon	YKTC	décembre 1999
	Cour des petites créances	YKSM	mai 2004
	Tribunal pour adolescents	YKYC	janvier 2001

APPENDIX C / ANNEXE C

C. CASELAW REPORTERS ~ RECUEILS DE JURISPRUDENCE

(C-1) Canadian Official reporters ~ *Recueils officiels canadiens*

Always cite to these reporters after the neutral citation (if available). Official reporters are published by the Queen's Printer. Whenever there is a discrepancy between two different versions of the same case, the version in the following reporters will be given precedence.

Only two reporters are still published today: the **Federal Court Reports** and the **Canada Supreme Court Reports**.

Ex CR	Canada Law Reports: Exchequer Court of Canada (1923-1970)
	Reports of the Exchequer Court of Canada (1875-1922)
FC	Federal Court Reports (1971 – present)
SCR	Canada Supreme Court Reports (1970 – present)
	Canada Law Reports: Supreme Court of Canada (1923-1969)
	Canada Supreme Court Reports (1876-1922)

Toujours faire référence aux recueils officiels après la référence neutre (si elle existe). Les recueils officiels sont publiés par l'Imprimeur de la Reine. En cas de disparité entre un recueil officiel et un autre recueil, la version du recueil officiel a préséance.

Seuls deux recueils sont toujours publiés de nos jours : les **Recueils des arrêts de la Cour fédérale du Canada** et les **Recueils des arrêts de la Cour suprême du Canada**.

CF	Recueils des arrêts de la Cour fédérale du Canada (1971 à aujourd'hui)
RC de l'É	Recueils des arrêts de la Cour de l'Échiquier (1875-1922)
	Rapports judiciaires du Canada : Cour de l'Échiquier (1923-1970)
RCS	Recueils des arrêts de la Cour suprême du Canada (1877-1922)
	Rapports judiciaires du Canada : Cour suprême (1923-1969)
	Recueils des arrêts de la Cour suprême du Canada (1970 à aujourd'hui)

(C-2) Canadian Semi-Official Reporters ~ *Recueils canadiens semi-officiels*

The following reporters are published under the auspices of the local Law Society. Always cite to these reporters before any other, except the SCR, FC, or Ex CR.

Les recueils suivants sont publiés sous l'égide du barreau de la province ou du territoire en question. Faire référence à ces recueils après les CF, les RC de l'É et les RCS.

Alta LR	Alberta Law Reports (only between 1908-1932 / seulement entre 1908-1932)
AR	Alberta Reports (1976 – present / 1976 à aujourd'hui)
BCR	British Columbia Reports (1867-1947)
BR	Recueils de jurisprudence du Québec : Cour du Banc de la Reine/du Roi (1942-1969) Rapports judiciaires officiels de Québec : Cour du Banc de la Reine/du Roi (1892-1941)
CA	Recueils de jurisprudence du Québec : Cour d'appel (1970-1985)
CBES	Recueils de jurisprudence du Québec : Cour du bien-être social (1975-1985)
CP	Recueils de jurisprudence du Québec : Cour provinciale (1975-1987)
CS	Recueils de jurisprudence du Québec: Cour supérieure (1967 – present / 1967 à aujourd'hui) Rapports judiciaires officiels de Québec : Cour supérieure (1892-1966)
CSP	Recueils de jurisprudence du Québec : Cour des Sessions de la paix (1975 – present / 1974 à aujourd'hui)
Man R	Manitoba Reports (1883-1961)
NBR	New Brunswick Reports (2d) (only since 1969 / seulement depuis 1969)
Nfld & PEIR	Newfoundland & Prince Edward Island Reports (1971 – present / 1971 à aujourd'hui)
NSR	Nova Scotia Reports (2d) (1969 – present / 1969 à aujourd'hui) Nova Scotia Reports (1965-1969) *NB: Not official from 1834-1929 / N.B. non officiel de 1834 à 1929*
NWTR	Northwest Territories Reports (1983-1998)
OLR	Ontario Law Reports (1900-1931)
OR	Ontario Reports (2d) (1973 – present / 1973 à aujourd'hui) Ontario Reports (1931-1973) *NB: Unofficial from 1882-1900 / N.B. non officiel de 1882 à 1900*
OWN	Ontario Weekly Notes (1909-1962)
RJQ	Recueils de jurisprudence du Québec (1975 – present / 1975 à aujourd'hui)
Sask LR	Saskatchewan Law Reports (1907-1931)

Terr LR	Territories Law Reports (1885-1907)
TJ	Recueils de jurisprudence du Québec : Tribunal de la jeunesse (1975 – present / 1975 à aujourd'hui)
YR	Yukon Reports (1986-1989)

(C-3) Other Reporters ~ *Autres recueils*

➢ For a more detailed list of Law Reports, consult the latest edition of *Bieber's Dictionary of Legal Abbreviations*.

➢ If an English reporter is reprinted in whole or in part in the *English Reports*, the applicable volume(s) are indicated.

➢ For the most part, selected reporters with recent jurisprudence have been included from all countries represented in this *Guide*, while selected reporters with both historical and recent jurisprudence have been included for Canada and the UK.

➢ French *Cahiers de droit* and yearbooks containing both doctrine and jurisprudence may be found in **Appendix D**.

➢ Because reporters may cover a large time period during which many names have existed for a jurisdiction, the jurisdiction listed in the jurisdiction column is always the most recent name for the jurisdiction covered by the reporter.

➢ This list only contains printed reporters. Decisions of many courts and administrative bodies are now available online. Follow the rules in Chapter 3 when citing decisions obtained online.

➢ Pour une liste plus détaillée des *Law Reports*, consulter la dernière édition du Prince, Bieber's Dictionary of Legal Abbreviations.

➢ Si un recueil anglais est reproduit entièrement ou en partie dans les *English Reports*, indiquer le volume approprié.

➢ La plupart des recueils de jurisprudence récents sont disponibles dans ce *Manuel*. Les recueils qui contiennent de la jurisprudence plus ancienne ne sont indiqués que pour le Canada et le Royaume-Uni.

➢ Pour les *Cahiers de droit* et les annuaires français de la doctrine et de la jurisprudence, voir l'**annexe D**.

➢ Puisque les recueils peuvent couvrir une longue période de temps durant laquelle le nom de la juridiction a pu changer, la liste ci-dessous représente le nom le plus récent de la juridiction.

➢ Seuls les recueils imprimés sont inclus dans cette liste. Les décisions de plusieurs cours et organes administratifs sont maintenant diponibles en ligne.

Abbreviation / Abréviation	Title of Reporter / *Titre du recueil*	Jurisdiction / *Indication géographique*	Dates
A	Atlantic Reporter	US / É-U	1855-1938
A (2d)	Atlantic Reporter, Second Series	US / É-U	1938-
A & N	Alcock and Napier's Reports	I	1831-1833
A Crim R	Australian Criminal Reports	Austl	1980-
Act	Acton's Prize Cases (ER vol 12)	US / É-U	1809-1811
A Int'l LC	American International Law Cases	US / É-U	1793-
ANWTYTR	Alberta, Northwest Territories & Yukon Tax Reporter	Can	1973-
AALR	Australian Argus Law Reports	Austl	1960-1973
AAR	Administrative Appeals Reports	Austl	1984-
AAS	Arbitrage – Santé et services sociaux	Can (QC)	1983-
ABC	Australian Bankruptcy Cases	Austl	1928-1964
ABD	Canada, Public Service Commission, Appeals and Investigation Branch, Appeal Board Decisions	Can	1979-1999
AC	Law Reports, Appeal Cases	UK / R-U	1890-
ACA	Australian Corporate Affairs Reporter	Austl	1971-1982
ACLC	Australian Company Law Cases	Austl	1971-
ACLP	Australian Company Law and Practice	Austl	1981-1991
ACLR	Australian Company Law Reports	Austl	1974-1989
ACLR	Australian Construction Law Reporter	Austl	1982-1997
ACSR	Australian Corporations and Securities Reports	Austl	1989-
ACTR	Australian Capital Territory Reports	Austl (ACT)	1973-
ACWS	All Canada Weekly Summaries	Can	1970-1979
ACWS (2d)	All Canada Weekly Summaries (Second Series)	Can	1980-1986
ACWS (3d)	All Canada Weekly Summaries (Third Series)	Can	1986-
AD	South African Law Reports, Appellate Division	S Afr du sud	1910-1946
Adam	Adam's Justiciary Cases	Scot	1893-1916
Add	Addams's Reports (ER vol 162)	UK / R-U	1822-1826
ADIL	Annual Digest and Reports of Public International Law Cases	Int'l	1919-1949
Admin LR	Administrative Law Reports	Can	1983-1991
Admin LR (2d)	Administrative Law Reports (Second Series)	Can	1992-1998
Admin LR (3d)	Administrative Law Reports (Third Series)	Can	1998-2003
Admin LR (4th)	Administrative Law Reports (Fourth Series)	Can	2003-
Ad & El	Adolphus & Ellis's Reports (ER vols 110-113)	US / É-U	1834-1842
ADR	Australian De Facto Relationships Law	Austl	1985-

AEBR	Australian Business & Assets Planning Reporter	Austl	1986-
AEBCN	Australian Business & Estate Planning Case Notes	Austl	1979-1981
AEUB	Alberta Energy and Utilities Board Decisions	Can (AB)	1995-
Afr LR (Comm)	African Law Reports: Commercial	Afr	1964-1980
Afr LR (Mal)	African Law Reports: Malawi Series	E Afr de l'est	1923-1972
Afr LR (SL)	African Law Reports: Sierra Leone Series	W Afr de l'ouest	1920-1936 1957-1960 1964-1966 1972-1973
AFTR	Australian Federal Tax Reporter	Austl	1969-
AILR	Australian Indigenous Law Reporter	Austl	1996-
A imm app	Affaires d'immigration en appel	Can	1967-1970
A imm app (ns)	Affaires d'immigration en appel (nouvelle série)	Can	1969-1977
AIN	Australian Industrial and Intellectual Property Cases	Austl	1982-
AJDA	Actualité juridique, droit administratif	France	1955-
AJDI	Actualité juridique, droit immobilier	France	1997-
AJDQ	Annuaire de jurisprudence et de doctrine du Québec	Can (QC)	1989-
AJPI	Actualité juridique, propriété immobilière	France	1955-1997
AJQ	Annuaire de jurisprudence du Québec	Can (QC)	1937-1988
Al	Aleyn's Select Cases (ER vol 82)	UK / R-U	1646-1649
Ala	Alabama Reports	US / É-U	1840-1946
Ala (NS)	Alabama Reports (New Series)	US / É-U	1846-1975
Alaska Fed	Alaska Federal Reports	US / É-U	1869-1937
Alaska R	Alaska Reports	US / É-U	1884-1958
ALD	Administrative Law Decisions	Austl	1976-
ALJR	Australian Law Journal Reports	Austl	1958-
All ER	All England Reports	UK / R-U	1936-
All ER (Comm)	All England Law Reports (Commercial Cases)	UK / R-U	1999-
All ER (EC)	All England Law Reports (European Cases)	UK / R-U	1995-
All ER Rep	All England Reports Reprints	UK / R-U	1558-1935
All ER Rep Ext	All England Reprints Extension Volumes	UK / R-U	1861-1935
ALLR	Australian Labour Law Reporter	Austl	1977-
ALMD	Australian Legal Monthly Digest	Austl	1967-
Alta BAA	Alberta Board of Arbitration, Arbitrations under the Alberta Labour Act	Can (AB)	1980-
Alta BAAA	Alberta Board of Adjudication, Adjudications and Arbitrations under the Public Service Employee Relations Act	Can (AB)	1980-1986

Alta BIR	Alberta Board of Industrial Relations Decisions	Can (AB)	1961-1982
Alta ERCB	Alberta Energy Resources Conservation Board (Decisions and Reports) *(formerly / anciennement Alberta Oil and Gas Conservation Board)*	Can (AB)	1971-
Alta HRCR	Alberta Human Rights Commission, Reports of Boards of Inquiry	Can (AB)	1972-1982
Alta LR	Alberta Law Reports	Can (AB)	1908-1933
Alta LR (2d)	Alberta Law Reports (Second Series)	Can (AB)	1976-1992
Alta LR (3d)	Alberta Law Reports (Third Series)	Can (AB)	1992-2002
Alta LR (4th)	Alberta Law Reports (Fourth Series)	Can (AB)	2002-2009
Alta LR (5th)	Alberta Law Reports (Fifth Series)	Can (AB)	2009-
Alta LRBD	Alberta Labour Relations Board Decisions	Can (AB)	1982-1986
Alta LRBR	Alberta Labour Relations Board Reports	Can (AB)	1986-
Alta OGCB	Alberta Oil and Gas Conservation Board Decisions *(formerly / anciennement Petroleum and Natural Gas Conservation Board of Alberta)*	Can (AB)	1957-1971
Alta PSERB	Alberta Public Service Employee Relations Board Decisions	Can (AB)	1981-1986
Alta PSGAB	Alberta Public Services Grievance Appeal Board Adjudications and Arbitrations	Can (AB)	1980-1985
Alta PUB	Alberta Public Utilities Board Decisions	Can (AB)	1976-
ALR	Administrative Law Reports in the British Journal of Administrative Law	UK / R-U	1954-1957
ALR	American Law Reports	US / É-U	1919-1948
ALR	Argus Law Reports	Austl	1895-1959
ALR	Australian Law Reports	Austl	1973-
ALR (2d)	American Law Reports (Second Series)	US / É-U	1948-1965
ALR (3d)	American Law Reports (Third Series)	US / É-U	1965-1980
ALR (4th)	American Law Reports (Fourth Series)	US / É-U	1980-1991
ALR (5th)	American Law Reports (Fifth Series)	US / É-U	1992-
Amb	Ambler's Reports, Chancery (ER vol 27)	UK / R-U	1716-1783
AMC	American Maritime Cases	US / É-U	1923-
And	Anderson's Common Law Conveyancing and Equity (ER vol 123)	UK / R-U	1534-1605
Andr	Andrews' Reports (ER vol 95)	UK / R-U	1738-1739
Ann Conv Eur DH	Annuaire de la Convention européenne des droits de l'Homme	EU / UE	1958-
Anst	Anstruther's Reports (ER vol 145)	UK / R-U	1792-1797
App Cas	Appeal Cases	UK / R-U	1875-1890
App Div	New York Appellate Division Reports	UK / R-U	1896-1956
App Div (2d)	New York Appellate Division Reports (Second Series)	US / É-U	1956-

APR	Atlantic Provinces Reports	Can	1975-
Arb Serv Rep	Arbitration Services Reporter	Can	1977-
Ariz	Arizona Reports	US / É-U	1866-
Ark	Arkansas Reports	US / É-U	1837-
Ark App	Arkansas Appellate Reports	US / É-U	1981-
Arn	Arnold's Reports	UK / R-U	1838-1839
Arn & H	Arnold and Hodges's Reports	UK / R-U	1840-1841
AR	Alberta Reports	Can (AB)	1976-
ASLC	Australian Securities Law Cases	Austl	1971-
ASC Sum	Alberta Securities Commission Summaries	Can (AB)	1975-
Asp MLC	Aspinall's Maritime Law Cases	UK / R-U	1870-1940
ATB	Canada Air Transport Board Decisions	Can	1944-1967
ATC	Australian Tax Cases	Austl	1969-
Atk	Atkyns's Reports, Chancery (ER vol 26)	UK / R-U	1736-1755
Av Cas	Aviation Cases	US / É-U	1822-
AWLD	Alberta Weekly Law Digest	Can (AB)	1982-
B & Ad	Barnewall & Adolphus's Reports, King's Bench (ER vols 109-110)	UK / R-U	1830-1834
B & Ald	Barnewall & Alderson's Reports, King's Bench (ER vol 106)	UK / R-U	1817-1822
B & CR	Reports of Bankruptcy and Companies Winding-Up Cases	UK / R-U	1918-1941
B & Cress	Barnewall & Cresswell's Reports, King's Bench (ER vols 107-109)	UK / R-U	1822-1830
B & S	Best & Smith's Reports (ER vols 121-122)	UK / R-U	1861-1865
BA	Book of Awards (Arbtration Court, Court of Appeal)	NZ / N-Z	1894-1991
Ball & B	Ball and Beatty's Reports	I	1807-1814
Barn C	Barnardiston's Chancery Reports (ER vol 27)	UK / R-U	1740-1741
Barn KB	Barnardiston's King's Bench Reports (ER vol 94)	UK / R-U	1726-1735
Barnes	Barnes's Notes (ER vol 94)	UK / R-U	1732-1760
Batt	Batty's Reports	I	1825-1826
BC Empl Standards Bd Dec	British Columbia Employment Standards Board Decisions	Can (BC)	1981-1983
BC En Comm'n Dec	British Columbia Energy Commission Decisions	Can (BC)	1977-1980
BCHRC Dec	British Columbia Human Rights Commission Decisions	Can (BC)	1975-1982
BCSCW Summ	British Columbia Securities Commission Weekly Summary	Can (BC)	1987-
BC Util Comm'n	British Columbia Utilities Commission Decisions	Can (BC)	1980-

BCAC	British Columbia Appeal Cases	Can (BC)	1991-
BCAVC	British Columbia, Director of Trade Practices, Assurances of voluntary compliance pursuant to section 15 of the Trade Practices Act (Decisions)	Can (BC)	1974-1978
BCD	Bulletin des contributions directes, de la taxe sur la valeur ajoutée et des impôts indirects	France	1961-1974
BCLR	British Columbia Law Reports	Can (BC)	1977-1986
BCLR (2d)	British Columbia Law Reports (Second Series)	Can (BC)	1986-1995
BCLR (3d)	British Columbia Law Reports (Third Series)	Can (BC)	1995-2001
BCLR (4th)	British Columbia Law Reports (Fourth Series)	Can (BC)	2002-
BCLRB Dec	British Columbia Labour Relations Board Decisions	Can (BC)	1979-
B Const LR	Butterworths Constitutional Law Reports	S Afr du sud	1994-
BCR	British Columbia Reports	Can (BC)	1867-1947
BCWCR	British Columbia Workers' Compensation Reporter	Can (BC)	1973-
BDM	Bulletin de droit municipal	Can (QC)	1994-
Bd Rwy Comm'rs Can	Board of Railway Commissioners for Canada – Judgments, Orders, Regulations and Rulings	Can	1911-1938
Bd Trans Comm'rs Can	Board of Transport Commissioners for Canada – Judgments, Orders, Regulations, and Rulings (formerly / anciennement Board of Railway Commissioners for Canada)	Can	1938-1967
Beat	Beatty's Reports	I	1813-1830
Beaubien	Beaubien	Can (QC)	1905-1906
Beav	Beavan's Reports (ER vols 48-55)	UK / R-U	1838-1866
Bel	Bellewe's Reports (ER vol 72)	UK / R-U	1378-1400
Bell	Bell's Reports (ER vol 169)	UK / R-U	1858-1860
Ben & D	Benloe & Dalison's Reports (ER vol 123)	UK / R-U	1486-1580
Benl	Benloe's Reports (ER vol 73)	UK / R-U	1531-1628
BILC	British International Law Cases	UK / R-U	1964-
Bing	Bingham's Reports (ER vols 130-131)	UK / R-U	1822-1834
Bing NC	Bingham's New Cases (ER vols 131-133)	UK / R-U	1834-1840
BISD	Basic Instruments and Selected Documents	GATT	1952-
Bla H	H Blackstone Reports	UK / R-U	1788-1796
Bla W	W Blackstone Reports	UK / R-U	1746-1779
BLE	Bulletin du libre-échange	Can	1990-1996
Bli	Bligh's Reports, House of Lords (ER vol 4)	UK / R-U	1819-1821
Bli NS	Bligh's Repors (New Series) (ER vols 4-6)	UK / R-U	1826-1837
BLR	Business Law Reports	Can	1977-1990
BLR (2d)	Business Law Reports (Second Series)	Can	1991-1999

BLR (3d)	Business Law Reports (Third Series)	Can	2000-2005
BLR (4th)	Business Law Reports (Fourth Series)	Can	2005-
Bos & Pul	Bosanquet & Puller's Reports (ER vols 126-127)	UK / R-U	1796-1804
Bos & Pul NR	Bosanquet & Puller's New Reports (ER vol 127)	UK / R-U	1804-1807
BR	Recueils de jurisprudence du Québec: Cour du Banc de la Reine / du Roi	Can (QC)	1892-1941
BR	Rapports judiciaires officiels de Québec : Cour du Banc de la Reine / du Roi	Can (QC)	1942-1969
BREF	Décisions du Bureau de révision de l'évaluation foncière	Can (QC)	1980-1998
Bridg	Sir John Bridgman's Reports	UK / R-U	1613-1621
Bridg Conv	Sir Orlando Bridgman's Conveyances	UK / R-U	1600-1667
Bridg J	Sir J Bridgman's Reports (ER vol 123)	UK / R-U	1613-1621
Bridg O	Sir O Bridgman's Reports (ER vol 124)	UK / R-U	1660-1667
Bro CC	Brown's Chancery Cases (by Belt) (ER vols 28-29)	UK / R-U	1778-1794
Bro PC	Brown's Parliamentary Cases (ER vols 1-3)	UK / R-U	1702-1800
Brod & Bing	Broderip & Bingham's Reports (ER vol 129)	UK / R-U	1819-1822
Brooke NC	Brooke's New Cases (ER vol 73)	UK / R-U	1515-1558
Brown & Lush	Browning & Lushington's Admiralty Reports (ER vol 167)	UK / R-U	1863-1865
Brownl	Brownlow & Goldesborough's Reports (ER vol 123)	UK / R-U	1569-1624
Bull CVMQ	Bulletin – Commission des valeurs mobilières du Québec	Can (QC)	1970?-
Bull civ	Bulletin des arrêts de la Cour de cassation, Chambres civiles	France	1798-
Bull Concl fisc	Bulletin des conclusions fiscales	France	1992-
Bull Crim	Bulletin des arrêts de la Cour de cassation, Chambre criminelle	France	1798-
Bull OSC	Bulletin of the Ontario Securities Commission	Can (ON)	1981-
Bulst	Bulstrode's Reports, King's Bench (ER vols 80-81)	UK / R-U	1609-1626
Bunb	Bunbury's Reports, Exchequer (ER vol 145)	UK / R-U	1713-1741
Burr	Burrow's Reports (ER vols 97-98)	UK / R-U	1756-1772
Burrell	Burrell's Reports (ER vol 167)	UK / R-U	1584-1839
C & J	Crompton & Jervis's Reports (ER vols 148-149)	UK / R-U	1830-1832
C & M	Crompton & Meeson's Reports (ER vol 149)	UK / R-U	1832-1834
C & S	Clarke and Scully's Drainage Cases	Can (ON)	1898-1903
CA	Recueils de jurisprudence du Québec : Cour d'appel	Can (QC)	1970-1985

CAC	Canada Citizenship Appeal Court, Reasons for Judgment	Can	1975-1977
CACM	Recueil des arrêts de la Cour d'appel des cours martiales du Canada	Can	1957-
CAEC	Commission d'appel des enregistrements commerciaux, Sommaires des décisions	Can (ON)	1971-?
CAI	Décisions de la Commission d'accès à l'information	Can (QC)	1984-
Cal	California Reports	US / É-U	1850-1934
Cal (2d)	California Reports (Second Series)	US / É-U	1934-1969
Cal (3d)	California Reports (Third Series)	US / É-U	1969-1991
Cal (4th)	California Reports (Fourth Series)	US / É-U	1991-
CALP	Décisions de la Commission d'appel en matière de lésions professionnelles	Can (QC)	1986-1998
CALR	Criminal Appeals Law Reporter	Can	1993-
Calth	Calthrop's Reports (ER vol 80)	UK / R-U	1609-1618
Cameron PC	Cameron's Constitutional Decisions of the Privy Council	Can	1867-1915
Cameron SC	Cameron's Supreme Court Cases	Can	1880-1900
Camp	Campbell's Reports (ER vols 170-171)	UK / R-U	1807-1816
Cape SCR	Supreme Court Reports (Cape)	S Afr du sud	1880-1910
CAQ	Causes en appel au Québec	Can (QC)	1986-1995
CAR	Commonwealth Arbitration Reports	Austl	1905-
Car & K	Carrington & Kirwan Reports (ER vols 174-175)	UK / R-U	1843-1853
Car & M	Carrington & Marshman Reports (ER vol 174)	UK / R-U	1840-1842
Car & P	Carrington & Payne (ER vols 171-173)	UK / R-U	1823-1841
Carey	Carey's Manitoba Reports	Can (MB)	1875
Cart BNA	Cartwright's Cases on the British North America Act, 1867	Can	1882-1897
Carter	Carter's Reports, Common Pleas (ER vol 124)	UK / R-U	1664-1676
Carth	Carthew's Reports, King's Bench (ER vol 90)	UK / R-U	1686-1701
Cary	Cary's Chancery Reports (ER vol 21)	UK / R-U	1557-1604
CAS	Décisions de la Commission des affaires sociales	Can (QC)	1975-1997
Cas t Hard	Cases temp Hardwicke (ER vol 95)	UK / R-U	1733-1738
Cas t Talb	Cases temp Talbot (ER vol 25)	UK / R-U	1733-1738
CB	Common Bench Reports (ER vols 135-139)	UK / R-U	1845-1856
CB (NS)	Common Bench Reports (New Series) (ER vols 140-144)	UK / R-U	1856-1866
CBES	Recueils de jurisprudence du Québec : Cour du bien-être social	Can (QC)	1975-1977

CBR	Copyright Board Reports	Can	1990-1994
CBR	Canadian Bankruptcy Reports	Can	1920-1960
CBR (NS)	Canadian Bankruptcy Reports (New Series)	Can	1960-1990
CBR (3d)	Canadian Bankruptcy Reports (Third Series)	Can	1991-1998
CBR (4th)	Canadian Bankruptcy Reports (Fourth Series)	Can	1998-2004
CBR (5th)	Canadian Bankruptcy Reports (Fifth Series)	Can	2004-
CCC	Cahiers du Conseil constitutionnel	France	1996-
CCC	Canadian Criminal Cases	Can	1898-1962
CCC (NS)	Canadian Criminal Cases (New Series)	Can	1963-1970
CCC (2d)	Canadian Criminal Cases (Second Series)	Can	1971-1983
CCC (3d)	Canadian Criminal Cases (Third Series)	Can	1983-
CCEL	Canadian Cases on Employment Law	Can	1983-1994
CCEL (2d)	Canadian Cases on Employment Law (Second Series)	Can	1994-2000
CCEL (3d)	Canadian Cases on Employment Law (Third Series)	Can	2000-
CCL	Canadian Current Law	Can	1948-1990
CCL	Canadian Current Law: Jurisprudence / sommaires de la jurisprudence	Can	1991
CCL	Canadian Current Law: Case Law Digests / sommaires de la jurisprudence	Can	1992-1996
CCL	Canadian Current Law: Case Digests / sommaires de la jurisprudence	Can	1996-
CCL Législation	Canadian Current Law: Annuaire de la législation	Can	1989-
CCL Legislation	Canadian Current Law: Legislation Annual	Can	1989-
CCLI	Canadian Cases on the Law of Insurance	Can	1983-1991
CCLI (2d)	Canadian Cases on the Law of Insurance (Second Series)	Can	1991-1998
CCLI (3d)	Canadian Cases on the Law of Insurance (Third Series)	Can	1998-
CCLR	Canadian Computer Law Reporter	Can	1983-1992
CCLS	Canadian Cases on the Law of Securities	Can	1993-1998
CCLT	Canadian Cases on the Law of Torts	Can	1976-1990
CCLT (2d)	Canadian Cases on the Law of Torts (Second Series)	Can	1990-2000
CCLT (3d)	Canadian Cases on the Law of Torts (Third Series)	Can	2000-
CCPB	Canadian Cases on Pensions and Benefits	Can	1994-
CCRI	Conseil canadien des relations industrielles, motifs de décision	Can	1999-

CCRTD	Conseil canadien des relations du travail, décisions	Can	1949-1974
CCRTDI	Conseil canadien des relations du travail, décisions et informations	Can	1974-1998
CCTCTD	Commission canadienne des transports, comité des télécommunications – décisions	Can	1973-1976
CCTCTEP	Commission canadienne des transports, comité des transports par eau – permis	Can	1976
CCTCTO	Commission canadienne des transports, comité des télécommunications – ordonnances	Can	1975-1976
CCTO	Commission canadienne des transports – ordonnances	Can	1972-1987
CDB-C	Collection de décisions du Bas-Canada	Can (QC)	1847-1891
CEB	Canadian Employment Benefits and Pension Guide Reports	Can	1995-
CEDH	Cour européenne des Droits de l'Homme	EU / UE	1960-
CEDH (Sér A)	Publications de la Cour européenne des Droits de l'Homme : Série A : Arrêts et décisions *(autre titre / other title: Recueil des arrêts et décisions de la Cour européenne des droits de l'homme)*	EU / UE	1960-1999
CEDH (Sér B)	Publications de la Cour européenne des Droits de l'Homme : Série B : Mémoires, plaidoiries et documents	EU / UE	1961-1999
CEGSB	Crown Employees Grievance Settlement Board Decisions	Can (ON)	1976-1997
CELR	Canadian Environmental Law Reports	Can	1978-1985
CELR (NS)	Canadian Environmental Law Reports	Can	1986-
CER	Canadian Customs and Excise Reports	Can	1980-1989
CFLC	Canadian Family Law Cases	Can	1959-1977
CFP	Recueil des décisions des comités d'appel de la fonction publique	Can (QC)	1980-1989
Ch	Law Reports, Chancery	UK / R-U	1891-
Ch App	Law Reports, Chancery Division	UK / R-U	1865-1874
Ch CR	Chancery Chambers Reports	Can (ON)	1857-1872
Ch Ca	Cases in Chancery (ER vol 22)	UK / R-U	1660-1698
Ch D	Law Reports, Chancery Division	UK / R-U	1875-1890
Ch R	Chancery Reports (ER vol 21)	UK / R-U	1625-1710
Chan Cas	Chancery Cases (ER vol 22)	UK / R-U	1615-1710
Chit	Chitty's Practice Reports, King's Bench	UK / R-U	1770-1822
Choyce Ca	Choyce Cases in Chancery (ER vol 21)	UK / R-U	1557-1606
CHRR	Canadian Human Rights Reporter	Can	1980-
CICB	Criminal Injuries Compensation Board Decisions	Can (ON)	1971-1989
CIJ Mémoires	Cour internationale de justice : Mémoires, plaidoiries et documents	Int'l	1946-

CIJ Rec	Cour internationale de justice : Recueil des arrêts, avis consultatifs et ordonnances	Int'l	1946-
CIPOO (M)	Commissaire à l'information et à la protection de la vie privée, Ontario, Orders, M Series	Can (ON)	1988-1998
CIPOO (P)	Commissaire à l'information et à la protection de la vie privée, Ontario, Orders, P Series	Can (ON)	1992-1998
CIPOS	Commissaire à l'information et à la protection de la vie privée, Ontario, Sommaires	Can (ON)	1990-1992
CIPR	Canadian Intellectual Property Reports	Can	1984-1990
CIRB	Canada Industrial Relations Board, Reasons for Decision	Can	1999-
CJCE	Recueil de la jurisprudence de la cour et du tribunal de première instance, Cour de justice des communautés européennes	EU / UE	1954-
Cl & F	Clark & Finnelly's Reports, House of Lords (ER vols 6-8)	UK / R-U	1831-1846
CLAS	Canadian Labour Arbitration Summaries	Can	1986-
CLASN	Criminal Law Aid Scheme News	Sing	
CLD	Commercial Law Digest	Can	1987-1990
CLL	Canadian Current Law: Canadian Legal Literature	Can	1991-
CLLC	Canadian Labour Law Cases	Can	1944-
CLLR	Canadian Labour Law Reporter	Can	1982-
CLP	Décisions de la Commission des lésions professionnelles	Can (QC)	1998-
CLR	Commonwealth Law Reports	Austl	1903-
CLR	Construction Law Reports	Can	1983-1992
CLR (2d)	Construction Law Reports (Second Series)	Can	1992-2000
CLR (3d)	Construction Law Reports (Third Series)	Can	2000-
CLRBD	Canada Labour Relations Board Decisions	Can	1949-1974
CLRBR	Canadian Labour Relations Board Reports	Can	1974-1982
CLRBR (NS)	Canadian Labour Relations Board Reports (New Series)	Can	1983-1989
CLRBR (2d)	Canadian Labour Relations Board Reports (Second Series)	Can	1989-
CM & R	Crompton, Meeson & Roscoe's Reports (ER vols 149-150)	UK / R-U	1834-1835
CMAR	Canada Court Martial Appeal Reports	Can	1957-
CMR	Common Market Law Reports	EU / UE	1962-1988
CMR	Common Market Reporter	EU / UE	1988-1997
CNLC	Canadian Native Law Cases	Can	1763-1978
CNLR	Canadian Native Law Reporter	Can	1979-
Coll	Collyer's Reports (ER vol 63)	UK / R-U	1844-1846

Colles	Colles's Reports, House of Lords (ER vol 1)	UK / R-U	1697-1713
COHSC	Canadian Occupational Health and Safety Cases	Can	1989-1993
Com	Comyns's Reports (ER vol 92)	UK / R-U	1695-1740
Comb	Comberbach's Reports (ER vol 90)	UK / R-U	1685-1699
Comm Eur DHDR	Décisions et rapports de la Commission européenne des Droits de l'Homme	EU / UE	1975-1999
Comm LR	Commercial Law Reports	Can	1903-1905
Comp Trib dec	Competition Tribunal, decisions	Can	1986-?
Conc Bd Rpts	Conciliation Board Reports	Can	1966-1974
Conc Comm'r Rpts	Conciliation Commissioner Reports	Can	1975
Cons sup N-F	Inventaire des jugements et délibérations du Conseil supérieur de la Nouvelle-France	Can / US	1717-1760
Cook Adm	Cook's Vice-Admiralty Reports	Can (QC)	1873-1874
Cooke CP	Cooke's Reports (Common Pleas) (ER vol 125)	UK / R-U	1706-1747
Coop Ch Ch	Cooper's Chancery Chambers Reports	Can (ON)	1866
Coop Pr Ca	Cooper's Practice Cases, Chancery (ER vol 47)	UK / R-U	1822-1838
Coop t Br	Cooper, temp Brougham's Reports, Chancery (ER vol 47)	UK / R-U	1833-1834
Coop t Cott	Cooper, temp Cottenham's Reports, Chancery (ER vol 47)	UK / R-U	1846-1848
Coop G	Cooper's Cases in Chancery (ER vol 35)	UK / R-U	1792-1815
Co Rep	Coke's Reports, King's Bench (ER vols 76-77)	UK / R-U	1572-1616
Cowp	Cowper's Reports (ER vol 98)	UK / R-U	1774-1778
Cox	Cox's Equity Reports (ER vols 29-30)	UK / R-U	1783-1796
CP	Recueils de jurisprudence du Québec : Cour provinciale	Can (QC)	1975-1985
CPC	Carswell's Practice Cases	Can	1976-1985
CPC (2d)	Carswell's Practice Cases (Second Series)	Can	1985-1992
CPC (3rd)	Carswell's Practice Cases (Third Series)	Can	1992-1997
CPC (4th)	Carswell's Practice Cases (Fourth Series)	Can	1997-2001
CPC (5th)	Carswell's Practice Cases (Fifth Series)	Can	2001-
CPC (Olmstead)	Canadian Constitutional Decisions of the Judicial Committee of the Privy Council (Olmstead)	Can	1873-1954
CPC (Plaxton)	Canadian Constitutional Decisions of the Judicial Committee of the Privy Council (Plaxton)	Can	1930-1939
CPD	Law Reports, Common Pleas Division	UK / R-U	1875-1880
CPDR	Cape Provincial Division Reports	S Afr du sud	1910-1946
CPJI (Sér A)	Publications de la Cour permanente de justice internationale: Série A: Recueil des arrêts	Int'l	1922-1930

CPJI (Sér B)	Publications de la Cour permamente de justice internationale : Série B : Recueil des avis consultatifs	Int'l	1922-1930
CPJI (Sér A/B)	Publications de la Cour permamente de justice internationale : Série A/B : Arrêts, ordonnances et avis consultatifs	Int'l	1931-1940
CPJI (Sér C)	Publications de la Cour permanente de justice internationale : Série C : Plaidoiries, exposés oraux et documents	Int'l	1922-1940
CPR	Canadian Patent Reporter	Can	1941-1971
CPR (2d)	Canadian Patent Reporter (Second Series)	Can	1971-1984
CPR (3d)	Canadian Patent Reporter (Third Series)	Can	1985-1999
CPR (4th)	Canadian Patent Reporter (Fourth Series)	Can	1999-
CPRB	Procurement Review Board of Canada, decisions	Can	1990-?
CPTA	Décisions de la Commission de protection du territoire agricole	Can (QC)	1984-1987
CR	Criminal Reports	Can	1946-1967
CR (3rd)	Criminal Reports (Third Series)	Can	1978-1991
CR (4th)	Criminal Reports (Fourth Series)	Can	1991-1996
CR (5th)	Criminal Reports (Fifth Series)	Can	1997-2002
CR (6th)	Criminal Reports (Sixth Series)	Can	2002-
CR (NS)	Criminal Reports (New Series)	Can	1967-1978
CRAC	Canadian Reports: Appeal Cases: appeals allowed or refused by the Judicial Committee of the Privy Council	Can	1828-1913
CRAT	Commercial Registration Appeal Tribunal – Summaries of Decisions	Can (ON)	1971-1979
CRC	Canadian Railway Cases	Can	1902-1939
CRD	Charter of Rights Decisions	Can	1982-
CRMPC	Commission de révision des marchés publics du Canada, décisions	Can	1990-?
CRNZ	Criminal Reports of New Zealand	NZ / N-Z	1983-
CRR	Canadian Rights Reporter	Can	1982-1991
CRR (2d)	Canadian Rights Reporter	Can	1991-
CRRBDI	Canada Labour Relations Board Decisions and Information	Can	1974-1998
CRT	Canadian Radio-Television and Telecommunications decisions and policy statements	Can	1975-1985
CRTC	Canadian Railway and Transport Cases	Can	1940-1966
CS	Recueils de jurisprudence du Québec : Cour supérieure	Can (QC)	1967-1985

CS	Rapports judiciaires officiels de Québec : Cour supérieure	Can (QC)	1892-1966
CSD	Canadian Sentencing Digest	Can	1980-1994
CSP	Recueils de jurisprudence du Québec : Cour des Sessions de la paix	Can (QC)	1975-1985
CT	Jurisprudence en droit du travail : Décisions des commissaires du travail	Can (QC)	1969-1981
CT Cases	Canadian Transport Cases	Can	1966-1977
CTAB	Canada Tax Appeal Board Cases	Can	1949-1966
CTAB (NS)	Canada Tax Appeal Board Cases (New Series)	Can	1967-1971
CTBR	Canada Tariff Board Reports	Can	1937-1988
CTC	Canada Tax Cases Annotated	Can	1917-1971
CTC (NS)	Canada Tax Cases (New Series)	Can	1972-
CTC	Canadian Transport cases	Can	1966-1977
CTCATC	Canadian Transport Commission, Air Transport Committee Decisions	Can	1967-1987
CTCDO	Canadian Transport Commission, Decisions and Orders Summary	Can	1970-1976
CTCMVTCD	Canadian Transport Commission, Motor Vehicle Transport Committee Decisions	Can	1973-1987
CTCMVTCO	Canadian Transport Commission, Motor Vehicle Transport Committee Orders	Can	1972-1987
CTCOA	Canadian Transport Commission, Orders (Air)	Can	1967-1987
CTCR	Canadian Transport Commission Reports	Can	1978-1986
CTCRCD	Canadian Transport Commission, Review Committee Decisions	Can	1971-1987
CTCRTC	Canadian Transport Commission Railway Transport Committee – Judgments, Orders, Regulations, and Rulings *(formerly / anciennement Board of Transport Commissioners for Canada)*	Can	1967-1987
CTCTCD	Canadian Transport Commission, Telecommunication Committee Decisions	Can	1973-1976
CTCTCO	Canadian Transport Commission, Telecommunication Committee Orders	Can	1975-1976
CTCWTCD	Canadian Transport Commission, Water Transport Committee, Decisions	Can	1972-1987
CTCWTCL	Canadian Transport Commission, Water Transport Committee, Licences	Can	1976
CTCWTCO	Canadian Transport Commission, Water Transport Committee, Orders	Can	1979-1987
CTR	Canadian Tax Reporter	Can	1972-
CTR	Cape Times Reports	S Afr du sud	1891-1910
CTR	Commission du tarif registre	Can	1981-1988
CTR	De Boo Commodity Tax Reports	Can	1987-1989

CTST	Canada Trade and Sales Tax Cases	Can	1989-1991
CTTT	Décisions du Commissaire du travail et du Tribunal du travail	Can (QC)	1982-1993
CTTTCRAA	Décisions du Commissaire du travail, du Tribunal du travail et de la Commission de reconnaissance des associations d'artistes	Can (QC)	1994-1997
Cun	Cunningham's Reports (ER vol 94)	UK / R-U	1734-1736
Curt	Curteis's Reports (ER vol 163)	UK / R-U	1834-1844
D	Recueil Dalloz	France	1945-1965
DA	Recueil analytique de jurisprudence et de législation (Dalloz)	France	1941-1944
Dan	Daniell's Reports (ER vol 159)	UK / R-U	1817-1820
Davis	Davis's Reports (Ireland) (ER vol 80)	I	1604-1612
DC	Recueil critique Dalloz	France	1941-1945
DCA	Canada, Commission de la fonction publique du Canada, décisions du comité d'appel	Can	1979-1999
DCA	Décisions de la cour d'appel / Queen's Bench Reports (Dorion)	Can (QC)	1880-1886
DCDRT	Décisions sur des conflits de droit dans les relations du travail	Can (QC)	1964-1970
DCL	Décisions de la Commission des loyers	Can (QC)	1975-1981
DCR	New Zealand District Court Reports	NZ / N-Z	1980-
DCRM	Commission de révision des marchés publics du Canada, décisions	Can	1990-?
DDCP	Décisions disciplinaires concernant les corporations professionnelles	Can (QC)	1974-
DDOP	Décisions disciplinaires concernant les ordres professionnels	Can (QC)	1995-
Dea & Sw	Deane & Swabey's Reports (ER vol 164)	UK / R-U	1855-1857
Dears	Dearsly's Crown Cases (ER vol 169)	UK / R-U	1852-1856
Dears & B	Dearsly and Bell's Crown Cases (ER vol 169)	UK / R-U	1856-1858
Déc B-C	Décisions des Tribunaux du Bas-Canada	Can (QC)	1851-1867
Déc trib Mont	Précis des décisions des tribunaux du district de Montréal	Can (QC)	1853-1854
De G & J	De Gex & Jones's Reports (ER vols 44-45)	UK / R-U	1857-1859
De G & Sm	De Gex & Smale's Reports (ER vols 63-64)	UK / R-U	1846-1849
De G F & J	De Gex, Fisher & Jones's Reports (ER vol 45)	UK / R-U	1859-1862
De G J & S	De Gex, Jones & Smith's Reports (ER vol 46)	UK / R-U	1863-1865
De G M & G	De Gex, Macnaghten & Gordon's Reports (ER vols 42-44)	UK / R-U	1851-1857
DELD	Dismissal and Employment Law Digest	Can	1986-
DELEA	Digest of Environmental Law and Environmental Assessment	Can	1992-

Den	Denison's Crown Cases (ER vols 1-2)	UK / R-U	1844-1852
Dés OAL	Décisions des orateurs de l'Assemblée législative de la province de Québec (Desjardins)	Can (QC)	1867-1901
DFQE	Droit fiscal québécois express	Can (QC)	1977-
DH	Recueil hebdomadaire Dalloz	France	1924-1940
Dick	Dickens's Reports (ER vol 21)	UK / R-U	1559-1798
DJC	Canadian Current Law : Documentation juridique au Canada	Can	1991-
DJG	Dalloz jurisprudence générale	France	1845-1923
DLQ	Droits et libertés au Québec	Can (QC)	1986-1987
DLR	Dominion Law Reports	Can	1912-1955
DLR (2d)	Dominion Law Reports (Second Series)	Can	1956-1968
DLR (3d)	Dominion Law Reports (Third Series)	Can	1969-1984
DLR (4th)	Dominion Law Reports (Fourth Series)	Can	1984-
DOAL	Décisions des orateurs, assemblé législative	Can (NB)	1923-1982
Dods	Dodson's Reports (ER vol 165)	UK / R-U	1811-1822
Donn	Donnelly's Reports (ER vol 47)	UK / R-U	1836-1837
Doug	Douglas's Reports (ER vol 99)	UK / R-U	1778-1785
Dow	Dow's Reports (ER vol 3)	UK / R-U	1812-1818
Dow & Cl	Dow & Clark's Reports (ER vol 6)	UK / R-U	1827-1832
Dowl & Ry	Dowling & Ryland's Reports (ER vol 171)	UK / R-U	1821-1827
DP	Recueil périodique et critique de jurisprudence (Dalloz)	France	1924-1940
Drap	Draper's King's Bench Reports	Can (ON)	1829-1831
Drew	Drewry's Reports (ER vols 61-62)	UK / R-U	1851-1859
Drew & Sm	Drewry & Smale's Reports (ER vol 62)	UK / R-U	1860-1865
DRL	Décisions de la Régie du logement	Can (QC)	1982-1993
DS / D	Recueil Dalloz et Sirey	France	1965-
DTC	Dominion Tax Cases	Can	1920-
DTE	Droit du travail Express	Can (QC)	1982-
Dy	Dyer's Reports, King's Bench (ER vol 73)	UK / R-U	1513-1582
E & A	Grant's Upper Canada Error and Appeals Reports	Can (ON)	1846-1866
E Afr CAR	Eastern Africa Court of Appeals Reports	Afr	1934-1956
E Afr LR	Eastern Africa Law Reports	Afr	1957-1967
East	East's Reports (ER vols 102-104)	UK / R-U	1800-1812
ECHR	European Court of Human Rights	EU / UE	1960-
ECHR (Ser A)	Publications of the European Court of Human Rights : Series A : Judgments and Decisions	EU / UE	1960-1999

ECHR (Ser B)	Publications of the European Court of Human Rights: Series B Pleadings, Oral Arguments and Documents	EU / UE	1961-1999
ECR	European Court Reports : Reports of Cases before the Court	EU / UE	1954-
Eden	Eden's Reports, Chancery (ER vol 28)	UK / R-U	1757-1766
Edw	Edwards's Admiralty Reports (ER vol 165)	UK / R-U	1808-1812
E Distr LDR	Eastern Districts' Local Division Reports	S Afr du sud	1911-1946
E Distr R	Eastern Districts' Reports	S Afr du sud	1880-1910
EHRR	European Human Rights Reports	EU / UE	1979-
El & Bl	Ellis & Blackburn's Reports (ER vols 118-120)	UK / R-U	1852-1858
El & El	Ellis & Ellis's Reports, King's Bench (ER vols 120-121)	UK / R-U	1858-1861
El Bl & El	Ellis, Blackburn & Ellis's Reports (ER vol 120)	UK / R-U	1858
ELLR	Employment and Labour Law Reporter	Can	1991-
ELR	Eastern Law Reporter	Can	1906-1915
ELR	Environmental Law Reporter of New South Wales	Austl	1981-
EMLR	Entertainment and Media Law Reports	UK / R-U	1993-
Eq Ca Abr	Equity Cases Abridged, Chancery (ER vols 21-22)	UK / R-U	1667-1744
ER	English Reports	UK / R-U	1210-1865
ERNZ	Employment Reports of New Zealand	NZ / N-Z	1991-
Esp	Espinasse's Reports	UK / R-U	1793-1807
ETR	Estates and Trusts Reports	Can	1977-1994
ETR (2d)	Estates and Trusts Reports (Second Series)	Can	1994-2003
ETR (3d)	Estates and Trusts Reports (Third Series)	Can	2003-
EULR	European Union Law Reporter	EU / UE	1997-
Eur Comm'n HRCD	Collection of Decisions of the European Commission of Human Rights	EU / UE	1960-1974
Eur Comm'n HRDR	European Commission of Human Rights: Decisions and Reports	EU / UE	1975-1999
Ex CR	Exchequer Court of Canada Reports	Can	1875-1922
Ex CR	Canada Law Reports : Exchequer Court	Can	1923-1970
Ex D	Law Reports, Exchequer Division	UK / R-U	1875-1890
Exch Rep	Exchequer Reports	UK / R-U	1847-1856
F	Federal Reporter	US / É-U	1880-1924
F (2d)	Federal Reporter (Second Series)	US / É-U	1925-1993
F (3d)	Federal Reporter, Third Series	US / É-U	1993-
F	Session Cases (Fifth Series) (Fraser)	Scot / Écosse	1898-1906
F & F	Foster and Finalson's Reports (ER vol 168)	UK / R-U	1856-1867

Fam	Law Reports, Family Division	UK / R-U	1972-
Fam LR	Family Law Reports	Austl	1975-
Farm Products App Trib Dec	Farm Products Appeal Tribunal Decisions	Can (ON)	1990-1996?
F Cas	Federal Cases	US / É-U	1789-1880
FCAD	Federal Court of Appeal Decisions	Can	1981-1999?
FLD	Family Law Digest	Can	1968-1982
FCR	Federal Court Reports	Can	1971-
FCR	Federal Court Reports	Austl	1984-
FLR	Federal Law Reports	Austl	1956-
FLRAC	Family Law Reform Act Cases	Can (ON)	1978-1985
FLRR	Family Law Reform Reporter	Can	1978-1987
Fitz-G	Fitz-Gibbons' Reports (ER vol 94)	UK / R-U	1727-1732
Foord	Foord's Reports	S Afr	1880
Forrest	Forrest's Reports (ER vol 145)	UK / R-U	1800-1801
Fort	Fortescue's Reports (ER vol 92)	UK / R-U	1695-1738
Fost	Foster's Reports (ER vol 168)	UK / R-U	1743-1761
Fox Pat C	Fox's Patent, Trade mark, Design and Copyright Cases	Can	1940-1971
FPR	Fisheries Pollution Reports	Can	1980?
F Supp	Federal Supplement	US / É-U	1933-1998
F Supp (2d)	Federal Supplement (Second Series)	US / É-U	1998-
FTLR	Financial Times Law Reports	UK / R-U	1981-
FTLR	Free Trade Law Reports	Can	1989-1991
FTR	Federal Trial Reports	Can	1986-
FTU	Free Trade Update	Can	1990-1996
Gaz LR	Gazette Law Reports	NZ / N-Z	1898-1952
Gaz Pal	Gazette du Palais	France	1886-
Ghana LR	Ghana Law Reports (West Africa)	W Afr	1959-1966 1971-1978
Giff	Giffard's Reports (ER vols 65-66)	UK / R-U	1858-1865
Gilb Cas	Gilbert's Cases in Law & Equity (ER vol 93)	UK / R-U	1713-1715
Gilb Rep	Gilbert's Reports, Chancery (ER vol 25)	UK / R-U	1705-1727
GLR	Gazette Law Reports	NZ / N-Z	1898-1953
Godbolt	Godbolt's Reports (ER vol 78)	UK / R-U	1575-1638
Gould	Gouldsborough's Reports (ER vol 75)	UK / R-U	1586-1602
Gow	Gow's Reports (ER vol 171)	UK / R-U	1818-1820
Gr / UC Ch	Grant's Upper Canada Chancery Reports	Can (ON)	1849-1882

Greg R	Gregorowski's Reports (Orange Free State)	S Afr du sud	1883-1887
Griq WR	Griqualand West Reports (Cape of Good Hope)	S Afr du sud	1882-1910
GSTR	Canadian Goods and Services Tax Reporter / Reports / Monitor	Can	1989-
GTC	Canadian GST & Commodity Tax Cases	Can	1993-
H & C	Hurlstone & Coltman's Reports (ER vols 158-159)	UK / R-U	1862-1866
H & M	Hemming & Miller's Reports (ER vol 71)	UK / R-U	1862-1865
H & N	Hurlstone & Norman's Reports (ER vols 156-158)	UK / R-U	1856-1862
H & Tw	Hall & Twells' Reports (ER vol 47)	UK / R-U	1849-1850
H & W	Haszard & Warburton's Reports	Can (PEI)	1850-1882
Hag Adm	Haggard's Admiralty Reports (ER vol 166)	UK / R-U	1822-1838
Hag Con	Haggard's Consistory Reports (ER vol 161)	UK / R-U	1752-1821
Hag Ecc	Haggard's Ecclesiastical Reports (ER vol 162)	UK / R-U	1827-1833
Hague Ct Rep	Hague Court Reports (1916)	Int'l	1899-1915
Hague Ct Rep (2d)	Hague Court Reports (Second Series) (1932)	Int'l	1916-1925
Hardr	Hardres' Reports (ER vol 145)	UK / R-U	1655-1669
Hare	Hare's Reports (ER vols 66-68)	UK / R-U	1841-1853
Harr & Hodg	Harrison and Hodgins Municipal Report	Can (ON)	1845-1851
Hay & M	Hay & Marriott's Reports (ER vol 165)	UK / R-U	1776-1779
Her Tr Nor	Heresy Trials in the Diocese of Norwich	UK / R-U	1428-1431
Het	Hetley's Reports (ER vol 124)	UK / R-U	1627-1632
HL Cas	Clark's House of Lords Cases (ER vols 9-11)	UK / R-U	1847-1866
HL Cas	House of Lords Cases	UK / R-U	1847-1866
Hob	Hobart's Reports (ER vol 80)	UK / R-U	1603-1625
Hodg	Hodgins Election Cases	Can (ON)	1871-1878
Hodges	Hodges' Reports	UK / R-U	1835-1837
Holt	Holt's Reports (ER vol 171)	UK / RU	1815-1817
Holt, Eq	Holt's Equity Reports (ER vol 71)	UK / R-U	1845
Holt, KB	Holt's King's Bench Cases (ER vol 90)	UK / R-U	1688-1711
Hut	Hutton's Reports (ER vol 123)	UK / R-U	1612-1639
IAA	Industrial Arbitration Awards	NZ / N-Z	1901-
IAR	Industrial Arbitration Reports	Austl (NSW)	1902-
IBDD	Instruments de base et documents divers	GATT	1952-
ICC	Indian Claims Commission Decisions	US / É-U	1948-1978
I Ch R	Irish Chancery Reports	I	1852-1867

ICJ Pleadings	International Court of Justice: Pleadings, Oral Arguments, Documents	Int'l	1946-
ICJ Rep	International Court of Justice: Reports of Judgments, Advisory Opinions and Orders	Int'l	1946-
ICLR	Irish Common Law Reports	I	1852-1867
ICR	Industrial Cases Reports	UK / R-U	1972-
ICR	Industrial Court Reports	UK / R-U	1972-1974
ICSID	International Centre for Settlement of Investment Disputes (World Bank)	Int'l	1966-
ILR	Canadian Insurance Law Reporter	Can	1951-
ILR	Insurance Law Reporter	Can	1934-1950
ILR	International Law Reports	Int'l	1950-
ILR	Irish Law Reports	I	1838-1850
ILRM	Irish Law Reports Monthly	I	1981-
ILTR	Irish Law Times Reports	I	1867-
IMA	Institute of Municipal Assessors of Ontario, Court Decisions	Can (ON)	1974-1986
Imm ABD	Immigration Appeal Board Decisions	Can	1977-1988
Imm AC	Immigration Appeal Cases	Can	1968-1970
Imm AC (2d)	Immigration Appeal Cases (Second Series)	Can	1969-1977
Imm LR	Immigration Law Reporter	Can	1985-1987
Imm LR (2d)	Immigration Law Reporter (Second Series)	Can	1987-1999
Imm LR (3d)	Immigration Law Reporter (Third Series)	Can	1999-
Inter-Am Ct HR (Ser A)	Series A Judgments and Opinions	Int'l	1982-
Inter-Am Ct HR (Ser B)	Series B: Pleadings, Oral Arguments and Documents	Int'l	1983-
Inter-Am Ct HR (Ser C)	Series C: Decisions and Judgments	Int'l	1987-
IR	Irish Law Reports	I	1892-
IR Eq	Irish Reports, Equity Series	I	1867-1878
IRCL	Irish Reports, Common Law Series	I	1867-1878
InfoCRTC	Broadcasting decisions, public notices and policy statements / Décisions, avis publics et énoncés de politique sur la radiodiffusion	Can	1995-1998
J & H	Johnson & Hemming's Reports (ER vol 70)	UK / R-U	1860-1862
Jac	Jacob's Reports (ER vol 37)	UK / R-U	1821-1822
Jac & W	Jacob & Walker's Reports (ER vol 37)	UK / R-U	1819-1821
JCA	Judgments Under the Competition Act	Can	1984-
JCAP	Judgments Under the Competition Act and its Predecessors	Can	1904-

J-cl Admin	Juris-classeur Administratif	France	
J-cl BC	Juris-classeur Banque et crédit	France	
J-cl Brev	Juris-classeur Brevets d'invention	France	
J-cl C-C	Juris-classeur Concurrence-consommation	France	
J-cl C-D	Juris-classeur Contrats-distribution	France	
J-cl Civ	Juris-classeur Civil	France	Publication
J-cl Civ Annexe	Juris-classeur Civil annexe	France	créée en
J-cl Coll terr	Juris-classeur Collectivités territoriales	France	1907
J-cl Com gén	Juris-classeur Commercial général	France	Mises à
J-cl Constr	Juris-classeur Construction	France	jour
J-cl Coprop	Juris-classeur Copropriété	France	trimestrielles
J-cl Div	Juris-classeur Divorce	France	
J-cl Dr comp	Juris-classeur Droit comparé	France	
J-cl Dr de l'enfant	Juris-classeur Droit de l'enfant	France	
J-cl Dr Intl	Juris-classeur Droit International	France	
J-cl Env	Juris-classeur Environnement	France	
J-cl Eur	Juris-classeur Europe	France	
J-cl F com	Juris-classeur Fonds de commerce	France	
J-cl Fisc	Juris-classeur Fiscal	France	
J-cl Fisc imm	Juris-classeur Fiscalité immobilière	France	
J-cl Fisc intl	Juris-classeur Fiscal international	France	
J-cl Foncier	Juris-classeur Foncier	France	
J-cl Impôt	Juris-classeur Impôt sur la fortune	France	
J-cl MDM	Juris-classeur Marques, dessins et modèles	France	
J-cl Not Form	Juris-classeur Notarial formulaire	France	
J-cl Pén	Juris-classeur Pénal	France	
J-cl Proc	Juris-classeur Procédure	France	Publication
J-cl Proc coll	Juris-classeur Procédures collectives	France	founded
J-cl Proc fisc	Juris-classeur Procédures fiscales	France	in 1907
J-cl Proc pén	Juris-classeur Procédure pénale	France	Quarterly
J-cl Prop litt art	Juris-classeur Propriété littéraire et artistique	France	updates
J-cl Rép prat Dr priv	Juris-classeur Répertoire pratique de droit privé	France	
J-cl Resp civ Ass	Juris-classeur Responsabilité civile et Assurances	France	
J-cl Séc Soc	Juris-classeur Sécurité sociale	France	
J-cl Sociétés	Juris-classeur Sociétés	France	

J-cl Trav	Juris-classeur Travail	France	
JCP	Semaine Juridique	France	1937-
JE	Jurisprudence Express	Can (QC)	1977-
Jenk	Jenkins's Reports (ER vol 145)	UK / R-U	1220-1623
JL	Jurisprudence logement : Recueil trimestriel de jurisprudence sur le bail d'habitation comprenant des décisions de la Régie du logement et des tribunaux judiciaires en matière de logement	Can (QC)	1993-
JL	Jurisprudence Logement	Can (QC)	1982-
JM	Décisions du juge des mines du Québec	Can (QC)	1967-1972
Johns	Johnson's Reports (ER vol 70)	UK / R-U	1859
Jones, T	Jones, T, Reports (ER vol 84)	UK / R-U	1667-1685
Jones, W	Jones W, Reports (ER vol 82)	UK / R-U	1620-1641
JSST	Jurisprudence en santé et sécurité du travail	Can (QC)	1983-1985
JSSTI	Jurisprudence en santé et sécurité du travail, décisions en matière d'inspection	Can (QC)	1981-1983
K & J	Kay & Johnson's Reports (ER vols 69-70)	UK / R-U	1854-1858
Kay	Kay's Reports (ER vol 69)	UK / R-U	1853-1854
KB	Law Reports, King's Bench	UK / R-U	1901-1951
Keble	Keble's Reports (ER vols 83-84)	UK / R-U	1661-1679
Keen	Keen's Reports (ER vol 48)	UK / R-U	1836-1838
Keilway	Keilway's Reports (ER vol 72)	UK / R-U	1496-1531
Kel J / Kel	Kelyng, Sir John's Reports (ER vol 84)	UK / R-U	1662-1669
Kel W	Kelynge, William's Reports (ER vol 25)	UK / R-U	1730-1732
Keny	Kenyon's Reports (ER vol 96)	UK / R-U	1753-1759
Kenya LR	Kenya Law Reports	Kenya	1897-1956
KLR	Kenya Law Reports	Afr	1897-1956
Kn	Knapp's Appeal Cases (ER vol 12)	UK / R-U	1829-1836
LAC	Labour Arbitration Cases	Can (ON)	1948-1972
LAC (2d)	Labour Arbitration Cases (Second Series)	Can (ON)	1973-1981
LAC (3d)	Labour Arbitration Cases (Third Series)	Can (ON)	1982-1989
LAC (4th)	Labour Arbitration Cases (Fourth Series)	Can (ON)	1989-
Lane	Lane's Reports (ER vol 145)	UK / R-U	1605-1611
Lap Sp Dec	Laperrier's Speakers' Decisions	Can	
LAR	Labor Arbitration Reports	US / É-U	1946-
Latch	Latch's Reports, King's Bench (ER vol 82)	UK / R-U	1625-1628
LC Jur	Lower Canada Jurist	Can (QC)	1847-1891
LCBD	Land Compensation Board Decisions	Can (ON)	1971-1983

LCR	Land Compensation Reports	Can	1969-
LCR	Lower Canada Reports	Can (QC)	1851-1867
Leach	Leach's Cases on Crown Law (ER vol 168)	UK / R-U	1730-1815
L Ed	United States Supreme Court, Lawyers' Edition	US / E-U	1790-1955
L Ed (2d)	United States Supreme Court, Lawyers' Edition (Second Series)	US / E-U	1956-1979
Lee	Lee's Ecclesiastical Reports (ER vol 161)	UK / R-U	1752-1758
Leo	Leonard's Reports (ER vol 74)	UK / R-U	1540-1615
Lev	Levinz's Reports (ER vol 83)	UK / R-U	1660-1697
Lewin	Lewin's Crown Cases on the Northern Circuit (ER vol 168)	UK / R-U	1822-1838
Le & Ca	Leigh & Cave's Reports (ER vol 169)	UK / R-U	1861-1865
Ley	Ley's Reports (ER vol 80)	UK / R-U	1608-1629
Lilly	Lilly's Assize Cases	UK / R-U	1688-1693
Lit	Littleton's Reports (ER vol 120)	UK / R-U	1626-1632
Ll LR	Lloyd's List Law Reports	UK / R-U	1919-1950
Lloyd's LR	Lloyd's Law Reports	UK / R-U	1968-
Lloyd's Rep	Lloyd's List Law Reports	UK / R-U	1951-1967
Lloyd's Rep Med	Lloyd's Law Reports (Medical)	UK / R-U	1998-
LN	Legal News	Can (QC)	1878-1897?
LR A & E	Law Reports, Admiralty and Ecclesiastical Cases (ER vols 1-4)	UK / R-U	1865-1875
LR A & E	Law Reports, Admiralty and Ecclesiastical Cases	UK / R-U	1865-1875
LR CCR	Law Reports, Crown Cases Reserved	UK / R-U	1865-1875
LR CP	Law Reports, Common Pleas	UK / R-U	1865-1875
LR Ch App	Law Reports, Chancery Appeals	UK / R-U	1865-1875
LR Eq	Law Reports, Equity Cases	UK / R-U	1865-1875
LR Ex	Law Reports, Exchequer	UK / R-U	1865-1875
LRHL	Law Reports, English and Irish Appeal Cases	I/ UK / R-U	1865-1875
LR Ir	Law Reports, Ireland	I	1878-1893
LR P & D	Law Reports, Probate and Divorce	UK / R-U	1865-1875
LR QB	Law Reports, Queen's Bench	UK / R-U	1865-1875
LR RP	Law Reports, Restrictive Practices	UK / R-U	1957-1972
LR Sc & Div	Scotch and Divorce Appeal Cases	UK / R-U	1866-1875
LRPC	Law Reports, Privy Council	UK / R-U	1865-1875
Lush	Lushington's Reports (ER vol 167)	UK / R-U	1859-1862
Lut	Lutwyche's Reports (ER vol 125)	UK / R-U	1682-1704
M & M	Moody & Malkin (ER vol 173)	UK / R-U	1826-1830

M & Rob	Moody & Robinson (ER vol 174)	UK / R-U	1831-1844
M & S	Maule & Selwyn's Reports (ER vol 105)	UK / R-U	1813-1817
M & W	Meeson & Welsby's Reports (ER vols 150-153)	UK / R-U	1836-1847
Mac & G	M'Naghten & Gordon's Reports (ER vols 41-42)	UK / R-U	1849-1851
Macl & R	Maclean & Robinson's Reports (ER vol 9)	UK / R-U	1839
MACMLC	Digest of the Selected Judgements of the Maori Appellate Court and Maori Land Court	NZ / N-Z	1858-1968
Madd	Maddock's Reports (ER vol 56)	UK / R-U	1815-1822
Man & G	Manning & Granger's Reports (ER vols 133-135)	UK / R-U	1840-1844
Man LR	Manitoba Law Reports (Queen's Bench)	Can (MB)	1884-1890
Man MTBD	Manitoba Motor Transport Board Decisions	Can (MB)	1985-
Man R	Manitoba Reports	Can (MB)	1883-1961
Man R (2d)	Manitoba Reports (Second Series)	Can (MB)	1979-
Man R temp Wood	Manitoba Reports temp Wood (ed Armour)	Can (MB)	1875-1883
Maori L Rev	Maori Law Review	NZ / N-Z	1993-
March, NR	March's New Cases (ER vol 82)	UK / R-U	1639-1642
MC	Malayan Cases	Sing	1939-?
MCC	Mining Commissioner's Cases	Can (ON)	1906-1979?
MCD	Magistrates' Court Decisions	NZ /N-Z	1939-1979
M'Cle	M'Cleland's Reports (ER vol 148)	UK / R-U	1824
M'Cle & Yo	M'Cleland & Younge's Reports (ER vol 148)	UK / R-U	1824-1825
MCR	Montreal Condensed Reports	Can (QC)	1853-1854
MCR	Précis des décisions des tribunaux du district de Montréal	Can (QC)	1853-1854
MCR	Magistrates' Court Reports	NZ / N-Z	1939-1979
Mer	Merivale's Reports (ER vols 35-36)	UK / R-U	1815-1817
MHRC Dec	Manitoba Human Rights Commission Decisions	Can (MB)	1971-1982
MLB Dec	Man toba Labour Board Decisions	Can (MB)	1985-
MLJ	Malayan Law Journal	Sing	1932-
MLR (KB)	Montreal Law Reports, King's Bench	Can (QC)	1885-1891
MLR (QB)	Montreal Law Reports, Queen's Bench	Can (QC)	1885-1891
MLR (SC)	Montreal Law Reports, Superior Court	Can (QC)	1885-1891
Mod	Modern Reports (ER vols 86-88)	UK / R-U	1669-1732
Mont Cond Rep	Montreal Condensed Reports	Can (QC)	1853-1854
Moo Ind App	Moore's Reports, Indian Appeals, Privy Council (ER vols 18-20)	UK / R-U	1836-1872
Moo KB	Moore's Reports, King's Bench (ER vol 72)	UK / R-U	1519-1621

Moo PC	Moore's Reports, Privy Council (ER vols 12-15)	UK / R-U	1836-1862
Moo PCNS	Moore's Reports, Privy Council, (New Series) (ER vols 15-17)	UK / R-U	1862-1873
Mood	Moody's Reports (ER vols 168-169)	UK / R-U	1824-1837
Mos	Mosely's Reports (ER vol 25)	UK / R-U	1726-1731
MPLR	Municipal and Planning Law Reports	Can	1976-1990
MPLR (2d)	Municipal and Planning Law Reports (Second Series)	Can	1991-
MPR	Maritime Provinces Reports	Can	1929-1968
MVR	Motor Vehicle Reports	Can	1979-1988
MVR (2d)	Motor Vehicle Reports (Second Series)	Can	1988-1994
MVR (3d)	Motor Vehicle Reports (Third Series)	Can	1994-2000
MVR (4th)	Motor Vehicle Reports (Fourth Series)	Can	2000-
My & Cr	Mylne & Craig's Reports (ER vols 40-41)	UK / R-U	1835-1840
My & K	Mylne & Keen's Reports (ER vols 39-40)	UK / R-U	1832-1835
NACD	Native Appeal Court Selected Decisions (Natal and Transvaal)	S Afr du sud	1930-1948
NACR	Native Appeal Court Reports	S Afr du sud	1951-
NB Eq	New Brunswick Equity Reports (Trueman)	Can (NB)	1894-1911
NB Eq Cas	New Brunswick Equity Cases (Trueman)	Can (NB)	1876-1893
NBESTD	New Brunswick Employment Standards Tribunal Decisions	Can (NB)	1986-
NBHRC Dec	New Brunswick Human Rights Commission Decisions	Can (NB)	1974-1982
NBLLC	New Brunswick Labour Law Cases	Can (NB)	1965-1979
NBPPABD	New Brunswick Provincial Planning Appeal Board Decisions	Can (NB)	1973-1983
NBR	New Brunswick Reports	Can (NB)	1825-1928
NBR (2d)	New Brunswick Reports (Second Series)	Can (NB)	1969-
NE	Northeastern Reporter	US / É-U	1885-1936
NE (2d)	Northeastern Reporter (Second Series)	US / É-U	1936-
NEBD	National Energy Board – Reasons for Decision	Can	1970-
Nels	Nelson's Reports, Chancery (ER vol 21)	UK / R-U	1625-1693
Nfld & PEIR	Newfoundland and Prince Edward Island Reports	Can (NF/PEI)	1971-
Nfld LR	Newfoundland Law Reports	Can (NF)	1817-1949
NHRC Dec	Newfoundland Human Rights Commission Decisions	Can (NF)	1971-1977
NI	Northern Ireland Law Reports	NI / IN	1925-
NLR	Nigeria Law Reports	Nigeria	1881-1955
NLR	Nyasaland Law Reports (Malawi)	Malawi	1922-1952

NLR (OS)	Natal Law Reports (Old Series)	S Afr du sud	1867-1872
NLR (NS)	Natal Law Reports (New Series)	S Afr du sud	1879-1932
Noy	Noy's Reports (ER vol 74)	UK / R-U	1559-1649
NPDR	Natal Provincial Division Reports	S Afr du sud	1933-1946
NR	National Reporter	Can	1973-
NSHRC Dec	Nova Scotia Human Rights Commissions Decisions	Can (NS)	1972-1980
NSBCPU Dec	Nova Scotia Board of Commissioners of Public Utilities Decisions	Can (NS)	1923-1973
NSCGA Dec	Nova Scotia Compendium of Grievance Arbitration Decisions	Can (NS)	1978-
NSR	Nova Scotia Reports	Can	1834-1929 1965-1969
NSR (2d)	Nova Scotia Reports (Second Series)	Can (NS)	1969-
NSRUD	Reported and Unreported Decisions	Can (NS)	1979-1984
NSWSCR	New South Wales Supreme Court Reports	Austl (NSW)	1862-1976
NSW St R	New South Wales State Reports	Austl (NSW)	1901-1970
NSWLR	New South Wales Law Reports	Austl (NSW)	1880-1900 1971-
NSWR	New South Wales Reports	Austl (NSW)	1960-1970
NSWWN	New South Wales Weekly Notes	Austl (NSW)	1884-1970
NTAD (Air)	National Transportation Agency Decisions (Air)	Can	1988-1992
NTAD (Rwy)	National Transportation Agency Decisions (Railway)	Can	1988-1991
NTAO (Air)	National Transportation Agency Orders (Air)	Can	1988-1992
NTAR	National Transportation Agency of Canada Reports	Can	1988-1995
NTJ	Northern Territory Judgments	Austl (NT)	1951-1976
NTLR	Northern Territory Law Reports	Austl (NT)	1992-
NTR	Northern Territory Reports	Austl (NT)	1978-
NW	Northwestern Reporter	US / É-U	1879-1942
NW (2d)	Northwestern Reporter (Second Series)	US / É-U	1942-
NWTR	Northwest Territories Reports	Can (NWT)	1983-1998
NWTSCR	Northwest Territories Supreme Court Reports	Can (NWT)	1889-1900
NY	New York Reports	US / É-U	1885-1955
NY (2d)	New York Reports (Second Series)	US / É-U	1956-
NYS (2d)	New York Supplement (Second Series)	US / É-U	1956-
NZHRC Dec	New Zealand Human Rights Commission Decisions	NZ / N-Z	1979-?
NZAC	Judgments of the Arbitration Court of New Zealand	NZ /N-Z	1979-1986

NZAR	New Zealand Administrative Reports	NZ / N-Z	1976-
NZBLC	New Zealand Business Law Cases	NZ / N-Z	1984-
NZFLR	New Zealand Family Law Reports	NZ / N-Z	1981-
NZILR	New Zealand Industral Law Reports	NZ / N-Z	1987-1990
NZIPR	New Zealand Intellectual Property Reports	NZ / N-Z	1967-1987
NZLR	New Zealand Law Reports	NZ / N-Z	1883-
NZPCC	New Zealand Privy Council Cases	NZ / N-Z	1840-1932
NZTC	New Zealand Tax Cases	NZ / N-Z	1973-
OAC	Ontario Appeal Cases	Can	1984-
OAR	Ontario Appeal Reports	Can (ON)	1876-1900
OELD	Ontario Environmental Law Digest	Can (ON)	1996-
OFLR	Ontario Family Law Reporter	Can (ON)	1987-
OHRCBI	Ontario Human Rights Commission – Board of Inquiry	Can (ON)	1963-1996
OHRC Dec	Ontario Human Rights Commission Decisions	Can (ON)	1956-1995?
OHRC Transcr	Ontario Human Rights Commission, Trancripts of Selected Hearings	Can (ON)	1968-1973
OIC Arb	Ontario Insurance Commission – Arbitration Cases	Can (ON)	1995-
Olmsted PC	Olmsted's Privy Council Decisions	Can	1867-1954
OLR	Ontario Law Reports	Can (ON)	1900-1931
OLRB Rep	Ontario Labour Relations Board Reports	Can (ON)	1944-
OMB Dec	Ontario Municipal Board Decisions	Can (ON)	1953-1994
OMB Index	Ontario Municipal Board Index to Applications Disposed of	Can (ON)	1969-1992
OMBEAB	Joint Board of the Ontario Municipal Board and the Environmental Assessment Board Decisions	Can (ON)	1984-
OMBR	Ontario Municipal Board Reports	Can (ON)	1973-
ONED	Office national de l'énergie, décisions	Can	1970-
Ont Building Code Comm'n Rulings	Ontario Building Code Commission Rulings	Can (ON)	1980-?
Ont CIP OM	Commissaire à l'information et à la protection de la vie privée de l'Ontario, ordonnances, série M	Can (ON)	1988-1998
Ont CIP OP	Commissaire à l'information et à la protection de la vie privée de l'Ontario, ordonnances, série P	Can (ON)	1989-1998
Ont CIP somm app	Commissaire à l'information et à la protection de la vie privée de l'Ontario, sommaires des appels	Can (ON)	1990-1992
ONTD (aérien)	Office national des transports du Canada décisions (transport aérien)	Can	1988-1992
ONTD (chemins de fer)	Office national des transports du Canada décisions (chemins de fer)	Can	1988-1991

Appendices / Annexes

Ont D Crim	Ontario Decisions – Criminal	Can (ON)	1997-1999
Ont D Crim Conv	Ontario Decisions – Criminal Convictions Cases	Can (ON)	1980-1996
Ont D Crim Sent	Ontario Decisions – Criminal Sentence Cases	Can (ON)	1984-1996
Ont Educ Rel Comm'n Grievance Arb	Ontario Education Relations Commission Grievance Arbitrations	Can (ON)	1970-1985
Ont Elec	Ontario Election Cases	Can (ON)	1884-1900
Ont En Bd Dec	Ontario Energy Board Decisions	Can (ON)	1961-
Ont Envtl Assessment Bd Dec	Ontario Environmental Assessment Board Decisions	Can (ON)	1980-
Ont Health Disciplines Bd Dec	Ontario Health Disciplines Board Decisions	Can (ON)	1980-
Ont IPC OM	Ontario Information and Privacy Commissioner, Orders, M Series	Can (ON)	1988-1998
Ont IPC OP	Ontario Information and Privacy Commissioner, Orders, P Series	Can (ON)	1989-1998
Ont IPC Sum App	Ontario Information and Privacy Commissioner, Summaries of Appeals	Can (ON)	1990-1992
Ont Lab-Mgmt Arb Comm'n Bull	Ontario Labour-Management Arbitration Commission Bulletin	Can (ON)	1978-1986
Ont Liquor Licence App Trib Dec	Ontario Liquor Licence Appeal Tribunal, Summaries of Decisions	Can (ON)	1977-1981
Ont Min Community & Soc Serv Rev Bd Dec	Ontario Ministry of Community and Social Services Review Board Decisions	Can (ON)	1974-1978
Ont Pol R	Ontario Police Reports	Can (ON)	1980-
OPR	Ontario Practice Reports	Can (ON)	1848-1901
OR	Ontario Reports	Can (ON)	1882-1900 1931-1973
OR (2d)	Ontario Reports (Second Series)	Can (ON)	1973-1990
OR (3d)	Ontario Reports (Third Series)	Can (ON)	1991-
Orange Free State Prov Div R	Orange Free State Provincial Division Reports	S Afr du sud	1910-1946
OSC Bull	Ontario Securities Commission Bulletin	Can (ON)	1949-
OSCWS	Ontario Securities Commission Weekly Summary	Can (ON)	1967-1980
OWCAT Dec	Ontario Workers' Compensation Appeals Tribunal Decisions	Can (ON)	1986-1989
Ow	Owen's Reports (ER vol 74)	UK / R-U	1556-1615
OWN	Ontario Weekly Notes	Can (ON)	1909-1962
OWR	Ontario Weekly Reporter	Can (ON)	1902-1916

P	Law Reports, Probate, Divorce, and Admiralty Division	UK / R-U	1891-1971
P	Pacific Reporter	US / É-U	1883-1931
P (2d)	Pacific Reporter (Second Series)	US / É-U	1931-2000
P (3d)	Pacific Reporter (Third Series)	US / É-U	2000-
P Wms	Peere Williams's Reports (ER vol 24)	UK / R-U	1695-1735
Palm	Palmer's Reports (ER vol 81)	UK / R-U	1619-1629
Park	Parker's Reports (ER vol 145)	UK / R-U	1743-1767
Patr Elec Cas	Patrick's Election Cases (Upper Canada / Canada West)	Can (ON)	1824-1849
PCIJ (Ser A)	Publications of the Permanent Court of International Justice: Series A, Collection of Judgments	EU / UE	1922-1930
PCIJ (Ser B)	Publications of the Permanent Court of International Justice: Series B, Collection of Advisory Opinions	EU / UE	1922-1930
PCIJ (Ser A/B)	Publications of the Permanent Court of International Justice: Series A/B, Judgments, Orders and Advisory Opinions	EU / UE	1931-1940
PCIJ (Ser C)	Publications of the Permanent Court of International Justice, Series C, Pleadings, Oral Statements and Documents	EU / UE	1922-1940
PD	Law Reports, Probate and Divorce	UK / R-U	1875-1890
Peake	Peake's Reports (ER vol 170)	UK / R-U	1790-1812
Peake Add Cas	Peake's Reports (Additional Cases) (ER vol 170)	UK / R-U	1790-1912
PEI	Prince Edward Island Supreme Court Reports	Can (PEI)	1850-1882
PER	Pay Equity Reports	Can (ON)	1990-
Per CS	Extraits ou précédents des arrêts tirés des registres du Conseil supérieur de Québec (Perrault)	Can (QC)	1727-1759
Perr P	Extraits ou précédents des arrêts tirés des registres de la prévosté de Québec	Can (QC)	1753-1854
Peters	Peters' Prince Edward Island Reports	Can (PEI)	1850-1872
PFP	Pandectes françaises périodiques	France	1791-1844
Ph	Phillips' Reports (ER vol 41)	UK / R-U	1841-1849
Phill Ecc	Phillimore's Reports (ER vol 161)	UK / R-U	1809-1821
Pl Com	Plowden's Commentaries (ER vol 75)	UK / R-U	1550-1580
PNGCB Alta	Petroleum and Natural Gas Conservation Board of Alberta	Can (AB)	1938-1957
Pollex	Pollexfen's Reports (ER vol 86)	UK / R-U	1669-1685
Pop	Popham's Reports (ER vol 79)	UK / R-U	1592-1627
PPR	Planning and Property Reports	Can (ON)	1960-1963
PPSAC	Personal Property Security Act Cases	Can	1977-1990

PPSAC (2d)	Personal Property Security Act Cases (Second Series)	Can	1991-2000
PPSAC (3d)	Personal Property Security Act Cases (Third Series)	Can	2001-
PRBC	Procurement Review Board of Canada Decisions	Can	1990-?
PRBR	Pension Review Board Reports	Can	1972-1986
Prec Ch	Precedents in Chancery (T Finch) (ER vol 24)	UK / R-U	1689-1722
Price	Price's Reports (ER vols 145-147)	UK / R-U	1814-1824
Pyke	Pyke's Reports	Can (QC)	1809-1810
QAC	Québec Appeal Cases	Can (QC)	1986-1995
QB	Queen's Bench Reports (ER vols 113-118)	UK / R-U	1841-1852
QBD	Law Reports, Queen's Bench Division	UK / R-U	1875-1890
Qc Comm dp déc	Québec Commission des droits de la personne, décisions des tribunaux	Can (QC)	1977-1981
Qld Lawyer Reps	Queensland Lawyer Reports	Austl (Qld)	1973-
QLR	Quebec Law Reports	Can (QC)	1875-1891
QPR	Québec Practice Reports	Can (QC)	1896-1944
QR	Queensland Reports	Austl (Qld)	1958-
Q St R	Queensland State Reports	Austl (Qld)	1902-1957
RAC	Ramsay, Appeal Cases	Can (QC)	1873-1886
RAT	Recueil d'arrêts sur les transports	Can	1966-1977
Raym Ld	Raymond, Lord Reports (ER vols 91-92)	UK / R-U	1694-1732
Raym T	Raymond, Sir T Reports (ER vol 83)	UK / R-U	1660-1684
RCCT	Recueil des décisions de la Commission canadienne des transports	Can	1978-1986
RCDA	Recueil des décisions de la Commission du droit d'auteur	Can	1990-1994
RCDA	Recueil de jurisprudence canadienne en droit des assurances	Can	1983-1991
RCDA (2e)	Recueil de jurisprudence canadienne en droit des assurances (deuxième série)	Can	1991-1998
RCDA (3e)	Recueil de jurisprudence canadienne en droit des assurances (troisième série)	Can	1998-
RCDE	Recueil de jurisprudence canadienne en droit de l'environnement	Can	1978-1985
RCDE (ns)	Recueil de jurisprudence canadienne en droit de l'environnement (nouvelle série)	Can	1986-
RC de l'É	Recueil des arrêts de la Cour de l'Échiquier	Can	1875-1922
RC de l'É	Rapports judiciaires du Canada : Cour de l'Échiquier	Can	1823-1970
RCDF	Recueil de jurisprudence canadienne en droit de la faillite		1920-1960

RCDF (2e)	Recueil de jurisprudence canadienne en droit de la faillite (deuxième série)	Can	1960-1990
RCDF (3e)	Recueil de jurisprudence canadienne en droit de la faillite (troisième série)	Can	1991-1998
RCDF (4e)	Recueil de jurisprudence canadienne en droit de la faillite (quatrième série)	Can	1998-
RCDSST	Recueil de jurisprudence canadienne en droit de la santé et de sécurité au travail	Can	1989-1993
RCDT	Recueil de jurisprudence canadienne en droit du travail	Can	1983-1994
RCDT (2e)	Recueil de jurisprudence canadienne en droit du travail (deuxième série)	Can	1994-2000
RCDT (3e)	Recueil de jurisprudence canadienne en droit du travail (troisième série)	Can	2000-
RCDVM	Recueil de jurisprudence canadienne en droit des valeurs mobilières	Can	1993-1998
RCE / Rec / Recueil Lebon	Recueil des arrêts du Conseil d'Etat statuant au contentieux et du Tribunal des conflits, des arrêts des cours administratives d'appel et des jugements des tribunaux administratifs *(nom le plus récent du recueil / most recent name of the reporter)*	France	1821-
RCF	Recueil des décisions des Cours fédérales	Can	1971-
RCRAS	Recueil de jurisprudence canadienne en matière de retraite et d'avantages sociaux	Can	1994-
RCRC	Recueil de jurisprudence canadienne en responsabilité civile	Can	1976-1990
RCRC (2e)	Recueil de jurisprudence canadienne en responsabilité civile (deuxième série)	Can	1990-2000
RCRC (3e)	Recueil de jurisprudence canadienne en responsabilité civile (troisième série)	Can	2000-
RCRP	Recueil des arrêts du Conseil de révision des pensions	Can	1972-1986
RCS	Rapports judiciaires du Canada : Cour suprême	Can	1923-1969
RCS	Recueils des arrêts de la Cour suprême du Canada	Can	1877-1922 1970-
RCTC	Rapports de la Commission de Tarif	Can	1937-1988
RDCC	Recueil des décisions du Conseil constitutionnel	France	1959-
RDCFQ	Recueil des décisions, Commission de la fonction publique et Comité d'appel de la fonction publique	Can (QC)	1990-
RDF	Recueil de droit de la famille	Can	1986-
RDFQ	Recueil de droit fiscal québécois	Can (QC)	1977-
RDI	Recueil de droit immobilier	Can (QC)	1986-
RDJ	Revue de droit judiciaire	Can (QC)	1983-1996
RDJC	Recueil de droit judiciaire de Carswell	Can	1976-1985

RDJC (2e)	Recueil de droit judiciaire de Carswell (deuxième série)	Can	1985-1992
RDJC (3e)	Recueil de droit judiciaire de Carswell (troisième série)	Can	1992-1997
RDJC (4e)	Recueil de droit judiciaire de Carswell (quatrième série)	Can	1997-2001
RDJC (5e)	Recueil de droit judiciaire de Carswell (cinquième série)	Can	2001-
RDP	Revue de droit pénal	Can (QC)	1978-1983
RDRTQ	Recueil des décisions, Régie des télécommunications du Québec	Can (QC)	1990-
RDT	Revue de droit du travail	Can (QC)	1963-1976
RECJ	Records of the Early Courts of Justice of Upper Canada	Can (ON)	1789-1984
Rép pén & proc pén	Encyclopédie juridique Dalloz : Répertoire de droit pénal et de procédure pénale	France	1951-
Rép admin	Encyclopédie juridique Dalloz : Répertoire de contentieux administratif	France	1951-
Rep Ch	Reports in Chancery (ER vol 21)	UK / R-U	1615-1710
Rép civ	Encyclopédie juridique Dalloz: Répertoire de droit civil	France	1951-
Rép com	Encyclopédie juridique Dalloz : Répertoire de droit commercial	France	1951-
Rép commun	Encyclopédie juridique Dalloz : Répertoire de droit communautaire	France	1957-
Rép proc civ	Encyclopédie juridique Dalloz : Répertoire de procédure civile	France	1951-
Rép soc	Encyclopédie juridique Dalloz : Répertoire des sociétés	France	1951-
Rep t Finch	Reports, temp Finch (Nelson's folio Reports) (ER vol 23)	UK / R-U	1673-1681
Rép tr	Encyclopédie juridique Dalloz: Répertoire de droit du travail	France	1951-
Rev serv arb	Revue des services d'arbitrage	Can	1977-
RFL	Reports of Family Law	Can	1971-1978
RFL (2d)	Reports of Family Law (Second Series)	Can	1978-1986
RFL (3d)	Reports of Family Law (Third Series)	Can	1986-1994
RFL (4th)	Reports of Family Law (Fourth Series)	Can	1994-2000
RFL (5th)	Reports of Family Law (Fifth Series)	Can	2000-
Rhod & NLR	Rhodesia & Nyasaland Law Reports	E Afr	1956-1963
Rhod LR	Rhodesian Law Reports	Zimb	1964-1979
Ridg t Hard	Ridgeway, temp Hardwicke's Reports (ER vol 27)	UK / R-U	1733-1745
RIAA	Report of International Arbitral Award	Int'l	1948-

Ritch Eq Rep	Ritchie's Equity Reports	Can (NS)	1873-1882
RJ imm	Recueil de jurisprudence en droit de l'immigration	Can	1985-1987
RJ imm (2e)	Recueil de jurisprudence en droit de l'immigration (deuxième série)	Can	1987-1999
RJ imm (2e)	Recueil de jurisprudence en droit de l'immigration (deuxième série)	Can	1999-
RJC	Revue de jurisprudence commerciale	France	1957-
RJC	Recueil de jurisprudence en droit criminel	Can	1946-1967
RJC (ns)	Recueil de jurisprudence en droit criminel (nouvelle série)	Can	1967-1978
RJC (3e)	Recueil de jurisprudence en droit criminel (troisième série)	Can	1978-1991
RJC (4e)	Recueil de jurisprudence en droit criminel (quatrième série)	Can	1991-1996
RJC (5e)	Recueil de jurisprudence en droit criminel (cinquième série)	Can	1997-
RJDA	Recueil de jurisprudence en droit des affaires	Can	1977-1990
RJDA (2e)	Recueil de jurisprudence en droit des affaires (deuxième série)	Can	1991-
RJDA (2e)	Recueil de jurisprudence en droit des affaires (deuxième série)	Can	1991-1999
RJDA (3e)	Recueil de jurisprudence en droit des affaires (troisième série)	Can	2000-
RJDC	Recueil de jurisprudence en droit de la construction	Can	1983-1992
RJDC (2e)	Recueil de jurisprudence en droit de la construction (deuxième série)	Can	1992-2000
RJDC (3e)	Recueil de jurisprudence en droit de la construction (troisième série)	Can	2000-
RJDI	Recueil de jurisprudence en droit immobilier	Can	1977-1989
RJDI (2e)	Recueil de jurisprudence en droit immobilier (deuxième série)	Can	1989-1996
RJDI (3e)	Recueil de jurisprudence en droit immobilier (troisième série)	Can	1996-
RJDM	Recueil de jurisprudence en droit municipal	Can	1976-1990
RJDM (2e)	Recueil de jurisprudence en droit municipal (deuxième série)	Can	1991-
RJDT	Recueil de jurisprudence en droit du travail	Can (QC)	1998-
RJF	Revue de jurisprudence fiscale (ancien titre / former title : Bulletin des contributions directes, de la taxe sur la valeur ajoutée et des impôts indirects)	France	1975-
RJF	Recueil de jurisprudence en droit de la famille	Can	1971-1978
RJF (2e)	Recueil de jurisprudence en droit de la famille (deuxième série)	Can	1978-1986

RJF (3e)	Recueil de jurisprudence en droit de la famille (troisième série)	Can	1986-1994
RJF (4e)	Recueil de jurisprudence en droit de la famille (quatrième série)	Can	1994-2000
RJF (5e)	Recueil de jurisprudence en droit de la famille (cinquième série)	Can	2000-
RJO (3e)	Recueil de jurisprudence de l'Ontario (troisième série) (1882-1991 : voir *Ontario Reports*)	Can (ON)	1991-
RJQ	Recueils de jurisprudence du Québec	Can (QC)	1875-1891 1975-
RJS	Revue de jurisprudence sociale	France	1989-
RL	Revue légale	Can (QC)	1869-1892
RL	Revue légale	Can (QC)	1943-
RL (ns)	Revue légale (nouvelle série)	Can (QC)	1895-1943
RNB (2d)	Recueil des arrêts du Nouveau Brunswick (deuxième série) (1825-1928 : voir *New Brunswick Reports*)	Can (NB)	1969-
Rob / Rob Chr	Robinson, C's Reports (ER vol 165)	UK / R-U	1798-1808
Rob Ecc	Robertson's Ecclesiastical Reports (ER vol 163)	UK / R-U	1844-1853
Rolle	Rolle's Reports (ER vol 81)	UK / R-U	1614-1625
RONTC	Recueil des décisions de l'office national des transports du Canada	Can	1988-
Roscoe	Roscoe's Reports	S Afr du sud	1861-1878
RPC	Reports of Patent Cases	UK / R-U	1884-1955
RPC	Reports of Patent, Design and Trademark Cases	UK / R-U	1957-
RPEI	Reports of cases determined in the Supreme Court, Court of Chancery and Court of Vice-Admiralty of Prince Edward Island	Can (PEI)	1850-1872
RPQ	Rapports de pratique de Québec	Can (QC)	1897-1982
RPR	Real Property Reports	Can	1977-1989
RPR (2d)	Real Property Reports (Second Series)	Can	1989-1996
RPR (3d)	Real Property Reports (Third Series)	Can	1996-
RPTA	Recueil en matière de protection du territoire agricole	Can (QC)	1990-
RR	Revised Reports	UK / R-U	1785-1865
RRA	Recueil en responsabilité et assurance	Can (QC)	1986-
RS	Recueil Sirey	France	1955?-1965
RSA	Recueil de sentences arbitrales	Can (QC)	1981-1983
RSE	Recueil des sentences de l'éducation	Can (QC)	1974-
RSF	Recueil de jurisprudence en droit des successions et des fiducies	Can	1977-1994

RSF (2e)	Recueil de jurisprudence en droit des successions et des fiducies (deuxième série)	Can	1994-
RSP	Recueil des ordonnances de la régie des services publics	Can (QC)	1973-1978
RTC	Décisions et énoncés de politique sur la radiodiffusion et les télécommunications canadiennes	Can	1975-1985
Russ	Russell's Reports (ER vol 38)	UK / R-U	1823-1829
Russ & M	Russell & Mylne's Reports (ER vol 39)	UK / R-U	1829-1831
Russ & Ry	Russell & Ryan's Crown Cases (ER vol 168)	UK / R-U	1799-1823
Russ ER	Russell's Election Reports	Can (NS)	1874
SAFP	Sentences arbitrales de la fonction publique	Can (QC)	1983-
S Afr LR	South African Law Reports	S Afr du sud	1947-
SAG	Sentences arbitrales de griefs	Can (QC)	1970-1981
Salk	Salkeld's Reports (ER vol 91)	UK / R-U	1689-1712
SALR	South Australia Law Reports	Austl	1865-
Sarbah	Sarbah's Fanti Law Reports	Ghana	1845-1903
SARB Dec	Social Assistance Review Board Selected Decisions	Can (ON)	1975-1986
SARB Sum	Social Assistance Review Board Summaries of Decisions	Can (ON)	1988-1994
Sask C Comp B	Saskatchewan Crimes Compensation Board, Awards	Can (SK)	1968-1992
Sask Human Rights Comm'n Dec	Saskatchewan Human Rights Commission Decisions	Can (SK)	1973-1981
Sask LR	Saskatchewan Law Reports	Can (SK)	1907-1931
Sask LRBD	Saskatchewan Labour Relations Board Decisions	Can (SK)	1945-1977
Sask LRBDC	Saskatchewan Labour Relations Board, Decisions and Court Cases	Can (SK)	1945-1964
Sask LRBR	Saskatchewan Labour Relations Board, Report of Meetings	Can (SK)	1967-1973
Sask R	Saskatchewan Reports	Can	1980-
Sask SC Bull	Saskatchewan Securities Commission Monthly Bulletin	Can (SK)	1984-
SASR	South Australia State Reports	Austl (SA)	1921-
Sav	Savile's Reports (ER vol 123)	UK / R-U	1580-1594
Say	Sayer's Reports (ER vol 96)	UK / R-U	1751-1756
SCC Cam	Canada Supreme Court Cases (Cameron) (Published / publié 1918)	Can	1887-1890
SCC Cam (2d)	Canada Supreme Court Reports (Cameron) (Published / publié 1925)	Can	1876-1922
SCC Coutl	Canada Supreme Court Cases (Coutlée)	Can	1875-1907

SCCB	Supreme Court of Canada Bulletin of Proceedings	Can	1970-
SCCD	Supreme Court of Canada Decisions	Can	1978-
SCCR	Supreme Court of Canada Reports Service	Can	1971-
Scot LR	Scottish Law Reporter	Scot / Écosse	1865-1924
SCR	Canada Law Reports: Supreme Court of Canada	Can	1923-1969
SCR	Canada Supreme Court Reports	Can	1877-1922 1970-
S Ct	Supreme Court Reporter	US / É-U	1882-
SE	South Eastern Reporter	US / É-U	1887-1939
SE (2d)	South Eastern Reporter (Second Series)	US / É-U	1939-1988
Searle	Searle's Reports	S Afr du sud	1850-1867
SEC Dec	Securities and Exchange Commission Decisions	US / É-U	1934-
Sel Ca t King	Select Cases, temp King (ER vol 25)	UK / R-U	1724-1733
Sem Jur	Semaine Juridique	France	1927-1936
Sess Cas	Session Cases	UK / R-U	1710-1748
Sess Cas	Session Cases	Scot / Écosse	1906-
Sess Cas S	Session Cases (Shaw & Balantine)	Scot / Écosse	1821-1838
Sess Cas D	Session Cases (Second Series) (Dunlop)	Scot / Écosse	1838-1862
Sess Cas F	Session Cases (Fifth Series) (Fraser)	Scot / Écosse	1898-1906
Sess Cas M	Sess on Cases (Third Series) (Macpherson)	Scot / Écosse	1862-1873
Sess Cas R	Session Cases (Fourth Series) (Rettie)	Scot / Écosse	1873-1898
Show KB	Shower's Reports, King's Bench (ER vol 89)	UK / R-U	1678-1695
Show PC	Shower's Reports, Privy Council (ER vol 1)	UK / R-U	1694-1699
Sid	Siderfin's Reports, King's Bench (ER vol 82)	UK / R-U	1657-1670
Sim	Simons's Reports (ER vols 57-60)	UK / R-U	1826-1852
Sim (NS)	Simons's New Reports (ER vol 61)	UK / R-U	1850-1852
Sim & St	Simons & Stuart's Reports (ER vol 57)	UK / R-U	1822-1826
SLLR	Sierra Leone Law Reports	W Afr	1960-1963
SLT	Scots Law Times	Scot / Écosse	1893-
SLR	Singapore Law Reports	Sing	1946-
SLR (R)	Singapore Law Reports (Reissue)	Sing	1965-2002
Skin	Skinner's Reports (ER vol 90)	UK / R-U	1681-1698
Sm & G	Smale & Giffard's Reports (ER vol 65)	UK / R-U	1852-1857
Sm & S	Smith and Sager's Drainage Cases	Can (ON)	1901-1913
SNB & B	Sarawak, North Borneo and Brunei Supreme Court Reports	Malay	1952-1963
So	Southern Reporter	US / É-U	1887-1941

So (2d)	Southern Reporter (Second Series)	US / É-U	1941-
SOLR	Sexual Offences Law Reporter	Can	1994-
Sp Ecc & Ad	Spinks's Ecclesiastical & Admiralty Reports (ER vol 164)	UK / R-U	1853-1855
Sp PC	Spinks' Prize Court Cases (ER vol 164)	UK / R-U	1854-1856
SRLA	Speakers' Rulings, Legislative Assembly	Can (NB)	1923-1982
SSC	Sarawak Supreme Court Reports	Malay	1928-1953
SSLR	Straits Settlements Law Reports	Sing	1893-1942
Stark	Starkie's Reports (ER vol 171)	UK / R-U	1814-1820
St-MSD	Saint-Maurice's Speakers' Decisions	Can (QC)	1868-1885
Str	Strange's Reports (ER vol 93)	UK / R-U	1716-1749
STR	Canadian Sales Tax Reporter	Can	1968-1989
Stu Adm	Stuart's Vice-Admiralty Reports (Lower Canada)	Can (QC)	1836-1874
Stu KB	Stuart's Reports (Lower Canada)	Can (QC)	1810-1835
Sty	Style's Reports (ER vol 82)	UK / R-U	1646-1655
Sudan LR	Sudan Law Reports	Sudan	1956-1971
SW	South Western Reporter	US / É-U	1979-
SW (2d)	South Western Reporter (Second Series)	US / É-U	1928-
Sw & Tr	Swabey & Tristram's Reports (ER vol 164)	UK / R-U	1858-1865
Swab	Swabey's Reports (ER vol 166)	UK / R-U	1855-1859
Swans	Swanston's Reports (ER vol 36)	UK / R-U	1818-1819
TA	Décisions du Tribunal d'arbitrage	Can (QC)	1982-1997
Talb	Talbot's Cases temp (ER vol 25)	UK / R-U	1733-1738
Taml	Tamlyn's Reports (ER vol 48)	UK / R-U	1829-1830
TAAT	Tribunal d'appel des accidents du travail	Can (ON)	1985-1997
TAQ	Décisions du Tribunal administratif du Québec	Can (QC)	1998-
Tas LR	Tasmanian Law Reports	Austl (Tas)	1896-1940
Tas R	Tasmania Reports	Austl (Tas)	1979-
Tas SR	Tasmania State Reports	Austl (Tas)	1941-1978
Taun	Taunton's Reports (ER vols 127-129)	UK / R-U	1807-1819
Tax ABC	Tax Appeal Board Cases	Can	1949-1966
Tax ABC (NS)	Tax Appeal Board Cases (New Series)	Can	1967-1972
TBR	Tariff Board Reports	Can	1937-1988
TBRD	Taxation Board of Review Decisions	Austl	1939-1949
TBRD (NS)	Taxation Board Review Decisions (New Series)	Austl	1950-1968
TCD	Tribunal de la Concurrence, décisions	Can	1986-
TCT	Canadian Trade and Commodity Tax Cases	Can	1989-1992

TE	Recueils de jurisprudence du tribunal de l'expropriation	Can (QC)	1972-1986
Terr LR	Territories Law Reports	Can (NWT)	1885-1907
TJ	Recueils de jurisprudence du Québec : Tribunal de la jeunesse	Can (QC)	1978-1985
TLLR	Tenant and Landlord Law Repors	Can (ON)	1983-1988
TLR	Times Law Reports	UK / R-U	1884-1952
TMR	Trademark Reporter	US / É-U	1911-
Toth	Tothill's Reports (ER vol 21)	UK / R-U	1559-1646
TPEI	Tucker's Select Cases of Prince Edward Island	Can (PEI)	1817-1828
TR	Term Reports (ER vols 99-101)	UK / R-U	1785-1800
Trib conc déc	Tribunal de la concurrence, décisions	Can	1986-?
TSPAAT	Tribunal d'appel de la sécurité professionnelle et de l'assurance contre les accidents du travail	Can (ON)	1998-
TTC	Hunter's Torrens Title Cases	Austl, Can, NZ N-Z, UK R-U	1865-1893
TTJ	Jurisprudence en droit du travail : Tribunal du travail	Can (QC)	1970-1981
TTR	Trade and Tariff Reports	Can	1990-1996
TTR (2d)	Trade and Tariff Reports (Second Series)	Can	1996-
Turn & R	Turner & Russell's Reports, Chancery (ER vol 37)	UK / R-U	1822-1824
UC Chamb Rep	Upper Canada Chambers Reports	Can (ON)	1846-1852
UCCP	Upper Canada Common Pleas Reports	Can (ON)	1850-1882
UCE & A	Upper Canada Error and Appeal Reports (Grant)	Can (ON)	1846-1866
UCKB	Upper Canada King's Bench Report (Old Series)	Can (ON)	1831-1844
UCQB	Upper Canada Queen's Bench Reports (New Series)	Can (ON)	1842-1882
UCQB (OS)	Upper Canada Queen's Bench Reports (Old Series)	Can (ON)	1831-1838
Uganda LR	Uganda Law Reports	E Afr	1904-1973
UIC Dec Ump	Unemployment Insurance Commission – Decisions of the Umpire	Can	1943-
UIC Selec Dec Ump	Unemployment Insurance Commission – Selected Decisions of the Umpire	Can	1943-1949
US	United States Reports	US / É-U	1754-
US App DC	United States Court of Appeals Reports	US / É-U	1941-
USLW	United States Law Week	US / É-U	1933-
Vaugh	Vaughan's Reports (ER vol 124)	UK / R-U	1665-1674
Vent	Ventris's Reports (ER vol 86)	UK / R-U	1666-1688

Vern	Vernon's Reports (ER vol 23)	UK / R-U	1680-1719
Ves & Bea	Vesey & Beames' Reports (ER vol 35)	UK / R-U	1812-1814
Ves Jr	Vesey Junior's Reports (ER vols 30-34)	UK / R-U	1789-1817
Ves Sr	Vesey Senior's Reports (ER vols 27-28)	UK / R-U	1746-1755
VLR	Victorian Law Reports	Austl (Vic)	1886-1956
VR	Victorian Reports	Austl (Vic)	1870-1872 1957-
WAC	Western Appeal Cases	Can	1991-
WALR	Western Australia Law Reports	Austl (WA)	1899-1959
WAR	Western Australia Reports	Austl (WA)	1960-1990
WAR (NS)	Western Australia Reports (New Series)	Austl (WA)	1990-
WCAT Dec	Workers' Compensation Appeal Tribunal Decisions	Can (NF)	1987-
WCATR	Workers Compensation Appeals Tribunal Reporter	Can (ON)	1986-1997
WCB	Weekly Criminal Bulletin	Can	1976-1986
WCB (2d)	Weekly Criminal Bulletin (Second Series)	Can	1986-
WDCP	Weekly Digest of Civil Procedure	Can	1985-1989
WDCP (2d)	Weekly Digest of Civil Procedure (Second Series)	Can	1990-1994
WDCP (3d)	Weekly Digest of Civil Procedure (Third Series)	Can	1994-
WDFL	Weekly Digest of Family Law	Can	1982-
Welsb H & G	Welsby, Hurlstone & Gordon's Exchequer Reports (ER vols 154-156)	UK / R-U	1847-1856
West, t Hard	West, temp Hardwicke Reports (ER vol 25)	UK / R-U	1736-1739
West	West's Reports (ER vol 9)	UK / R-U	1839-1841
West's Alaska	West's Alaska Digest	Can (AB)	1987-
Wight	Wightwick's Reports (ER vol 145)	UK / R-U	1810-1811
Will Woll & H	Willmore, Wollaston & Hodges's Reports	UK / R-U	1838-1839
Willes	Willes's Reports (ER vol 125)	UK / R-U	1737-1760
Wilm	Wilmot's Reports (ER vol 97)	UK / R-U	1757-1770
Wils Ch	Wilson's Reports, Chancery (ER vol 37)	UK / R-U	1818-1819
Wils Ex	Wilson's Reports, Exchequer (ER vol 159)	UK / R-U	1805-1817
Wils KB	Wilson's Reports, King's Bench (ER vol 95)	UK / R-U	1742-1774
Winch	Winch's Reports (ER vol 124)	UK / R-U	1621-1625
WLAC	Western Labour Arbitration Cases	Can	1966-1985
WLR	Weekly Law Reports	UK / R-U	1953-
WLR	Western Law Reporter	Can	1905-1917
WLRBD	Canadian Wartime Labour Relations Board Decisions	Can	1944-1948

WLTR	Western Law Times and Reports	Can	1890-1896
Wms Saund	Williams' & Saunders's Reports (ER vol 85)	UK / R-U	1666-1673
W Rob	W Robinson's Reports (ER vol 166)	UK / R-U	1838-1850
WSIATR	Workplace Safety and Insurance Appeals Tribunal Reporter	Can (ON)	1998-
W W & A'B	Wyatt, Webb & A'Beckett's Reports (Supreme Court of Victoria)	Austl	1866-1871
WWR	Western Weekly Reports	Can	1911-1950 1971-
WWR (NS)	Western Weekly Reports (New Series)	Can	1951-1970
YAD / Young Adm	Young's Admiralty Decisions	Can (NS)	1864-1880
Y & C Ex	Younge & Collyer's Reports (ER vol 160)	UK / R-U	1834-1842
Y & CCC	Younge & Collyer's Chancery Cases (ER vols 62-63)	UK / R-U	1841-1843
Y & J	Younge & Jervis's Reports (ER vol 148)	UK / R-U	1826-1830
YB Eur Conv HR	Yearbook of the European Convention on Human Rights	EU / UE	1955-
YR	Yukon Reports	Can	1986-1989
Yel	Yelverton's Reports (ER vol 80)	UK / R-U	1603-1613
You	Younge's Reports (ER vol 159)	UK / R-U	1830-1832

APPENDIX D / ANNEXE D

D. Periodicals and Yearbooks ~ *périodiques et annuaires*

Abbreviations ~ *Abréviations*

Name of Periodical or Yearbook / *Nom du périodique ou de l'annuaire*	Abbreviation / *Abréviation*
Across Borders	Across Borders
Acta Criminologica	Acta Crim
Actualités du droit	Actualités
Actualités juridiques, droit administratif	Actualités jur dr admin
Actualités-Justice	Actualités-Justice
Actualité et droit international	Actualité & dr int
Actualités de la délégation pour l'Union Européenne	Actualités dél UE
Actualités d'Unidroit	Actualités d'Unidroit
Adelaide Law Review	Adel LR
Adelphia Law Journal	Adelphia LJ
Administrative & Regulatory Law News	Admin & Reg L News
Administrative Law Journal of the American University (*formerly / anciennement Administrative Law Journal*)	Admin LJ Am U
Administrative Law Review	Admin L Rev
Advocate	Advocate
Advocate (Idaho)	Advocate (Idaho)
Advocates' Quarterly	Advocates' Q
Advocates' Society Journal	Advocates' Soc J
African-American Law and Policy Report	Afr-Am L & Pol'y Rep
Air Force Law Review	AFL Rev
Air & Space Law	Air & Space L
Air & Space Lawyer	Air & Space Law
Akron Law Review	Akron L Rev
Akron Tax Journal	Akron Tax J
Alabama Law Review	Ala L Rev
Alaska Law Review	Alaska L Rev
Albany Law Environmental Outlook	Alb L Envtl Outlook
Albany Law Journal of Science & Technology	Alb LJ Sci & Tech
Albany Law Review	Alb L Rev
Alberta Law Quarterly	Alta L Q

Alberta Law Review	Alta L Rev
Alternatives Journal	Alt J
American Association of Law Libraries Spectrum	AALL Spec
American Bankruptcy Institute Journal	Am Bankr Inst J
American Bankruptcy Institute Law Review	Am Bankr Inst L Rev
American Bankruptcy Law Journal	Am Bank LJ
American Bar Association Antitrust Law Journal	ABA Antitrust LJ
American Bar Association Criminal Justice	ABA Criminal J
American Bar Association Entertainment & Sports Lawyer	ABA Ent & Sports Law
American Bar Association Family Advocate	ABA Fam Advocate
American Bar Association Family Law Quarterly	ABAFam LQ
American Bar Association Journal	ABA J
American Bar Association Law Practice Management	ABAPM
American Bar Association Section of Intellectual Property Law	ABAIPL
American Bar Association Tort and Insurance Law Journal	ABA Tort & Ins LJ
American Business Law Journal	Am Bus LJ
American Criminal Law Review	Am Crim L Rev
American Indian Law Review	Am Indian L Rev
American Intellectual Property Law Association Quarterly Journal	AIPLAQJ
American Journal of Comparative Law	Am J Comp L
American Journal of Criminal Law	Am J Crim L
American Journal of International Arbitration	Am J Int'l Arb
American Journal of International Law	AJIL / Am J Int'l L
American Journal of Jurisprudence	Am J Juris
American Journal of Law & Medicine	Am J L & Med
American Journal of Legal History	Am J Legal Hist
American Journal of Tax Policy	Am J Tax Pol'y
American Journal of Trial Advocacy	Am J Trial Advoc
American Law and Economics Review	Am L & Econ Rev
American Review of International Arbitration	Am Rev Int'l Arb
American Society International Law Review	Am Soc Int'l L Rev
American University International Law Review (formerly / anciennement American University Journal of International Law & Policy)	Am U Int'l L Rev
American University Journal of Gender, Social Policy & the Law (formerly / anciennement American University Journal of Gender & the Law)	Am U J Gender Soc Pol'y & L

American University Journal of International Law & Policy	Am U J Int'l L & Pol'y
American University Law Review	Am U L Rev
Analyse de politiques	Anal de pol
Anglo-American Law Review	Anglo-Am L Rev
Animal Law	Animal L
Annales de droit aérien et spacial	Ann Air & Sp L
Annales de droit de Louvain	Ann dr Louv
Annales de la propriété industrielle artistique et littéraire	Ann pr ind art & lit
Annales de l'Université des sciences sociales de Toulouse	Ann de l'UssT
Annals of Air and Space Law	Ann Air & Sp L
Annals of Health Law	Annals Health L
Annuaire canadien de droit international	ACDI
Annuaire canadien des droits de la personne	ACDP
Annuaire de la Convention européenne des droits de l'Homme	Ann Conv Eur DH l'Homme
Annuaire de droit aérien et spatial	Ann dr aér & spat
Annuaire de droit maritime et aérien	Ann dr marit & aér
Annuaire de droit maritime et aéro-spatial	Ann dr marit & aéro-spat
Annuaire des collectivités locales	Ann coll loc
Annuaire français de droit international	AFDI
Annuaire français des droits de l'Homme	Ann fr DH
Annuaire français du transport aérien	Ann fr transp aér
Annuaire de la Haye de droit international	Ann Haye dr int
Annuaire de l'Institut de droit international	Ann inst dr int
Annuaire international de justice constitutionnelle	Ann int j c
Annuaire de la Société des Nations	Ann SN
Annuaire de la Société française de droit aérien et spatial	Ann S fr dr aér & spat
Annuaire de législation étrangère	Ann lég étrang
Annuaire de législation française	Ann lég fr
Annuaire de philosophie de droit	Ann phil dr
Annuaire des Nations Unies	Ann NU
Annuaire suisse de droit international	Ann suisse dr int
Annual Review of Banking Law	Ann Rev Banking L
Annual Survey of American Law	Ann Surv Am L
Annual Survey of Australian Law	Ann Surv Austl L
Annual Survey of Commonwealth Law	Ann Surv Commonwealth L
Annual Survey of English Law	Ann Surv Engl L

Annual Survey of International & Comparative Law	Ann Surv Int'l & Comp L
Annual Survey of South African Law	Ann Surv S Afr L
Antitrust	Antitrust
Antitrust Bulletin	Antitrust Bull
Antitrust Law and Economics Review	Antitrust L & Econ Rev
Antitrust Law Journal	Antitrust LJ
Anuario Mexicano de Derecho Internacional	An Mex Der Int'l
Appeal: Review of Current Law and Law Reform	Appeal
Arab Law Quarterly	Arab LQ
Arbitration International	Arb Int'l
Archiv des Oeffentlichen Rechts	AOR
Archiv fuer die civilistische Praxis	ACP
Archiv für rechts- und Sozialphilosophie	ARSP
Arizona Bar Journal	Ariz Bar J
Arizona Journal of International & Comparative Law	Ariz J Int'l & Comp L
Arizona Law Review	Ariz L Rev
Arizona State Law Journal	Ariz St LJ
Arkansas Law Review	Ark L Rev
Art, Antiquity, and the Law	Art Ant & L
Artificial Intelligence and Law	AI & L
Army Lawyer	Army Law
Asian Law Journal	Asian LJ
Asia Pacific Journal of Environmental Law	Asia Pac J Envtl L
Asia-Pacific Journal of Human Rights and the Law	Asia Pac J HR & L
Asia Pacific Journal of International Law	Asia Pac J Int'l L
Asia Pacific Law Review	Asia Pac L Rev
Asian-Pacific American Law Journal (formerly / anciennement Asian American Pacific Islands Law Journal)	Asian Pac Am LJ
Asian-Pacific Law & Policy Journal	Asian Pac L & Pol'y J
Atomic Energy Law Journal	AELJ
Auckland University Law Review	Auckland UL Rev
Australian & New Zealand Journal of Criminology	Austl Crim & NZJ
Australian Bar Review	Austl Bar Rev
Australian Business Law Review	Austl Bus L Rev
Australian Competition and Consumer Law Journal	Austl Comp & Cons LJ
Austalian Insurance Law Journal	Austl Ins LJ
Australian Journal of Contract Law	Austl J Contract L

Australian Journal of Corporate Law	Austl J Corp L
Australian Journal of Family Law	Austl J Fam L
Australian Journal of Human Rights	Austl J H R
Australian Journal of Labour Law	Austl J Lab L
Australian Journal of Legal History	Austl J Legal Hist
Australian Law Journal	Austl L J
Australian Property Law Journal	Austl Prop LJ
Australian Torts Law Journal	Aust Torts LJ
Austrian Journal of Public and International Law	Aus J Pub & Int'l L
Austrian Review of International and European Law	Aus Rev Int'l & Eur L
Baltimore Law Review	Baltimore L Rev
Banking and Finance Law Review	BFLR
Banking Law Journal	Banking LJ
Banking Policy Report	Banking Pol'y Rep
Bankruptcy Developments Journal	Bankr Dev J
Banque et droit	B & dr
Bar & Bench News Digest	Bar & Bench ND
Baylor Law Review	Baylor L Rev
Barrister	Barrister
Behavioural Sciences and the Law	Behav Sci & L
Berkeley Journal of Employment and Labour Law	Berkeley J Emp & Lab L
Berkeley Journal of Health Care Law	Berkeley J Health Care L
Berkeley Journal of International Law	Berkeley J Int'l L
Berkeley Technology Law Journal	Berkeley Tech LJ
Berkeley Women's Law Journal	Berkeley Women's LJ
Biotechnology Law Report	Biotech L Rep
Boletin Mexicano de Derecho Comparado	Bol Mex Der Comp
Boston Bar Journal	Boston Bar J
Boston College Environmental Affairs Law Review	BC Envtl Aff L Rev
Boston College International & Comparative Law Review	BC Int'l & Comp L Rev
Boston College Law Review	BCL Rev
Boston College Third World Law Journal	BC Third World LJ
Boston University International Law Journal	BU Int'l LJ
Boston University Journal of Science & Technology Law	BUJ Sci & Tech L
Boston University Journal of Tax Law	BUJ Tax L
Boston University Law Review	BUL Rev
Boston University Public Interest Law Journal	BU Pub Int LJ

Brandeis Law Journal	Brandeis LJ
Briefly Speaking	Brief Speaking
Brigham Young University Education & Law Journal	BYU Educ & LJ
Brigham Young University Law Review	BYUL Rev
British Columbia Law Notes	BCLN
British Institute of International and Comparative Law	Brit Inst Int'l & Comp L
British Journal of Criminology	Brit J Crim
British Medical Journal	Brit Med J
British Tax Review	Brit Tax Rev
British Yearbook of International Law	Brit YB Int'l L
Brooklyn Journal of International Law	Brook J Int'l L
Brooklyn Law Review	Brook L Rev
Buffalo Criminal Law Review	Buff Crim L Rev
Buffalo Environmental Law Journal	Buff Envtl LJ
Buffalo Human Rights Law Review	Buff HRL Rev
Buffalo Law Review	Buff L Rev
Buffalo Public Interest Law Journal	Buff Pub Int LJ
Buffalo Women's Law Journal	Buff Women's LJ
Bulletin canadien VIH-SIDA et droit	Bull can VIH-SIDA & D
Bulletin of Legal Developments	Bull Leg Dev
Bulletin d'information sur les activités juridiques (Conseil de l'Europe)	Bull infoact jur
Bullettino dell'Istituto di diritto romano	Bull Inst dirrom
Bureau of National Affairs Patent, Trademark and Copyright Journal	BNA Patent, TM & Copyright J
Business and the Law	Bus & L
Business Law Review	Bus L Rev
Business Lawyer	Bus Law
Business Quarterly	Bus Q
BYU Journal of Public Law	BYUJ Pub L
Cahiers de droit	C de D
Cahiers de droit de l'entreprise	C de D entr
Cahiers de droit européen	C de D eur
Cahiers du Conseil Constitutionnel	C du Cons Const
Cahiers de l'Institut québécois d'administration judiciaire	CIQAJ
Cahiers de propriété intellectuelle	CPI
California Bankruptcy Journal	Cal Bankr J

California Criminal Law Review	Cal Crim L Rev
California Law Review	Cal L Rev
California Regulatory Law Reporter	Cal Reg L Rep
California State Bar Journal	Cal St BJ
California Western International Law Journal	Cal W Int'l LJ
California Western Law Review	Cal WL Rev
Cambridge Law Journal	Cambridge LJ
Cambridge Yearbook of European Legal Studies	Cambridge YB Eur Legal Stud
Campbell Law Review	Campbell L Rev
Canada Law Journal	Can LJ
Canada-United States Law Journal	Can-USLJ
Canadian Bar Association Papers	CBA Papers
Canadian Bar Association Year Book	CBAYB
Canadian Bar Journal	Can Bar J
Canadian Bar Review	Can Bar Rev
Canadian Bioethics Report	Can Bioethics R
Canadian Business Law Journal	Can Bus LJ
Canadian Business Review	Can Bus Rev
Canadian Class Action Review	Can Class Action Rev
Canadian Communications Law Review	Can Comm L Rev
Canadian Community Law Journal	Can Community LJ
Canadian Competition Policy Record	Can Compet Pol'y Rec
Canadian Competition Record	Can Comp Rec
Canadian Council on International Law: Proceedings	Can Council Int'l L Proc
Canadian Criminal Law Review	Can Crim L Rev
Canadian Criminology Forum	Can Crim Forum
Canadian Current Tax	Can Curr Tax
Canadian Environmental Law News	Can Envtl LN
Canadian Family Law Quarterly	Can Fam LQ
Canadian HIV/AIDS Policy & Law Review	Can HIV/AIDS Pol'y & L Rev
Canadian Human Rights Advocate	Can HR Advoc
Canadian Human Rights Yearbook	Can Hum Rts YB
Canadian Intellectual Property Review	CIPR
Canadian International Lawyer	Can Int'l Law
Canadian Journal of Administrative Law & Practice	Can J Admin L & Prac
Canadian Journal of Corrections	Can J Corr
Canadian Journal of Criminology	Can J Crim

Canadian Journal of Criminology and Corrections	Can J Crim & Corr
Canadian Journal of Family Law	Can J Fam L
Canadian Journal of Insurance Law	Can J Ins L
Canadian Journal of International Buseness Law and Policy	Can J Int'l Bus L & Pol'y
Canadian Journal of Law and Jurisprudence	Can JL & Jur
Canadian Journal of Law and Society	CJLS
Canadian Journal of Law and Technology	CJLT
Canadian Journal of Women and the Law	CJWL
Canadian Labour & Employment Law Journal	CLELJ
Canadian Law Libraries	Can L L
Canadian Law Review	Can L Rev
Canadian Law Times	Can LT
Canadian Lawyer	Can Law
Canadian Legal Studies	Can Legal Stud
Canadian Medical Association Journal	Can Med Assoc J
Canadian Municipal Journal	Can Mun J
Canadian Native Law Bulletin	Can NL Bull
Canadian Public Policy	Can Pub Pol'y
Canadian Tax Foundation (Conference Report / Rapport de conférence)	Can Tax Found
Canadian Tax Highlights	Can Tax Highlights
Canadian Tax Journal	Can Tax J
Canadian Tax News	Can Tax N
Canadian Taxation: A Journal of Tax Policy	Can Tax'n: J Tax Pol'y
Canadian Yearbook of International Law	Can YB Int'l Law
Capital University Law Review	Capital UL Rev
Cardozo Arts & Entertainment Law Journal	Cardozo Arts & Ent LJ
Cardozo Electronic Law Bulletin	Cardozo EL Bull
Cardozo Journal of International & Comparative Law *(formerly / anciennement New Europe Law Review)*	Cardozo J Int'l & Comp L
Cardozo Law Review	Cardozo L Rev
Cardozo Studies in Law and Literature	Cardozo Stud L & Lit
Cardozo Women's Law Journal	Cardozo Women's LJ
Caribbean Law Review	Caribbean L Rev
Carolina Law Journal	Car LJ
Case Western Reserve Journal of International Law	Case W Res J Int'l L
Case Western Reserve Law Review	Case W Res L Rev
Catholic Lawyer	Cath Law

Catholic University Law Review	Cath U L Rev
Chapman Law Review	Chapman L Rev
Chicago Journal of International Law	Chicago J Int'l L
Chicago-Kent Law Review	Chicagio-Kent L Rev
Chicano-Latino Law Review *(formerly / anciennement Chicano Law Review)*	Chicano-Latino L Rev
Chicago Lawyer	Chicago Law
Chicago Legal Forum	Chicago Legal F
Children's Legal Rights Journal	Child Legal Rts J
China Law Reporter	China L Rep
Chinese Yearbook of International Law and Affairs	Chinese YB Int'l L & Aff
Chitty's Law Journal	Chitty's LJ
Circles: Buffalo Women's Journal of Law & Social Policy	Circles
Civil Liberties Review	Civ Lib Rev
Civil Justice Quarterly	CJQ
Cleveland State Law Review	Clev St L Rev
Cleveland-Marshall Law Review	Clev-Marshall L Rev
Clinical Law Review	Clinical L Rev
Coastal Management	Coastal Mgmt
Codicillus	Codicillus
Colorado Journal of International Environmental Law & Policy	Colo J Int'l Envtl L & Pol'y
Colorado Lawyer	Colo Law
Columbia Business Law Review	Colum Bus L Rev
Columbia Human Rights Law Review	Colum HRL Rev
Columbia Journal of Asian Law *(formerly / anciennement Journal of Chinese Law)*	Colum J Asian Law
Columbia Journal of East European Law	Colum J E Eur L
Columbia Journal of Environmental Law	Colum J Envtl L
Columbia Journal of European Law	Colum J Eur L
Columbia Journal of Gender and Law	Colum J Gender & L
Columbia Journal of Law and Social Problems	Colum JL & Soc Probs
Columbia Journal of Transnational Law	Colum J Transnat'l L
Columbia Law Review	Colum L Rev
Columbia Science and Technology Law Review	Colum Sci & Tech L Rev
Columbia-VLA Journal of Law & the Arts	Colum-VLA J L & Arts
Commercial Law Journal	Com LJ
Commercial Leasing Law and Strategy	Com Leasing L & Strategy

Common Law World Review	C L World Rev
Common Market Law Review	CML Rev
Commonwealth Law Bulletin	Commonwealth L Bull
Commonwealth Legal Education	Commonwealth Legal Educ
Communication Law & Policy	Comm L & Pol'y
Communications Lawyer	Comm Law
Communiqué – International Court of Justice	Communiqué ICJ
Comparative and International Law Journal of Southern Africa	Comp & Int'l LJS Afr
Comparative Juridical Review	Comp Jurid Rev
Comparative Labor Law & Policy Journal *(formerly / anciennement Comparative Labor Law Journal)*	Comp Lab L & Pol'y J
Comptes rendus sténographiques des débats (Conseil de l'Europe)	Débats
Computer Law and Security Report	Computer L & Sec R
Computer Law Review and Technology Journal	Computer L Rev & TJ
Computer Lawyer	Computer Law
Congressional Digest	Cong Dig
Connecticut Bar Journal	Conn BJ
Connecticut Insurance Law Journal	Conn Ins LJ
Connecticut Journal of International Law	Conn J Int'l L
Connecticut Law Review	Conn L Rev
Connecticut Probate Law Journal	Conn Prob LJ
Constitutional Commentary	Const Commentary
Constitutional Forum Constitutionnel	Const Forum Const
Constitutional Review	Const Rev
Consumer Finance Law Quarterly Report	Cons Fin LQ Rep
Construction Law Journal	Construction LJ
Construction Lawyer	Construction Law
Continuity and Change	Continuity & Change
Copyright Bulletin	Copyright Bull
Cooley Law Review	Cooley L Rev
Cornell International Law Journal	Cornell Int'l LJ
Cornell Journal of Law & Public Policy	Cornell JL & Pub Pol'y
Cornell Law Review	Cornell L Rev
Cornell Law Journal	Cornell LJ
Corporate Management Tax Conference	Corp Mgmt Tax Conf
Corporate Taxation	Corp Tax'n

Corpus Juris Secundum	CJS
Correspondances judiciaires	Corr jud
Counsellor: The New York Law School Journal	Counsellor
Cours de perfectionnement du notariat	CP du N
Creighton Law Review	Creighton L Rev
Crime, Law and Social Change	Crime, L & Soc Change
Criminal Law Forum	Crim LF
Criminal Law Quarterly	Crim LQ
Criminal Law Review	Crim L Rev
Criminologie	Criminol
Criminology	Criminol
Critical Criminology	Crit Criminol
Croation Arbitration Yearbook	Croation Arb YB
Croatian Critical Law Review	Croat Crit L Rev
Crown Counsel's Review	Crown Coun Rev
Cumberland Law Review	Cumb L Rev
Current Law Yearbook	Curr LYB
Current Legal Problems	Curr Legal Probs
Current Medicine for Attorneys	Current Med for Att'ys
Currents: International Trade Law Journal	Currents
Cyberspace Law Journal	Cyberspace LJ
Cyberspace Lawyer	Cyberspace Law
Dalhousie Journal of Legal Studies	Dal J Leg Stud
Dalhousie Law Journal	Dal LJ
Defense Counsel Journal	Def Couns J
Delaware Journal of Corporate Law	Del J Corp L
Delaware Law Review	Del L Rev
Delaware Lawyer	Del Law
Denver Journal of International Law & Policy	Denv J Int'l L & Pol'y
Denver University Law Review (formerly / anciennement Denver Law Journal)	Denv UL Rev
Department of State Bulletin	Dep't St Bull
DePaul Business Law Journal	DePaul Bus LJ
DePaul International Law Journal	DePaul Int'l LJ
DePaul Journal of Health Care Law	DePaul J Health Care L
DePaul Law Review	DePaul L Rev
DePaul-LCA Journal of Art and Entertainment Law and Policy	DePaul-LCA J Art & Ent L & Pol'y

Deutsche Richterzeitung	DRiZ
Deutsches und Europäisches Familienrecht	DEFR
Dickinson Journal of Environmental Law & Policy	Dick J Envtl L & Pol'y
Dickinson Journal of International Law	Dick J Int'l L
Dickinson Law Review	Dick L Rev
Digital Technology Law Journal	DTLJ
Dispute Resolution Journal *(formerly / anciennement Arbitration Journal)*	Disp Resol J
District of Columbia Law Review	DCL Rev
Documents juridiques internationaux	DJI
Documents (Working Papers) (Council of Europe)	Documents
Documents de séance (Conseil de l'Europe)	Documents
Drake Journal of Agricultural Law	Drake J Agric L
Drake Law Review	Drake L Rev
Droit africain du travail	DAT
Droit des sociétés	Dr soc
Droit et Cultures	Dr et Cult
Droit et patrimoine	Dr et pat
Droit et pratique du commerce international	DPCI
Droit et Société	Dr et Soc
Droit européen des transports	Dr eur transp
Droit Maritime Français	Dr Marit Fr
Droit polonais contemporain	Dr polon contemp
Droit Social	Dr social
Droits	Droits
Duke Environmental Law & Policy Forum	Duke Envtl L & Pol'y F
Duke Journal of Comparative & International Law	Duke J Comp & Int'l L
Duke Journal of Gender Law & Policy	Duke J Gender L & Pol'y
Duke Law Journal	Duke LJ
Duke Law and Technology Review	Duke L & Tech Rev
Duquesne Business Law Journal	Duq Bus LJ
Duquesne Law Review	Duq L Rev
East European Business Law	E Eur Bus L
East European Constitutional Review	E Eur Const Rev
East European Human Rights Review	E Eur HR Rev
Ecology Law Quarterly	Ecology LQ
Edinburgh Law Review	Ed L Rev

Education & Law Journal	Educ & LJ
Elder Law Journal	Elder LJ
Election Law Journal	Election LJ
Electronic Journal of Comparative Law	EJCL
Emory International Law Review *(formerly / anciennement Emory Journal of International Dispute Resolution)*	Emory Int'l L Rev
Emory Law Journal	Emory LJ
Employee Rights & Employment Policy Journal	Employee Rts & Employment Pol'y J
Energy Law Journal	Energy LJ
Entertainment & Sports Lawyer	Ent & Sports Law
Entertainment Law & Finance	Ent L & Fin
Environmental Law	Envtl L
Environmental Law and Management	Envtl L & Mgmt
Environmental Law and Policy Journal	Envtl L & Pol'y J
Environmental Law Journal	Envtl LJ
Environmental Lawyer	Envtl Law
Environmental Policy and Law	Envtl Pol'y & L
Environmentally Friendly: The Journal of the Pace Center for Environmental Legal Studies	Envtlly Friendly
Environs Environmental Law and Policy Journal	Environs Envtl L & Pol'y J
Estates and Trusts Journal	E & TJ
Estates and Trusts Quarterly	E & TQ
Estates Trusts & Pensions Journal	ETPJ
Ethics	Ethics
Europarecht	EuR
Europäische Zeitschrift für Privatrecht	EZPR
European Business Law Review	Eur Bus L Rev
European Competition Law Review	Eur Comp L Rev
European Environmental Law Review	Eur Envtl L Rev
European Environment Yearbook	Eur Env YB
European Human Rights Law Review	Eur HRL Rev
European Intellectual Property Review	Eur IP Rev
European Journal of Health Law	Eur J Health L
European Journal of Law & Economics	Eur J L & Econ
European Journal of Law Reform	Eur J L Ref
European Journal of International Law	EJIL
European Journal for Education Law and Policy	Eur J Educ L & Pol'y

European Journal of Migration and Law	Eur J Migr & L
European Journal of Social Security	Eur J Soc Sec
European Journal of Criminal Policy & Research	Eur J Crim Pol'y & Research
European Journal of Crime, Criminal Law, and Criminal Justice	Eur J Crime, Crim L & Crim J
European Law Journal	Eur LJ
European Law Review	Eur L Rev
European Legal Forum	Eur Leg F
European Review of Private Law	ERPL
European Transport Law	Eur Transp L
Examiner	Examiner
FAA Aviation New	FAA Av N
Family Court Review (formerly / anciennement Family & Conciliation Courts Review)	Fam Ct Rev
Family Law Quarterly	Fam LQ
Family Law Review	Fam L Rev
Federal Bar News & Journal	Fed B News & J
Federal Circuit Bar Journal	Fed Circuit BJ
Federal Communications Law Journal	Fed Comm LJ
Federal Courts Law Review	Fed Cts L Rev
Federal Lawyer	Fed Law
Federal Litigator	Fed Litigator
Federal Rules Decisions	FRD
Feminist Legal Studies	Fem Legal Stud
Florida Bar Journal	Fla BJ
Florida Coastal Law Journal	Fla Coastal LJ
Florida International Law Journal	Fla Int'l LJ
Florida Journal of International Law	Fla J Int'l L
Florida Law Review (formerly / anciennement University of Florida Law Review)	Fla L Rev
Florida State Journal of Transnational Law & Policy	Fla St J Transnat'l L & Pol'y
Florida State University Journal of Land Use & Environmental Law	Fla St UJ Land Use & Envtl L
Florida State University Law Review	Fla St UL Rev
Florida Tax Review	Fla Tax Rev
Food & Drug Law Journal	Food & Drug LJ
Fordham Environmental Law Journal	Fordham Envtl LJ
Fordham Finance, Securities & Tax Law Forum	Fordham Fin Sec & Tax LF

Fordham Intellectual Property, Media & Entertainment Law Journal	Fordham IP Media & Ent LJ
Fordham International Law Journal	Fordham Int'l LJ
Fordham Journal of Corporate and Finance Law	Fordham J Corp & Fin L
Fordham Law Review	Fordham L Rev
Fordham Urban Law Journal	Fordham Urb LJ
International Law FORUM du droit international	FORUM
George Mason Law Review *(formerly / anciennement George Mason University Law Review and George Mason Independent Law Review)*	Geo Mason L Rev
George Mason University Civil Rights Law Journal	Geo Mason U Civ Rts LJ
George Washington International Law Review *(formerly / anciennement George Washington Journal of International Law and Economics)*	Geo Wash Int'l L Rev
George Washington Law Review	Geo Wash L Rev
Georgetown Immigration Law Journal	Geo Immig LJ
Georgetown International Environmental Law Review	Geo Int'l Envtl L Rev
Georgetown Journal of Gender and the Law	Geo J Gender & L
Georgetown Journal of International Law	Geo J Int'l L
Georgetown Journal of Legal Ethics	Geo J Legal Ethics
Georgetown Journal on Poverty Law & Policy *(formerly / anciennement Georgetown Journal on Fighting Poverty)*	Geo J on Poverty L & Pol'y
Georgetown Law Journal	Geo LJ
Georgetown Public Policy Review	Geo Pub Pol'y Rev
Georgia Journal of International and Comparative Law	Ga J Int'l & Comp L
Georgia Law Review	Ga L Rev
Georgia State University Law Review	Ga St U L Rev
Global Journal on Crime and Criminal Law	Global J on Crime & Crim L
Global Law Review	Global L Rev
Golden Gate University Law Review	Golden Gate UL Rev
Gonzaga Law Review	Gonz L Rev
Great Plains Natural Resources Journal	Great Plains Nat Resources J
Griffith Law Review	Griffith LR
Hague Yearbook of International Law	Hague YB Int'l L
Hamline Journal of Public Law and Policy	Hamline J Pub L & Pol'y
Hamline Law Review	Hamline L Rev
Harvard BlackLetter Law Journal	Harv BlackLetter LJ
Harvard Civil Rights-Civil Liberties Law Review	Harv CR-CLL Rev
Harvard Environmental Law Review	Harv Envtl L Rev

Harvard Human Rights Journal *(formerly / anciennement Harvard Human Rights Yearbook)*	Harv Hum Rts J
Harvard International Law Journal	Harv Int'l LJ
Harvard Journal of Law and Gender	Harv J L & Gender
Harvard Journal of Law and Public Policy	Harv JL & Pub Pol'y
Harvard Journal of Law & Technology	Harv JL & Tech
Harvard Journal on Legislation	Harv J on Legis
Harvard Law Review	Harv L Rev
Harvard Negotiation Law Review	Harv Negot L Rev
Harvard Women's Law Journal	Harv Women's LJ
Hastings Communications & Entertainment Law Journal	Hastings Comm & Ent LJ
Hastings Constitutional Law Quarterly	Hastings Const LQ
Hastings International and Comparative Law Review	Hastings Int'l & Comp L Rev
Hastings Law Journal	Hastings LJ
Hastings West-Northwest Journal of Environmental Law and Policy	Hastings W-Nw J Envtl L & Pol'y
Hastings Women's Law Journal	Hastings Women's LJ
Hawaii Bar Journal	Haw BJ
Hawaiil Law Review	Haw L Rev
Health and Human Rights	Health & Hum Rts
Health Law in Canada	Health L Can
Health Law Journal	Health LJ
Health Lawyer	Health Law
Health Matrix	Health Matrix
Heidelberg Journal of International Law	Heidelberg J Int'l L
High Technology Law Journal	High Tech LJ
Hitotsubashi Journal of Law and Politics	HJLP
Hofstra Labor & Employment Law Journal	Hofstra Lab & Empl LJ
Hofstra Law Review	Hofstra L Rev
Hofstra Property Law Journal	Hofstra Prop LJ
Holdsworth Law Review	Hold LR
Hong Kong Law Journal	Hong Kong LJ
Houston Journal of International Law	Hous J Int'l L
Houston Law Review	Hous L Rev
Howard Journal of Criminal Justice	How J Crim Justice
Howard Law Journal	How LJ
Howard Scroll: The Social Justice Law Review	How Scroll
Human Rights Internet Reporter	HRIR

Human Rights Law Journal	HRLJ
Human Rights Case Digest	Hum Rts Case Digest
Human Rights in Development	Hum Rts Dev
Human Rights in Developing Countries	Hum Rts Dev Countries
Human Rights Journal	Hum Rts J
Human Rights Quarterly	Hum Rts Q
Human Rights Tribune	Hum Rts Trib
Humboldt Forum Recht	Humboldt FR
ICSID Review	ICSID Rev
Idaho Law Review	Idaho L Rev
IDEA: The Journal of Law and Technology	IDEA
Illinois Bar Journal	Ill BJ
Illinois Law Quarterly	Ill LQ
ILSA Journal of International & Comparative Law	ILSA J Int'l & Comp L
Immigration and Nationality Law Review	Immig & Nat'lity L Rev
Impact Labour Law & Management Practices	Impact
Indiana International and Comparative Law Review	Ind Int'l & Comp L Rev
Indiana Journal of Global Legal Studies	Ind J Global Legal Stud
Indiana Law Journal	Ind LJ
Indiana Law Review	Ind L Rev
Indigenous Law Journal	Indigenous LJ
Industrial Law Journal	Indus LJ
Industrial Relations Law Journal	Indus Rel LJ
Industrial & Labor Relations Review	Indus & Lab Rel Rev
Information Bulletin on Legal Affairs (Council of Europe)	Inf Bull
Information and Communications Technology Law	I & Comm T L
Insolvency Bulletin	Ins Bull
Intellectual and Comparative Law Quarterly	ICLQ
Intellectual Property Journal	IPJ
Intellectual Property Law Bulletin	IPL Bull
Intellectual Property Law Newsletter	IPL Newsl
Intellectual Property & Technlology Forum	IP & T F
Intellectual Property & Technology Law Review	IP & T L Rev
International Arbitration Law Review	Int'l Arb L Rev
International Business Law Journal	IBLJ
International Business Lawyer	Int'l Bus Law
International Commercial Litigation	Int'l Com Lit

International Commission of Jurists Review	Int'l Comm Jur Rev
International Company and Commercial Law Review	Int'l Co & Com L Rev
International and Comparative Corporate Law Journal	Int'l & Comp Corp LJ
International and Comparative Law Quarterly	ICLQ
International and Comparative Law Review	Int'l & Comp L Rev
International Criminal Law Review	Int'l Crim L Rev
International Financial Law Review	Int'l Fin L Rev
International Insights	Int'l Insights
International Insurance Law Review	Int'l Ins L Rev
International Journal	Int'l J
International Journal for the Semiotics of Law	Int'l J Sem L
International Journal of Children's Rights	Int'l J Child Rts
International Journal of Communications Law & Policy	Int'l J Comm L & Pol'y
International Journal of Comparative Labour Law and Industrial Relations	Int'l J Comp Lab L & Ind Rel
International Journal of Conflict Management	Int'l J Confl Mgmt
International Journal of Cultural Property	Int'l J Cult Prop
International Journal of Franchising and Distribution Law	Int'l J Franch & Distrib L
International Journal of Human Rights	Int'l JHR
International Journal of Offender Therapy and Comparative Criminology	Int'l J Off Ther & Comp Crim
International Journal of Law Policy and the Family	Int'l JL Pol'y & Fam
International Journal of Law and Information Technology	Int'l JL & IT
International Journal of Law and Psychiatry	Int'l J L & Psychiatry
International Journal of Legal Information	Int'l J Legal Info
International Journal of Marine and Coastal Law	Int'l J Mar & Coast L
International Journal of the Sociology of Law	Int'l J Soc L
International Journal of Refugee Law	Int'l J Refugee L
International Journal of the Sociology of Law	Int'l J Soc L
International Lawyer	Int'l Law
International Legal Materials	ILM
International Legal Perspectives	Int'l Legal Persp
International Legal Practitioner	Int'l Leg Practitioner
International Legal Theory	Int'l L Theory
International Maritime and Commercial Law Yearbook	Int'l Mar & Com L YB
International Review of Criminal Policy	Int'l Rev Crim Pol'y
International Review of Industrial Property and Copyright Law	Int'l Rev Ind Prop & C'right L

International Review of Law Computers & Technology	Int'l Rev L Comp & Tech
International Review of Law & Economics	Int'l Rev L & Econ
International Review of the Red Cross	Int'l Rev Red Cross
International Tax and Business Lawyer	Int'l Tax & Bus Law
International Trade Law and Practice	Int'l Trade L & Pract
International Trade Law & Regulation	Int'l Trade L Reg
International Trade Law Quarterly	ITLQ
Iowa Law Review	Iowa L Rev
Irish Jurist	Ir Jur
Islamic Law & Society	Islamic L & Soc
Israel Law Review	Isr LR
Issues in Law & Medicine	Issues L & Med
ITU News	ITU N
Jahrbuch für Recht und Ethik	JBRE
Jersey Law Review	J L Rev
Jewish Law Report	Jewish LR
John Marshall Journal of Computer & Information Law	J Marshall J Computer & Info L
John Marshall Law Quarterly	J Marshall LQ
John Marshall Law Review	J Marshall L Rev
Journal des juges provinciaux	JJ prov
Journal des Tribunaux	J Tribun
Journal de Droit Européen	J Droit Eur
Journal du Barreau	J Barreau
Journal du droit des jeunes	J dr jeunes
Journal du droit international	JDI
Journal of Affordable Housing & Community Development Law	J Aff Housing & Community Dev L
Journal of African Law	J Afr L
Journal of Agricultural Law	J Agric L
Journal of Air Law	J Air L
Journal of Air Law and Commerce	J Air L & Com
Journal of Animal Law	J Animal L
Journal of Animal Law and Ethics	J Animal L & Ethics
Journal of Appellate Practice & Process	J App Pr & Pro
Journal of Art & Entertainment Law	J Art & Ent L
Journal of BioLaw & Business	J BioLaw & Bus
Journal of Business Law	J Bus L
Journal of Catholic Legal Studies	J Cath Legal Stud

Journal of Chinese Law	J Chinese L
Journal of College & University Law	JC & UL
Journal of Commonwealth Law and Legal Education	J Commonwealth L & Legal Educ
Journal of Comparative Business and Capital Market Law	J Comp Bus & Cap Mkt L
Journal of Conflict and Security Law	J Confl & Sec L
Journal of Conflict Resolution	J Confl Resolution
Journal of Constitutional Law in Eastern and Central Europe	J Const LE & Cent Eur
Journal of Contemporary Health Law & Policy	J Contemp Health L & Pol'y
Journal of Contemporary Law	J Contemp L
Journal of Contemporary Legal Issues	J Contemp Legal Issues
Journal of Corporate Taxation	J Corp Tax'n
Journal of Corporation Law	J Corp L
Journal of Criminal Justice Education	J Crim J Educ
Journal of Criminal Law	J Crim L
Journal of Criminal Law & Criminology	J Crim L & Criminology
Journal of Dispute Resolution	J Disp Resol
Journal of Empirical Legal Studies	J Empirical Legal Stud
Journal of Energy Law & Policy	J Energy L & Pol'y
Journal of Energy, Natural Resources & Environmental Law	J Energy, Nat'l Res & Envtl L
Journal of Environmental Law	J Envtl L
Journal of Environmental Law & Practice	J Envtl L & Prac
Journal of Environmental Law & Litigation	J Envtl L & Litig
Journal of European Integration	J Eur Int
Journal of Family Law	J Fam L
Journal of Gender, Race & Justice	J Gender Race & Just
Journal of Health and Hospital Law	J Health & Hosp L
Journal of Health Care Law & Policy	J Health Care L & Pol'y
Journal of Health Politics, Policy & Law	J Health Pol
Journal of the History of International Law	J Hist Int'l L
Journal of the Indian Law Institute	JILI
Journal of Informaion, Law and Technology	JILT
Journal of the Institute for the Study of Legal Ethics	JISLE
Journal of Intellectual Property	J Intell Prop
Journal of Intellectual Property Law	J Intell Prop L
Journal of International Arbitration	J Int'l Arb
Journal of International Banking Law	JIBL

Journal of International Economic Law	J Int'l Econ L
Journal of International Financial Markets	J Int'l Fin Markets
Journal of International Law & Business	J Int'l L & Bus
Journal of International Legal Studies	J Int'l Legal Stud
Journal of International Taxation	J Int'l Tax
Journal of International Wildlife Law and Policy	J Int'l Wildlife L & Pol'y
Journal of Juvenile Law	J Junvenile L
Journal of Land Use & Environmental Law	J Land Use & Envtl L
Journal of Land, Resources & Environmental Law *(formerly / anciennement Journal of Energy, Natural Resources & Environmental Law)*	J Land Resources & Envtl L
Journal of Law & Commerce	JL & Com
Journal of Law & Economics	JL & Econ
Journal of Law, Economics & Organization	JL Econ & Org
Journal of Law & Education	JL & Educ
Journal of Law and Environment	JL & Env't
Journal of Law and Equality	JL & Equality
Journal of Law & Family Studies	JL & Fam Stud
Journal of Law & Health	JL & Health
Journal of Law & Information Science	J L & Info Sci
Journal of Law & Policy	JL & Pol'y
Journal of Law & Politics	JL & Pol
Journal of Law & Religion	JL & Religion
Journal of Law and Social Policy	J L & Soc Pol'y
Journal of Law and Society	JL & Soc'y
Journal of Law in Society	JL in Soc'y
Journal of Law & Technology	JL & Tech
Journal of Law, Medicine & Ethics	JL Med & Ethics
Journal of Legal Advocacy & Practice	J Legal Advoc & Prac
Journal of Legal Economics	J Legal Econ
Journal of Legal Education	J Legal Educ
Journal of Legal History	J Legal Hist
Journal of Legal Medicine	J Legal Med
Journal of Legal Pluralism and Unofficial Law *(formerly / anciennement Journal of Legal Pluralism)*	J Legal Pluralism
Journal of Legal Studies	J Legal Stud
Journal of Legislation	J Legis
Journal of Legislation & Public Policy	J Legis & Pub Pol'y

Journal of Maritime Law & Commerce	J Mar L & Com
Journal of Medicine and Law	J Med & L
Journal of Mineral Law & Policy	J Min L & Pol'y
Journal of Multistate Taxation	J Multistate Tax'n
Journal of Natural Resources & Environmental Law *(formerly / anciennement Journal of Mineral Law & Policy)*	J Nat Resources & Envtl L
Journal of Partnership Taxation	J Partnership Tax'n
Journal of Personal Injury Litigation	J Pers Inj Lit
Journal of Pharmacy & Law	J Pharmacy & L
Journal of Planning & Environmental Law	J Plan & Envtl L
Journal of Private International Law	J P Int'l L
Journal of Products Liability	J Prod Liab
Journal of Proprietary Rights	J Proprietary Rts
Journal of Science & Technology Law	J Sci & Tech L
Journal of Small & Emerging Business Law	J Small & Emerging Bus L
Journal of Social Welfare Law	J Soc Welfare L
Journal of Social Welfare and Family Law	J Soc Welfare & Fam L
Journal of South Pacific Law	J S Pac L
Journal of Southern Legal History	JS Legal Hist
Journal of Space Law	J Space L
Journal of Taxation	J Tax'n
Journal of Technology Law & Policy	J Tech L & Pol'y
Journal of the Institute for the Study of Legal Ethics	J Inst for Study Legal Ethics
Journal of the Law Society of Scotland	JLSS
Journal of the Legal Profession	J Legal Prof
Journal of the Patent & Trademark Office Society	J Pat & Trademark Off Soc'y
Journal of the Suffolk Academy of Law	J Suffolk Academy L
Journal of Transnational Law & Policy	J Transnat'l L & Pol'y
Journal of World Trade	J World Trade
Journal of World Trade Law, Economics and Policy	J World Trade L Econ & Pol'y
Journal Officiel des Communautés européennes: Communications et informations	JOC
Journal Officiel des Communautés européennes: Débats du Parlement européen	JOD
Journal Officiel des Communautés européennes: Législation	JOL
Judicature	Judicature
Juridical Review	Jurid Rev
Kansas Journal of Law & Public Policy	Kan JL & Pub Pol'y

Kansas Law Review	Kan L Rev
Kentucky Children's Rights Journal	Ky Children's Rts J
Kentucky Law Journal	Ky LJ
Korean Journal of Air and Space Law	Korean J Air & Sp L
Korean Journal of Comparative Law	Korean J Comp L
Korean Journal of International and Comparative Law	Korean J Int'l & Comp L
La Raza Law Journal	La Raza LJ
Labor Law Journal	Lab LJ
Labor Lawyer	Lab Law
Land and Water Law Review	Land & Water L Rev
Law & Contemporary Problems	Law & Contemp Probs
Law & Inequality	Law & Inequality
Law and History Review	LHR
Law and Philosophy	Law & Phil
Law and Philosophy: an International Journal for Jurisprudence and Legal Philosophy	Law & Phil Int'l J
Law & Policy	Law & Pol'y
Law & Policy in International Business	Law & Pol'y Int'l Bus
Law and Politics Book Review	Law & Pol Book Rev
Law & Practice of International Courts & Tribunals	Law & Prac Int'l Courts & Trib
Law & Psychology Review	Law & Psychol Rev
Law & Sexuality: A Review of Lesbian & Gay Legal Issues	Law & Sexuality
Law & Social Inquiry	Law & Soc Inquiry
Law & Society Review	Law & Soc'y Rev
Law Department Management	Law Dep't Mgmt
Law Firm Partnership & Benefits Report	Law Firm Partnership & Ben Rep
Law Librarian	Law Librn
Law Library Journal	Law Libr J
Law Office Management & Administration Report	Law Off Mgmt & Admin Rep
Law Office Technology Review	Law Off Tech Rev
Law Practice Management *(formerly / anciennement Legal Economics)*	Law Prac Mgmt
Law Quarterly Review	Law Q Rev
Law Review of Michigan State University Detroit College of Law	Law Rev Mich St U Det CL
Law Society Gazette (Law Society of Upper Canada)	L Soc'y Gaz
Law Society's Gazette and Guardian Gazette	L Soc'y Gaz & Guardian Gaz

Law Technology and Insurance	Law Tech & Ins
Law, Text, Culture	Law Text Culture
Lawyers Journal *(formerly / anciennement Pittsburgh Legal Journal)*	Pittsburgh Legal J
Legal History Review	Legal Hist Rev
Legal Information Management	Legal Info Mgmt
Legal Issues of Economic / European Integration	LIEI
Legal Medical Quarterly	L Med Q
Legal Reference Services Quarterly	Legal Ref Serv Q
Legal Studies	LS
Legal Theory	Legal Theory
Leiden Journal of International Law	Leiden J Int'l L
Lex Electronica: Revue du droit des technologies de l'information	Lex Electronica
Lloyd's Maritime and Commercial Law Quarterly	LMCLQ
Local Courts' and Municipal Gazette (Toronto)	Local Ct Gaz
Los Angeles Lawyer	LA Law
Louisiana Bar Journal	La BJ
Louisiana Law Review	La L Rev
Lower Canada Jurist	LC Jurist
Lower Canada Law Journal	LCLJ
Loyola Consumer Protection Journal	Loy Con Prot J
Loyola Law Review (New Orleans)	Loy L Rev
Loyola of Los Angeles Entertainment Law Journal	Loy LA Ent LR
Loyola of Los Angeles International & Comparative Law Journal	Loy LA Int'l & Comp LJ
Loyola of Los Angeles Law Review	Loy LA L Rev
Loyola Poverty Law Journal	Loy Poverty LJ
Loyola University of Chicago Law Journal	Loy U Chicago LJ
Maastricht Journal of European and Comparative Law	MJECL
Macquarie Jornal of International and Comparative Environmental Law	Macq J Int'l & CEnvtl L
Maine Law Review	Me L Rev
Malaya Law Review	Mal L Rev
Malayan Law Journal	MLJ
Manitoba Bar News	Man Bar N
Manitoba Law Journal	Man LJ
Maori Law Review	Maori L Rev

Marquette Intellectual Property Law Review	Marq Intell Prop L Rev
Marquette Law Review	Marq L Rev
Marquette Sports Law Review	Marq Sports LJ
Maryland Journal of Contemporary Legal Issues	Md J Contemp Legal Issues
Maryland Journal of International Law and Trade	Md J Int'l L & Trade
Maryland Law Review	Md L Rev
Massachusetts Law Review	Mass L Rev
McGeorge Law Review (formerly / anciennement Pacific Law Journal)	McGeorge L Rev
McGill International Journal of Sustainable Development Law and Policy	JSDLP
McGill Journal of Law and Health (formerly McGill Health Law Publication)	McGill JL & Health
McGill Law Journal	McGill LJ
Media Law & Policy	Media L & Pol'y
Medicine, Science and the Law	Med Sci Law
Medical Law Review	Med L Rev
Medicine & Law	Med & L
Medico-Legal Journal	Med Leg J
Melbourne University Law Review	Melbourne UL Rev
Mercer Law Review	Mercer L Rev
Mexico Trade & Law Reporter	Mex Trade & L Rep
Michigan Bar Journal	Mich BJ
Michigan Business Law Journal	Mich Bus LJ
Michigan Journal of Gender & Law	Mich J Gender & L
Michigan Journal of International Law	Mich J Int'l L
Michigan Journal of Law Reform	Mich JL Reform
Michigan Journal of Race & Law	Mich J Race & L
Michigan Law & Policy Review	Mich L & Pol'y Rev
Michigan Law Journal	Mich LJ
Michigan Law Review	Mich L Rev
Michigan State University – DCL Journal of International Law	MSU-DCL J Int'l L
Michigan Telecommunications & Technology Law Review	Mich Telecomm & Tech L Rev
Military Law Review	Mil L Rev
Minnesota Intellectual Property Review	Minn Intell Prop Rev
Minnesota Journal of Global Trade	Minn J Global Trade
Minnesota Law Review	Minn L Rev
Mississippi College Law Review	Miss CL Rev

Mississippi Law Journal	Miss LJ
Mississippi Law Review	Miss L Rev
Missouri Environmental Law & Policy Review	Mo Envtl L & Pol'y Rev
Missouri Law Review	Mo L Rev
Modern Law Review	Mod L Rev
Monash University Law Review	Monash UL Rev
Monde Juridique	Monde Jur
Money Laundering Law Report	Money Laundering L Rep
Montana Law Review	Mont L Rev
Montana Lawyer	Mont Law
Monthly Labor Review	Monthly Lab Rev
Murdoch University Electronic Journal of Law	Murdoch UEJL
NAFTA Law & Business Review of the Americas	NAFTA L & Bus Rev Am
National Banking Law Review	Nat'l Banking L Rev
National Black Law Journal	Nat'l Black LJ
National Insolvency Review	Nat'l Insolv Rev
National Institute of Justice Journal	Nat'l Inst Just J
National Journal of Constitutional Law	NJCL
National Journal of Sexual Orientation Law	Nat'l J Sexual Orientation L
National Law Journal	Nat'l LJ
National Law Review	Nat'l L Rev
National Real Property Law Review	Nat'l Real PLR
National Tax Journal	Nat'l Tax J
Natural Resources & Environment	Nat Resources & Env't
Natural Resources Journal	Nat Resources J
Naval Law Review	Nav L Rev
Nebraska Law Review	Neb L Rev
Neptunus: Maritime and Oceanic Law Review	Neptunus
Netherlands International Law Review	Nethl Int'l L Rev
Netherlands Quarterly of Human Rights	Nethl QHR
New England International and Comparative Law Annual	New Eng Int'l & Comp L Ann
New England Journal of Medicine	New Eng J Med
New England Journal on Criminal & Civil Confinement	New Eng J on Crim & Civ Confinement
New England Law Review	New Eng L Rev
New Europe Law Review	New Eur L Rev
New Jersey Lawyer	NJ Law

New Law Journal	New LJ
New Mexico Law Review	NML Rev
New York City Law Review	NY City L Rev
New York International Law Review	NY Int'l L Rev
New York Law Journal	NYLJ
New York Law Review	NYL Rev
New York Law School Journal of Human Rights	NYL Sch J Hum Rts
New York Law School Journal of International & Comparative Law	NYL Sch J Int'l & Comp L
New York Law School Law Review	NYL Sch L Rev
New York State Bar Journal	NY St BJ
New York University Clinical Law Review	NYU Clin L Rev
New York University East European Constitutional Review	E Eur Const Rev
New York University Environmental Law Journal	NYU Envtl LJ
New York University International Journal of Constitutional Law	NYU Int'l J Cont L
New York University Journal of International Law & Politics	NYUJ Int'l L & Pol
New York University Journal of Legislation & Public Policy	NYUJ Legis & Pub Pol'y
New York University Law Review	NYUL Rev
New York University Review of Law & Social Change	NYU Rev L & Soc Change
New Zealand Law Journal	NZLJ
New Zealand Law Review	NZL Rev
New Zealand Universities Law Review	NZUL Rev
NEXUS: A Journal of Opinion	NEXUS: J Opinion
Non-Profit Law Yearbook	Non-Profit L Yearbook
Non-State Actors and International Law	Non-State Act & Int'l L
Nordic Journal of International Law	Nordic J Int'l L
North Carolina Central Law Journal	NC Centr LJ
North Carolina Journal of International Law & Commercial Regulation	NCJ Int'l L & Com Reg
North Carolina Law Review	NCL Rev
North Dakota Law Review	NDL Rev
Northern Illinois University Law Review	N Ill UL Rev
Northern Ireland Legal Quarterly	N Ir Legal Q
Northern Kentucky Law Review	N Ky L Rev
Northwestern Journal of International Law & Business	Nw J Int'l L & Bus
Northwestern University Law Review	Nw UL Rev
Notarius International	Notarius Int'l

Notre Dame International Law Review	Notre Dame Int'l L Rev
Notre Dame Journal of Law Ethics & Public Policy	Notre Dame JL Ethics & Pub Pol'y
Notre Dame Law Review	Notre Dame L Rev
Nova Law Review	Nova L Rev
Nuclear Law	Nuclear L
Ocean & Coastal Law Journal *(formerly / anciennement Territorial Sea Journal)*	Ocean & Coastal LJ
Ocean Development & International Law	Ocean Devel & Int'l L
OECD Journal of Competition Law and Policy	OECD J Comp L & Pol'y
Official Journal of the European Communities: Debates of the European Parliament	OJD
Official Journal of the European Communities: English Special Edition	OJ Sp Ed
Official Journal of the European Communities: Information and Notices	OJI
Official Journal of the European Communities: Legislation	OJL
Official Report of Debates (Council of Europe)	Debates
Ohio Northern University Law Review	Ohio NUL Rev
Ohio State Journal on Dispute Resolution	Ohio St J Disp Resol
Ohio State Law Journal	Ohio St LJ
Oklahoma City University Law Review	Okla City UL Rev
Oklahoma Law Review	Okla L Rev
Ombudsman Journal	Ombudsman J
Ontario Family Law Bulletin	Ont Fam L Bull
Ontario Lawyers Gazette	Ont Law Gaz
Ontario Securities Commission Bulletin	OSC Bull
Ordres du jour et procès-verbaux (Conseil de l'Europe)	Ordres
Orders of the Day and Minutes of Proceedings (Council of Europe)	Orders
Oregon Law Review	Or L Rev
Osaka University Law Review	Osaka UL Rev
Osgoode Hall Law Journal	Osgoode Hall LJ
Osteuropa-Recht	Osteurop-R
Otago Law Review	Otago L Rev
Ottawa Law Review	Ottawa L Rev
Oxford Journal of Legal Studies	Oxford J Legal Stud
Oxford University Commonwealth Law Journal	OUCLJ
Pace Environmental Law Review	Pace Envtl L Rev

Pace International Law Review *(formerly / anciennement Pace Yearbook of International Law)*	Pace Int'l L Rev Pace YB Int'l L
Pace Law Review	Pace L Rev
Pacific Law Journal	Pac LJ
Pacific Rim Law & Policy Journal	Pac Rim L & Pol'y J
Państwo i Prawo	Panstwo i Prawo
Patent Law Annual	Pat L Ann
Penn State Law Review	Penn St L Rev
Pepperdine Law Review	Pepp L Rev
The Philanthropist	Philanthropist
Philippine Law Journal	Philippine LJ
Pittsburgh Legal Journal	Pittsburgh Legal J
Polish Contemporary Law	Polish Contemp L
Polish Yearbook of International Law	Polish YB Int'l L
Potomac Law Review	Potomac L Rev
Probate & Property	Prob & Prop
Probate Law Journal	Prob LJ
Procurement Lawyer	Procurement Law
Products Liability Law Journal	Prod Liab LJ
Provincial Judges Journal	Prov Judges J
Psychology, Public Policy & Law	Psychol Pub Pol'y & L
Public Contract Law Journal	Pub Cont LJ
Public Interest Law Review	Pub Int L Rev
Public Land Law Review	Pub Land L Rev
Public Land & Resources Law Review	Pub Land & Resources L Rev
Public Law	PL
QLR *(formerly / anciennement Bridgeport Law Review)*	QLR
Queen's Law Journal	Queen's LJ
Quinnipiac Health Law Journal	Quinnipiac Health LJ
Quinnipiac Law Review	Quinnipac L Rev
Quinnipiac Probate Law Journal *(formerly / anciennement Connecticut Probate Law Journal)*	Quinnipiac Prob L J
Ratio Juris	Ratio Juris
Real Estate Law Journal	Real Est LJ
Real Estate Law Report	Real Est L Rep
Real Property, Probate & Trust Journal	Real Prop Prob & Tr J
Recueil des Cours	Rec des Cours
Reform	Reform

Regent University Law Review	Regent UL Rev
Relations Industrielles	RI
Res Communes Vermont's Journal of the Environment	Res Communes: Vermont's J Env't
Responsa Meridiana	Responsa Merid
Responsabilité civile et assurances	Resp civ et assur
Restitution Law Review	RLR
Review of Central and East European Law	Rev cent & E Eur L
Review of Constitutional Studies	Rev Const Stud
Review of European Community and International Environmental Law	RECIEL
Review of Litigation	Rev Litig
Revista Europea de Derecho de la Navegación Marítima y Aeronáutica	REDNMA
Revista Jurídica de la Universidad Interamericana de Puerto Rico	Rev Jur UIPR
Revista Jurídica de la Universidad de Puerto Rico	Rev Jur UPR
Revue administrative	Rev admin
Revue africaine de droit international et comparé	RADIC
Revue algérienne des sciences juridiques, économiques et politiques	Rev ASJEP
Revue belge de droit constitutionnel	Rev BD Const
Revue belge de droit international	Rev BDI
Revue canadienne de criminologie	Rev can dr crim
Revue canadienne de droit communautaire	Rev can dr commun
Revue canadienne de droit de commerce	Rev can dr comm
Revue canadienne de droit familial	Rev Can D Fam
Revue canadienne de droit international	RCDI
Revue canadienne de droit pénal	RCDP
Revue canadienne droit et société	RCDS
Revue canadienne de propriété intellectuelle	RCPI
Revue canadienne du droit d'auteur	RCDA
Revue critique	Rev crit
Revue critique de droit international privé	Rev crit dr int privé
Revue critique de jurisprudence belge	RCJB
Revue critique de législation et de jurisprudence du Canada	RCLJ
Revue de la common law en français	RCLF
Revue de droit de l'ULB	Rev dr ULB
Revue de droit d'Ottawa	RD Ottawa

Revue de droit de l'Université de Sherbrooke	RDUS
Revue de droit de l'Université du Nouveau-Brunswick	RD UN-B
Revue de droit de McGill	RD McGill
Revue de droit des affaires internationales	RDAI
Revue de droit immobilier	RD imm
Revue de droit international de sciences diplomatiques et politiques	RDISDP
Revue de droit international et de droit comparé	Rev DI & DC
Revue de droit et santé de McGill *(formerly / anciennement Publication en droit de la santé de McGill)*	RD & santé McGill
Revue de droit social	RDS
Revue de droit uniforme	Rev DU
Revue de jurisprudence	R de J
Revue de l'arbitrage	Rev arb
Revue de législation et de jurisprudence	R de L
Revue de planification fiscale et successorale	RPFS
Revue du Barreau	R du B
Revue du Barreau canadien	R du B can
Revue d'études constitutionnelles	R études const
Revue d'études juridiques	REJ
Revue d'histoire du droit	Rev hist dr
Revue d'histoire du droit international	Rev hist dr int
Revue d'intégration européenne	RIE
Revue du droit	R du D
Revue du droit de l'Union Européenne	RDUE
Revue du droit public et de la science politique en France et à l'étranger	Rev DP & SP
Revue du Notariat	R du N
Revue de la Recherche Juridique	RRJ
Revue de planification fiscale et successorale	RPFS
Revue des Juristes de l'Ontario	Rev juristes de l'Ont
Revue des sociétés	Rev sociétés
Revue égyptienne de droit international	Rev EDI
Revue européenne de droit privé	RED privé
Revue européenne de droit public	RED public
Revue européenne de philosophie et droit	REPD
Revue Femmes et Droit	RFD
Revue française de droit administratif	Rev fr dr admin

Revue française de droit aérien et spatial	Rev fr dr aérien
Revue française de droit constitutionnel	Rev fr dr constl
Revue générale de droit	RGD
Revue générale de droit international public	RGDIP
Revue générale du droit des assurances	RGDA
Revue hellénique de droit international	RHDI
Revue historique de droit français et étranger	Rev hist dr fr & étran
Revue interdisciplinaire d'études juridiques	Rev interdiscipl ét jur
Revue internationale de droit comparé	RIDC
Revue internationale de droit économique	RID écon
Revue internationale de droit pénal	Rev IDP
Revue internationale de droit et politique de développement durable de McGill	RDPDD
Revue internationale de la Croix-Rouge	RICR
Revue internationale de la propriété industrielle et artistique	RIPIA
Revue internationale de politique criminelle	Rev IPC
Revue internationale du droit d'auteur	RIDA
Revue internationale de sémiotique juridique	RISJ
Revue juridique de l'environnement	RJE
Revue juridique des étudiants et étudiantes de l'Université Laval	RJEUL
Revue juridique La femme et le droit	Rev jur femme dr
Revue juridique Thémis	RJT
Revue nationale de droit constitutionnel	RNDC
Revue québécoise de droit international	RQDI
Revue suisse de droit international et de droit européen	SZIER
Revue suisse de jurisprudence	RSJ
Revue trimestrielle de droit civil	RTD civ
Revue trimestrielle de droit commercial et de droit économique	Rev trim dr com
Revue trimestrielle de droit européen	RTD eur
Revue universelle des droits de l'homme	RUDH
Richmond Journal of Global Law & Business	Rich J Global L & Bus
Richmond Journal of Law & Technology	Rich JL & Tech
Richmond Journal of Law and the Public Interest	Rich JL & Pub Int
Rivista di Diritto Internazionale	RDI
Roger Williams University Law Review	Roger Williams U L Rev
Roma e America Diritto Romano Comune	Dir Rom Com

Rutgers Computer & Technology Law Journal	Rutgers Computer & Tech LJ
Rutgers-Camden Law Journal	Rutgers-Camden LJ
Rutgers Journal of Law and Religion	Rutgers JL & Religion
Rutgers Law Journal	Rutgers LJ
Rutgers Law Review	Rutgers L Rev
Rutgers Race and the Law Review	Rutgers Race & L Rev
Saint John's Journal of Legal Commentary	St John's J Legal Comment
Saint John's Law Review	St John's L Rev
Saint Louis University Law Journal	Saint Louis ULJ
Saint Louis University Public Law Review	St Louis U Pub L Rev
Saint Louis-Warsaw Transatlantic Law Journal	St Louis-Warsaw Transatlantic LJ
Saint Mary's Law Journal	St Mary's LJ
Saint Thomas Law Review	St Thomas L Rev
San Diego Law Review	San Diego L Rev
San Joaquin Agricultural Law Review	San Joaquin Agric L Rev
Santa Clara Computer & High Technology Law Journal	Santa Clara Computer & High Tech LJ
Santa Clara Law Review	Santa Clara L Rev
Saskatchewan Bar Review	Sask Bar Rev
Saskatchewan Law Review	Sask L Rev
Scandinavian Studies in Law	Scand Stud L
Scottish Current Law Yearbook	Scot Curr LYB
Schweizerische Juristen-Zeitung	SJZ
Schweizerische Zeitschrift für internationales und europäisches Recht	SYIER
Seattle University Law Review (formerly / anciennement University of Puget Sound Law Review)	Seattle UL Rev
Securities Regulation Law Journal	Sec Reg LJ
Seton Hall Constitutional Law Journal	Seton Hall Const LJ
Seton Hall Journal of Sport Law	Seton Hall J Sport L
Seton Hall Law Review	Seton Hall L Rev
Seton Hall Legislative Journal	Seton Hall Legis J
Sherbrooke Law Review	Sherbrooke L Rev
Singapore Academy of Law Annual Review	Sing Ac L Ann Rev
Singapore Academy of Law Journal	Sing Ac LJ
Singapore Journal of International & Comparative Law	Sing JICL
Singapore Journal of Legal Studies	Sing JLS

Singapore Law Review	Sing L Rev
Singapore Year Book of International Law	SYBIL
SMU Law Review	SMU L Rev
Social and Legal Studies	Soc & Leg Stud
South African Journal on Human Rights	SAJHR
South African Law Journal	SALJ
South African Yearbook of International Law	SAYB Int'l L
South Carolina Environmental Law Journal	SC Envtl LJ
South Carolina Law Review	SCL Rev
South Dakota Law Review	SDL Rev
South Texas Law Review *(formerly / anciennement South Texas Law Journal)*	S Tex L Rev
Southern California Interdisciplinary Law Journal	S Cal Interdisciplinary LJ
Southern California Law Review	S Cal L Rev
Southern California Review of Law and Women's Studies	S Cal Rev L & Women's Stud
Southern California Sports & Entertainment Law Journal	S Cal Sports & Ent LJ
Southern Illinois University Law Journal	S Ill ULJ
Southern University Law Review	SUL Rev
Southwestern Journal of Law & Trade in the Americas	Sw J Trade Am
Southwestern University Law Review	Sw UL Rev
Space Policy	Space Pol'y
Special Lectures of the Law Society of Upper Canada	Spec Lect LSUC
Sports Lawyers Journal	Sports Law J
Stanford Environmental Law Journal	Stan Envtl LJ
Stanford Journal of Animal Law and Policy	Stan J Animal L & Pol'y
Stanford Journal of International Law	Stan J Int'l L
Stanford Journal of Law, Business & Finance	Stan JL Bus & Fin
Stanford Journal of Legal Studies	Stan J Legal Stud
Stanford Law & Policy Review	Stan L & Pol'y Rev
Stanford Law Review	Stan L Rev
Stanford Technology Law Review	Stan Tech L Rev
Statute Law Review	Stat L Rev
Stetson Law Review	Stetson L Rev
Studia Canonica	Stud Canon
Suffolk Journal of Trial & Appellate Advocacy	Suffolk J Trial & Appellate Advoc
Suffolk Transnational Law Review *(formerly / anciennement Suffolk Transnational Law Journal)*	Suffolk Transnat'l L Rev

Suffolk University Law Review	Suffolk UL Rev
Supreme Court Economic Review	Sup Ct Econ Rev
Supreme Court Review	Sup Ct Rev
Supreme Court Law Review	Sup Ct L Rev
Sydney Law Review	Sydney L Rev
Syracuse Journal of International Law & Commerce	Syracuse J Int'l L & Com
Syracuse Law Review	Syracuse L Rev
Syracuse University Law and Technology Journal	Syracuse UL & TJ
Tax Law Review	Tax L Rev
Telecommunications & Space Journal	Telecom & Space J
Temple Environmental Law & Technology Journal	Temp Envtl L & Tech J
Temple International & Comparative Law Journal	Temp Int'l & Comp LJ
Temple Law Review (formerly / anciennement Temple Law Quarterly)	Temp L Rev
Temple Political & Civil Rights Law Review	Temp Pol & Civ Rts L Rev
Tennessee Law Review	Tenn L Rev
Texas Bar Journal	Tex BJ
Texas Forum on Civil Liberties & Civil Rights	Tex F on CL & CR
Texas Hispanic Journal of Law & Policy (formerly / anciennement Hispanic Law Journal)	Tex Hispanic J L & Pol'y
Texas Intellectual Property Law Journal	Tex Intell Prop LJ
Texas International Law Journal	Tex Int'l LJ
Texas Journal of Business Law	Tex J Bus L
Texas Journal of Women & the Law	Tex J Women & L
Texas Law Review	Tex L Rev
Texas Review of Law & Politics	Tex Rev L & Pol
Texas Wesleyan Law Review	Tex Wesleyan L Rev
Texas Tech Law Review	Tex Tech L Rev
Textes adoptés par l'Assemblée (Conseil de l'Europe)	Textes adoptés
Texts Adopted by the Assembly (Council of Europe)	Texts Adopted
Theoretical Inquiries in Law	Theor Inq L
Third World Legal Studies	Third World Legal Stud
Thomas Jefferson Law Review	Thomas Jefferson L Rev
Thomas M Cooley Journal of Practical & Clinical Law	TM Cooley J Prac & Clinical L
Thomas M Cooley Law Review	TM Cooley L Rev
Thurgood Marshall Law Review	T Marshall L Rev
Tilburg Foreign Law Review	Tilburg Foreign L Rev

Toledo Journal of Great Lakes' Law, Science & Policy	Tol J Great Lakes' L Sci & Pol'y
Tolley's Communications Law	Tolley's Comm L
Tort & Insurance Law Journal	Tort & Ins LJ
Touro Environmental Law Journal	Touro Envtl LJ
Touro International Law Review	Touro Int'l L Rev
Touro Law Review	Touro L Rev
Trade Law Topics	Trade L Topics
Transnational Law & Contemporary Problems	Transnat'l L & Contemp Probs
Transnational Lawyer	Transnat'l Law
Transportation Law Journal	Transp LJ
Travaux de l'Association Henri Capitant des amis de la culture juridique française	Travaux de l'assoc Henri Capitant
Tribal Law Journal	Tribal LJ
Tribune des droits humains	Trib dr hum
Trust Law International	Trust L Int'l
Trusts & Estates	Trusts & Est
Tulane Environmental Law Journal	Tul Envtl LJ
Tulane European & Civil Law Forum	Tul Eur & Civ LF
Tulane Journal of International & Comparative Law	Tul J Int'l & Comp L
Tulane Journal of Law and Sexuality	Tul JL & Sexuality
Tulane Law Review	Tul L Rev
Tulane Maritime Law Journal	Tul Mar LJ
Tulsa Journal of Comparative & International Law	Tulsa J Comp & Int'l L
Tulsa Law Journal	Tulsa LJ
UC Davis Journal of International Law & Policy	UC Davis J Int'l L & Pol'y
UC Davis Law Review	UC Davis L Rev
UCLA Asian Pacific American Law Journal	UCLA Asian Pac Am LJ
UCLA Bulletin of Law and Technology	UCLA Bull L & T
UCLA Entertainment Law Review	UCLA Ent L Rev
UCLA Journal of Environmental Law & Policy	UCLA J Envtl L & Pol'y
UCLA Journal of International Law and Foreign Affairs	UCLA J Int'l L & Foreign Aff
UCLA Law Review	UCLA L Rev
UCLA Pacific Basin Law Journal	UCLA Pac Basin LJ
UCLA Women's Law Journal	UCLA Women's LJ
UMKC Law Review	UMKC L Rev
UNCTAD Law Review: Journal on Law, Trade and Development	UNCTAD L Rev
Uniform Commercial Code Law Journal	Unif Comm Code L J

Uniform Law Conference of Canada: Proceedings	Unif L Conf Proc
Uniform Law Review	Unif L Rev
United States-Mexico Law Journal	US-Mex LJ
University of Arkansas at Little Rock Law Review	U Ark Little Rock L Rev
University of Baltimore Intellectual Property Law Journal	U Balt Intell Prop LJ
University of Baltimore Journal of Environmental Law	U Balt J Envtl L
University of Baltimore Law Forum	U Balt LF
University of Baltimore Law Review	U Balt L Rev
University of British Columbia Law Review	UBC L Rev
University of California at Davis Law Review	UC Davis L Rev
University of Chicago Law Review	U Chicago L Rev
University of Chicago Law School Roundtable	U Chicago L Sch Roundtable
University of Chicago Legal Forum	U Chicago Legal F
University of Cincinnati Law Review	U Cin L Rev
University of Colorado Law Review	U Colo L Rev
University of Dayton Law Review	U Dayton L Rev
University of Detroit Mercy Law Review	U Det Mercy L Rev
University of Florida Journal of Law & Public Policy	U Fla JL & Pub Pol'y
University of Ghana Law Journal	UGLJ
University of Hawaii Law Review	U Haw L Rev
University of Illinois Law Review	U Ill L Rev
University of Kansas Law Review	U Kan L Rev
University of Malaya Law Review	U Mal L Rev
University of Memphis Law Review	U Mem L Rev
University of Miami Business Law Review	U Miami Bus L Rev
University of Miami Entertainment & Sports Law Review	U Miami Ent & Sports L Rev
University of Miami Inter-American Law Review	U Miami Inter-Am L Rev
University of Miami International & Comparative Law Review *(formerly / anciennement University of Miami Yearbook of International Law)*	U Miami Int'l & Comp L Rev
University of Miami Law Review	U Miami L Rev
University of Michigan Journal of Law Reform	U Mich JL Ref
University of New Brunswick Law Journal	UNBLJ
University of New South Wales Law Journal	UNSWLJ
University of Pennsylvania Journal of Constitutional Law	U Pa J Const L
University of Pennsylvania Journal of International Economic Law	U Pa J Int'l Econ L
University of Pennsylvania Journal of Labor and Employment Law	U Pa J Lab & Employment L

University of Pennsylvania Law Review	U Pa L Rev
University of Pittsburgh Law Review	U Pitt L Rev
University of Queensland Law Jounal	UQLJ
University of Richmond Law Review	U Rich L Rev
University of San Francisco Law Review	USF L Rev
University of San Francisco Journal of Law and Social Challenges	USF JL & Soc Challenges
University of San Francisco Maritime Law Journal	USF Mar LJ
University of Tasmania Law Review	U Tasm L Rev
University of the District of Columbia Law Review *(formerly / anciennement District of Columbia Law Review)*	UDC L Rev
University of Toledo Law Review	U Tol L Rev
University of Toronto Faculty of Law Review	UT Fac L Rev
University of Toronto Law Journal	UTLJ
University of Western Australia Law Review	UWA L Rev
University of Western Ontario Law Review	UWO L Rev
Upper Canada Law Journal	UCLJ
Utah Bar Journal	Utah BJ
Valparaiso University Law Review	Val U L Rev
Vanderbilt Journal of Entertainment Law & Practice	Vand J Ent L & Prac
Vanderbilt Journal of Transnational Law	Vand J Transnat'l L
Vanderbilt Law Review	Vand L Rev
Vermont Bar Journal	Vt BJ
Vermont Law Review	Vt L Rev
Victoria University of Wellington Law Review	VUWLR
Vietnam Law & Legal Forum	Vietnam L & Legal Forum
Villanova Environmental Law Journal	Vill Envtl LJ
Villanova Law Review	Vill L Rev
Villanova Sports and Entertainment Law Journal	Vill Sports & Ent LJ
Virginia Environmental Law Journal	Va Envtl LJ
Virginia Journal of International Law	Va J Int'l L
Virginia Journal of Law & Technology	Va JL & Tech
Virginia Journal of Social Policy & Law	Va J Soc Pol'y & L
Virginia Journal of Sports and the Law	Va J Sports & L
Virginia Law Review	Va L Rev
Virginia Tax Review	Va Tax Rev
Waikato Law Review: Taumauri	Waikato L Rev
Wake Forest Law Review	Wake Forest L Rev

Waseda Bulletin of Comparative Law	Waseda Bull Comp L
Washburn Law Journal	Washburn LJ
Washington & Lee Race & Ethnic Ancestry Law Journal *(formerly / anciennement Race & Ethnic Ancestry Law Journal and Race & Ethnic Ancestry Law Digest)*	Wash & Lee Race & Ethnic Ancestry LJ
Washington & Lee Law Review	Wash & Lee L Rev
Washington Law Review	Wash L Rev
Washington University Journal of Law & Policy	Wash UJL & Pol'y
Washington University Journal of Urban and Contemporary Law	Wash UJ Urb & Contemp L
Washington University Law Quarterly	Wash ULQ
Wayne Law Review	Wayne L Rev
Web Journal of Current Legal Issues	Web JCLI
West Virginia Journal of Law & Technology	W Va J L & T
West Virginia Law Review	W Va L Rev
West Virginia Lawyer	W Va Law
West's Education Law Reporter	W Ed Law Rep
Western Law Review (San Francisco)	West L Rev
Western Law Review (Canada)	West LR
Western Ontario Law Review	West Ont L Rev
Western New England Law Review	W New Eng L Rev
Western State University Law Review	W St U L Rev
Widener Journal of Public Law	Widener J Pub L
Widener Law Symposium Journal	Widener L Symp J
Willamette Journal of International Law & Dispute Resolution	Willamette J Int'l & Disp Resol
Willamette Law Review	Willamette L Rev
William & Mary Bill of Rights Journal	Wm & Mary Bill Rts J
William & Mary Environmental Law & Policy Review	Wm & Mary Envtl L & Pol'y Rev
William & Mary Journal of Women and the Law	Wm & Mary J Women & L
William & Mary Law Review	Wm & Mary L Rev
William Mitchell Law Review	Wm Mitchell L Rev
Windsor Review of Legal and Social Issues	Windsor Rev Legal Soc Issues
Windsor Yearbook of Access to Justice	Windsor YB Access Just
Wisconsin Environmental Law Journal	Wis Envtl LJ
Wisconsin International Law Journal	Wis Int'l LJ
Wisconsin Law Review	Wis L Rev
Wisconsin Women's Law Journal	Wis Women's LJ
Women's Rights Law Reporter	Women's Rts L Rep

World Arbitration and Mediation Report	World Arb & Mediation Rep
World Trade and Arbitration Materials	WTAM
Wyoming Law Review (formerly / anciennement Land & Water Law Review)	Wyo L Rev
Yale Human Rights & Development Law Journal	Yale Human Rts & Dev LJ
Yale Journal of International Law	Yale J Int'l L
Yale Journal of Law & Feminism	Yale JL & Feminism
Yale Journal of Law & the Humanities	Yale JL & Human
Yale Journal on Regulation	Yale J on Reg
Yale Law & Policy Review	Yale L & Pol'y Rev
Yale Law Journal	Yale LJ
Yearbook: Commercial Arbitration	YB Comm Arb
Yearbook of Air and Space Law	YB Air & Sp L
Yearbook of Copyright and Media Law	YB Copyright & Media L
Yearbook of European Law	YB Eur L
Yearbook of International Law	YB Int'l L
Yearbook of International Environmental Law	YB Int'l Env L
Yearbook of International Humanitarian Law	YB Int'l Human L
Yearbook of Maritime Law	YB Marit L
Yearbook of the Canadian Bar Association	YB CBA
Yearbook of the European Convention on Human Rights	YB Eur Conv HR
Yearbook of the Institute of International Law	YB Inst Int'l L
Yearbook of the International Court of Justice	YBICJ
Yearbook of the United Nations	YBUN
Yearbook on Human Rights	YBHR
Zeitschrift für ausländisches öffentliches Recht und Völkerrecht	ZaöRV
Zeitschrift für das gesamte Familienrecht	Fam R Z
Zeitschrift für Europäisches Privatrecht	Z Eu P
Zeitschrift für Luft- und Weltraumrecht	ZLW
Zeitschrift für Rechtspolitik	ZRP
Zeitschrift für Rechtsvergleichung	ZRV
Zeitschrift für Unternehmens- und Gesellschaftsrecht	ZUG
Zeitschrift für Vergleichende Rechtswissenschaft	Z Vgl RWiss
Zeitschrift für Wirtschaftsrecht	ZW

APPENDIX E / ANNEXE E

E. ELECTRONIC SERVICES ~ *SERVICES ÉLECTRONIQUES*

Abreviations ~ *Abréviations*

Australasian Legal Information Institute	AustLII
Azimut (produced by / *produit par* SOQUIJ)	Azimut
British and Irish Legal Information Institute	BAILII
Butterworths Services	Butterworths
Canadian Legal Information Institute / *Institut canadien d'information juridique*	CanLII
Hong Kong Legal Information Institute	HKLII
Justis	Justis
KluwerArbitration	Kluwer
Lawnet (Singapore)	Lawnet
Legal Information Institute	LII
Legifrance	Legifrance
LexisNexis	Lexis
LexUM	LexUM
New Zealand Legal Information Institute	NZLII
Pacific Islands Legal Information Institute	PacLII
Quicklaw	QL
Répertoire électronique de jurisprudence du Barreau	REJB
Southern African Legal Information Institute	SAFLII
Taxnet Pro	TaxnetPRO
Westlaw (US)	WL
Westlaw Canada	WL Can
Westlaw International	WL Int
Westlaw UK	WL UK
World Legal Information Institute	WorldLII